Study Guide for use with

Essentials of Understanding Psychology

Second Canadian Edition

Robert S. Feldman
University of Massachusetts–Amherst

Joan E. Collins
Sheridan College

Judy M. Green
Sheridan College

Prepared by

Robert S. Feldman
University of Massachusetts-Amherst

Harry Webster
Vanier College

Barbara Radigan
Community College of Allegheny County, Pennsylvania

McGraw-Hill Ryerson

Toronto Montréal Boston Burr Ridge, IL Dubuque, IA Madison, WI New York San Francisco
St. Louis Bangkok Bogotá Caracas Kuala Lumpur Lisbon London Madrid
Mexico City Milan New Delhi Santiago Seoul Singapore Sydney Taipei

Study Guide for use with
Essentials of Understanding Psychology
Second Canadian Edition

ISBN: 0-07-088963-5

2 3 4 5 6 7 8 9 10 CP 0 9 8 7 6

Printed and bound in Canada.

Care has been taken to trace ownership of copyright material contained in this text; however, the publisher will welcome any information that enables them to rectify any reference or credit for subsequent editions.

Vice President, Editorial and Media Technology: Patrick Ferrier
Executive Sponsoring Editor: James Buchanan
Developmental Editor: Darren Hick
Production Coordinator: Andrée Davis
Supervising Editor: Anne Nellis
Printer: Canadian Printco, Ltd.

Table of Contents

Preface

This *Student Study Guide* has been prepared with several very important student concerns in mind. First, the students' needs for a comprehensive guide that is meant to supplement Robert Feldman's *Essentials of Understanding Psychology, 2nd Canadain Edition,* in such a way as to take advantage of the many features in the book that support effective study habits. Second, students need practice and drill work that focuses on the full content of each chapter and presents practice questions that are similar to those provided in the instructor's *Test Bank*. Key term definitions in the text were used to develop the key term drills found throughout the study guide in the *Evaluate* sections. Three practice tests have been created for each chapter. The first two tests are composed of questions that are primarily factual in nature. The third test is composed of difficult factual, applied, and conceptual questions. A complete set of answer explanations for both the right and wrong answers to all of the multiple choice questions are available at the end of each chapter.

You will also find three practice essay questions for each chapter. These questions are intended to provide you opportunities to practice writing and critical analysis skills. In each chapter's answer key, a list of points that should be covered in your answer to each question has been provided. These questions are meant to be difficult and to require you to draw on both conceptual and factual knowledge. Some require that you apply concepts to situations, and others may require that you compare several ideas. New in this edition students will discover "Keys to Excellence: Study Skills" section and counterpart end-of-chapter sections called "Spotlight on Terminology and Language—ESL Pointers" for the reader who may be less experienced in American usages of the English language.

The introduction explains the organization of the *Study Guide* and offers tips on how to use the features of the *Study Guide* to improve your study skills and make your time spent with the text more effective.

Introduction

Using *Essentials of Understanding Psychology:* Strategies for Effective Study

Essentials of Understanding Psychology has been written with the reader in mind, and it therefore includes a number of unique features that will help you to maximize your learning of the concepts, theories, facts, and other kinds of information that make up the field of psychology. To take advantage of these features, there are several steps that you should take when reading and studying the book. The *Student Study Guide* was designed to help the student take full advantage of the features in the textbook, and the steps recommended for the text have been incorporated into this *Study Guide*. By following these steps, you will not only get the most from reading and studying *Essentials of Understanding Psychology*, but you will also develop habits that will help you to study other texts more effectively and to think critically about material you are learning. Among the most important steps to follow:

■ *Familiarize yourself with the logic of the book's structure.* Begin by reading the Table of Contents. It provides an overview of the topics that will be covered and gives a sense of the way the various topics are interrelated. Next, review the Preface, which describes the book's major features. Note how each chapter is divided into three or four self-contained units; these provide logical starting and stopping points for reading and studying. Also note the major highlights of each chapter: a chapter-opening outline, a Prologue, a Looking Ahead section that includes chapter objectives, A P.O.W.E.R. learning system, which will include chapter goals, the organizational format, a Work section, an Evaluate section, and a Rethink section to help you, the student, to increase you ability to learn and retain information and to think critically. At the end of each chapter there are chapter tests so that you can review and evaluate those skills you have acquired while studying each chapter. Answers to all of the work and evaluation sections are located at the end of each chapter along with answers to the practice tests. Because every chapter is structured in the same way, you are provided with a set of familiar landmarks as you chart your way through new material, allowing you to organize the chapter's content more readily. This study guide is designed to lead you through each of these steps.

■ *Title Bars* Each chapter is divided by title bars like the one shown below, and each title bar provides recommendations for what can be done with the material provided.

Practise Questions

Test your knowledge of the chapter material by answering the **Multiple Choice Questions**. These questions have been placed in three Practise Tests. The first two tests are composed of questions that will test your recall of factual knowledge. The third test contains questions that are challenging and primarily test for conceptual knowledge and your ability to apply that knowledge. Check your answers and review the feedback using the Answer Key at the end of each chapter of the *Study Guide.*

■ **The new "*Keys to Excellence*" *Study Skills* and *Spotlight on Terminology and Language—Cultural Idioms* sections** are intended to facilitate the comprehension and retention of the text material by non-native speakers of English, focusing on 490-plus key terms and concepts in *Essentials of Understanding Psychology, 2nd Canadian Edition*. The *Keys to Excellence: Study Skills* section in the front of the Study Guide provides tips to identifying in-text language cues and organizing study materials accordingly. And the *Spotlight on Terminology and Language* sections in each chapter provide clarification of a great number of content-specific idiomatic phrases by defining them in context.

■ The new edition of *Essentials of Understanding Psychology's Student Study Guide* provides students with the option of using *P.O.W.E.R. Learning*, a systematic approach to learning and studying based on five key steps (*P*repare, *O*rganize, *W*ork, *E*valuate, and *R*ethink). Based on empirical research, *P.O.W.E.R. Learning* systematizes the acquisition of new material by providing a learning framework. The system stresses the importance of learning objectives, self-evaluation, and critical thinking. The elements of the *P.O.W.E.R. Learning* can also be used in conjunction with other learning systems, such as *SQ3R*.

The *P.O.W.E.R.* learning strategy includes five key steps: *P*repare, *O*rganize, *W*ork, *E*valuate, and *R*ethink. *P.O.W.E.R. Learning* systematizes the acquisition of new material by providing a learning framework. It stresses the importance of learning objectives and appropriate preparation prior to beginning to study, as well as the significance of self-evaluation and the incorporation of critical thinking into the learning process. Specifically, use of the P.O.W.E.R. Learning system entails the following steps:

- *Prepare.* Before starting any journey, we need to know where we are headed. Academic journeys are no different; we need to know what our goals are. The *Prepare* stage consists of thinking about what we hope to attain from reading a particular section of the text by identifying specific goals that we seek to accomplish. In your *Essentials of Understanding Psychology Student Study Guide,* these goals are presented in the form of broad questions that start each major section.

- *Organize.* Once we know what our goals are, we need to develop a route to accomplish those goals. The *Organize* stage involves developing a mental roadmap of where we are headed. *Essentials of Understanding Psychology Student Study Guide* highlights the organization of each upcoming section. Read the outline to get an idea of what topics are covered and how they are organized.

- *Work.* The heart of the P.O.W.E.R. Learning system entails actually reading and studying the material presented in the book. In some ways *Work* is the easy part, because, if you have carried out the steps in the preparation and organization stage, you'll know where you're headed and how you'll get there. Of course it's not so simple—you'll need the motivation to conscientiously read and think about the material presented in the chapter. And remember, the main text isn't the only material that you need to read and think about. It's also important to read the boxes, the marginal glossary terms, and the special sections in order to gain a full understanding of the material, so be sure to include them as part of the *Work* of reading the chapter and then use the *Work* section of your study guide to support your text reading.

- *Evaluate.* The fourth step, *Evaluate*, provides you with the opportunity to determine how effectively you have mastered the material. ***Essentials of Understanding Psychology Student Study Guide*** has matching tests following each *Work* section that permits a rapid check of your understanding of the material. Evaluating your progress is essential to assessing your degree of mastery of the material.

- *Rethink.* The final step in *P.O.W.E.R. Learning* involves critical thinking, which entails reanalyzing, reviewing, questioning, and challenging assumptions. It provides the opportunity to look at the big picture by thinking about how material fits with other information that you have already learned. Every major section of ***Essentials of Understanding Psychology, 5/e,*** ends with a *Rethink* section that contains thought-provoking questions. Answering them will help you understand the material more fully and at a deeper level.

If you want to maximize your potential to master the material in ***Essentials of Understanding Psychology, 5/e***, use *P.O.W.E.R. Learning*. Taking the time and effort to work through the steps of the system is a proven technique for understanding and learning the material.

Supplementing *P.O.W.E.R. Learning* with *SQ3R*

Although *P.O.W.E.R. Learning* is the learning strategy that is built into the book and consequently easiest to use, it is not the only system compatible with the book. For example, some readers may wish to supplement the *P.O.W.E.R. Learning* system with the *SQ3R* method, which includes a series of five steps, designated by the initials *S-Q-R-R-R*. The first step is to *survey* the material by reading the chapter outlines, chapter headings, figure captions, recaps, and Looking Ahead and Looking Back sections, providing yourself with an overview of the major points of the chapter. The next step—the "Q" in SQ3R—is to *question*. Formulate questions about the material—either aloud or in writing—prior to actually reading a section of the material. The queries posed in the *Prepare* sections and the *Evaluate* and *Rethink* questions that end each part of the chapter are also a good source of questions.

The next three steps in *SQ3R* ask you to *read, recite,* and *review* the material. *Read* carefully and, even more important, read actively and critically. While you are reading, answer the questions you have asked yourself. Critically evaluate material by considering the implications of what you are reading, thinking about possible exceptions and contradictions, and examining underlying assumptions. The *recite* step involves describing and explaining to yourself (or to a friend) the material you have just read and answering the questions you have posed earlier. Recite aloud; the recitation process helps to identify your degree of understanding of the material you have just read. Finally, *review* the material, looking it over, reading the Looking Back summaries, and answering the in-text review questions.

Final Comments

- *Find a location and time.* The last aspect of studying that warrants mention is that *when* and *where* you study are in some ways as important as *how* you study. One of the truisms of the psychological literature is that we learn things better, and are able to recall them longer, when we study material in small chunks over several study sessions, rather than massing our study into one lengthy period. This implies that all-night studying just prior to a test is going to be less effective—and a lot more tiring—than employing a series of steady, regular study sessions.

In addition to carefully timing your studying, you should seek out a special location to study. It doesn't really matter where it is, as long as it has minimal distractions and is a place that you use *only* for studying. Identifying a special "territory" allows you to get in the right mood for study as soon as you begin.

- *Use a study strategy.* Although we are expected to study and ultimately to learn a wide array of material throughout our schooling, we are rarely taught any systematic strategies that permit us to study more effectively. Yet, just as we wouldn't expect a physician to learn human anatomy by trial and error, it is the unusual student who is able to stumble upon a truly effective studying strategy Each chapter is divided by title bars like those shown, and each provides recommendations for what can be done with the material provided

The *P.O.W.E.R. Learning* system (as well as *SQ3R)* provides a proven means of increasing your study effectiveness. Yet you need not feel tied to a particular strategy. You might want to combine other elements into your own study system. For example, learning tips and strategies for critical thinking will be presented throughout ***Essentials of Understanding Psychology***, such as in Chapter 6 when the use of mnemonics (memory techniques for organizing material to help its recall) are discussed. If these tactics help you to successfully master new material, stick with them.

By using the proven *P.O.W.E.R. Learning* system, you will maximize your understanding of the material in this book and will master techniques that will help you learn and think critically in all of your academic endeavors. More important, you will optimize your understanding of the field of psychology. It is worth the effort. The excitement, challenge, and promise that psychology holds for you is immense.

Robert Feldman
Barbara Radigan
Harry Webster

Keys To Excellence: Study Skills

The following study strategies will help you to think deeply and critically about what you read. Non-native speakers of English should find this section especially helpful.

Words are the instruments of communication, learning, and thinking. Use key words to trigger your consolidation of material. One key word can initiate the recall of a whole cluster of ideas. A few key words can form a chain from which you can reconstruct an entire lecture.

Learning involves digesting what you read and actively using the information. *Digesting*: Give yourself time for a thinking pause after you finish a paragraph and summarize it. The thinking pause will provide time for the main idea to sink in and connect with information you already know.

Using New Information: Consciously rehearse what you've learned. Repetition can often be the key to remembering. Always strive to link what you learn to what you already know. Reinforce new ideas by associating them with the things close to you in your own life.

Recognizing Patterns of Organization

Organizational patterns help to organize a reader's thoughts and help you to better comprehend key concepts. As your brain works to make sense of the world around you, it tries to fit everything into a recognizable shape and pattern that has meaning for you. Placing work into reasonable blocks of information makes it easier for your brain to understand and remember information.

There are four basic approaches, or *patterns*, that writers use in presenting concepts:

- Describing the concept in the form of a generalization
- Explaining the similarities and/or differences of the concept as compared to other concepts
- Using cause and effect to show the active relationship of the concept to other concepts and to a bigger picture – for instance, a theory
- Including a series of events or steps – breaking the concept down into digestible pieces

Familiarize yourself with the organizational pattern the text author is using. By recognizing the structure of the author's writing style, you will be better prepared to organize your studying and note taking strategy. Recognizing patterns helps you to anticipate information that is coming and to incorporate and assimilate it within your existing knowledge base. You become more involved in your own learning process by focusing on the presentation of the material. You can think of yourself as a partner with the author as you learn this new information.

Use Signal Words to Organize Reading

Words can be used as obvious indicators of the direction of a writer's thoughts. These signal words for patterns can also be referred to as transitional words. Writers use these words to mark the shifts and turns in their thinking. Following these signal words, readers can identify when the writer is moving from one idea to the next. Using signal words and phrases imposes a recognizable order on ideas, facts, and details.

Different kinds of signal words can alert you to what type of material is to follow. For example, the following *comparison and contrast* signal words and phrases can be used to explain similarities and/or differences:

- However
- Although
- Rather
- Conversely
- Different from
- In contrast
- Instead
- More than

- But
- While
- Yet
- Less than
- On the other hand
- One difference
- Unlike
- Another major difference

When you read sentences, make full use of signal words and organizational clues. If you see "on the one hand," watch for the key words "on the other hand," which introduces the other side of the argument.

The following are *cause and effect* signal words and phrases that call attention to a concept's connection to other concepts and its role in an overriding theme:

Some signal words demonstrating this pattern are:

- Therefore
- As a result
- Accordingly
- Consequently
- Because

Sequencing signal words help you to notice important events and the logical progression of material. Sequence word and phrase examples are:

- Near
- Until
- First
- For the next
- Then
- Finally

- After
- Last
- While
- Later
- Before
- The following

Signal words that are used to add *emphasis*, and in doing so distinguish important points to take note of, are:

- Most important
- Remember that
- Pay attention to
- Above all
- A key (component, feature, etc.)
- The main idea
- Of primary concern
- Most significant
- In conclusion

Creating Study Cards

Use 3" x 5" note cards to learn your vocabulary words by recitation and repetition. Select a word you want to remember and write the word on the front of a card. On the back of the card, write the complete sentence in which the word occurs in the text. Then, write the same word in a meaningful context that is familiar with you. This will reinforce your use of the term and help you incorporate it more fully into your current vocabulary base.

To study the word, always look first at the front of the card. Pronounce the word. Think about the word and how you would define it. Put the word in a new sentence, and then check the use and definition of the word on the back of the card. The best part about using these study cards is that you can take them just about anywhere and use them for review in your spare moments!

Understanding and Applying the Steps of Marking A Text

The purpose of making marks in a text is to create your own personal road map to make navigating through the material easier. Marking a textbook will help you to accumulate information in an orderly and systematic way. You can underline important words and sentences and makes notes in the margins about them. Paraphrase important statements in the top and bottom margins of your text to simplify concepts into kernels of important information. Circle words, phrases, and theorists' names where they appear or rewrite them in the margin if they seem meaningful or are difficult to grasp. Seeing these words stand out on the page will draw you back to review them. Use memory-jogging abbreviations to stimulate your recall of information. Circle numbers that indicate a series of arguments, facts, or ideas – either main or supporting. Develop visual diagrams of the concepts when you can. Consider all blank spaces as flexible note-taking areas. By marking your book, you are turning your textbook into your own custom-made study guide. Referring back to your marginal notes, you will be able to review the essential material at a glance just by flipping back through the pages.

Using special marks and colours, you can highlight and differentiate between different types of material. By creating a key of marks and colours, you can easily identify where certain types of information can be found. You might chose to highlight key terms in yellow marker or draw squares around theorists' names. One successful method of marking is to star (*) the beginning of a sentence, paragraph, questions, etc. that you believe your instructor may quiz you on. Instructors may suggest, through their emphasis in class, that certain information is likely to appear on an exam. Finding the coverage of this material in your text and starring it will distinguish it as a potential test question. Then, when you revisit your text, you can better focus your studying time.

Vocabulary

Knowing the meaning of prefixes, roots, and suffixes can unlock the meaning of unfamiliar words. Common word parts are building blocks used in forming many English words. Increasing your awareness of these basic word parts help to unlock the meaning of unfamiliar words.

Root
A root is a basic word part to which prefixes, suffixes, or both are added.

Prefix
A prefix is a word part added to the beginning of a word. Here is a list of some common prefixes with their meanings:

PREFIX	MEANING
A-	in, on, at
Ab-	from, away
Ad-, a-	to, toward
An-, a-	not, without
Ambi-, amphi-	around, both
Ana-	back, opposite
Ante-	before
Anti-	against, opposite
Cata-	break down
Circum-	around
Con-	with, together
Contra-	against
Dia-	through
Dis-	apart
Dys-	ill
Extra-	beyond
Fore-	before
Hyper-	over, beyond
Hypo-	under
Inter-	between
Intra	within
Para-	beside
Post-	after
Re-	before
Retro-	backward
Sub-	under
Super-	over
Trans-	across
Ultra-	beyond

- Un-   not

Suffix

A suffix is a word part added to the end of a word. While a suffix may affect a word's meaning slightly, it is more likely to affect how the word is used in a sentence.

Introduction to Psychology

1

Chapter Overview

Chapter 1 defines psychology as the scientific study of behaviour and mental processes. The diversity of the field of psychology is illustrated by listing several of the subfields of psychology. This is followed by samples of questions that each psychological subfield attempts to answer.

A portrait of psychologists is presented that illustrates both the types of psychologists and the educational requirements for those who choose careers in the field of psychology.

Attention is also given to some of the unique ways in which the profession of psychology in Canada differs from and is similar to psychology in the United States. These differences and similarities are discussed in terms of their historical roots and the ways in which the profession of psychology is required to address specific needs in the Canadian community, which often differ in important ways from those in the United States. For example, these include differences in political systems, cultural make-up, and outlook on societal issues.

The historical roots of psychology are discussed with attention to the roles that women have played in the development of the discipline. The chapter then goes on to trace the events that led to the five basic perspectives in psychology today. These are the biological perspective, the psychodynamic perspective, the cognitive perspective, the behavioural perspective, and the humanistic perspective.

Next, the five key issues in psychology today are presented: nature versus nurture, conscious versus unconscious causes of behaviour, observable behaviour versus internal mental processes, free will versus determinism, and individual differences versus universal principles. These key issues are used to understand how culture, ethnicity, and race influence behaviour.

The chapter than goes on to investigate how psychologists reach conclusions about the unknown. First the scientific method that is used to pose and answer questions of psychological interest is examined. This is followed by a description of the ways in which psychologists develop suppositions and test theories. Consideration is then given to the specific means that researchers use in doing research. These include archival research, naturalistic observation, survey research, case studies, correlational research and experimental research. Next, the major techniques used in carrying out research are discussed and the benefits and limitations of each type of research are listed.

Finally, the ethics of doing psychological research are discussed. Attention is given to using both humans and animals as subjects. The discussion poses questions on when it is and when it is not appropriate to design experiments using human subjects and/or animals.

To further investigate the topics covered in this chapter, you can access the related websites by visiting the following link: http://www.mcgrawhill.ca/college/feldman.

Prologue: From Terrorism to Heroism
Looking Ahead

Section 1: Psychologists at Work
The Subfields of Psychology: Psychology's Family Tree
Working at Psychology

Section 2: A Science Evolves: The Past, the Present, and the Future
The Roots of Psychology
Today's Perspectives

> **Applying Psychology in the 21st Century:** Psychology and the Reduction of Violence

Section 3: Psychology's Key Issues
Psychology's Future

Section 4: Research in Psychology
The Scientific Method
Psychological Research

> **Pathways Through Psychology:** Wendy Josephson: Associate Professor of Psychology, University of Manitoba

Section 5: Research Challenges: Exploring the Process
The Ethics of Research
Should Animals Be Used in Research?
Threats to Experiments: Experimenter and Participant Expectations

> **Psychology at Work:** Alexandra Kitty, Journalist and Professor, Mohawk College

> **Becoming an Informed Consumer of Psychology:** Thinking Critically About Research

Learning Objectives	

These are the concepts and the learning objectives for Chapter 1. Read them carefully as part of your preliminary survey of the chapter.

Psychologists at Work

1. Define psychology, including its scope, goals, and methods. (p. 4)

2. Name and describe the different subfields of psychology and distinguish between them by giving examples of the work and workers in each field. (pp. 6–8)

3. Identify and describe two newer fields of psychology. (p. 8)

4. Identify the significant demographic trends of the profession, including place of employment, educational background and the different focus of the profession in Canada compared to the United States (pp. 8–10)

A Science Evolves: The Past, the Present, and the Future

5. Discuss the history of the science of psychology and the approaches taken by early psychologists, including the pioneering contributions of women (pp. 11–13)

6. Name and outline the key characteristics of each of the five current perspectives in psychology, including practical applications (pp. 13-15)

Psychology's Key Issues

7. List the key issues for psychology and identify statements that represent each issue. (pp 17, 18)

8. Discuss the trends that are emerging within psychology. (p. 19)

Research in Psychology

9. Describe the scientific method approach. (p. 20-22)

10. Distinguish between theory and hypothesis and describe the role of each in scientific inquiry. (pp. 21–22)

11. Define research and distinguish between archival, naturalistic observation, survey, and case

study research methods. (pp. 22–24)

12. Describe how correlational research determines the relationship between two sets of variables. (pp. 25–26)

13. Define the key elements common to all experiments, including independent and dependent variables, experimental and control groups, random assignment of participants, and a hypothesis that links the variables. (pp. 26–28)

14. Discuss the importance of statistical techniques used to establish whether the outcome of an experiment is significant. (pp. 29–31)

15. Discuss the importance of replicating experiments and testing the limits of theories and hypotheses for proving the existence of a causal relationship between variables in specific circumstances. (p. 31)

Research Challenges: Exploring the Process

16. Describe the ethical concerns involving the welfare of human and animal participants in scientific research. (pp. 32–35)

17. Identify the possible sources of experimental bias and discuss techniques used to safeguard against them. (pp. 33, 35–36)

18. Apply the knowledge of scientific methods to evaluate how well research supports particular findings. (pp. 36–37)

SECTION 1: Psychologists at Work

Prepare

- *What is the science of psychology?*
- *What are the major specialties in the field of psychology?*
- *Where do psychologists work?*

Organize

- *The Subfields of Psychology*
- *Working at Psychology*

Work

[a] _____ is defined as the scientific study of behaviour and mental processes. Psychologists investigate what people do as well as their thoughts, feelings, perceptions, reasoning processes, and memories. They also investigate the biological foundations of these processes. Psychology relies upon the scientific method to discover ways of explaining, predicting, modifying, and improving behaviour. The study of behaviour and mental processes

involves examining animal as well as human subjects to find the general laws that govern the behaviour of all organisms.

Contrary to the mistaken view held by many people that psychology is interested only in abnormal behaviour, psychologists examine a wide array of behaviours and mental processes. The speciality areas are described in the order in which they appear throughout the text.

[b] _____ explores the relationship between fundamental biological processes and behaviour. The study is focused on the brain and the nervous system, and both diseases and healthy functions are examined for their contribution to the understanding of behaviour.

[c] _____ *psychology* is both a speciality and a task undertaken by most psychologists. The scientific work of psychology requires experimental methods to be applied wherever possible. **[d]** _____ *psychology* is a speciality within experimental psychology that focuses on higher mental functions like thought, language, memory, problem solving, reasoning, and decision making, among other processes.

Emerging areas of psychology include: **[e]** _____ psychology, an area that seeks to identify behaviour patterns that are a result of our genetic inheritance;

[f] _____ unites the areas of biopsychology and clinical psychology. It focuses on the relationship between biological factors and psychological disorders. This speciality area has led to promising new medications to treat psychological disorders; and

[g] _____ psychology, the study of how physical environments influence behaviour; **[h]** _____ psychology, is the study of law and psychology. It has changed many of the methods and techniques used in the criminal justice field today;

[i] _____ psychology, is the branch investigating applications of psychology to sports and athletic activity.

Evaluate

_____ 1. biopsychology

_____ 2. experimental psychology

_____ 3. cognitive psychology

_____ 4. developmental psychology

_____ 5. personality psychology

a. The branch that studies the processes of sensing, perceiving, learning, and thinking about the world.

b. The branch that studies consistency and change in a person's behaviour over time as well as the individual traits that differentiate the behaviour of one person from another when each confronts the same situation.

c. The branch that specializes in the biological basis of behaviour.

d. The branch that studies how people grow and change throughout the course of their lives.

e. The branch that focuses on the study of higher mental processes, including thinking, language, memory, problem solving, knowing, reasoning, judging, and decision making.

Rethink

1. Why might the study of twins who were raised together and twins who were not be helpful in distinguishing the effects of heredity and environment?

2. Suppose you know a 7-year-old child who is having problems learning to read and you want to help. Imagine that you can consult as many psychologists as you want. How might each type of psychologist approach the problem?

SECTION 2: A Science Evolves: The Past, the Present, and the Future

Prepare

- *What are the historical roots of the field of psychology?*
- *What are the major approaches used by contemporary psychologists?*

Organize

- *The Roots of Psychology*
- *Today's Perspectives*

Work

Trephining (drilling holes in the skull to let evil spirits escape), Hippocrates' theory of humors, Gall's "science" of phrenology (the association of bumps on the head with traits), and Descartes' concept of animal spirits reflect some of the most forward thought of past times. The era of scientific psychology is usually dated from the establishment of an experimental psychology laboratory by Wilhelm Wundt in 1879.

The perspective associated with Wundt's laboratory is called **[a]** _____. It focused on the elements, or building blocks, that constitute the foundation of perception, thinking, and emotions. Structuralism utilized a technique called **[b]** _____ to examine these elements. Introspection required the subject to report how a stimulus was experienced. A perspective called **[c]** _____ replaced structuralism, and instead of focusing on the structure of mental elements, it focused on how the mind works and how people adapt to environments. William James was the leading functionalist in the early 1900s, and one of the leading educators, John Dewey, took a functionalist approach in his development of school psychology. **[d]** _____ was another reaction to structuralism that developed in the early 1900s. The gestalt approach examines phenomena in terms of the whole experience rather than the individual elements, and gestalt psychologists are identified with the maxim "the whole is greater than the sum of the parts."

Several early female contributors to the field of psychology were Leta Stetter Hollingworth, known for her focus on adolescent development and for an early focus on women's issues, and June Etta Downey, who studied personality traits in the 1920s. Also among the early contributors were Karen Horney, who focused on the social and cultural factors behind the development of personality, and Anna Freud, whose contributions were in the field of abnormal behaviour. In Canada, the work of **[e]** _____ was in the field of mental health and it contributed to the plan for deinstitutionalized psychiatric patients. Brenda Milner was a pioneer in Montreal in the field of **[f]** _____ and continues her work at the Montreal Neurological Institute.

Contemporary psychology is now dominated by five major conceptual perspectives. The **[g]** _____ perspective is focused on the study of the relationship between biological processes and behaviour. The **[h]** _____ perspective views behaviour as motivated by inner and unconscious forces over which the individual can exert little control. The psychodynamic perspective, developed by Sigmund Freud in the early 1900s, has been a major influence in twentieth-century thinking and continues to have an influence in the treatment of mental disorders. The **[i]** _____ perspective has evolved the structuralists' concern with trying to understand the mind into a study of how we internally represent the outside world and how this representation influences behaviour. This includes how we think and how we understand. The **[j]** _____ perspective began as a reaction to the failure of other early perspectives to base the science of psychology on observable phenomena. John B. Watson developed behaviourism as a study of how environmental forces

influence behaviour. He suggested that observable behaviour, measured objectively, should be the focus of the field. His views were shared by B. F. Skinner, probably the best-known psychologist. The newest perspective, the **[k]** _____ perspective, rejects the deterministic views of the other perspectives and instead focuses on the unique ability of humans to seek higher levels of maturity and fulfilment and to express **[l]** _____ .
All the major perspectives have active practitioners and continuing research programs.

Evaluate

_____ 1. biological perspective

_____ 2. psychodynamic perspective

_____ 3. cognitive perspective

_____ 4. behavioural perspective

_____ 5. humanistic perspective

a. The psychological perspective that suggests that observable behaviour should be the focus of study.

b. The psychological perspective that views behaviour from the perspective of biological functioning.

c. The psychological perspective based on the belief that behaviour is motivated by inner forces over which the individual has little control.

d. The psychological perspective that suggests that people are in control of their lives.

e. The psychological perspective that focuses on how people think, understand, and know the world.

Rethink

3. How might today's major perspectives of psychology be related to the earliest perspectives, such as structuralism, functionalism, and gestalt psychology?

4. Select one of the five major perspectives in use today (biological, psychodynamic, cognitive, behavioural, or humanistic), and describe the sorts of research questions and studies that researchers using that perspective might pursue.

SECTION 3: Psychology's Key Issues

Prepare

- *What are psychology's key issues and controversies?*
- *What is the future of psychology likely to hold?*

Organize

- *Psychology's Future*

Work

Few psychologists identify exclusively with one perspective. However, not every branch can utilize any perspective equally well. Biopsychology is far more focused on the biological perspective than on others. Social psychologists are more likely to find the cognitive perspective to be more useful than the biological perspective.

Major issues and questions form a common ground for psychology. The question of

[a] _____ places perspectives that focus on the environmental influences on behaviour against the perspectives that focus on inheritable traits. The perspective to which a psychologist subscribes determines the view taken concerning this issue. The question of whether

behaviour is determined by **[b]** _____ forces also separates psychological perspectives. The psychodynamic perspective interprets behaviour as influenced by unconscious forces whereas the cognitive perspective may attribute abnormal behaviour to faulty (conscious) reasoning. The issue of observable behaviour versus internal mental processes places the behavioural perspective against the cognitive perspective. The very controversial

question of free choice versus **[c]** _____ raises such issues as whether abnormal behaviour is a result of intentional choice. Finally, interests in individual differences conflict with the desire to find universal principles. These five key issues should not be viewed in an either-or manner, but instead they should be understood as creating a continuum along which psychologists would place themselves.

Evaluate

_____ 1. Nature versus nurture

_____ 2. Free will versus determinism

_____ 3. Observable behaviour versus internal mental process

_____ 4. Conscious versus unconscious behaviour

_____ 5. Individual differences versus universal principles

a. How much of our behaviour is produced by forces we are aware of, and how much is due to unconscious activity?

b. Should psychology focus on behaviour that can be observed by outside observers, or should it focus on unseen thinking processes?

c. How much of our behaviour is unique and how much reflects the culture and society in which we live?

d. How much behaviour is choice by the individual and how much is produced by factors beyond our control?

e. How much behaviour is due to heredity and how much is due to environment?

Rethink

5.   "The fact that some businesses now promote their ability to help people 'expand their mind beyond virtual reality' shows the great progress psychology has made lately."

Criticize this statement in light of what you know about professional psychology and pseudopsychology.

6.   How do some of the key issues identified in this chapter relate to law enforcement and criminal justice?

Section 4: Research in Psychology

Prepare

- **What is the scientific method, and how do psychologists use theory and research to answer questions of interest?**
- **What are the different research methods employed by psychclogists?**
- **How do psychologists establish cause-and-effect relationships in research studies?**

Organize

- **The Scientific Method**
- **Psychological Research**

Work

The cases of the Scarborough rape victim and Kitty Genovese illustrate the complex task of conducting research in order to explain phenomena that otherwise appear inexplicable. Research into the question of why bystanders fail to help—and under what conditions they are more likely to offer help—is used throughout the chapter to illustrate research methods.

A major aim of research in psychology is to discover which of our assumptions about human behaviour is correct. First, questions that interest psychologists must be set into the proper framework so that a systematic inquiry may be conducted to find the answer to the question.

Psychologists use an approach called the **[a]** _____ to conduct their inquiry. The scientific method has three main steps: (1) identifying questions of interest; (2) formulating an explanation; and (3) carrying out research designed to lend support or refute the explanation.

[b] _____ are broad explanations and predictions about phenomena that interest the scientist. Because psychological theories grow out of the diverse models (presented in Chapter 1), they vary in breadth and detail. Psychologists' theories differ from our informal theories by being formal and focused. Latané and Darley proposed a theory of *diffusion of responsibility* to account for why bystanders and onlookers did not help Kitty Genovese.

After formulating a theory, the next step for Latané and Darley was to devise a way of testing the theory. They began by stating a **[c]** _____, a prediction stated in a way that allows it to be tested. Latané and Darley's hypothesis was: The greater the number of people who witness an emergency situation, the less likely it is that help will be given to a victim.

Formal theories and hypotheses allow psychologists to organize separate bits of information and to move beyond the facts and make deductions about phenomena not yet encountered.

Research is systematic inquiry aimed at the discovery of new knowledge. It is the means of actually testing hypotheses and theories. In order to research a hypothesis, the hypothesis must be stated in a manner that is testable. **[d]** _____ refers to the translation of a hypothesis into specific, testable procedures that can be observed and measured. If we examine scientific methods closely, we can then make more critically informed and reasoned judgments about everyday situations.

[e] _____ requires examining existing records and collecting data regarding the phenomena of interest to the researcher. Latané and Darley would have begun by examining newspaper clippings and other records to find examples of situations like those they were studying.

[f] _____ involves the researcher observing naturally occurring behaviour without intervening in the situation. Unfortunately, the phenomena of interest may be infrequent. Furthermore, when people know they are being watched, they may act differently.

In **[g]** _____, participants are chosen from a larger population and asked a series of questions about behaviour, thoughts, or attitudes. Techniques are sophisticated enough now that small samples can be drawn from large populations to make predictions about how the entire population will behave. The potential problems are that some people may not remember how they felt or acted at a particular time, or they may give answers they believe that the researcher wants to hear. Also, survey questions can be formulated in such a way as to bias the response.

When the phenomena of interest is uncommon, psychologists may use a

[h] _____, an in-depth examination of an individual or small group of people. Insight gained through a case study must be done carefully because the individuals studied may not be representative of a larger group.

[i] _____ examines the relationship between two factors and the degree to which they are associated, or "correlated." The correlation is measured by a mathematical score ranging from +1.0 to -1.0. A positive correlation says that when one factor _increases_, the other correlated factor also _increases_. A negative correlation says that as one factor _increases_, the other negatively correlated factor _decreases_. When little or no relationship exists between two factors, the correlation is close to 0. Correlation can show that two factors are related and that the presence of one predicts another, but it cannot prove that one causes the other. Correlation research cannot rule out alternative causes when examining the relationship between two factors.

Experiments must be conducted in order to establish cause-and-effect relationships. A formal

[j] _____ examines the relationship of two or more factors in a setting that is deliberately manipulated to produce a change in one factor and then to observe how the change affects other factors. This **[k]** _____ allows psychologists to detect the relationship between these factors. These factors, called **[l]** _____, can be behaviours, events, or other characteristics that can change or vary in some way. The first step in developing an experiment is to operationalize a hypothesis (as did Latané and Darley). At least two groups of participants must be observed. One group receives the

[m] _____ , the manipulated variable, and is called the

[n] _____ . The other group is called the [o] _____ and is not exposed to the manipulated variable. Latané and Darley created a bogus emergency and then varied the number of bystanders present, in effect creating several different treatment groups. The variable that is manipulated is the [p] _____ —the condition that distinguishes the treatment groups—and in this example it was the number of people present.

The [q] _____ is the variable that is measured to reveal the effect of the manipulation. In this example, the dependent variable was how long it took the *participant* to offer help.

In order to be assured that some characteristics of the participant do not influence the outcome of an experiment, a procedure called [r] _____ must be used to assign participants to treatment or control groups. The objective of random assignment is to make each group comparable.

Latané and Darley utilized a trained *confederate*, who feigned an epileptic seizure, to create the bogus emergency. The results of their experiment suggested that the size of the audience did indeed influence the time it took for participants to offer help. To be sure, they had to analyze their results according to statistical procedures to prove that it was unlikely that their results were caused by chance. Also, to be certain of their results, other psychologists must try to repeat the experiment under the same or similar circumstances and test other variations of the hypothesis.

The process is called [s] _____ .

Evaluate

_____ 1. naturalistic observation

_____ 2. survey research

_____ 3. independent variable

_____ 4. operational definition

_____ 5. experimental group

_____ 6. random assignment

a. The group in an experiment that receives the effect of the independent variable.

b. A precise definition that allows other researchers to replicate an experiment.

c. The study of behaviour in its own setting, with no attempt to alter it

d. The variable manipulated by a researcher to determine its effects on the dependent variable.

e. Assignment of experimental participants to two or more groups on the basis of chance.

f. A research method that involves

_____ 7. correlation
coefficient

manipulating independent variables to determine how they affect dependent variables.

_____ 8. experimental
research

g. An in-depth study of a single person, that can provide suggestions for future research

_____ 9. case study

h. A number ranging from +1.00 and -1.00 that represents the degree and direction of the relationship between two variables.

i. A research method that involves collecting information from a group of people who are representative of a larger group.

Rethink

7. Starting with the theory that diffusion of responsibility causes responsibility for helping to be shared among bystanders, Latané and Darley derived the hypothesis that the more people who witness an emergency situation, the less likely it is that help will be given to a victim. How many other hypotheses can you think of based on the same theory of diffusion of responsibility?

8. Can you describe how a researcher might use naturalistic observation, case study methods, and survey research to investigate gender differences in aggressive behaviour in the workplace? First state a hypothesis, than describe your research approaches. What positive and negative features does each method have?

Section 5: Research Challenges: Exploring the Process

Prepare

- ***What major issues underlie the process of conducting research?***

Organize

- ***The Ethics of Research***
- ***Should Animals Be Used in Research?***
- ***Threats to Experiments***

Work

There are issues other than the quality of research that are of concern to psychologists. The ethics of certain research practices come into question when there exists a possibility of harm to a participant. Guidelines have been developed for the treatment of human and animal participants, and most proposed research is now reviewed by a panel to assure that guidelines are being met.

The concept of **[a]** _____ has become a key ethical principle. Prior to participating in an experiment, participants must sign a form indicating that they have been told of the basic outlines of the study and what their participation will involve.

For proper and meaningful generalizations of research results, a selection of participants that reflects the diversity of human behaviour is necessary. Also, ethical guidelines call for assurance that animals in experiments do not suffer as a consequence of being participants in the experiment.

Researchers must all address the issue of **[b]** _____, the factors that distort the experimenter's understanding of the relationship between the independent and dependent variables. **[c]** _____ *expectations* occur when the experimenter unintentionally conveys cues about how the participants should behave in the experiment.

[d] _____ *expectations* are the participant's expectations about the intended goal of the experiment. The participant's guesses about the hypothesis can influence behaviour and thus the outcomes. One approach is to disguise the true purpose of the experiment. Another is to use a **[e]** _____ with the control group so that the participants remain unaware of whether or not they are being exposed to the experimental condition. The *double-blind procedure* guards against these two biases by informing neither the experimenter nor the participant about which treatment group the participant is in.

Psychologists utilize statistical procedures to determine if the results of a research study are significant. A **[f]** _____ means that the results of the experiment were not likely to be a result of chance.

Evaluate

_____ 1. bias

_____ 2. placebo

_____ 3. informed consent

_____ 4. representative sample

a. A written agreement by a subject and the researcher in an experiment signed after receiving information about the researcher's specific procedures.

b. A sample that is selected so that it reflects the characteristics of a population that the research is interested in studying.

c. Beliefs that interfere with a researcher's objectivity

d. In drug research, the positive effects that are associated with a person's beliefs about a drug even when it contains no active ingredients.

Rethink

9.   A pollster studies people's attitudes toward welfare programs by circulating a questionnaire via the Internet. Is this study likely to reflect accurately the views of the general population? Why or why not?

10.   A researcher believes that college professors in general show female students less attention and respect in the classroom than they show male students. She sets up an experimental study involving the observation of classrooms in different conditions. In explaining the study to the professors and students who will participate, what steps should the researcher take to eliminate experimental bias based on both experimenter expectations and participant expectations?

Practise Tests

Test your knowledge of the chapter material by answering these questions. These questions have been placed in three Practise Tests. The first two tests are composed of questions that will test your recall of factual knowledge. The third test contains questions that are challenging and primarily test for conceptual knowledge and your ability to apply that knowledge. Check your answers and review the feedback using the Answer Key on the following pages of the *Study Guide*.

PRACTISE TEST 1:

1.   The humanistic perspective places a major emphasis on:
   a.   observable behaviour.
   b.   inner forces.
   c.   free will.
   d.   understanding concepts.

2.   A psychodynamic psychologist would be most interested in:
   a.   the learning process.
   b.   our perceptions of the world around us.
   c.   dreams.
   d.   the functioning of the brain.

3.   Which of the following sources of evidence would be the least acceptable to behaviourist like John B. Watson?
   a.   Evidence gathered using introspection.
   b.   Evidence from intelligence tests.
   c.   Evidence regarding emotional growth and development.
   d.   Evidence from perception and sensation experiments.

4.   The influence of inherited characteristics on behaviour would be studied with the:
   a.   cognitive perspective.
   b.   psychodynamic perspective.
   c.   behavioural perspective.
   d.   biological perspective.

5.   "The whole is greater than the sum of the parts" is a postulate of:
   a.   structuralism.
   b.   functionalism.
   c.   gestalt psychology.
   d.   behaviourism.

6. Which of the following techniques distinguishes the kind of inquiry used by scientists from that used by professionals in nonscientific areas like literature, art, and philosophy?
    a. intuitive thought
    b. scientific methods
    c. common sense
    d. construction of new theoretical models

7. Which of the following psychological speciality areas would be considered as the most coherent?
    a. psychodynamic psychology
    b. cross-cultural psychology
    c. experimental psychology
    d. counseling psychology

8. The focus of developmental psychology is on:
    a. applications such as improving the parenting skills of adults.
    b. understanding growth and changes occurring throughout life.
    c. development and maintenance of healthy interpersonal relationships as in friendships, co-worker relationships, and marriages.
    d. identifying behavioural consistencies throughout life.

9. Psychology was established formally in 1879 when:
    a. Sigmund Freud began psychoanalysis.
    b. the American Psychological Association was founded.
    c. William James, an American, published his first major book.
    d. Wilhelm Wundt founded his psychology laboratory in Germany.

10. According to the discussion in the text, the profession of psychology in Canada differs from that in the United States in terms of:
    a. their early historical beginnings.
    b. professionalism.
    c. increasing the ethnic sensitivity of counseling and clinical psychologists.
    d. academic credentials.

11. Theories tend to be _____ while hypotheses are _____.
    a. general statements; specific statements
    b. specific statements; general statements
    c. provable; impossible to disprove
    d. factual; based on speculation

12. The technique of conducting an in-depth interview of an individual in order to understand that individual better and to make inferences about people in general is called a:
    a. focused study.
    b. generalization study.
    c. case study.
    d. projection study.

13. When the strength of a relationship is represented by a mathematical score of +.87 we are dealing with a:
    a. dependent variable.
    b. manipulation.
    c. correlation.
    d. treatment.

14. The group that receives no treatment in an experiment using two or more groups serves as:
    a. a control.
    b. a case.
    c. an independent variable.
    d. a measured variable.

15. In an experiment, the event that is measured and expected to change is the:
    a. dependent variable.
    b. independent variable.
    c. control variable.
    d. confounding variable.

_____ 16. scientific method

_____ 17. theories

_____ 18. hypothesis

_____ 19. research

_____ 20. operationalization

a. Systematic inquiry aimed at discovering new knowledge.

b. The assignment of participants to given groups on a chance basis alone.

c. A prediction stated in a way that allows it to be tested.

d. The process of translating a hypothesis into specific testable procedures that can be measured and observed.

e. The process of appropriately framing and properly answering questions, used by scientists to come to an understanding about the world.

f. Broad explanations and predictions concerning phenomena of interest.

21. The assignment of participants to given groups based on a chance basis alone is

_____.

22. _____ are defined as broad explanations and predictions concerning phenomena of interest

23. Psychologists who focus on the effects of physical maltreatment by mothers and fathers on the level of aggression in their children are working in the field of_____psychopathology..

24. Children who are abused and become abusers are part of what researchers have termed the "the _____."

25. To reduce the number of rapes, researchers have developed programs aimed at teaching _____ that make aggression less likely to occur.

26. Describe the perspective—or conceptual model—that best fits your current understanding of why people behave the way that they do. Be sure to explain why you selected this particular perspective. Which perspectives do you reject? Why?

PRACTISE TEST 2:

1. Although their interests are diverse, psychologists share a common:
    a. concern for applying their knowledge to social situations.
    b. interest in mental processes or behaviour.
    c. respect for the ideas of psychoanalyst Sigmund Freud.
    d. interest in the study of animals' behaviour.

2. Of the following, an environmental psychologist would be most likely to study:
    a. the impact of smoking on health.
    b. experimental ethics.

    c.   the effects of crowding on behaviour.

    d.   program effectiveness.

3. During legislative hearings to review the state's insanity laws, lawmakers are likely to seek the advice of:

    a.   social psychologists.

    b.   counseling psychologists.

    c.   clinical psychologists.

    d.   forensic psychologists.

4. The largest proportion of psychologists are employed:

    a.   privately at their own independent practises.

    b.   in hospitals or mental institutions.

    c.   at colleges or universities.

    d.   in private businesses or industries.

5. Which of these questions would most interest a functionalist?

    a.   What are the best human values?

    b.   What are the contents of the mind?

    c.   How do nerves work?

    d.   How do the person's thoughts help her to get along in daily life?

6. John B. Watson was the first American psychologist to follow the:

    a.   behavioural perspective.

    b.   humanistic perspective.

    c.   cognitive perspective.

    d.   psychodynamic perspective.

7. Which of the following types of psychologists would be most interested in the "unconscious" side of the conscious versus unconscious determinants of behaviour issue?

    a.   a behavioural experimental psychologist

    b.   a humanistic psychologist

    c.   a psychodynamic clinical psychologist

    d.   a sports psychologist

8. Sigmund Freud believed that behaviour is motivated by:

    a.   subconscious inner forces.

    b.   a desire to achieve personal fulfilment.

    c.   the natural tendency to organize data through perception.

    d.   inherited characteristics.

9. Books that promise cheap, quick cures for psychological problems should be doubted because:

    a.   if the procedures worked as stated, they would already be applied widely.

    b.   only medically based therapies are fast.

    c.   the American Psychological Association would suppress any procedures that would cut back on the income earned by therapists.

    d.   the books' authors are overqualified to write on those topics.

10.   A theory is:

    a.   a broad explanation of phenomena of interest.

    b.   the step of identifying phenomena of interest.

    c.   observation that occurs without intervention by the observer.

    d.   a prediction stated in such a way that it can be tested.

11. If you decide that love is measured by the amount of touching that a couple engages in, then you have _____ love.
    a. archived
    b. operationalized
    c. theorized
    d. correlationalized

12. Suppose that a psychology professor joins the circus and gets a job working with the elephants in order to study the treatment of animals in the circus. Which research method is being applied?
    a. archival research
    b. correlational research
    c. naturalistic observation
    d. experimentation

13. Whether a behavioural scientist uses human or animal participants in an experiment, there are _____ that the scientist must satisfy in order not to violate the rights of the participants.

    a. moral obligations
    b. religious principles
    c. professional standards
    d. ethical guidelines

14. Neither the dentist nor the participant in a toothpaste study is told which of four toothpastes assigned to participants has the fluoride in order to:
    a. keep the confederate from influencing other participants.
    b. eliminate dependent variables.
    c. control the placebo effect.
    d. eliminate participant and experimenter expectations.

15. When a researcher reports that a study's outcome was statistically significant, this suggests that:
    a. efforts to replicate the results will succeed.
    b. a theory has been proven true.
    c. the results will have a noticeable social impact.
    d. the results were unlikely to have happened by chance.

_____ 16. experimental manipulation

_____ 17. experimental group

_____ 18. control group

_____ 19. independent variable

_____ 20. dependent variable

a. The variable that is manipulated in an experiment.

b. The research group receiving the treatment, or manipulation.

c. The manipulation implemented by the experimenter to influence results in a segment of the experimental population.

d. The variable that is measured and is expected to change as a result of experimenter manipulation.

e. The research group receiving no treatment.

21. The _____ perspective of psychology states that actions, feelings, and thoughts are associated with bodily events.

22. _____ developed psychoanalysis.

23. The father of modern psychology is _____.

24. A perspective in psychology that was developed to enhance human potential is the _____ perspective.

25. A behaviour or an event that can be manipulated in an experiment is referred to as an _____.

26. Select two of the key issues for psychology and describe how the resolution of these issues one way or the other would change the way you view yourself and others, your goals, and your immediate responsibility for your own success.

PRACTISE TEST 3: Conceptual, Applied, and Challenging Questions

1. What kind of psychologist would have a special interest in studying the aspects of an earthquake that people are most likely to recall?
   a. social psychologist
   b. consumer psychologist
   c. educational psychologist
   d. cognitive psychologist

2. Professor Gaipo has identified a trait he calls persistence, and he has begun to conduct research on the consistency of this trait in various situations. Professor Gaipo is most likely:
   a. a social psychologist.
   b. a cross-cultural psychologist.
   c. an educational psychologist.
   d. a personality psychologist.

3. Laura's car stalls on the highway on a cold, windy, and snowy night. Which type of psychologist would be most interested in whether other motorists offered assistance?
   a. a social psychologist
   b. an environmental psychologist
   c. a clinical psychologist
   d. an industrial-organizational psychologist

4. An architect interested in designing an inner-city apartment building that would not be prone to vandalism might consult with:
   a. a clinical psychologist.
   b. a school psychologist.
   c. a forensic psychologist.
   d. an environmental psychologist.

5. The procedure for studying the mind, in which structuralists train people to describe carefully, in their own words, what they experienced upon being exposed to various stimuli, is called:
   a. cognition.
   b. mind expansion.
   c. perception.
   d. introspection.

6. Today's scientists believe that the purpose of trephining was to:
   a. enable one person to read another's mind.
   b. allow evil spirits to escape.
   c. increase telekinetic powers.
   d. heal the patient of mental illness.

7. The major distinction between educational and school psychology is that:
   a. educational psychology is devoted to improving the education of students who have special needs, and school psychology is devoted to increasing achievement in all students.

b.　school psychology is devoted to improving the schooling of students who have special needs, and educational psychology is devoted to better understanding of the entire educational system.

c.　school psychology attempts to examine the entire educational process, and educational psychology looks at individual students.

d.　educational psychology attempts to examine the entire educational process, and school psychology is devoted to assessing and correcting academic and school-related problems of students.

8.　In an experiment, participants are placed in one of several rooms, each with a different colour scheme. In each setting, the participants are given a problem-solving task that has been shown to be challenging and often results in increased tension while the problem-solver attempts to solve the problem. Researchers have hypothesized that some colours may reduce stress and improve problem solving. In this study, the colour schemes of the rooms would be considered:

a.　irrelevant.

b.　the independent variable.

c.　the dependent variable.

d.　the confounding variable.

9.　In an experiment, participants are placed in one of several rooms, each with a different colour scheme. In each setting, the participants are given a problem-solving task that has been shown to be challenging and often results in increased tension while the problem-solver attempts to solve the problem. Researchers have hypothesized that some colours may reduce stress and improve problem solving. In this study, the levels of stress experienced by the participants would be considered to be:

a.　due to a combination of the problem and the colour schemes.

b.　the confounding variable.

c.　the independent variable.

d.　irrelevant.

10.　In an experiment, participants are placed in one of several rooms, each with a different colour scheme. In each setting, the participants are given a problem-solving task that has been shown to be challenging and often results in increased tension while the problem-solver attempts to solve the problem. Researchers have hypothesized that some colours may reduce stress and improve problem solving. In this study, the time required for each participant to solve the problem could be used as:

a.　the control condition.

b.　the independent variable.

c.　the dependent variable.

d.　the confounding variable.

11.　Professor Cooper is particularly interested in explanations of an individual's ability to make decisions based on a free choice. She is exploring a number of factors that may influence or determine choices, but she is very hopeful that she will be able to show that some non-determined choices can be demonstrated. Which of the following combinations best represents the two perspectives that would be supported by her research?

a.　the psychoanalytic and biological perspectives

b.　the behavioural and the humanistic perspectives

c.　the humanistic and cognitive perspectives

e.　the cognitive and behavioural perspectives

12.　Professor Murphy is convinced that his theory claiming that voters are more easily influenced by negative campaign messages is a correct theory. Which of the following would be his first step in demonstrating the theory's claims to be correct?

a.　Professor Murphy must find ways to measure the negativity of messages and voter behaviour.

b.　Professor Murphy must define the correlation coefficients.

c.　Professor Murphy must collect data about voters and campaigns.

    d.   Professor Murphy must select the appropriate statistical analyses to utilize.

13. Which of the following statements requires the least modification in order to produce testable predictions?
    a.   Decreases in physical exercise are associated with higher rates of heart-related diseases.
    b.   Intelligence declines dramatically as people age.
    c.   Disgruntled employees are likely to steal from their employers.
    d.   Smiling can make you feel happy.

14. For several years, Professor Lane has been studying the effects of light on the ability of monkeys to tolerate stress. Each experiment varies the conditions slightly, but usually only one factor is altered each time. Dr. Lane is most likely trying to
    a.   develop a new statistical test.
    b.   operationalize her hypothesis.
    c.   formulate a new hypothesis.
    d.   test the limits of her theory.

15. Dr. Liefeld has analyzed the death rates reported in several hundred studies of AIDS. She has compared the statistical results from each study and been able to create a summary analysis. To complete her analysis, she most likely has used:
    a.   significant outcomes.   c.   correlational research.
    b.   meta-analysis.   d.   experimental techniques.

_____ 16. archival research

_____ 17. naturalistic observation

_____ 18. survey research

_____ 19. case study

_____ 20. correlational research

a.   Observation without intervention, in which the investigator records information about a naturally occurring situation and does not intervene in the situation.

b.   The examination of existing records for the purpose of confirming a hypothesis.

c.   An in-depth interview of an individual in order to understand that individual better and to make inferences about people in general.

d.   Research to determine whether there is a relationship between two sets of factors, such as certain behaviours and responses.

e.   Sampling a group of people by assessing their behaviour, thoughts, or attitudes, then generalizing the findings to a larger population.

21. Wilhelm Wundt asked his subjects to observe, analyze, and describe in detail what they were experiencing when they were exposed to a stimulus. This was known as _____.

22. The_____ view , developed principally by Freud, proposed that patients' symptoms were due to past conflicts and that emotional traumas were too threatening to be remembered consciously.

23. The_____ perspective looks to the environment to explain the behaviour of the organism. This contrasts with the other four perspectives, which look inside the organism to explain behaviour.

24. Study participants are invited to receive a _____ , in which they are given an explanation of the study and the part they played in it.

25. When scientists use animals in research, they must strive to avoid physical discomfort to the animals and strive to promote their _____ well being.

26. Explain how you would respond to the comment that psychology is just common sense. Define critical thinking and demonstrate how it is used in psychological research.

27. One criticism of psychological experiments using college students as participants is that the average college student is not representative of the _____ at large.

Spotlight on Terminology and Language—
Cultural Idioms
Psychologists at Work

Page 5 "**Methodically**—and painfully—**recounting** events that occurred in his youth, the college student **discloses** a childhood secret that he has revealed previously to no one."

The college student arranged the way he told his story, so that he told it in a systematic and orderly method. He told it **methodically**. To **recount** is to review, call to mind, and tell the particular details of this secret. When you **recount** and narrate an event, people now know about it. As it is **disclosed**, he has revealed his secret. Are there some events in your life that you have **recounted methodically** as you have **disclosed** them?

Page 5 "Each of these episodes describes work carried out by **contemporary** psychologists." Health psychologists, developmental psychologists, cognitive psychologists, clinical neuropsychologists, evolutionary psychologists, and clinical psychologists are just a few of the major subfields of psychology of a **contemporary** psychologist.

Pages 5-6 "For example, they might examine the link between specific sites in the brain and the muscular **tremors** of people affected by Parkinson's disease or attempt to determine how our emotions are related to physical sensations."

When your body shakes as a result of physical weakness or emotional stress, it's an involuntary **trembling**, or quivering of voluntary muscle. These **tremors** vary in intensity and duration.

Page 6 "If you have every wondered why you are susceptible to **optical** illusions, how your body registers pain, or how you can study with the greatest effectiveness, an experimental psychologist can answer your questions."

Anything **optic** pertains to the eye or vision. An **optical** illusion is a misleading image presented to the vision.

Page 7 "The complex networks of social **interrelationships** that are part of our world are the focus of study for a number of subfields of psychology."

The prefix **inter** means between, among, in the midst of something. When we talk about **interrelationships**, we mean carried on between groups, occurring between and shared by the groups. What are some of the social **interrelationships** you have as part of your lifestyle?

Page 8 "Candidates must have the ability to establish a **rapport** with senior business executives and to help them find innovative, practical, and psychologically sound solutions to problems concerning people and organizations."

When you establish **rapport** with someone, it means you develop a relationship. Psychologists need to be able to establish **rapport** with a patient so that the patient has confidence in the psychologist. The establishment of **rapport** is an important initial component of successful psychotherapy.

Page 9 "For instance, many people in business, nursing, law, social work, and other professions report that an undergraduate background in psychology has proven **invaluable** in their careers."

Invaluable means to have a worth beyond measure. Psychology training has a high degree of value in every career.

Page 9 "Furthermore, undergraduates who specialize in psychology typically have good **analytical** skills, are trained to think critically, and are able to synthesize and evaluate information well—skills that are held in high regard by employers in business, industry, and the government."

A student who has good **analytical** skills is able to separate and break up an event into its component parts or ingredients. Can you **analyze**, or carefully determine the procedures you use to check your competence in learning the psychology text material?

Psychology's Key Issues

Page 11 "Franz Josef Gall, an eighteenth-century physician, argued that a trained observer could **discern** intelligence, moral character, and other basic personality characteristics from the shape and number of bumps on a person's skull."

To **discern** means to be able to detect, usually with senses other than vision. Can you **discern** an unfamiliar odor in a room? Are you capable of **discerning**, revealing insight and understanding, when you are in an uncomfortable situation?

Page 11 "Psychology's roots can be traced back to the ancient Greeks and Romans, and philosophers argued for hundreds of years about some of the questions psychologists **grapple** with today."

To **grapple** is to struggle and to work to come to grips with. As we **grapple** to understand what we are reading, we cope with the new knowledge and deal with needing to understand it by working to make sense of it—by synthesizing and analyzing the new information.

Page 12 "Such drawbacks led to the evolution of new approaches, which largely **supplanted** structuralism."

To **supplant** is to replace. Structuralism was **supplanted** with the evolution of new approaches to understand the fundamental elements of the mind."

Page 12 "Instead of considering the individual parts that make up thinking, gestalt psychologists took the opposite **tack**, concentrating on how people consider individual elements together as units or wholes."

When you take the opposite **tack**, you move in a different direction, or shift your focus. Generally when you are trying a new method of action, you are trying a new **tack**.

Page 12 "Their **credo** was 'The whole is different from the sum of its parts,' meaning that, when considered together, the basic elements that compose our perception of objects produce something greater and more meaningful than those individual elements alone."

When you have a **credo**, you have a belief system that you use to guide your actions and achievements. Many psychologists have a **credo** of usefulness to society. What is the **credo** of gestalt psychologists?

Page 12 "Karen Horney focused on the social and cultural factors behind personality, and June Etta Downey **spearheaded** the study of personality traits and became the first woman to head a psychology department at a state university."

To **spearhead** means to be the leading element, to take a leading role. Often, the person who **spearheads** an activity is the leader and the leading force. Have you **spearheaded** any efforts to improve your community or your academic institution?

Page 14"**Proponents** of the psychodynamic **perspective** believe that behaviour is motivated by inner forces and conflicts about which we have little awareness or control."

A **proponent** is an advocate, someone who argues in favour of something, such as a legislative measure or a doctrine. Are you a **proponent** of one specific psychological perspective?

Page 14 "As we will see, the behavioural **perspective** crops up along every **byway** of psychology."

A **perspective** is a way of regarding, viewing, or evaluating information, ideas, objects, etc. Issues in psychology can be viewed from five different, general perspectives. By being able to view any problem from several perspectives we are potentially able to understand it better than viewing it from one perspective alone.

Something **crops up** when it appears suddenly, unexpectedly, and often, similar to weeds.

A **byway** is generally a secondary aspect. The behavioural perspective is used to explain much of how people learn behaviours, and in

designing programs to implement change.

Page 17 "As you consider the many topics and perspectives that make up psychology, which range from a narrow focus on minute biochemical influences on behaviour to a broad focus on social behaviours, you might find yourself thinking that the discipline lacks **cohesion**."

Cohesion involves seeing how something sticks together. The field of psychology has **cohesion** because the five theoretical perspectives (cognitive, psychodynamic, humanistic, biological, and behavioural) are consistently used to explain and predict behaviour.

Page 20 "Probably the best known case of **bystander** inaction involved a young woman named Kitty Genovese"

A **bystander** is someone who is present but not taking part in an event. He or she would be a spectator. Would there be any **bystanders** in a nuclear disaster or a snowstorm?

Page 21 The scientific theory "consists of three main steps: (1) identifying questions of interest, (2) formulating an explanation, and (3) carrying out research designed to lend support or to **refute** the explanation."

To **refute** is to be able to prove something is false. In the courtroom, evidence and proof are used to **refute** statements. Psychological research is often used to refute assumptions people believe are true.

Page 21 "If you have ever asked yourself why a particular teacher is so easily annoyed, why a friend is always late for appointments, or how your dog understands your commands, you have been **formulating** questions about behaviour."

You **formulate** hypotheses in psychology as you state your observations or questions you can test statistically.

Page 22 "Psychologists Bibb Latané and John Darley, responding specifically to the Kitty

Genovese case, developed a theory based on a phenomenon they called **diffusion** of responsibility."

Diffusion means to spread out and to make more widespread. When there is a **diffusion** of responsibility among a group of people, it means that so many people are witness to an event that each feels a lessened responsibility to report the event or to act on it because they can tell themselves the next person will do this. Have you experienced the phenomenon of **diffusion** of responsibility on a crowded road following an accident, where people see an accident as an inconvenience instead of an opportunity to help?

Page 22 "Hypotheses stem from theories; they help to test the underlying **validity** of theories."

When a hypothesis has **validity**, the way the hypothetical prediction has been stated makes this statement capable of measuring, predicting, or representing what it has been designed to measure.

Page 22 "For one thing, theories and hypotheses allow psychologists to make sense of unorganized, separate observations and bits of information by permitting them to place the pieces with a structured and **coherent** framework."

When you are told you are thinking **coherently**, your thinking has logical consistency and an order to it. As you learn the psychological theories, you have a structured and **coherent** framework for explaining behaviour.

Research in Psychology

Page 23 "The media constantly **bombard** us with claims about research studies and findings."

When a person gets **bombarded**, he or she feels attacked or assaulted. Students often question their professors persistently with questions on interesting topics; they are **bombarding** their professors with questions as they delve into learning and understanding the material.

Page 23 "The important point to remember about naturalistic observation is that the researcher is **passive** and simply records what occurs."

Passive means not acting and not operating, but rather receptive to outside influences or impressions. When psychologists conduct naturalistic observation, they hope that their presence does not impact the environment. They do not want to make a change in the situations. But rather, they wish to **passively** observe and record.

Page 24 "Asking people directly about their behaviour seems in some ways the most straightforward approach to understanding what people do, but survey research has several potential **drawbacks**."

A **drawback** is an objectionable feature because it is a hindrance to our progress. When we have a **drawback** with the research we are conducting, it may mean that our very presence or behaviour or questions are influencing the responses we are recording. Influencing your results is a definite **drawback** of some ways of collecting data. In survey research the researcher must be careful not to use questions that lead the respondent into specific types of answers. If the manner in which a question was phrased impacted the honesty of the responses of the survey participants, this would be a **drawback** of the research design.

Research Challenges: Exploring the Process

Page 33 "…College students are used so frequently in experiments that psychology has been called—somewhat **contemptuously**—the 'science of the behaviour of the college sophomore.'"

When you do something with **contempt**, you are suggesting that you have no respect or regard for it. Contempt here refers to disrespect for the research results conducted with the college sophomore research population. Persons **contemptuously** point out that the college student population is a very contained and limited grouping.

■ CHAPTER 1: ANSWER KEY

Section 1:	Section 2:	Section 3:	Section 4:	Evaluate	Section 5:
[a] Psychology	[a] structuralism	[a] nurture	[a] scientific method	1. c	[a] informed
[b] Biopsychology	[b] introspection	[b] unconscious	[b] Theories	2. i	consent
[c] Experimental	[c] functionalism	[c] determinism	[c] hypothesis	3. d	[b] experimental
[d] Cognitive	[d] Gestalt psychology		[d] Operationalization	4. b	bias
[e] evolutionary	[e] Reva Gerstein	Evaluate	[e] Archival research	5. a	[c] Experimenter
psychology	[f] neuropsychology	1. e	[f] Naturalistic observation	6. e	[d] Participant
[f] clinical	[g] biological	2. d	[g] survey research	7. h	[e] placebo
neuropsychology	[h] psychodynamic	3. b	[h] case study	8. f	[f] significant
[g] environmental	[i] cognitive	4. a	[i] Correlational research	9. g	outcome
[h] forensic	[j] behavioural	5. c	[j] experiment		
[i] sport and exercise	[k] humanistic		[k] experimental		Evaluate
	[l] free will		manipulation		1. c
			[l] variables		2. d
			[m] treatment		3. a
Evaluate	Evaluate		[n] experimental group		4. b
1. c	1. b		[o] control group		
2. a	2. c		[p] independent variable		
3. e	3. e		[q] dependent variable		
4. d	4. a		[r] random assignment to		
5. b	5. d		condition		
			[s] replication		

Selected Rethink Answers

1. Twins share a similar genetic makeup. If they do not share the same environment, questions can be explored about whether or not behaviour is nature (heredity) or nurture (behavioural characteristics that are created and maintained by the environment).

2. List those psychologists (biological, school, developmental, cognitive, behavioural, etc.) that you believe may study issues (poor nutrition, lack of maturity, inability to perceive the written word correctly, etc.) related to a 7 year old's inability to read. State the viewpoint/perspective that each would have about a 7 year old's inability to read. Discuss how each would go about identifying and correcting the problem.

3. List the basic ideas early researchers had when developing structuralism, functionalism and gestalt psychology. List the five major psychological perspectives in psychology (behavioural, cognitive, psychodynamic, humanistic, biological) and describe the basic tenets of each perspective. Note the similarities in the approaches used.

4. Identify a psychological perspective, (e.g.., the biological perspective, the study of the relationship of the mind and the body). Research questions are then based on this mind-body connection. Are issues like alcoholism, aggression and violence, and shyness determined by things such as genetics, diet and nutrition, amount of sleep, exercise, etc.? Studies to address this might include experiments that manipulate a certain group's daily diet, sleep, or exercise habits. Other studies/surveys might look at family histories of alcoholism, aggression, etc. Also, studies that look at the use of drugs to manipulate the behaviours that have been mentioned would all be areas that might be pursued by a researcher with a biological perspective.

6. Law enforcement and the criminal justice field both work to identify the causes of criminal behaviour. They study people's unconscious motivations for committing offences. They are also interested in whether or not people are born (nature) with certain personality traits or live in environments (nurture) that support criminal behaviours. Researchers in these fields try to find ways to both understand and change certain behaviours. Each of the five contemporary psychologists would have their own approach

8. State an operational definition for what you would consider aggression in the workplace. In naturalistic observation, researchers could get jobs at the workplace being studied in order to experience, or not experience, the aggression. In a case study, a very thorough and detailed history of the situation could be taken from a selected few who had experienced this behaviour. Design a survey to gather information from a wide group of people. List the positive features of each and the negative features. Which would you select and why?

9.. The general population does not use the Internet, only a select portion of citizens fall into this survey group. Information gathered here would have to be presented as "People who use the Internet and filled out an attitude survey on welfare" had the following views on the topic. Your sample must reflect characteristics of the population being studied.

Practise Test 1:

1. c   obj. 6   p. 15
a. Incorrect. This is the focal interest of behaviourists and experimental psychologists.
b. Incorrect. Inner forces are the focal interest of psychodynamic psychologists.
*c. Correct. Humanistic psychologists are indeed interested in the individual's power to make choices on their own, in other words, the individual's free will.
d. Incorrect. Concepts are the domain of cognitive psychologists.

2. c   obj. 6   p. 14
a. Incorrect. While not central, the learning process would be of some interest to psychodynamic psychologists.
b. Incorrect. While not central, the perceptions are of interest to psychodynamic psychologists.
*c. Correct. As dreams reflect the activity of the unconscious elements of the mind, they would be of great interest to psychodynamic psychologists.
d. Incorrect. While not central, the functioning of the brain has been of some interest to some psychodynamic psychologists.

3. a   obj. 6   pp. 14, 15
*a. Correct. Above all things, Watson abhorred the use of information derived from consciousness and other unobservable phenomena.
b. Incorrect. If gathered through observable events, this is acceptable.
c. Incorrect. If gathered through observable events, this is acceptable.
d. Incorrect. If gathered through observable events, this is acceptable.

4. d   obj. 6   pp. 13, 14
a. Incorrect. The cognitive model focuses on understanding thought processes.
b. Incorrect. The psychodynamic model focuses upon understanding the role of unconscious motivation and primitive forces in behaviour.
c. Incorrect. The behavioural model focuses upon understanding how behaviour is conditioned and modified by stimuli and reinforcements.
*d. Correct. The biological model examines the role of genetics in all aspects of human behaviour.

5. c   obj. 5   p. 12
a. Incorrect. This statement is completely associated with gestalt psychology.
b. Incorrect. This statement is completely associated with gestalt psychology.
*c. Correct. This statement reflects the gestalt view that the mind organizes perceptions as it adds information to them.

d. Incorrect. This statement is completely associated with gestalt psychology.

6. b   obj. 9   pp. 20, 21
a. Incorrect. Intuitive thought describes something other than an approach to collecting data, referring perhaps to thinking about intuitions.
*b. Correct. Scientists refer to their systematic methods for collecting and analyzing data as the scientific method.
c. Incorrect. Common sense is an approach available to all, and does not necessarily have the qualities of systematic and rigourous data collection and analysis associated with science.
d. Incorrect. Literature, art, and philosophy often construct theories of interpretation or truth, or may utilize theories to account for evil, and so on.

7. a   obj. 6   p. 13, 14
*a. Correct. Psychodynamic psychology follows a coherent conceptual perspective.
b. Incorrect. Cross-cultural psychology involves a collection of approaches.
c. Incorrect. Experimental psychology involves a collection of theoretical approaches, though all utilize experimental methods.
d. Incorrect. Counseling psychology involves a wide range of approaches.

8. b   obj. 2   p. 9
a. Incorrect. Parenting skills comprise only a minor interest of developmental psychology.
*b. Correct. "Development" refers to growth, maturation, and change through life.
c. Incorrect. Peer relationships and marriage comprise only a minor interest of developmental psychology.
d. Incorrect. This too may be considered only a minor interest of developmental psychology.

9. d   obj. 5   p. 11
a. Incorrect. Freud did not have a laboratory, and his work began in the 1880s.
b. Incorrect. The APA was founded long after the beginning of psychology.
c. Incorrect. James established a lab in 1875 and some students conducted research in it.
*d. Correct. Wundt is given this credit because of his 1879 laboratory, complete with funding and graduate students.

10. d   obj. 4   pp. 9, 10
a. Incorrect. They are similar.
b. Incorrect. They both have equally high standards
c. Incorrect. Being sensitive to ethnic origins of ones clients is not compared between Canada and the U.S..
*d. Correct. In Canada most psychologists with a doctoral degree have a Ph.D. In the U.S. clinical psychologists

who focus on treatment may have a PsyD instead.

11. a   obj. 10   p. 21, 22
*a.   Correct. Typically, theories are general statements about the relationships among the phenomena of interest, while hypotheses are specific statements about those relationships.
b.   Incorrect. This is opposite the general trend.
c.   Incorrect. All theories are potentially provable, but hypotheses can be disproved.
d.   Incorrect. If it were a fact, it would not be a theory.

12. c   obj. 11   p. 24
a.   Incorrect. This is not a term in psychology, except as it may refer to the way students should study for exams.
b.   Incorrect. Perhaps a learning theorist may conduct a study to test the generalization of stimuli or responses, but such would not fit the definition given.
*c.   Correct. This definition describes a case study.
d.   Incorrect. This is not a term in psychology.

13. c   obj. 12   p. 25
a.   Incorrect. A dependent variable is that variable that changes as a result of changes in the independent variable.
b.   Incorrect. The experimenter manipulates variables during an experiment.
*c.   Correct. This defines a correlation.
d.   Incorrect. The manipulation of variables is sometimes called a treatment.

14. a   obj. 13   p. 27
*a.   Correct. The experiment must compare the behaviour of one group to that of another in order to demonstrate that a specific variable caused the difference. The group receiving no treatment is one in which the variable should not change.
b.   Incorrect. A case may refer to one instance of the event.
c.   Incorrect. An independent variable is the variable that is changed in order to be "treated."
d.   Incorrect. All variables should be measured, even those in the "no treatment" group.

15. a   obj. 13   pp. 27, 28
*a.   Correct. The dependent variable changes as a result of a change in the independent variable.
b.   Incorrect. The independent variable is manipulated by the experimenter and it causes the change in the dependent variables.
c.   Incorrect. The control involves a group that does not receive the treatment, and the dependent variable is not expected to change.
d.   Incorrect. A confounding variable is a variable that causes change in the dependent variable unexpectedly.

16. e   obj. 9   p. 21
17. f   obj. 10   p. 21, 22
18. c   obj. 10   p. 22
19. a   obj. 11   p. 21
20. d   obj. 11   p. 23
21. b. randomization   obj. 13   p. 28
22. theories   obj. 10   p. 21, 22

23. developmental psychopathology   obj. 6   p. 16
24. cycle of violence   obj. 6   p. 16
25. values education   obj. 6   p. 16

26.
• Identify the key principle of the perspectives you have chosen. For instance, in the psychodynamic perspective, one of the key principles is unconscious motivation. For the biological perspective, the focus is on the physiological and organic basis of behaviour.
• Offer a reason, perhaps an example, that illustrates why you like this perspective. Asserting that you just "liked it" or that "it makes the most sense" is not a sufficient answer.

Practise Test 2:
1. b   obj. 1   p. 4
a.   Incorrect. Not all psychologists seek to apply their knowledge to social situations.
*b.   Correct. Mental processes and behaviour constitute the area of study of psychology.
c.   Incorrect. Few psychologists appear to respect the ideas of Freud.
d.   Incorrect. Only special areas of psychology are interested in animal behaviour.

2. c   obj. 2   p. 6
a.   Incorrect. This is of interest to physiological and health psychology.
b.   Incorrect. The ethics involved in experimentation affect every psychologist and would be of interest to all, though primarily experimental psychologists.
*c.   Correct. Environmental psychologists claim the study of crowding as their domain.
d.   Incorrect. The determination of program effectiveness is the domain of psychologists concerned with program evaluation.

3. d   obj. 2   p. 6
a.   Incorrect. Social psychologists are not interested in the insanity laws of the state.
b.   Incorrect. Counseling psychologists are not interested in the insanity laws of the state.
c.   Incorrect. Clinical psychologists are not interested in the insanity laws of the state.
*d.   Correct. Forensic psychologists study legal issues and behaviour.

4. c   obj. 4   p. 8
a.   Incorrect.
b.   Incorrect.
*c.   Correct..
d.   Incorrect.

5. d   obj. 5   p. 12
a.   Incorrect. This is probably an issue for existential and humanistic psychology.
b.   Incorrect. This was structuralism's concern.
c.   Incorrect. The neurological psychologist would be more interested in neuron function.
*d.   Correct. The functionalists were primarily interested in the adaptive work of the mind.

6.   a   obj. 6   pp. 14, 15
*a. Correct. Not only was he the first, but he was the founder of the perspective called behaviourism.
b.   Incorrect. Abraham Maslow and Carl Rogers share this honour.
c.   Incorrect. Since this has to do with mind, Watson probably would reject such an association.
d.   Incorrect. Not only does it have to do with the mind, psychoanalysis attends to the unconscious mind, a double error for Watson.

7.   c   obj. 6   p. 14
a.   Incorrect. Behavioural experimental psychology has little interest in the unconscious whatsoever.
b.   Incorrect. The humanistic perspective has little interest in the unconscious whatsoever.
*c. Correct. The psychodynamic approach explores the unconscious in order to understand behaviour.
d.   Incorrect. A sports psychologist may have some interest in how subconscious influences performance, but the role is not significant.

8.   a   obj. 6   p. 14
*a. Correct. Dreams provide important insight into these subconscious forces because the powers that inhibit their expression are weakest during sleep.
b.   Incorrect. This reflects the interests of humanistic psychology more than psychoanalysis.
c.   Incorrect. This is an area of study of cognitive psychology.
d.   Incorrect. Biopsychology is concerned with inherited characteristics and their role in behaviour.

9.   a   obj. 18   p. 37
*a. Correct. Inexpensive solutions would be self-extinguishing!
b.   Incorrect. Few therapies are fast, and medical therapies are not typically among that group.
c.   Incorrect. This action would be very unethical.
d.   Incorrect. More likely, the authors are less qualified than practitioners.

10. a   obj. 10   p. 21
*a. Correct. This answer defines a theory.
b.   Incorrect. This is the first step in the scientific method, and it may lead to the formulation of a hypothesis.
c.   Incorrect. This is the definition of naturalistic observation.
d.   Incorrect. A hypothesis formulates the theory into a testable prediction.

11. b   obj. 11   pp. 22, 23
a.   Incorrect. "Archived" means to store in a secure place.
*b. Correct. "To operationalize" is to make something measurable and thus testable.
c.   Incorrect. "To theorize" is to speculate about causal or other relationships.
d.   Incorrect. This is not a word.

12. c   obj. 11   pp. 23, 24
a.   Incorrect. Archival research involves searching records and libraries.
b.   Incorrect. Correlational research involves a statistical analysis of pairs of data sets.
*c. Correct. One means of naturalistic observation is to blend into the situation and be unnoticed.
d.   Incorrect. An experiment requires careful subject selection and control of variables.

13. d   obj. 16   p. 32
a.   Incorrect. Moral refers to "right and wrong" and thus does not quite fit this context.
b.   Incorrect. Behavioural scientist may chose not to undertake a kind of study on personal, religious grounds, but this does not describe the relationship to subjects.
c.   Incorrect. "Professional standards" refers to a broad category of standards that apply to the conduct of a professional.
*d. Correct. The American Psychological Association has published a set of ethical guidelines that are meant to ensure the welfare of subjects in research.

14. d   obj. 17   p. 35
a.   Incorrect. Often it is the goal of a confederate to influence subjects in an experiment.
b.   Incorrect. An experiment must have dependent variables, otherwise it would not be an experiment.
c.   Incorrect. The placebo effect can occur under many conditions, even the double-blind procedure.
*d. Correct. This is the only procedure that will guarantee that both subject and experimenter expectations are eliminated.

15. d   obj. 14   pp. 29-31
a.   Incorrect. The results can be analyzed as significant, disconfirmed, but the theory may still be up for grabs.
b.   Incorrect   This is not true.
c.   Incorrect. Statistical significance does not imply social importance.
*d. Correct. Statistical significance judges the probability that the results occurred due to chance.

16. c   obj. 13   p. 26
17. b   obj. 13   p. 26
18. e   obj. 13   p. 26
19. a   obj. 13   p. 27
20. d   obj. 13   p. 27
21. biological   obj. 6   pp. 13, 14
22. Freud   obj. 6   p. 14
23. Wundt   obj. 5   p. 11
24. humanistic   obj. 6   p. 15
25. independent variable   obj. 13   p. 27

26. For this answer, "freedom of choice versus determinism" is used as the example.
■   The selection of the freedom of choice side of this answer reflects how most people would chose. However, it suggests that all of our actions are thus our responsibility—even our boredom and our

mistakes. We should be unable to attribute any causes for our behaviour to others than ourselves.

- Should the issue be resolved in favour of determinism, then we should be able to understand all of human behaviour as flowing from some root cause. Many religions have this kind of view, and some theorists and philosophers believe that science should be able to find causes. For psychology, this view is most compatible with behaviourism and psychoanalysis.

Practise Test 3:

1. d obj. 2 pp. 6, 7
a. Incorrect. A social psychologist would more likely study the prosocial behaviours (helping) exhibited shortly after an earthquake.
b. Incorrect. A consumer psychologist might be interested in the aspects of consumer behaviour that are affected by a natural disaster.
c. Incorrect. An educational psychologist might have an interest on how information regarding earthquakes could be transmitted most effectively.
*d. Correct. A cognitive psychologist would be interested in memory phenomena, and an earthquake may have elements of such phenomena as the flashbulb memory.

2. d obj. 2 pp. 6, 7
a. Incorrect. A social psychologist does not study traits directly, but may be interested in the role of groups as they may influence such a trait.
b. Incorrect. The only interest that a cross-cultural psychologist may have is whether the trait was common to more than one cultural group.
c. Incorrect. An educational psychologist would probably be interested in whether the trait could be acquired for learning purposes.
*d. Correct. The study of traits is specifically the domain of personality psychologists.

3. a obj. 2 pp. 6,7
*a. Correct. The helping behaviour studied by social psychologists is called prosocial behaviour.
b. Incorrect. An environmental psychologist may be remotely interested in determining whether the climatic conditions influence prosocial behaviour.
c. Incorrect. This would not be of interest to a clinical perspective.
d. Incorrect. This would not be of interest to an I/O psychologist.

4. d obj. 2 pp. 6, 7
a. Incorrect. A clinical psychologist could not offer this kind of consultation.
b. Incorrect. A school psychologist conducts assessment and recommends corrective measures for students.
c. Incorrect. A forensic psychologist is more interested in the legal system than in the hall system.
*d. Correct. Environmental psychologists examine factors like crowding and architectural design to understand the influences they may have on behaviours like aggression.

5. d obj. 5 p. 11

a. Incorrect. Cognition is a speciality area of psychology and refers to how we perceive, process, and store information; it is not a method of investigation.
b. Incorrect. Though it may lead to some kind of "mind expansion," such is not the psychological research technique.
c. Incorrect. Perception refers to any processing of sensory stimuli.
*d. Correct. This does define the concept of introspection and the way that Tichener sought to utilize the procedure.

6. b obj. 5 p. 11
a. Incorrect. There is no evidence that the purpose was to enable mind-reading.
*b. Correct. Trephining for the purpose of letting evil spirits out has been the conclusion of most anthropologists, though it has never been shown that having a hole in ones head does not actually let the evil spirits in.
c. Incorrect. There is no evidence that the purpose of these holes was to increase telekinetic powers.
d. Incorrect. Since mental illness was probably viewed as possession by evil spirits, choice "b" is a better answer.

7. d obj. 2 p. 6
a. Incorrect. This responses has the two types switched.
b. Incorrect. The school psychologist does more than promote the needs of special students.
c. Incorrect. The difference is not one of a group versus the individual, as this option suggests.
*d. Correct. Both halves of this statement are indeed true, and they reflect the broadest formulation of the goals of the two areas.

8. b obj. 13 p. 27
a. Incorrect. If colours are a key to problem solving, then they must be very relevant.
*b. Correct. The hypothesis suggests that colour scheme influences tension, so varying the schemes would serve as the independent variable.
c. Incorrect. The level of tension is the dependent variable.
d. Incorrect. A confounding variable would be some factor not found in the design of the experiment.

9. a obj. 13 pp. 27, 28
*a. Correct. Tension would depend upon both the colour scheme and the challenge of the problem.
b. Incorrect. A confounding variable would be some fact or not found in the design of the experiment.
c. Incorrect. The colour scheme is the independent variable.
d. Incorrect. Levels of stress are quite relevant to the hypothesis.

10. c obj. 13 pp. 27, 28
a. Incorrect. The control would be something like a neutral colour scheme.
b. Incorrect. The colour scheme is the independent variable.
*c. Correct. Time would indicate the amount of tension and how it impedes the solving of the problems.

d.   Incorrect. A confounding variable would be some factor not found in the design of the experiment.

11. c   obj. 6   p. 14, 15
a.   Incorrect. These two perspectives are both highly deterministic.
b.   Incorrect. The behavioural approach is highly deterministic, while the humanistic approach is focused on free choices.
*c. Correct. Both of these approaches would accept self-determination in decision making.
d.   Incorrect. While the cognitive approach would allow for free will, the behavioural approach is highly determined.

12. a   obj. 10   pp. 21, 22
*a. Correct. The first step after one has formulated a theory is to create a testable hypothesis.
b.   Incorrect. One does not define correlation coefficients for specific studies.
c.   Incorrect. True, but before collecting the data, it is necessary to define what data need to be collected.
d.   Incorrect. This will come after the data have been defined and collected.

13. a   obj. 10   p. 21
*a. Correct. Both the amount of physical exercise and the decline in heart-related disease can be measured and recorded.
b.   Incorrect. "Dramatically" is not very well defined.
c.   Incorrect. "Disgruntled" needs careful definition.
d.   Incorrect. "Happy" is not well defined.

14. d   obj. 15   p. 31
a.   Incorrect. No statistical test was mentioned or suggested in this scenario.
b.   Incorrect. The amount of light and the levels of stress would need to be operationalized from the very beginning.

c.   Incorrect. A hypothesis would already need to be in place for this series of studies to have any meaning.
*d. Correct. Often researchers will repeat their studies with slight variations as they test the limits of their theories.

15. b   obj. 15   p. 31
a.   Incorrect. Significant outcomes would have been reported in the studies, but so would results without significance.
*b. Correct. The use of other studies is the foundation for the procedure known as meta-analysis.
c.   Incorrect. True, correlational data would be used, but as a part of the procedure known as meta-analysis.
d.   Incorrect. Experimental techniques require controlled situations.

16. b   obj. 11   p. 23
17. a   obj. 11   pp. 23, 24
18. e   obj. 11   p. 24
19. c   obj. 11   p. 24
20. d   obj. 11   pp. 25, 26
21. Introspection   obj. 5   p. 13
22. Psychodynamic   obj 6.   p. 15
23. behaviouristic   obj. 6   p. 14
24. debriefing   obj. 16   p. 32
25. psychological   obj. 16   pp. 34, 35

26. Give examples of things that we believe because they are "common sense" or that you believe because of intuition.
■   Critical thinking is the ability and willingness to assess claims and make objective judgments on the basis of well-supported reasons.
■   Next, define the scientific approach. Explain how stating a hypothesis and than gathering information/facts to support the hypothesis through careful, methodical scientific methods will elicit a more exact measure of what is being studied.

27. population   obj. 16   p. 33

The Biology
Underlying Behaviour

2

Chapter Overview

This chapter focuses on the biological structures of the body that are of interest to biopsychologists. Initially the discussion will be on nerve cells, called neurons, which allow messages to travel through the brain and the body. Psychologists are increasing their understanding of human behaviour and are uncovering important clues in their efforts to cure certain kinds of diseases through their growing knowledge of these neurons and the nervous system. Then a review of the structure and the main divisions of the nervous system will lead to a discussion on how the different areas work to control voluntary and involuntary behaviours. The chapter also examines how the various parts of the nervous system operate together in emergency situations to produce lifesaving responses to danger.

Next, the brain itself will be considered by examining its major structures and the ways in which these affect behaviour. The brain controls movement, our senses, and our thought processes. It is also fascinating to focus on the idea that the two halves of the brain may have different specialties and strengths and so this area will be discussed and the research presented. Finally, the chemical messenger system of the body, the endocrine system, will be studied.

To further investigate the topics covered in this chapter, you can access the related websites by visiting the following link: http://www.mcgrawhill.ca/college/feldman.

Prologue: The Fight of His Life
Looking Ahead

Section 1: Neurons: The Elements of Behaviour

The Structure of the Neuron
Firing the Neuron
Where Neurons Meet: Bridging the Gap
Neurotransmitters: Multitalented Chemical Couriers

Section 2: The Nervous System

Central and Peripheral Nervous Systems
The Evolutionary Foundations of the Nervous System
Behavioural Genetics

Section 3: The Brain

Studying the Brain's Structure and Functions: Spying on the Brain
The Central Core: Our "Old Brain"

> **Applying Psychology in the 21st Century:** Mind over Cursor: Using Brain Waves to Overcome Physical Limitations

The Limbic System: Beyond the Central Core
The Cerebral Cortex: Our "New Brain"
Mending the Brain
The Specialization of the Hemispheres: Two Brains or One?

> **Exploring Diversity:** Human Diversity and the Brain

The Split Brain: Exploring the Two Hemispheres
The Endocrine System: Of Chemicals and Glands

> **Becoming an Informed Consumer of Psychology:** Learning to Control Your Heart—and Mind—through Biofeedback

Learning Objectives

These are the concepts and the learning objectives for Chapter 2. Read them carefully as part of your preliminary survey of the chapter.

Neurons: The Elements of Behaviour

1. Understand the significance of the biology that underlies behaviour and identify reasons why psychologists study these biological underpinnings, especially the brain and the nervous system. (p. 44)

2. Describe the structure of the neuron and its parts. (pp. 45–46)

3. Describe the all-or-none law of neural transmission, the resting state and action potential of the neuron, as well as the complete transmission of a message from initial stimulation to transmission across the synapse. (pp. 46–48)

4. Name key neurotransmitters and their functions and describe their known or suspected roles

in behaviour as well as in illnesses. (pp. 48–51)

The Nervous System

5.   Describe the major divisions of the nervous system, including the central and the peripheral, the autonomic and somatic, and the sympathetic and parasympathetic divisions. (pp. 51–53)

6.   Outline the major developments in the evolution of the nervous system and describe the associated fields of evolutionary psychology and behavioural genetics. (pp. 53–55)

The Brain

7.   Name the techniques used to map and study the brain. (pp. 57–58)

8.   Name the components of the central core and the limbic system and describe the functions of their individual parts. (pp. 59–62)

9.   Name the major areas of the cerebral hemispheres, especially the lobes and the cortex areas, and describe the roles of each area in behaviour. (pp. 63–66)

The Specialization of the Hemispheres: Two Brains or One?

10.   Discuss the issues involved with brain plasticity, brain specialization, brain lateralization, and the split-brain operation, including what has been learned about the two hemispheres from that procedure. (pp. 67–70)

11.   Discuss differences in brain lateralization as influenced by gender and culture. (pp. 67–70)

The Endocrine System: Of Chemicals and Glands

12.   Describe the function of the endocrine system, including its relationship to the hypothalamus and the functions of the pituitary gland. (pp. 71)

13.   Describe how biofeedback can be used to control some of the basic biological processes. (p. 71–73)

SECTION 1: Neurons: The Elements of Behaviour

Prepare

- *Why do psychologists study the brain and the nervous system?*
- *What are the basic elements of the nervous system?*
- *How does the nervous system communicate electrical and chemical messages from one part to another?*

Organize

- *The Structure of the Neuron*
- *Firing the Neuron*
- *Where Neurons Meet*
- *Neurotransmitters*

Work

Psychologists' understanding of the brain has increased dramatically in the past few years. Neuroscientists examine the biological underpinnings of behaviour, and

[a] _____ explore the ways the biological structures and functions of the body affect behaviour.

Specialized cells called [b] _____ are the basic component of the nervous system. Every neuron has a nucleus, a cell body, and special structures for

communicating with other neurons. [c] _____ are the receiving structures

and [d] _____ are the sending structures. The message is communicated in one direction from the dendrites, through the cell body, and down the axon to the

[e] _____. A fatty substance known as the [f] _____ surrounds the axons of most neurons and serves as an insulator for the electrical signal being transmitted down the axon. It also speeds the signal. Certain substances necessary for the maintenance of the cell body travel up the axon to the cell body in a reverse flow. Amyotrophic lateral sclerosis (ALS), or Lou Gehrig's disease, is a failure of the neuron to work in this reverse direction.

The neuron communicates its message by "firing," which refers to its changing from a

[g] _____ to an [h] _____. Neurons express the

action potential following the [i] _____ law, that is, firing only when a certain level of stimulation is reached. Just after the action potential has passed, the neuron cannot fire again for a brief period. The thicker the myelin sheath and the larger the diameter of the axon, the faster the action potentials travels down the axons. A neuron can fire as many as 1,000 times per second if the stimulus is very strong. However, the communicated message is a matter of how frequently or infrequently the neuron fires, not the intensity of the action potential, since the action potential is always the same strength.

The message of a neuron is communicated across the **[j]** _____ to the receiving neuron by the release of **[k]** _____ . The synapse is the small space between the terminal button of one neuron and the dendrite of the next. Neurotransmitters can either excite or inhibit the receiving neuron. The exciting neurotransmitter makes

[l] _____ and the inhibiting neurotransmitter makes **[m]** _____ . Once the neurotransmitters are released, they lock into special sites on the receiving neurons.

They must then be reabsorbed through **[n]** _____ into the sending neuron or deactivated by enzymes.

About 100 neurotransmitters have been found. Neurotransmitters can be either exciting or inhibiting depending on where in the brain they are released. The most common neurotransmitters are _acetylcholine (ACh), gamma-amino butyric acid (GABA), dopamine (DA), serotonin, adenosine triphosphate (ATP),_ and _endorphins._

Evaluate

_____ 1. neurons

_____ 2. dendrites

_____ 3. axon

_____ 4. terminal buttons

_____ 5. myelin sheath

a. Specialized cells that are the basic elements of the nervous system that carry messages.

b. Small branches at the end of an axon that relay messages to other cells.

c. A long extension from the end of a neuron that carri[] messages to other cells through the neuron.

d. An axon's protective coating, made of fat and protei[]

e. Clusters of fibers at one end of a neuron that receive messages from other neurons.

Rethink

1. Can you use your knowledge of psychological research methods to suggest how researchers can study the effects of neurotransmitters on human behaviour?

2. In what ways might endorphins help produce the placebo effect? Is there a difference between believing that one's pain is reduced and actually experiencing reduced pain? Why or why not?

SECTION 2: The Nervous System

Prepare

- *How are the structures of the nervous system tied together?*

Organize

- *The Central and Peripheral Nervous Systems*
- *The Evolutionary Foundations of the Nervous System*
- *Behavioural Genetics*

Work

The nervous system is divided into the **[a]** _____—composed of the brain and the spinal cord—and the peripheral nervous system. The

[b] _____ is a bundle of nerves that descend from the brain. The main purpose of the spinal cord is as a pathway for communication between the brain and the body.

Some involuntary behaviours, called **[c]** _____, involve messages that do not travel to the brain but instead stay entirely within the spinal cord.

[d] _____ neurons bring information from the periphery to the brain.

[e] _____ neurons carry messages to the muscles and glands of the body.

[f] _____, a third type of neurons, connect the sensory and the motor neurons, carrying messages between them. The spinal cord is the major carrier of sensory and motor information. Its importance is evident in injuries that result in *quadriplegia* and

paraplegia. The **[g]** _____ branches out from the spinal cord. It is divided

into the **[h]** _____, which controls muscle movement, and the

[i] _____, which controls basic body functions like heartbeat, breathing, glands, and lungs.

The role of the autonomic nervous system is to activate the body through the

[j] _____ and then to modulate and calm the body through the

[k] _____. The sympathetic division prepares the organism for stressful situations; and the parasympathetic division returns the body to help the body recover after the emergency has ended.

The branch of psychology known as **[l]** _____ attempts to provide answers concerning how our genetic inheritance from our ancestors influences the structure and function of our nervous system and influences everyday behaviour. The new field known as

[m] _____ studies the effects of heredity on behaviour.

Evaluate

_____ 1. peripheral nervous system

_____ 2. somatic division

_____ 3. autonomic division

_____ 4. sympathetic division

_____ 5. parasympathetic division

a. The part of the autonomic division of the peripheral nervous system that calms the body, bringing functions back to normal after an emergency has passed.

b. All parts of the nervous system *except* the brain and the spinal cord (includes somatic and autonomic divisions).

c. The part of the nervous system that controls involuntary movement (the actions of the heart, glands, lungs, and other organs).

d. The part of the autonomic division of the peripheral nervous system that prepares the body to respond in stressful emergency situations.

e. The part of the nervous system that controls voluntary movements of the skeletal muscles.

Rethink

3. How might communication within the nervous system result in human consciousness?

4. How is the "fight or flight" response helpful to organisms in emergency situations?

SECTION 3: The Brain

Prepare

- *How do researchers identify the major parts and functions of the brain?*
- *What are the major parts of the brain, and for what behaviours is each part responsible?*
- *How do the two halves of the brain operate interdependently?*
- *How can an understanding of the nervous system help us find ways to relieve disease and pain?*

Organize

- *Studying the Brain's Structure and Functions*
- *The Central Core*
- *The Limbic System*
- *The Cerebral Cortex*
- *Mending the Brain*
- *The Specialization of the Hemisphere*
- *The Split Brain*
- *The Endocrine System*

Work

Because it evolved very early, the **[a]** _____ of the brain is referred to as the old brain. It is composed of the *medulla*, which controls functions like breathing and heartbeat; the *pons*, which transmits information helping to coordinate muscle activity on the right and left halves of the body; and the **[b]** _____, which coordinates muscle activity. The **[c]** _____ is a group of nerve cells extending from the medulla and the pons that serve to alert other parts of the brain to activity. The central core also includes the **[d]** _____, which transmits sensory information, and the **[e]** _____, which maintains *homeostasis* of the body's environment. The hypothalamus also plays a role in basic survival behaviours like eating, drinking, sexual behaviour, aggression, and child–rearing behaviour.

The **[f]** _____ is a set of interrelated structures that includes pleasure centres, structures that control eating, aggression, reproduction, and self-preservation. Intense pleasure is felt through the limbic system. The limbic system also plays important roles in learning and memory. The limbic system is sometimes called the "animal brain" because its structures and functions are so similar to those of other animals.

The **[g]** _____ is identified with the functions that allow us to think and remember. The cerebral cortex is deeply folded in order to increase the surface area of the covering. The cortex is divided into four main sections, or **[h]** _____. They are the *frontal lobes*, the *parietal lobes*, the *temporal lobes*, and the *occipital lobes*. The lobes are separated by deep grooves called sulci. The cortex and its lobes have been divided into three major areas, the motor area, the sensory area, and the association area.

The **[i]** _____ area of the brain is responsible for the control and direction of voluntary muscle movements. There are three areas devoted to the **[j]** _____ area, that of touch, called the *somatosensory area*; that of sight, called the *visual area*; and that of hearing, called the *auditory area*. The **[k]** _____ area takes up most of the cortex and is devoted to mental processes like language, thinking, memory, and speech.

The two halves of the brain called **[l]** _____ are lateralized. The left hemisphere concentrates on verbal-based skills and controls the right side of the body. The right hemisphere deals with spatial understanding and pattern recognition and controls the left side of the body. This **[m]** _____ appears to vary greatly with individuals. The major difference that has been discovered is that the connecting fibers between the two hemispheres, called the *corpus callosum*, have different shapes in men and women.

Roger Sperry pioneered the study of the surgical separation of the two hemispheres for cases of severe epilepsy. Those who have had the procedure are called

[n] _____ .

The **[o]** _____ is a chemical communication network that delivers

[p] _____ into the bloodstream which, in turn, influence growth and behaviour. Sometimes called the "master gland," the **[q]** _____ gland is the major gland of the endocrine system. The hypothalamus regulates the pituitary gland.

"Becoming an Informed Consumer of Psychology" discusses the use of

[r] _____ to control a variety of body functions. It has been successfully applied to the control of headaches, blood pressure, and other medical and physical problems.

Evaluate
Test A

_____ 1.   central core

_____ 2.   medulla

_____ 3.   pons

_____ 4.   cerebellum

_____ 5.   reticular formation

a. The part of the brain that joins the halves of the cerebellum, transmitting motor information to coordinate muscles and integrate movement between the right and left sides of the body.

b. The part of the central core of the brain that controls many important body functions, such as breathing and heartbeat.

c. The part of the brain that controls bodily balance.

d. The "old brain," which controls such basic functions as eating and sleeping and is common to all vertebrates.

e. A group of nerve cells in the brain that arouses the body to prepare it for appropriate action and screens out background stimuli.

Test B

_____ 1. limbic system

_____ 2. cerebral cortex

_____ 3. frontal lobes

_____ 4. temporal lobes

_____ 5. occipital lobes

a. The brain structure located at the front centre of the cortex, containing major motor and speech and reasoning centres.

b. The structures of the brain lying behind the temporal lobes; includes the visual sensory area.

c. The "new brain," responsible for the most sophisticated information processing in the brain; contains the lobes.

d. The portion of the brain located beneath the frontal and parietal lobes; includes the auditory sensory areas.

e. The part of the brain located outside the "new brain" that controls eating, aggression, and reproduction.

Rethink

5. How would you answer the argument that "psychologists should leave the study of neurons and synapses and the nervous system to biologists"?

6. Before sophisticated brain-scanning techniques were developed, biopsychologists' understanding of the brain was largely based on the brains of people who had died. What limitations would this pose, and in what areas would you expect the most significant advances once brain scanning techniques were possible?

7. Suppose that abnormalities in an association area of the brain were linked through research to serious criminal behaviour. Would you be in favour of mandatory testing of individuals and surgery to repair or remove those abnormalities? Why or why not?

8. Could personal differences in people's specialization of right and left hemispheres be related to occupational success? For example, might an architect who relies on spatial skills have a different pattern of hemispheric specialization than a writer?

Practise Questions

Test your knowledge of the chapter material by answering these questions. These questions have been placed in three Practise Tests. The first two tests are composed of questions that will test your recall of factual knowledge. The third test contains questions that are challenging and primarily test for conceptual knowledge and your ability to apply that knowledge. Check your answers and review the feedback using the Answer Key on the following pages of the *Study Guide*.

PRACTISE TEST 1:4

1. The function of a neuron's dendrites is to:
   a. frighten potential cellular predators.
   b. make waves in the liquid that bathes the neurons.
   c. give personality or uniqueness to each neuron.
   d. receive incoming signals relayed from other neurons.

2. Neurons communicate with each other through specialized structures known as:
   a. glial cells.
   b. myelin sheaths.
   c. somas.
   d. dendrites and axons.

3. The space between the end of the axon of neuron 'A' and the receptor site on the dendrite of neuron 'B', into which a neurotransmitter is released is a:
   a. terminal button.
   b. cell body.
   c. synapse.
   d. refractory period.

4. A neurotransmitter affects particular neurons, but not others, depending upon whether:
   a. the receiving neuron expects a message to arrive.
   b. a suit0able receptor site exists on the receiving neuron.
   c. the nerve impulse acts according to the all-or-none law.
   d. the receiving neuron is in its resting state.

5. The neural process of reuptake involves:
   a. the production of fresh neurotransmitters.
   b. the release of different neurotransmitter types by message-sending neurons.
   c. chemical breakdown of neurotransmitters by the receiving cell.
   d. soaking up of surplus neurotransmitters by the terminal button.

6. The portion of the nervous system that is particularly important for reflexive behaviour is the:
   a. brain.
   b. spinal cord.
   c. sensory nervous system.
   d. motor nervous system.

7. Reflexes:
   a. are learned from infancy.
   b. involve the peripheral nervous system.
   c. always involve both the peripheral and central nervous systems.
   d. Need not involve the cerebral cortex at all.

8. The autonomic nervous system controls:
   a. habitual, automatic movements such as applying the brakes of an automobile.
   b. the functions of the spinal cord.
   c. the body's response to an emergency or crisis.
   d. most of the spinal reflexes.

9. Which of the following is **not** likely to happen during activation of the sympathetic division of the nervous system?
    a. increase in digestion
    b. increase in heart rate
    c. increase in sweating
    d. increase in pupil sizes

10. Although "pleasure centres" are found at many brain sites, the most likely place to find them is in:
    a. the association areas of the cerebral cortex.
    b. the limbic system.
    c. the medulla.
    d. the cerebellum.

11. Which of the following controls important bodily functions such as heartbeat and breathing?
    a. medulla
    b. cerebellum
    c. thalamus
    d. hypothalamus

12. _____ in the cerebral cortex enhance(s) the most sophisticated integration of neural information by providing for much greater surface area and complex interconnections among neurons.
    a. Convolutions
    b. Mapping
    c. Lateralization
    d. Hemispheric dominance

13. When a person is unable to undertake purposeful, sequential behaviours, the condition is known as:
    a. dyslexia.
    b. aphasia.
    c. apraxia.
    d. paraplegia.

14. Sequential information processing is a characteristic of:
    a. the left cerebral hemisphere.
    b. the right cerebral hemisphere.
    c. the frontal lobes.
    d. the occipital lobes.

15. Which statement about the cerebral hemispheres does **not** apply to most right-handed people?
    a. The left hemisphere processes information sequentially.
    b. The right hemisphere processes information globally.
    c. The right hemisphere is associated with language and reasoning.
    d. Women display less hemispheric dominance than men, particularly with skills such as language.

____ 16. neurotransmitter

____ 17. excitatory message

____ 18. inhibitory message

____ 19. endorphins

____ 20. GABA

a. A chemical secretion that makes it more likely that a receiving neuron will fire and an action potential will travel down its axons.

b. A class of chemical secretions that behave like pain-killing opiates.

c. A chemical messenger that inhibits behaviours like eating and aggression.

d. A chemical secretion that prevents a receiving neuron from firing.

e. A chemical that carries the message from one neuron to another when secreted as the result of a nerve impulse.

21. The part of the brain's central core that transmits messages from the sense organs to the cerebral cortex and from the cerebral cortex to the cerebellum and medulla is the _____.

22. The _____ is located below the thalamus of the brain, and its major function is to maintain homeostasis.

23. The _____ is a bundle of fibers that connects one half of the brain to the other half.

24. One of the major areas of the brain, responsible for voluntary movement of particular parts of the body is called the _____.

25. _____ is the area within the cortex corresponding to the sense of touch.

26. Describe the specific benefits of our knowledge of brain function and the effect of injury on the brain. What are the possible consequences of research in neurotransmitters, biofeedback, and even sex differences in the brain?

PRACTISE TEST 2:

1. Which response listed below is least likely to be treated with biofeedback?
    a. impotence
    b. headaches
    c. high blood pressure
    d. problems with maintaining optimal skin temperature

2. Neurons share many structures and functions with other types of cells, but they also have a specialized ability to:
    a. be active yet consume almost no cellular energy.
    b. regenerate themselves even if injured very seriously.
    c. send messages to specific targets over long distances.
    d. live for a long time even after the official death of the body.

3. When an action potential has been fired, the neuron will be ready to fire again after_____:
    a. the resting state has been restored.
    b. the rising phase of the action potential has reached its peak.
    c. the reuptake of neurotransmitters has been completed.
    d. the direction of the nerve impulse within the axon has been reversed.

4. Generally, neural impulses travel:
    a. electrically between and within each neuron.
    b. chemically between and within each neuron.
    c. electrically between neurons and chemically within each neuron.
    d. chemically between neurons and electrically within each neuron.

5. Muscle tremors and rigidity result from _____ in neural circuits.
    a. excessive ACh
    b. not enough ACh
    c. excessive dopamine
    d. not enough dopamine

6. The peripheral nervous system consists of:
    a. the spinal cord and brain.
    b. all neurons with myelin sheath.
    c. all neurons other than those in the spinal cord or brain.
    d. entirely efferent neurons.

7. Sympathetic division is to parasympathetic division as:
    a. fight is to flight.   c. arousing is to calming.
    b. central is to peripheral.   d. helpful is to hurtful.

8. The _____ records the brain's ongoing neural activities via electrodes attached externally to the skull.
    a. electroencephalogram (EEG)   c. computerized axial tomography (CAT) scan
    b. magnetic resonance imaging (MRI) d. positron emission tomography (PET) scan

9. The capacities to think and remember probably best distinguish humans from other animals. These qualities are most closely associated with the function of the:
    a. cerebral cortex.   c. cerebellum.
    b. medulla.   d. limbic system.

10. The diagram with parts of the "little man" on the surface of the motor cortex of a cerebral hemisphere shows that:
    a. body structures requiring fine motor movements are controlled by large amounts of neural tissue.
    b. major motor functions are controlled by the right hemisphere.
    c. large body parts on the diagram (e.g., fingers on a hand) receive little motor input.
    d. certain areas of the body are more responsive to touch, temperature, and other stimulation.

11. Which area has the largest portion of the cortex?
    a. motor area   c. sensory area
    b. somatosensory area   d. association area

12. Appreciation of music, art, and dance, and understanding of spatial relationships are more likely to be processed in the:
    a. right side of the brain.   c. occipital lobes.
    b. left side of the brain.   d. temporal lobe.

13. Damage to which of the following areas is most likely to cause people to have difficulty with pattern recognition tasks and spatial memory?
    a. frontal lobe   c. right hemisphere
    b. left hemisphere   d. temporal lobe

14. Biofeedback is a technique to control internal biological states by:
    a. following the suggestions and strategies of a biologically trained facilitator or therapist.
    b. thinking positively about the biological responses to be modified.
    c. listening to a soothing audio cassette containing biorhythmic signals that alter biological responses in the brain.
    d. electronically monitoring biological responses so that adaptive tactics for changing those responses can be applied.

15. In multiple sclerosis, the _____ deteriorates, exposing parts of the _____. The result is a short circuit between the nervous system and muscle, which leads to difficulties with walking, vision, and with general muscle coordination.
    a. cell body; nucleus
    b. dendrite; terminal button
    c. terminal button; nucleus
    d. myelin sheath; axon

____ 16. synapse

____ 17. acetylcholine

____ 18. EEG

____ 19. reflex

a. An electrophysiological technique that involves monitoring the electrical activity of the brain.

b. The gap between neurons across which chemical messages are communicated.

c. Automatic behaviour that is a response to a specific stimulus.

d. A chemical secretion that transmits messages relating to skeletal muscles and may also be related to memory.

20. The gap between neurons is called the _____.

21. The division of the nervous system that is particularly important for "fight or flight" is the _____.

22. The most likely place to find "pleasure centre" in the brain is the _____.

23. The _____ controls important bodily functions such as heartbeat and breathing.

24. The _____ areas of the brain deal with thinking, language, and speech.

25. Several recent developments raise important questions for ethical consideration. What are the problems that arise when surgery separates the two hemispheres? What are the potential dangers of transplanting fetal tissue into the brain? Discuss these ethical and moral issues. Are there other issues?

Practise Test 3: Conceptual, Applied, and Challenging Questions

1. According to the textbook, a greater number of glial cells are more likely to be implicated in:
    a. action potentials occurring at a rate of 250 per second rather than a rate of 25 per second..
    b. action potentials occurring at a rate of 38 per second rather than a rate of 380 per second..
    c. action potentials travelling at 360 kilometres per hour rather than at 3 kilometres per hour.
    d. functions that do not directly concern the speed or rate of the action potential

2. In **most** cases, after neurotransmitters have sent their message to the receiving neuron, they are:
   a. deactivated by enzymes.
   b. reabsorbed by the terminal buttons.
   c. absorbed into the body and filtered through the kidneys.
   d. absorbed into the receiving neuron.

3. The word most closely associated with the function of the limbic system is:
   a. thinking.
   b. waking.
   c. emergency.
   d. emotion.

4. Which of the following may be the most critical structure for maintaining homeostasis, a steady internal state of the body?
   a. hippocampus
   b. cerebral cortex
   c. hypothalamus
   d. cerebellum

5. Damage to or lesions in which of the following brain structures would be most likely to cause dramatic changes in emotionality and behaviour?
   a. pons
   b. medulla
   c. cerebellum
   d. limbic system

6. Which of the following is true of both the sensory and motor areas of the cortex?
   a. They both contain pleasure centres.
   b. More cortical tissue is devoted to the most important structures.
   c. Electrical stimulation produces involuntary movement.
   d. Destruction of any one area affects all the senses.

7. Phineas was a shrewd, energetic business executive who persistently carried out all his plans of operation. After an injury to his head, he was no longer able to make plans or complete them. The dramatic changes in him following his accident suggest which area of his cerebral cortex was injured?
   a. neuromuscular
   b. association
   c. sensory-somatosensory
   d. motor

8. Which of the following is characterized by difficulty understanding the speech of others and producing coherent speech?
   a. Wernicke's aphasia
   b. Lou Gehrig's disease
   c. Broca's aphasia
   d. Phineas Gage's disease

9. Left hemisphere is to _____ function as right hemisphere is to _____ function.
   a. sequential; successive
   b. sequential; global
   c. successive; sequential
   d. global; sequential

10. Wernicke's aphasia is to _____ as Broca's aphasia is to _____ .
    a. spasticity; flaccidity
    b. motor cortex; sensory cortex
    c. overeating; irregular gait
    d. difficulty in comprehending words; searching for the correct word.

11. One primary difference in the organization of male and female brains is that:
    a. logical abilities are on the opposite sides in males and females.

    b.   language abilities are more evenly divided between the two hemispheres in females.

    c.   the right hemisphere is almost always dominant in females.

    d.   spatial abilities are on the opposite sides in males and females.

12.   In all cases, a split-brain patient has had:

    a.   a stroke.   c.   damage to one of the hemispheres.

    b.   the nerves between the hemispheres cut.   d.   epilepsy.

13.   Mr. Simpson has just been diagnosed with a disease that causes his neurons to die of starvation because they are unable to get chemical substances necessary for cell function to flow up the axon toward the cell body. The diagnosis is most likely:

    a.   Alzheimer's disease.   c.   multiple sclerosis.

    b.   Parkinson's disease.   d.   amyotrophic lateral sclerosis.

14.   In the middle of a sentence, Joseph becomes rigid and stares into space. After a few minutes he shakes a little bit and then seems to return to the discussion. He explains that he has a common neural disorder related to a shortage of a neurotransmitter. His disorder is probably:

    a.   Alzheimer's disease.   c.   multiple sclerosis.

    b.   Parkinson's disease.   d.   amyotrophic lateral sclerosis.

15.   Professor Daniels records the activity of a set of neurons. As the neurons in the set increase their activity, surrounding neurons seem to slow down. What kind of messages are these neurons most likely sending?

    a.   sensory   c.   inhibitory

    b.   motor   d.   autonomic

_____ 16. homeostasis

_____ 17. eating

_____ 18. terminal buttons

_____ 19. myelin sheath

_____ 20. reuptake

a.   The limbic system regulates a variety of motivated behaviours such as _____.

b.   Located at the end of the axon, their purpose is to store neurotransmitters before release.

c.   Characterized by the functioning of an optimal range of physiological processes, it is the tendency of the body to maintain a balanced state.

d.   Method of clearing the neurotransmitter from the synaptic cleft, transmitter returns to terminal buttons.

e.   Specialized cells of fat and protein that wrap themselves around the axon.

21.   The function of the neuron's _____ is to receive incoming signals relayed from other neurons.

22. The _____ is one of the major areas of the brain, the site of the higher mental processes, such as thought, language, memory, and speech.

23. The _____ hemisphere of the brain concentrates on tasks requiring verbal competence.
24. Music and emotional experiences are located in the _____ hemisphere.

25. Located in the occipital lobe, the _____ receives input of images from the eyes.

26. Discuss the role that the media might play in certain brain research. Consider what well-known celebrities have done for the research of their particular illness (M. J. Fox, Mohammed Ali, Janet Reno, Parkinson's disease; Christopher Reeves, spinal cord regeneration).

Spotlight on Terminology and Language—
Cultural Idioms

Neurons: The Elements of Behaviour

Page 45 "Neurons are physically held in place by glial cells, which provide nourishment and **insulate** them."

The glial cells **insulate** the neurons by shielding them and protecting them. To **insulate** is to place in a detached situation or in a state of isolation.

Page 45 "The myelin sheath also serves to increase the **velocity** with which the electrical impulses travel through the axons."

Velocity is speed. The myelin sheath increases the rapidity of movement.

Page 48 "When a nerve impulse comes to the end of the axon and reaches a terminal button, the terminal button releases a chemical **courier** called a neurotransmitter."

The chemical **courier**, the neurotransmitter, carries messages. One of the most common neurotransmitters is acetylcholine. This neurotransmitter transmits messages related to our skeletal muscle movement.

Page 48 "Like a boat that ferries passengers across a river, these chemical messengers move toward the **shorelines** of other neurons."

Shorelines suggest a zone of contact.

Page 48 "In the same way as a jigsaw puzzle can fit in only one specific location in a puzzle, so each kind of neurotransmitter has a distinctive **configuration** that allows it to fit into a specific type of receptor site on the receiving neuron."

Configuration has to do with the relative disposition or arrangement of parts—in this case the structure of the neurotransmitter.

Page 48 "**Excitatory** messages make it more likely that a receiving neuron will fire and an action potential will travel down its axon. **Inhibitory** messages, in contrast, do just the opposite; they provide chemical information that prevents or decreases the likelihood that the receiving neuron will fire."

Excitatory messages are messages that are likely to induce action. **Inhibitory** messages tend to reduce or suppress the activity of the receiving neuron.

Page 48 "Because the dendrites of a neuron receive both excitatory and inhibitory messages simultaneously, the neuron must **integrate** the messages by using a kind of chemical calculator."

Integrate means to interpret these messages and coordinate functions.

Page 48 "To solve this problem, neurotransmitters are either **deactivated** by enzymes or—more frequently—**reabsorbed** by the terminal button in an example of chemical recycling called reuptake. Like a vacuum cleaner sucking up dust, neurons reabsorb the neurotransmitters that are now **clogging** the synapse."

When neurotransmitters are **deactivated**, they are made inactive or ineffective. Your body is basically deprived of the chemical activity that would be occurring. When neurotransmitters are being **reabsorbed**, they are being reused. When the synapse is being **clogged**, activity is restricted or halted.

Pages 48, 50 "The same neurotransmitter, then, can cause a neuron to fire when it is **secreted** in one part of the brain and can inhibit the firing of neurons when it is produced in another part."

When a neurotransmitter is **secreted** it is deposited in the synapse.

Page 51 "Endorphins can also produce the **euphoric** feelings that runners sometimes experience after long runs."

Euphoria is a feeling of well-being or elation. What activities do you do that activate feelings of **euphoria**?

The Nervous System

Page 52 "As you can see from the **schematic** representation, the nervous system is divided into two main parts: the central nervous system and the peripheral nervous system."

When you see a **schematic**, you are seeing a diagram or a drawing that is being used to help illustrate what the author is discussing. It is important to look at all the **schematics** and review them.

Page 52 "The spinal cord is not just a communications **conduit**."

A **conduit** is a passage within or between parts.

Page 52 "Actor Christopher Reeve, who was injured in a horse-riding accident, suffers from **quadriplegia**, a condition in which voluntary muscle movement below the neck is lost. In a less severe but still debilitating condition, **paraplegia**, people are unable to voluntarily move any muscles in the lower half of their body."

Quadriplegia is paralysis of both arms and both legs. **Paraplegia** is paralysis of the lower half of the body with involvement of both legs usually due to disease of or injury to the spinal cord.

Page 53 "The **parasympathetic** division acts to calm the body after the emergency situation is resolved."

The **parasympathetic** division is the division of the autonomic nervous system that oversees digestion, elimination, and glandular function. It is the resting and digesting subdivision.

The Brain

Page 57 "Our brain is responsible for our **loftiest** thoughts-and our most primitive urges. It is the **overseer** of the intricate workings of the human body."

The **overseer** is the executor. To have **lofty** thoughts is to have great and superior thoughts. **Lofty** is often characterized by an elevation in character or speech.

Page 57 "The sheer quantity of nerve cells in the brain is enough to **daunt** even the most ambitious computer engineer."

Daunt refers to discouragement. The number of nerve cells in the brain is such a great number that it is **daunting** and intimidates some researchers.

Page 57 "…the most astounding thing about the brain is not its number of cells but its ability to allow human intellect to **flourish** as it guides our behaviour and thoughts."

Flourish means to thrive. Human intellect **flourishes** and increases.

Page 58 "Advances in brain scanning are also aiding the development of new methods for **harnessing** the brain's neural signals."

Harnessing means to control and direct. What is some research you would like to see conducted to **harness** some of the functions of the brain?

Page 59 "The portion of the brain known as the central **core** is quite similar to that found in all vertebrates (species with backbones)."

The central **core** is sometimes referred to as the 'old brain' because its evolutionary **underpinnings** can be traced back some 500 million years to primitive structures found in nonhuman species."

Core is the innermost or most important part. **Underpinnings** are something serving as a support or foundation. The legs are the **underpinnings** of the body.

Page 60 "The **cerebellum** is found just above the medulla behind the pons…Drinking too much alcohol seems to depress the activity of the cerebellum, leading to the unsteady **gait** and movement characteristic of drunkenness."

The **cerebellum** is the brain structure responsible for coordination and regulation of complex voluntary muscular movement. The **cerebellum** is the brain region most involved in producing smooth, coordinated skeletal muscle activity. The **cerebellum** is involved in the workings of the intellect. **Gait** is a particular way of walking, or running, or moving on foot. **Gait** controls the speed at which we walk and run.

Page 61 "Like an ever-**vigilant** guard, the reticular formation is made up of groups of nerve cells that can immediately activate other parts of the brain to produce general bodily arousal."

Vigilant is to be on the alert, or watchful. Can you describe some situations in your life when you have felt the need to be especially **vigilant**?

Page 61 "Although tiny—about the size of a fingertip—the hypothalamus plays an **inordinately** important role."

Inordinately means exceeding in scope the ordinary, reasonable, or prescribed limits. The small size of the hypothalamus belies the importance of its function.

Page 61 "In an **eerie** view of the future, some science fiction writers have suggested that people will someday routinely have electrodes implanted in their brains."

An **eerie** view suggests a supernatural view that would be strange and mysterious.

Page 62 "To identify the part of the brain that provides the complex and **subtle** capabilities that are uniquely human, we need to turn to another structure—the **cerebral cortex**.

Subtle is so slight that it is difficult to detect. The **cerebral cortex** is the outer gray matter region of the cerebral hemispheres.

■ CHAPTER 2: ANSWER KEY

GUIDED REVIEW

Section 1:	Section 2:	Section 3:	Evaluate
[a] biopsychologists	[a] central nervous system (CNS)	[a] central core	Test A
[b] neurons	[b] spinal cord	[b] cerebellum	1. d
[c] Dendrites	[c] reflexes	[c] reticular formation	2. b
[d] axons	[d] Sensory (afferent)	[d] thalamus	3. a
[e] terminal buttons	[e] Motor (efferent)	[e] hypothalamus	4. c
[f] myelin sheath	[f] Interneurons	[f] limbic system	5. e
[g] resting state	[g] peripheral nervous system	[g] cerebral cortex	Test B
[h] action potential	[h] somatic division	[h] lobes	1. e
[i] all-or-none	[i] autonomic division	[i] motor	2. c
[j] synapse	[j] sympathetic division	[j] sensory	3. a
[k] neurotransmitters	[k] parasympathetic division	[k] association	4. d
[l] excitatory messages	[l] evolutionary psychology	[l] hemispheres	5. b
[m] inhibitory messages	[m] behavioural genetics	[m] lateralization	
[n] reuptake		[n] split-brain patients	
		[o] endocrine system	
Evaluate	Evaluate	[p] hormones	
1. a	1. b	[q] pituitary	
2. e	2. e	[r] biofeedback	
3. c	3. c		
4. b	4. d		
5. d	5. a		

Selected Rethink Answers

1. Experiments could be designed to measure variables that define perceptual, motor, and behavioural characteristics of humans and the effects that certain neurotransmitters have on these characteristics. One group could be given medication to increase the amount of certain neurotransmitters in one's brain and the effects could be recorded. Done on several different subjects, patterns could develop that helped us understand the purpose and the activity of different neurotransmitters. Another way to look at the same issue would be to observe people who have a deficit of a certain neurotransmitter and record their behaviours. In Parkinson's disease, a great deal of data have now been collected on the effects of the lack of the neurotransmitter dopamine.

4 Fight or Flight. Part of the sympathetic division that acts to prepare the body for action in the case of a stressful situation. It engages the organs resources to respond to a threat: heart races, palms sweat, etc. Reactions occur at the physiological level.

6. In studying the brains of people who have died, we have only a limited opportunity to see the effects that parts of the brain have on certain behaviours. We can make assumptions from the damage that we observe about the cause of certain behaviours. This correlational study does not prove cause and effect. In studying subjects that are alive through the use of EEG, CAT, MRI, and PET scans, we have the advantage of actually looking at brain functions while the subject performs certain tasks. The assumption here would be that different tasks would produce effects on different areas of the brain.

7. If abnormalities in an association of the brain were linked to criminal behaviour it would only be correlational data. It would not show causation. Experimental methods would be necessary to prove causation. There may be many factors in combination that cause criminal behaviour. Research is not refined enough yet to make a direct cause and effect relationship. Even if a subject has the potential to be a criminal, we measure behaviour, not the potential for criminal behaviour or the possibility that a person might commit a crime. On the other hand, if a person knew this information about himself and chose to have the surgery, the issue may have to be studied from a different perspective. One could be as "Does an individual have the right to agree to surgery on his brain that will alter behaviour?" I think since we already allow the use of medications to alter the behaviour of individuals, surgical procedures would also be allowed.

Practise Test 1:

1. d   obj. 2   p. 45
a.   Incorrect. Cellular predators cannot be frightened.
b.   Incorrect. The only waving done in the body is with the hand.
c.   Incorrect. Indeed, each neuron has a unique number and distribution of dendrites, but this is not the purpose of the dendrites.
*d.   Correct. Dendrites act as the receivers for the neuron.

2. d   obj. 2   p. 45
a.   Incorrect. Glial cells are the cells that support neurons.
b.   Incorrect. The myelin sheath is the fatty substance that forms an insulating covering around axons.
c.   Incorrect. The soma is the cell body of the neuron.
*d.   Correct. Dendrites receive stimulation and axons convey information to the next neuron.

3. c   obj. 3   p. 48
a.   Incorrect. Although this is at the end of the axon branch.
b.   Incorrect. This is the part that contains the nucleus and metabolic units of the neuron.
*c.   Correct. The word "synapse" even means gap.
d.   Incorrect. A refractory period is a period at the conclusion of an action potential during which the neuron cannot fire again.

4. b   obj. 4   pp. 48-49
a.   Incorrect. Individual neurons do not exhibit the cognitive skill of "expectation."
*b.   Correct. Neurotransmitters lock into specific sites receptive to that type of neurotransmitter.
c.   Incorrect. All nerve impulses act according to the all-or-none law, thus this information would be irrelevant to the receiving neuron.
d.   Incorrect. If the neuron has the receptor sites, it always is affected by the neurotransmitter, whether it is firing or not.

5. d   obj. 4   p. 48
a.   Incorrect. The need for new production is minimized by reuptake.
b.   Incorrect. This is not reuptake.
c.   Incorrect. Some neurotransmitters are metabolized by enzymes in the synaptic cleft–this material may return to the neuron in another manner other than reuptake.
*d.   Correct. Reuptake is the reabsorption of unmetabolized neurotransmitters in the area of the synapse.

6. b   obj. 5   p. 52
a.   Incorrect. Actually, it could be said that the role of the brain is to override reflexes.
*b.   Correct. Many messages that are processed reflexively simply pass through the spinal cord and are not sent to the brain.
c.   Incorrect. We do indeed sense the stimuli that cause reflexes, but can actually have them without our sensation of them.
d.   Incorrect. However, without a motor system, we would not have reflexes. There is a better alternative.

7. d   obj. 5   p. 52
a.   Incorrect. Reflexes are inborn and not learned.
b.   Incorrect. They involve the peripheral nervous system and often the central nervous system.
c.   Incorrect. Some reflexes may not involve the central nervous system.
*d.   Correct. Fundamentally, reflexes are processed through the spinal cord or by lower parts of the brain.

8. c   obj. 5   p. 53
a.   Incorrect. These kinds of processes do involve the brain and the voluntary muscles.
b.   Incorrect. The autonomic nervous system is not responsible for spinal cord functions.
*c.   Correct. Of these choices, this is the only one included in the activity controlled by the autonomic system.
d.   Incorrect. The spinal reflexes involve the somatic system and voluntary muscles.

9. a   obj. 5   p. 53
*a.   Correct. The sympathetic division activates and energizes responses necessary for survival and quick responses, thus it shuts down the digestive processes.
b.   Incorrect. The sympathetic response increases heart rate in order to increase energy availability.
c.   Incorrect. The sympathetic response increases sweating in order to provide for additional cooling.
d.   Incorrect. The sympathetic response increases pupil sizes, probably to increase the available detail about the visible world.

10. b   obj. 8   pp. 61, 62
a.   Incorrect. Memory is stored here.
*b.   Correct. Most of the structures related to pleasure, especially the hypothalamus and the amygdala, are part of the limbic system.
c.   Incorrect. The medulla controls things like breathing.
d.   Incorrect. The cerebellum controls voluntary muscle movements.

11. a   obj. 8   pp. 59, 60
*a.   Correct. This is the medulla's role.
b.   Incorrect. The cerebellum helps control voluntary muscle and coordinate movement.
c.   Incorrect. The thalamus is responsible for handling incoming and outgoing messages for the cortex.
d.   Incorrect. The hypothalamus is responsible for regulating basic biological needs.

12. a   obj. 9   p. 59
*a.   Correct. The convolutions increase the surface area of the cortex dramatically.
b.   Incorrect. Mapping helps the neuroscientists but not the brain itself.
c.   Incorrect. Lateralization arises due to the cerebrum being divided into two hemispheres.
d.   Incorrect. Hemispheric dominance is not related to the amount of surface area of the cortex.

13. c   obj. 9   p. 66
a.   Incorrect. "Lexia" is related to the root of lexicon and refers to words.
b.   Incorrect. "Aphasia" refers to processing errors, like the inability to process language or the inability to produce speech.
*c. Correct. The root of "praxia" means practise or action.
d.   Incorrect. "Paraplegia" refers to paralysis in two limbs.

14. a   obj. 10   p. 68
*a. Correct. Logic, sequential, and many language functions are controlled in the left hemisphere.
b.   Incorrect. The right hemisphere has been associated more with spatial relations and emotional expression.
c.   Incorrect. The frontal lobes are more responsible for planning and physical movement.
d.   Incorrect. The occipital lobes are devoted to visual experience.

15. c   obj. 10   p. 68
a.   Incorrect. This is true of most right-handed people.
b.   Incorrect. This is true of most right-handed people.
*c. Correct. The left hemisphere is associated with language and reasoning.
d.   Incorrect. This applies to both left- and right-handed people.

16. e   obj. 3   p. 48
17. a   obj. 3   p. 48
18. d   obj.3   p. 48
19. b   obj. 4   p. 51
20. c   obj. 4   p. 50
21. thalamus   obj. 8   p. 61
22. hypothalamus   obj. 8   p. 61
23. pons obj. 8   p. 56
24. cerebellum   obj. 8   p. 60
25. The somatosensory area   obj. 9   p. 65

26.
■   Knowledge of the brain leads to improved medical and psychological therapies of the injured and of stroke sufferers.
■   Knowledge about brain function should provide greater knowledge about behaviour.
■   An understanding of neurotransmitter function can be applied to many phenomena, such as pain, drug abuse, healing processes, and thinking processes.
■   Knowledge of male and female differences will help us understand differences and similarities among individuals as well.

Practise Test 2:
1.   a   obj. 13   p. 71-73
*a. Correct. Of the four choices, the use of biofeedback to treat impotence has not proven effective.
b.   Incorrect. Biofeedback can be used effectively to treat headaches.

c.   Incorrect. Biofeedback can be used effectively to treat high blood pressure
d.   Incorrect. Biofeedback can be used effectively to treat skin temperature problems.

2.   c   obj. 2   p. 45
a.   Incorrect. Like any other cell, activity requires energy.
b.   Incorrect. Actually, they regenerate only in special circumstances.
*c. Correct. Many neurons have very long axons, and the axons are attached to specific target.
d.   Incorrect. Neurons live no longer than any other cells.

3.   a   obj. 3   p. 45
*a. Correct. During an absolute refractory period, prior to returning to the resting state, the neuron cannot fire.
b.   Incorrect. There is no "rising phase."
c.   Incorrect. Reuptake occurs continuously and independently of the firing of the neuron.
d.   Incorrect. The nerve impulse never reverses (though many neurons have feedback loops).

4.   d   obj. 3   p. 46
a.   Incorrect. A chemical process takes place between neurons.
b.   Incorrect. An electrical process carries the message within the neuron.
c.   Incorrect. The parts are reversed, try: chemically between neurons and electrically within each neuron.
*d. Correct. A neurotransmitter (chemical) passes between neurons; an electrical charge moves down neurons.

5.   d   obj. 4   p. 50
a.   Incorrect. The answer is insufficient dopamine.
b.   Incorrect. The answer is insufficient dopamine.
c.   Incorrect. The answer is insufficient dopamine.
*d. Correct. The answer is insufficient dopamine, and these symptoms are linked to Parkinson's disease.

6.   c   obj. 5   p. 53
a.   Incorrect. This is the central nervous system.
b.   Incorrect. Neurons with myelin sheath can be found in both the central and peripheral nervous system.
*c. Correct. The peripheral system consists of the voluntary and involuntary control systems of the body.
d.   Incorrect. It also includes efferent neurons.

7.   c   obj. 5   p. 53
a.   Incorrect. Fight and flight are the options available whenever the sympathetic system is activated.
b.   Incorrect. Both sympathetic and parasympathetic divisions are part of the peripheral system.
*c. Correct. The sympathetic division arouses and the parasympathetic division calms.
d.   Incorrect. Both divisions are necessary to survival (thus helpful?).

8.   a   obj. 7   p. 57
*a. Correct. EEG stands for electroencephalogram, or electrical recording of the brain.
b.   Incorrect. MRI scans use the magnetic fields of the object being scanned.
c.   Incorrect. CAT scans use computers and X-ray images.
d.   Incorrect. PET scans utilize recordings of the metabolism of isotopes of a special glucose.

9.   a   obj. 9   p. 63
*a. Correct. The cortex is rich in axons and dendrites that are very close together, thus supporting rapid processing of large amounts of information.
b.   Incorrect. The medulla controls unconscious functions like breathing and blood circulation.
c.   Incorrect. The cerebellum helps smooth and coordinate muscle movement.
d.   Incorrect. The limbic system includes a number of structures related to emotion, motivation, memory, pain, and pleasure.

10. a   obj. 9   p.64
*a. Correct. The parts of the little man are represented in proportion to the amount of surface area devoted to the feature controlled by that area.
b.   Incorrect. Motor functions are controlled by both hemispheres.
c.   Incorrect. The opposite is true.
d.   Incorrect. This is true, but this alternative is referring to the sensory cortex, not the motor cortex.

11. d   obj. 9   p. 66
a.   Incorrect. Compared to the association areas, the motor area is quite small.
b.   Incorrect. Compared to the association areas, the somatosensory area is quite small.
c.   Incorrect. Compared to the association areas, the sensory areas are quite small.
*d. Correct. All the areas not specifically associated with an identified function, like sensation, motor activity, or language, are called association areas.

12. a   obj. 10   p. 68
*a. Correct. The right side of the brain is often associated with more global processing and emotional or expressive information.
b.   Incorrect. The left side of the brain is more often associated with linear and logical processing.
c.   Incorrect. The occipital lobes are necessary for the visual information about art and dance, but their role is more specialized to visual processing.
d.   Incorrect. The temporal lobes are primarily responsible for hearing, and may contribute well to understanding dance and music, but less well to processing other forms of art.

13. c   obj. 10   p. 68
a.   Incorrect. The frontal lobe is responsible for higher-order thought and planning, among other activities.
b.   Incorrect. The left side of the brain is more often associated with linear and logical processing.

*c. Correct. The right side of the brain is often associated with more global processing, emotional or expressive information, and pattern recognition and spatial memory.
d.   Incorrect. The temporal lobes are primarily responsible for hearing.

14. d   obj. 13   pp. 71-73
a.   Incorrect. In order to begin, one must attend to the directions of the person attaching the machine, but that is the only suggestion required.
b.   Incorrect. This may be part of the process, but it is not the technique.
c.   Incorrect. This may be feedback, but it is not biofeedback.
*d. Correct. The technique does involve focusing upon electronic signals and attention to changes in them.

15. d   obj. 2   p. 46
a.   Incorrect. The myelin sheath deteriorates and the axon is then exposed to stimulation from other axons.
b.   Incorrect. The myelin sheath deteriorates and the axon is then exposed to stimulation from other axons.
c.   Incorrect. The myelin sheath deteriorates and the axon is then exposed to stimulation from other axons.
*d. Correct. The myelin sheath deteriorates and loses its insulating capacity, allowing the short circuits to occur.

16. b   obj. 3   p. 48
17. d   obj. 4   p. 50
18. a   obj. 7   p. 57
19. c   obj. 5   p. 52
20. synapse   obj. 3   p. 48
21. sympathetic division   obj. 5   p. 53
22. limbic system   obj. 8   pp. 61, 62
23. medulla   obj. 8   p. 59
24. association   obj. 9   p. 66

25.
■   Split brain research may actually create the phenomena observed, yet many people wish to use it to substantiate strong differences between left- and right-brain dominant individuals. Also, this research depends upon this operation.
■   The danger of transplanting tissue is not that it will create some monster, but that tissue needed may come from sources that raise questions, like fetal tissue.
■   You should identify moral and ethical reasons both for and against this research and related procedures.

Practise Test 3:
1.   c   obj. 3   pp. 45, 46
a.   Incorrect. Glial cells may be implicated in the rate of action potentials but this information is not in the text.
b.   Incorrect. See answer to a.
*c. Correct. Glial cells make up the myelin sheath that insulates axons. More myelin means greater speeds.
d.   Incorrect. see answer to c.

2.   b   obj. 3   p. 48

a. Incorrect. Deactivation by enzymes in the receiving cell happens to all neurotransmitters.
*b. Correct. Most are reabsorbed in the process called reuptake, some are broken down by enzymes in the area surrounding the synapse.
c. Incorrect. Some, but not most, are processed out of the body this way.
d. Incorrect. None are absorbed by the receiving neuron.

3. d   obj. 8   pp. 61, 62
a. Incorrect. Thinking is associated with the frontal lobes.
b. Incorrect. Waking is associated with the pons and the reticular formation.
c. Incorrect. Emergencies are associated with the sympathetic nervous system.
*d. Correct. The limbic system is associated with emotions as well as pain and pleasure, motivation, and memory.

4. c   obj. 8   p. 61
a. Incorrect. The hippocampus is associated with memory and motivation.
b. Incorrect. The cerebral cortex is associated with thinking.
*c. Correct. This describes the primary role of the hypothalamus.
d. Incorrect. The cerebellum is responsible for smoothing and coordinating voluntary muscle activity.

5. d   obj. 8   pp. 61, 62
a. Incorrect. Damage here might affect motor behaviour but not emotion, and the individual would probably have difficulty waking up from the coma.
b. Incorrect. Damage here would affect breathing and circulation, however, emotional expression would be limited by the mobility of the heart-lung machine.
c. Incorrect. The cerebellum is responsible for smoothing and coordinating voluntary muscle activity.
*d. Correct. The limbic system is associated with emotions as well as pain and pleasure, motivation, and memory.

6. b   obj. 9   p. 64, 65
a. Incorrect. Pleasure centres are in the limbic system.
*b. Correct. The amount of surface area correlates to the sensitivity or refinement of control of the associated function.
c. Incorrect. This is true only in the motor cortex.
d. Incorrect. Damage to the somatosensory area may affect all the bodily sensation for the corresponding body area, but it will not affect the motor control.

7. b   obj. 9   p. 66
a. Incorrect. The neuromuscular area is not very close to the area affected.
*b. Correct. The areas affected must have been association areas because they are important for planning.
c. Incorrect. The damage described does not relate to damage to the somatosensory areas.

d. Incorrect. The damage described does not relate to damage to the motor areas.

8. a   obj. 9   p. 66
*a. Correct. Wernicke's aphasia is associated with the comprehension of speech.
b. Incorrect. Lou Gehrig's disease does affect speech, but it affects motor control—not the comprehension of speech.
c. Incorrect. Broca's aphasia results in difficulty producing speech, while the sufferer may be able to understand the speech of others perfectly well.
d. Incorrect. Phineas Gage did not have a disease, he had an accident that effectively gave him a frontal lobotomy.

9. b   obj. 10   p. 68
a. Incorrect. Successive functioning sounds a lot like sequential functioning.
*b. Correct. In broad terms, these two choices reflect the description of the styles of activity associated with the hemispheres.
c. Incorrect. Successive functioning sounds a lot like sequential functioning.
d. Incorrect. The choices are reversed.

10. d   obj. 9   p. 66
a. Incorrect. Probably not, though the terms have a technical ring to them.
b. Incorrect. Actually, Wernicke's area is closely aligned with the sensory cortex and Broca's area is closely aligned with the motor cortex.
c. Incorrect. Overeating would be associated with the hypothalamus and other limbic structures, while an irregular gait could be associated with motor cortex damage or damage to the cerebellum.
*d. Correct. These choices describe the correct aphasias. Both aphasias have an effect on the production of speech.

11. b   obj. 10   p. 69
a. Incorrect. Just not true: Logic processing tends to occur in the left side of the brain for males and females.
*b. Correct. Language is more localized in males in the left hemisphere.
c. Incorrect. Not true. It may occasionally be dominant in left-handed people.
d. Incorrect. Just not true: spatial abilities tend to be processed in the right hemisphere for both males and females.

12. b   obj. 10   p. 70
a. Incorrect. The bundle of neural fibers called the corpus callosum has been severed in split-brain patients.
*b. Correct. The bundle of neural fibers called the corpus callosum has been severed in split-brain patients.
c. Incorrect. The bundle of neural fibers called the corpus callosum has been severed in split-brain patients, but not all patients had damage to a hemisphere.

d.   Incorrect. The bundle of neural fibers called the corpus callosum has not been cut in all patients with epilepsy.

13.   d   obj. 2   p. 45
a.   Incorrect. Alzheimer's disease has been associated with a deficiency of acetylcholine.
b.   Incorrect. Parkinson's disease has been associated with an underproduction of dopamine.
c.   Incorrect. Multiple sclerosis involves the deterioration of the myelin sheath.
*d.   Correct. Also known as Lou Gehrig's disease.

14.   b   obj. 4   p. 50
a.   Incorrect. Alzheimer's disease does not come and go.
*b.   Correct. Parkinson's disease has been associated with a shortage of dopamine, and one of the symptoms is this on and off type of behaviour.
c.   Incorrect. Multiple sclerosis involves the deterioration of the myelin sheath.
d.   Incorrect. Lou Gehrig's disease involves the failure of the reverse flow mechanism in the neurons.

15.   c   obj. 3   p. 48
a.   Incorrect. These kinds of messages do occur in sensory messages, but they do not define the sensory message.
b.   Incorrect. These kinds of messages do occur in motor messages, but they do not define the motor message.
*c.   Correct. This is what happens in inhibitory messages.
d.   Incorrect. The autonomic system utilizes both inhibitory and excitatory messages.

16. c   obj. 8   p. 61
17. a   obj. 8   p. 61, 62
18. b   obj. 2   p. 45
19. e   obj. 2   p. 45
20. d   obj. 3   p. 48
21. dendrites   obj. 2   p. 45
22. association   obj. 9   p. 66
23. left   obj. 10   p. 68
24. right obj. 10   p. 68
25. visual area   obj. 9   p. 63

26.
- The media helps us identify and understand different illnesses of the brain. News articles, movies of the week, and talk shows all make us aware of illnesses and their effects on human lives and the lives of their families.
- While it is unfortunate that famous people feel exploited, celebrity illnesses make good press. People like to read about those they know and like to watch their progress.
- Also celebrities can successfully raise money for a particular cause (because they have access that many of us don't to people with money and influence.)
- This has always been a lucrative avenue for those looking for research funding.

Sensation and Perception

3

Section 3: Hearing and the Other Senses

Sensing Sound
Smell and Taste

Psychology at Work:
Julia A. Mennella, Taste Researcher

The Skin Senses: Touch, Pressure, Temperature, and Pain

Pathways Through Psychology:
Patrick J. McGrath, Pediatric Pain Researcher

Becoming an Informed Consumer of Psychology:
Managing Pain

Section 4: Perceptual Organization: Constructing Our View of the World

The Gestalt Laws of Organization
Feature Analysis: Focusing on the Parts of the Whole
Top-Down and Bottom-Up Processing
Visual Processing and Action
Perceptual Constancy
Depth Perception: Translating 2-D to 3-D
Motion Perception: As the World Turns
Perceptual Illusions: The Deceptions of Perceptions

Exploring Diversity: Culture and Perception

Subliminal Perception

Learning Objectives

These are the concepts and the learning objectives for Chapter 3. Read them carefully as part of your preliminary survey of the chapter.

Sensing the World Around Us

1. Define sensation, perception, stimulus, and psychophysics. (pp. 80–81)

2. Distinguish between absolute threshold, just noticeable difference, and sensory adaptation. (pp. 81–82)

Vision: Shedding Light on the Eye

3. Describe the structural components of the eye, the initial processing of light, and adaptation to different light levels. (pp. 84–86)

4. Discuss how an image is conveyed from the eye to the brain, and the role of feature detection in processing visual information. (pp. 86,87)

5. Explain the trichromatic and opponent-process theories and how they account for colour vision. (pp. 88–90)

Hearing and the Other Senses

6. Describe the structural parts of the ear, the role of each part in detecting sound, and the basic physical properties of sound. (pp. 92–94)

7. Distinguish between the place theory and the frequency theory of hearing. (pp. 95–97)

8. Explain how semicircular canals detect motion and produce the sense of balance. (p. 97)

9. Describe the sensory mechanisms of smell and taste. (pp. 97–99)

10. Describe the skin senses of touch, pressure, and temperature, and explain the gate-control theory of pain. (pp. 99–102)

Perceptual Organization: Constructing Our View of the World

11. Distinguish figure from ground and perception from sensation. (pp. 103–104)

12. Distinguish between the gestalt approach and feature analysis. (pp. 104–107)

13. Distinguish between top-down and bottom-up processing. (pp. 107–108)

14. Explain perceptual constancy, depth perception, and motion perception. (pp. 108–110)

15. Describe and illustrate the major perceptual illusions, especially the Müller-Lyer illusion. (pp. 111–113)

16. Discuss the evidence for the existence of subliminal perception and extrasensory perception. (pp. 114–115)

SECTION 1: Sensing the World Around Us

Prepare

- *What is sensation, and how do psychologists study it?*
- *What is the relationship between the nature of a physical stimulus and the kinds of sensory responses that result from it?*

Organize

- *Absolute Thresholds*
- *Difference Thresholds*
- *Sensory Adaptation*

Work

A **[a]** _____ is the activity of the sense organ when it detects a stimulus. The difference between perception and sensation is that sensation involves the organism's first encounter with physical stimuli, and **[b]** _____ is the process of interpreting, analyzing, and integrating sensations.

We detect the world around us through our senses. A **[c]** _____ is any physical energy that can be detected by a sense organ. Stimuli vary in type and intensity. *Intensity* refers to the physical strength of the stimulus. **[d]** _____ studies the relationship between the strength of a stimulus and the nature of the sensory response it creates.

[e] _____ refers to the smallest amount of energy, the smallest intensity, needed to detect a stimulus. The absolute threshold for sight is illustrated by a candle burning at 30 miles away on a dark night; for hearing, the ticking of a watch 20 feet away in a quiet room; for taste, one teaspoon of sugar in two gallons of water; for smell, one drop of perfume in three rooms; and for touch, a bee's wing falling one centimetre onto a cheek. *Noise* refers to the background stimulation for any of the senses.

The ability to detect a stimulus is influenced not only by the stimulus but also by conditions like expectations and experience. **[f]** _____ attempts to explain the role of psychological factors in detecting stimuli. Two errors can be made while a subject is detecting stimuli: one, that a stimuli is present when it is not, and the other, that the stimuli is not present when it actually is. Signal detection theory has great practical importance, ranging from helping people who must distinguish various items on radar screens to improving how witnesses identify suspects in a police lineup.

The smallest noticeable difference between two stimuli is called the **[g]** _____, or the **[h]** _____. The amount of stimulus required for the just noticeable difference depends upon the level of the initial stimulus. **[i]** _____ states that the just noticeable difference is a constant proportion for each sense. Weber's law is not very accurate at extreme high or low intensities.

After prolonged exposure to a sensory stimulus, the capacity of the sensory organ adjusts to the stimulus in a process called **[j]** _____. The sensory receptor cells are most responsive to changes in stimuli, because constant stimulation produces adaptation. Context also affects judgments about sensory stimuli. People's reactions to sensory stimuli do not always accurately represent the physical stimuli that cause it.

Evaluate

_____ 1. sensation

_____ 2. intensity

_____ 3. absolute threshold

_____ 4. noise

_____ 5. difference threshold

a. The strength of a stimulus.

b. The smallest detectable difference between two stimuli.

c. The process of responding to a stimulus.

d. The smallest amount of physical intensity by which a stimulus can be detected.

e. Background stimulation that interferes with the perception of other stimuli.

Rethink

1. Do you think it is possible to have sensation without perception? Is it possible to have perception without sensation?

2. Do you think sensory adaptation is essential for everyday psychological functioning?

SECTION 2:   Vision: Shedding Light on the Eye

Prepare

- *What basic processes underlie the sense of vision?*
- *How do we see colours?*

Organize

- *Illuminating the Structure of the Eye*
- *Sending the Message from the Eye to the Brain*
- *Processing the Visual Message*
- *Colour Vision and Colour Blindness*

Work

The stimulus that produces vision is light. Light is the electromagnetic radiation that our visual apparatus is capable of detecting. The range of visible light is called the **[a]** _____ .

Light enters the eye through the **[b]** _____ , a transparent, protective window. It then passes through the **[c]** _____ , the opening in the

[d] _____ . The iris is the pigmented muscle that opens and closes the pupil depending on how much light is in the environment. The narrower the pupil is, the greater is the focal distance for the eye. After the pupil the light passes through the *lens*, which then bends and focuses the light on the back of the eye by changing its thickness, a process called

accommodation. The light then strikes the **[e]** _____ , a thin layer of nerve cells at the back of the eyeball. The retina is composed of light-sensitive cells called

[f] _____ , which are long and cylindrical, and

[g] _____ , which are shorter and conical in shape. The greatest concentration of cones is in the *fovea*, an area that is extremely sensitive. Cones are responsible for colour vision, and rods are insensitive to colour and play a role in *peripheral vision*, the ability to see objects to our side, and in night vision.

When a person goes into a dark room from a well-lit space, the person becomes, after a time, accustomed to the dark and experiences **[h]** _____ , an adjustment by the eyes to low levels of light. The changes that make this adjustment are chemical changes in the rods and cones.

Rods contain **[i]** _____ , a complex substance that changes chemically when struck by light. This chemical change sets off a reaction. The response is then transmitted to two other kinds of cells, first to the *bipolar cells* and then to *ganglion cells*. The ganglion cells organize and summarize the information and then convey it to the **[j]** _____ . Where the optic nerve goes from the retina back through the eyeball there are no rods or cones, which results in the blind spot. The optic nerves from both eyes meet behind the eyes at the

[k] _____ where each optic nerve splits. Nerve impulses from the right half of each eye go to the right side of the brain, and nerve impulses from the left half of each eye go to the left half of the brain. However, at the stage when the lens focused the image onto the retina, it reversed it from top to bottom and from left to right. Therefore, the result is that the nerve impulses going to the right side of brain from the right side of each retina, actually originated in the left field of vision of each eye. Likewise, the information going to the left side of the brain, originated in **[l]** _____ .

The visual message is processed from the beginning by ganglion cells, and continues to the visual cortex, where many neurons are highly specialized. Their roles are specialized to detect certain visual features, and the process is called **[m]** _____ .

Evaluate

_____ 1. pupil

_____ 2. cornea

_____ 3. iris

_____ 4. lens

_____ 5. retina

a. The coloured part of the eye.

b. The part of the eye that converts the electromagnetic energy of light into useful information for the brain.

c. A dark hole in the centre of the eye's iris that changes size as the amount of incoming light changes.

d. A transparent, protective window into the eyeball.

e. The part of the eye located behind the pupil that bends rays of light to focus them on the retina.

Rethink

3. If the eye were constructed with a second lens that "unreversed" the image hitting the retina, do you think there would be changes in the way people perceive the world?

4. From an evolutionary standpoint, why might the eye have evolved so that the rods, which we rely on in low light, do not provide sharp images? Are there any advantages to this system?

SECTION 3: Hearing and the Other Senses

Prepare

- **What role does the ear play in the senses of sound, motion, and balance?**
- **How do smell and taste function?**
- **What are the skin senses, and how do they relate to the experience of pain?**

Organize

- **Sensing Sound**
- **Smell and Taste**
- **The Skin Senses: Touch, Pressure, Temperature and Pain**

Work

[a] _____ is the movement of air that results from the vibration of objects. The outer ear collects sounds and guides them to the internal portions of the ear. Sounds are funneled into the auditory canal toward the [b] _____ . Sound waves hit the eardrum, which in turn transmits its vibrations into the [c] _____ . The middle ear contains three small bones: the hammer, the anvil, and the stirrup. These three bones transmit the vibrations to the [d] _____ . The inner ear contains the organs for transmitting the sound waves into nerve impulses as well as the organs for balance and position. The [e] _____ is a coiled tube that contains the [f] _____ . The basilar membrane is covered with [g] _____ that vibrate. Sound may also enter the cochlea through the bones that surround the ear.

Sound is characterized by *frequency*, or the number of waves per second, and *pitch* is our experience of this number as high or low. *Intensity* may be thought of as the size of the waves—how strong it is. Intensity is measured in *decibels*. The [h] _____ is based on the fact that parts of the basilar membrane are sensitive to different pitches. The

[i] _____ suggests that the entire basilar membrane vibrates in response to any sound, and the nerves send signals that are more frequent for higher pitches and less frequent for lower pitches.

The inner ear is also responsible for the sense of balance. The disturbance of the sense of balance is called *vertigo*. The structures responsible for balance are the [j] _____ , three tubes filled with fluid that move around in the tubes when the head moves. The fluid affects

[k] _____ , small motion-sensitive crystals in the semicircular canals.

We are able to detect about 10,000 different smells, and women have a better sense of smell than do men. Some animals can communicate using odor. Odor is detected by molecules of a substance coming into contact with the *olfactory cells* in the nasal passages. Each olfactory cell responds to a narrow band of odors. [l] _____ are chemicals that can produce a reaction in members of a species. These chemicals have a role in sexual activity and identification. Taste is detected by *taste buds* on the tongue. Taste buds detect sweet, sour, salty, or bitter flavous. The experience of taste also includes the odor and appearance of food.

The [m] _____ include touch, pressure, temperature, and pain. Receptor cells for each of these senses are distributed all over the body, though each sense is distributed in varying concentrations. The major theory of pain is called the

[n] _____ . This theory states that nerve receptors send messages to the brain areas related to pain, and whenever they are activated, a "gate" to the brain is opened and pain is experienced. The gate can be shut by overwhelming the nerve pathways with non-painful messages. It can also be closed by the brain producing messages to reduce or eliminate the experience of pain. *Acupuncture* may be explained by the first option in which the needles shut off the messages going to the brain. Endorphins may also close the gate.

Evaluate
Test A

____ 1. outer ear

____ 2. auditory canal

____ 3. eardrum

____ 4. middle ear

____ 5. oval window

a. The visible part of the ear that acts as a collector to bring sounds into the internal portions of the ear.

b. A tiny chamber containing three bones—the hammer, the anvil, and the stirrup—which transmit vibrations to the oval window.

c. The membrane that separates the outer ear from the middle ear and vibrates when sound waves hit it.

d. A thin membrane between the middle ear and the inner ear that transmits vibrations while increasing their strength.

e. A tubelike passage in the ear through which sound moves to the eardrum.

Test B

____ 1. cochlea

____ 2. basilar membrane

____ 3. hair cells

____ 4. frequency

____ 5. pitch

a. The number of wave crests occurring each second in any particular sound.

b. A structure dividing the cochlea into an upper and a lower chamber.

c. A coiled tube filled with fluid that receives sound via the oval window or through bone conduction.

d. The characteristic that makes sound "high" or "low."

e. Tiny cells that, when bent by vibrations entering the cochlea, transmit neural messages to the brain.

Rethink

5. Much research is being conducted on repairing faulty sensory organs through such devices as personal guidance systems, eyeglasses, and so forth. Do you think that researchers should attempt to improve normal sensory capabilities beyond their "natural" range (e.g., make human visual or audio capabilities more sensitive than normal)? What benefits might this bring? What problems might it cause?

6. Why might sensitivity to pheromones have evolved differently in humans than in other species? What cultural factors might have played a role?

SECTION 4: Perceptual Organization: Constructing Our View of the World

Prepare

- *What principles underlie our organization of the visual world, allowing us to make sense of our environment?*
- *How are we able to perceive the world in three dimensions when our retinas are capable of sensing only two-dimensional images?*
- *What clues do visual illusions give us about our understanding of general perceptual mechanisms?*

Organize

- *The Gestalt Laws of Organization*
- *Feature Analysis: Focusing on the Parts of the Whole*
- *Top-Down and Bottom-Up Processing*
- *Perceptual Constancy*
- *Depth Perception: Translating 2-D to 3-D*
- *Motion Perception: As the World Turns*
- *Perceptual Illusions: The Deceptions of Perceptions*
- *Subliminal Perception*

Work

Errors in perception occur because perception is an *interpretation* of sensory information. The distinction between *figure* and *ground* is crucial to perceptual organization. The tendency is to form an object in contrast to its ground, or background.

Through perception we try to simplify complex stimuli in the environment. This tendency toward simplicity and organization into meaningful wholes follows basic principles called the

[a] _____. *Gestalt* refers to a "pattern." Basic patterns identified by the gestalt psychologists are: (1) *closure*, groupings tend to be in complete or enclosed figures; (2) *proximity*, elements close together tend to be grouped together; (3) *similarity*, elements that are similar tend to be grouped together; and (4) *simplicity*, the tendency to organize patterns in a basic, straightforward manner.

The recent approach called [b] _____ suggests that we perceive first the individual components and then formulate an understanding of the overall picture. Specific neurons respond to highly specific components of stimuli, suggesting that each stimulus is made up of a series of component features. One theory has identified thirty-six fundamental components that form the basic elements of complex objects. Treisman has proposed that perception requires a two-stage process, first a *preattentive stage* and then a *focused-attention stage*.

Perception proceeds in two ways, though top-down or through bottom-up processing. In

[c] _____ perception is controlled by higher-level knowledge, experience, expectations, and motivation. Top-down processing helps sort through ambiguous stimuli or

missing elements. Context is critical for filling in missing information. Isolated stimuli illustrate how context is important for top-down processing. **[d]** _____ consists of recognizing and processing information about individual components. If we cannot recognize individual components, recognizing the complete picture would be very difficult.

One phenomena that contributes to our perception of the world is that of

[e] _____, the tendency for objects to be perceived as unvarying and consistent even as we see them from different views and distances. The rising moon is one example of how perceptual constancy works. The moon illusion is explained as resulting from the intervening cues of landscape and horizon, which give it context. When it rises, there are no context cues. Perceptual constancies occur with size, shape, and colour.

The ability to view the world in three dimensions is called **[f]** _____. The two slightly different positions of the eyes give rise to minute differences in the visual representation in the brain, a phenomenon called **[g]** _____. Discrepancy between the two images from the retinas gives clues to the distance of the object or the distance between two objects. The larger the disparity, the larger the distance. Other cues for visual depth perception can be seen with only one eye, and so they are called **[h]** _____.

The Parthenon in Athens is built with an intentional illusion to give the building a greater appearance of straightness and stability. **[i]** _____ are physical stimuli that produce errors in perception. Explanations of the **[j]** _____ focus on the apparatus of the eye and the interpretations made by the brain.

[k] _____ is the process of perceiving messages without our awareness of their being presented. Research has shown that the subliminal message does not lead to attitude or behaviour change. Another controversial area is that of *extrasensory perception* (*ESP*). Claims of ESP are difficult to substantiate.

Evaluate

_____ 1. gestalts

_____ 2. closure

_____ 3. proximity

_____ 4. similarity

_____ 5. simplicity

a. The tendency to group together those elements that are similar in appearance.

b. Patterns studied by the gestalt psychologists.

c. The tendency to perceive a pattern in the most basic, straightforward, organized manner possible—the overriding gestalt principle.

d. The tendency to group together those elements that are close together.

e. The tendency to group according to enclosed or complete figures rather than open or incomplete ones.

Rethink

7. Can you think of examples of the combined use of top-down and bottom-up processing in everyday life? Is one type of processing superior to the other?

8. In what ways do painters represent three-dimensional scenes in two dimensions on a canvas? Do you think artists in non-Western cultures use the same or different principles to represent three dimensionality? Why?

Practise Questions

Test your knowledge of the chapter material by answering these questions. These questions have been placed in three Practise Tests. The first two tests are composed of questions that will test your recall of factual knowledge. The third test contains questions that are challenging and primarily test for conceptual knowledge and your ability to apply that knowledge. Check your answers and review the feedback using the Answer Key on the following pages of the *Study Guide*.

PRACTISE TEST 1:

1. A focus of interest on the biological activity of the sense organ is typical in:
   a. sensory psychology.
   b. perceptual psychology.
   c. gestalt psychology.
   d. illusionary psychology.

2. Psychophysicists define absolute threshold as the:
   a. minimum amount of change in stimulation that is detectable.
   b. range of stimulation to which each sensory channel is sensitive.
   c. maximum intensity that is detectable to the senses.
   d. minimum magnitude of stimulus that is detectable.

3. On the day after his wedding, a groom is very conscious of the feeling of his wedding band on his finger, but two months later he does not notice the ring at all. This change has occurred because of the principle of:
   a. the difference threshold.
   b. sexual experience.
   c. bottom-up perceptual processing.
   d. sensory adaptation.

4. Feature detection is best described as the process by which specialized neurons in the cortex:
   a. identify fine details in a larger pattern.
   b. see things clearly that are far away.
   c. discriminate one face from another.
   d. recognize particular shapes or patterns.

5. The contemporary view of colour vision is that the _____ theory is true only for early stages of visual processing but the _____ theory applies correctly to both early and later stages.
   a. trichromatic; gate-control
   b. trichromatic; opponent-process
   c. place; gate-control
   d. opponent-process; trichromatic

6. The function of the three tiny bones of the middle ear is to:
    a. add tension to the basilar membrane.
    b. prevent the otoliths from becoming mechanically displaced.
    c. amplify sound waves being relayed to the oval window.
    d. minimize the disorienting effects of vertigo.

7. Compared with high-frequency sound, low-frequency sound:
    a. has more peaks and valleys per second.
    b. generates an auditory sensation of low pitch.
    c. has a lower decibel value.
    d. is heard by pets such as cats or dogs but not by humans.

8. The theory that certain nerve receptors lead to specific areas of the brain that sense pain is the:
    a. endorphin.
    b. opiate.
    c. opponent process.
    d. gate control.

9. The gestalt laws of organization are best described as:
    a. patterns of perceiving determined by specific functions of neural receptors.
    b. principles that describe how people perceive.
    c. an explanation for how neural networks in the sensory system operate.
    d. explanations of how people determine the quality of a work of art.

10. The fact that a number of instruments all blend together to form a symphony orchestra demonstrates:
    a. a figure/ground relationship.
    b. the law of similarity.
    c. that the whole is more than the sum of its parts.
    d. the law of perceptual constancy.

11. Perception that is guided by higher-level knowledge, experience, expectations, and motivations is called:
    a. top-down processing.
    b. bottom-up processing.
    c. perceptual constancy.
    d. feature analysis.

12. Suppose that a person's racial prejudices influenced whether she perceived people as workers or vagrants. This would best demonstrate:
    a. preattentive perceptual processing.
    b. bottom-up processing.
    c. gestalt perceptual organization.
    d. top-down perceptual processing.

13. Binocular disparity refers to the fact that:
    a. the world looks different with prescription glasses than without.
    b. objects appear closer when they are larger.
    c. the visual image on the retina of each eye is slightly different.
    d. objects progressing into the distance, such as railroad tracks, appear to converge.

14. The perception of messages about which the person is unaware is called:
    a. extrasensory perception.
    b. subliminal perception.
    c. cognition in the Ganzfeld.
    d. otolithic preprocessing.

15. The signals that allow us to perceive distance and depth with just one eye are called
    a. the gestalt principle of figure/ground.
    b. binocular disparity.
    c. monocular cues.
    d. motion parallax.

_____ 16. perceptual constancy

_____ 17. depth perception

_____ 18. binocular disparity

_____ 19. motion parallax

_____ 20. relative size

a. The ability to view the world in three dimensions and to perceive distance.

b. The change in position of the image of an object on the retina as the head moves, providing a monocular cue to distance.

c. The phenomenon by which, if two objects are the same size, the one that makes a smaller image on the retina is perceived to be farther away.

d. The phenomenon by which physical objects are perceived as unvarying despite changes in their appearance or the physical environment.

e. The difference between the images that reach the retina of each eye; this disparity allows the brain to estimate distance.

21. As the available light diminishes, the _____ gets larger.

22. _____ is the process that causes incoming images to be focused in the eye.

23. Cones are found primarily in the _____ of the retina.

24. A receptor called a _____ is used in peripheral vision.

25. The senses of taste and smell are alike in that they both depend on _____ as stimuli.

26. Consider what it would be like if our senses were not within their present limits. What visual problems might we face? What would we hear if our hearing had a different range? What if we were more sensitive to smell? What about the other senses?

PRACTISE TEST 2:

1. A dog's nose is more sensitive to smells than is a human's nose. It then would be expected that the absolute threshold for smell will be _____ amount of odorant for a dog than for a person.
    a. a much larger
    b. a moderately larger
    c. about the same
    d. a smaller

2. The function of the retina is to:
    a. turn the image of the object upside down.
    b. redistribute the light energy in the image.
    c. convert the light energy into neural impulses.
    d. control the size of the pupil.

3. The visual receptors most useful for night vision are called:
    a. buds.
    b. cones.
    c. ossicles.
    d. rods.

4. Dark adaptation refers to the fact that:
    a. our eyes are less sensitive to a dim stimulus when we look directly at it rather than slightly to the side of it.
    b. the colour of objects changes at dusk as light intensity decreases.
    c. the eyes become many times more sensitive after being exposed to darkness.
    d. some people have great difficulty seeing things under low levels of illumination.

5. According to the text, afterimages can best be explained by the:
    a. opponent-process theory of colour vision.
    b. trichromatic theory of colour vision.
    c. place theory of colour vision.
    d. receptive-field theory of colour vision.

6. People hear the sound of their own voice differently from the way others hear it primarily because of:
    a. bone conduction.
    b. tympanic vibrations.
    c. low-frequency vibrations.
    d. gradual hearing loss associated with age.

7. Which statement about the taste buds is accurate?
    a. Each receptor is able to respond to many basic tastes and to send the information to the brain.
    b. Over twelve types of receptors for different basic flavours have been described.
    c. Taste receptors for all the flavours, located on the tongue, the sides and roof of the mouth, and the top part of the throat, send complex information about taste to the brain, where it is interpreted.
    d. Receptors for the four basic flavours are located on different areas of the tongue, other parts of the mouth, and in the throat.

8. Look at these letters: *ppp ppp ppp ppp*. You see four groups, each containing three *p*'s, rather than a single row of twelve *p*'s because of the gestalt principle known as:
    a. similarity.
    b. proximity.
    c. closure.
    d. constancy.

9. Which principle of perceptual organization is used when we group items together that look alike or have the same form?
    a. proximity
    b. similarity
    c. figure/ground
    d. closure

10. Making sense of a verbal message by first understanding each word and then piecing them together is:
    a. top-down processing.
    b. bottom-up processing.
    c. selective attention.
    d. perceptual constancy.

11. When we perceive the characteristics of external objects as remaining the same even though the retinal image has changed, _____ has been maintained.
    a.   sensory adaptation
    b.   bottom-up processing
    c.   subliminal perception
    d.   perceptual constancy

12. The brain estimates the distance to an object by comparing the different images that it gets from the right and left retinas using:
    a.   the gestalt principle of figure/ground.
    b.   binocular disparity.
    c.   monocular cues.
    d.   motion parallax.

13. The Parthenon in Athens looks as if it:
    a.   is leaning backward from the viewer.
    b.   is completely upright with its columns formed of straight lines.
    c.   has bulges in the middle of the columns.
    d.   is ready to fall over.

14. Martin is able to read the message on the board even though part of each word has been erased. This is the gestalt principle of:
    a.   figure/group.
    b.   closure.
    c.   proximity.
    d.   similarity.

_____ 15. linear perspective

_____ 16. visual illusion

_____ 17. decibel

_____ 18. basilar membrane

_____ 19. figure/ground

a.   Figure refers to the object being perceived, whereas ground refers to the background or spaces within the object.

b.   A structure dividing the cochlea into an upper and a lower chamber

c.   The phenomenon by which distant objects appear to be closer together than nearer objects, a monocular cue.

d.   A physical stimulus that consistently produces errors in perception (often called an optical illusion).

e.   A measure of sound loudness or intensity.

20. The _____ holds that certain nerve receptors lead to specific areas of the brain that sense pain.

21. Perception that is guided by high-level knowledge, experience, expectations, and motivations is called _____.

22. _____ perspective makes railroad tracks appear to come closer together as they move away from the observer.

23. _____ is the study of the relationship between the physical nature of stimuli and a person's sensory responses to them.

24. The organ that gives your eyes their identifying colour is the _____ .

25. What are the basic differences between the gestalt organizational principles and the feature analysis approach to perception? Are there some phenomena that one or the other explains better? Are there phenomena that would be difficult for one to explain?

PRACTISE TEST 3: Conceptual, Applied, and Challenging Questions

1. _____ is to pinprick as _____ is to sharp pain.
   a. Threshold; just noticeable difference
   b. Stimulus; sensation
   c. Difference threshold; context
   d. Sensory adaptation; short-duration stimulation

2. Which statement about the rods and the cones of the retina is accurate?
   a. The rods are concentrated in the fovea of the retina; the cones are in the periphery.
   b. The rods are the receptors for dim illumination; the cones are for high illumination levels.
   c. The rods are responsible for the first 0–10 minutes of the dark adaptation curve; the cones are responsible for the remaining 11–40 minutes.
   d. Cones are found in larger numbers on the retina than are rods.

3. Professor Lobe is frequently distressed by the background noise in his classroom. If he were able to extract all the air from this noisy classroom he would:
   a. hear only the sound of his own voice.
   b. greatly diminish the background noise and hear himself.
   c. hear his own voice but the background noise would also be louder.
   d. be unable to hear either himself or background noise.

4. Suppose you could hear nothing but your own voice. Of the following, which might your physician suspect as the source of the problem?
   a. the cochlea.
   b. the basilar membrane.
   c. the auditory cortex.
   d. the middle ear.

5. On a piano keyboard, the keys for the lower-frequency sounds are on the left side; the keys for the higher-frequency sounds are on the right. If you first pressed a key on the left side of the keyboard, and then a key on the right side, you might expect that:
   a. pitch would depend on how hard the keys were struck.
   b. the pitch would be lower for the first key that was played.
   c. the pitch would be lower for the second key that was played.
   d. the pitch would be identical for each.

6. Intensity is to _____ as frequency is to _____ .
   a. resonance; loudness
   b. loudness; pitch
   c. acoustic nerve; auditory canal
   d. external ear; consonance

7. Which of the following would refer to the number of wave crests that occur in a second when a tuning fork is struck?
    a. pitch
    b. intensity
    c. decibel level
    d. frequency

8. Loudness is to _____ as frequency is to _____.
    a. decibels; cycles per second
    b. millimicrometres; loudness
    c. cycles per second; wavelength
    d. cochlea; auditory nerve

9. When a person suffers from vertigo, the symptoms would probably be:
    a. a strange taste in the mouth, described as garlic and seaweed.
    b. persistently heard voices, typically shouting for help.
    c. dizziness or motion sickness.
    d. phantom skin sensations, such as insects crawling up the arm.

10. The figure/ground principle:
    a. was formulated by gestalt psychologists to describe how objects seem to pop out from the background against which they are seen.
    b. states that figures are obscured by their backgrounds.
    c. suggests that elements that are located near to each other tend to be seen as part of the same perceptual unit, in most cases.
    d. states that individuals with attractive figures are likely to be viewed with interest.

11. An interesting reversible figure/ground stimulus for perceptual demonstrations:
    a. has a predominant ground.
    b. has a predominant figure.
    c. always gives the same dramatic visual image, no matter how it is viewed.
    d. has a figure and a ground that can alternate when viewed in certain ways.

12. First graders are asked to sort geometric puzzle pieces, such as circles, squares, and triangles. This activity illustrates the gestalt principle of:
    a. figure/group.
    b. closure.
    c. proximity.
    d. similarity.

13. As you look at a car, you can see only the last part of the make, reading "mobile." You determine that the car is probably an Oldsmobile. This illustrates:
    a. top-down processing.
    b. bottom-up processing.
    c. selective attention.
    d. feature analysis.

14. Which one of the following statements concerning depth perception is true?
    a. It is not always necessary to use two eyes to perceive depth.
    b. Distant objects appear smaller because of linear perspective.
    c. The greater the discrepancy between two retinal images, the more difficult it is to reconcile depth.
    d. If two objects are the same size, the one that projects the smaller image on the retina is closer.

15. Suppose that you happened upon two buffalo grazing in an open field, and one looked substantially larger than the other. Now suppose that the image of the smaller buffalo began to expand. You would probably assume that:
    a. it was growing.
    c. it was moving away from you.

b.   it was running toward you.   d.   it was turning sideways.

16. _____ is most important in order for major-league baseball players to be able to hit the ball when it reaches the plate.
    a.   Tracking
    b.   Focusing
    c.   Anticipation
    d.   Eye coordination

17. Matthew is interested in learning to speak French, so he purchases some tapes that he is supposed to play while he is asleep. The concept that supports the notion of being able to learn in this manner is called _____. According to the text, will his tapes work?
    a.   selective attention; yes
    b.   selective attention; no
    c.   subliminal perception; yes
    d.   subliminal perception; no

18. According to the text, which alternative below is **not** an important factor that influences illusions?
    a.   amount of formal education
    b.   cultural experiences
    c.   structural characteristics of the eye
    d.   interpretive errors of the brain

19.   The visual receptors most useful for night vision are called _____.

20.   The _____ is made up from the up of bundles axons from the ganglion cells.

21.   In the study of perception, patterns are referred to as "_____."

22.   Filling in the gaps is known as _____.

23.   _____ are chemical molecules that promote communication between members of a species.

24.   _____ is an organism's first encounter with a raw sensory stimulus.

25.   _____ is the process by which the stimulus is interpreted, analyzed, and integrated with other sensory information.

Spotlight on Terminology and Language—
Cultural Idioms

Page 80 " ...**Sensation** can be thought of as an organism's first encounter with a raw sensory stimulus, whereas **perception** is the process by which the stimulus is interpreted, analyzed, and integrated with other sensory information."

Sensation is our first awareness of some outside stimulus. **Perception** is your brain assembling thousands of individual **sensations** into the experience of a meaningful pattern or image.

Sensing the World Around Us

Page 77 "You would experience the dinner very differently from someone whose sensory **apparatus** was intact."

Apparatus is the set of materials or equipment designed for a particular use. What are some of the ways in which you use hearing and tasting senses?

Page 81 "Perhaps you were taught that there are just five senses—sight, sound, taste, smell, and touch—this **enumeration** is too modest."
To **enumerate** is to list. This list of the senses is simply not complete. Which senses would you add to the list?

Page 81 "An absolute threshold is the smallest **intensity** of a stimulus that must be present for it to be detected."

Intensity refers to the magnitude. Absolute threshold refers to the smallest amount of a stimulus that must be present for it to be determined that it exists.

Page 81 "If our ears were just slightly more **acute**, we would be able to hear the sound of air molecules in our ears knocking into our eardrum…."

Acute means more discerning or more perceptive. **Acute** hearing is hearing that is responsive to slight impressions or stimuli.

Page 82 "The reason you **acclimate** to the odor is sensory adaptation."
When an organism **acclimates** to something, it makes a physiological adjustment to environmental changes.

Vision: Shedding Light on the Eye

Page 84 "The ray of light we are tracing as it is reflected off the flower first travels through the cornea, a **transparent**, protective window."

When something is **transparent**, it has the property of transmitting light without appreciable scattering.

Page 84 "After moving through the cornea, the light **traverses** the pupil."

The light moves across the pupil.

Page 85 "The **dimmer** the surroundings, the more the pupil opens in order to allow more light to enter."

When you **dim** the lights, you reduce the light, or provide only a limited or insufficient amount of light.

Page 85 "The lens focuses light by changing its own thickness, a process called **accommodation**."

Accommodation is the change that occurs in existing experience or knowledge as a result of assimilating some new information.

Page 85 "The **retina** consists of a thin layer of nerve cells at the back of the eyeball."

The **retina** is a thin film lining the back of the eye. The **retina** consists of three layers, the third and deepest of which contains two kinds of photoreceptors, rods and cones, that change light waves into nerve impulses.

Page 86 "The rods play a key role in **peripheral** vision—seeing objects that are outside the main centre of focus—and in night vision."

Peripheral vision is the outer part of the field of vision. Do you have good **peripheral** vision?

Page 86 "Normally, this absence of nerve cells does not interfere with vision, because you automatically **compensate** for the missing part of your field of vision."

When we **compensate**, we are counterbalancing. We sometimes compensate for feelings of inferiority or failure in one field by achievement in another. We may **compensate** for an organic defect with the increased function of another organ.

Page 87 "Psychologists David Hubel and Torsten Wiesel won the Nobel Prize for their discovery that many neurons in the cortex are **extraordinarily** specialized, being activated only by visual stimuli of a particular shape or pattern—a process known as feature detection."

Extraordinary means exceptional to a very conspicuous degree. Some students have **extraordinary** powers of deduction; they have skills beyond what is usual in a college student.

Page 87 "Other cells are activated only by moving, as opposed to **stationary**, stimuli.

When something is **stationary**, it is in a fixed mode. It is unchanging in condition. A stationary bicycle is one that is motionless.

Page 85 "For most people with colour-blindness, the world looks quite **dull**."

Dull suggests a lack of sharpness or intensity. Vision that is **dull** may lack brightness or vividness.

Hearing and the Other Senses

Page 92 "This sense allows people to navigate their bodies through the world and maintain an **upright** position without falling."

Upright is vertically upward. You are **upright** when you are standing.

Page 93 "When sound enters the inner ear through the oval window, it moves into the **cochlea**, a coiled tube that looks something like a snail and is filled with fluid that can vibrate in response to sound. Inside the **cochlea** is the **basilar membrane**, a structure that runs through the centre of the **cochlea**, dividing it into an upper and a lower chamber."

The **cochlea** is a coiled, fluid-filled structure in the inner ear that contains the receptors for hearing. The function of the **cochlea** is to transform vibrations into nerve impulses (electrical signals) that are sent to the brain for processing into sound sensations. The **basilar membrane** is a membrane within the **cochlea** that contains the auditory receptors, or hair cells.

Perceptual Organization: Constructing Our View of the World

Page 106 "According to some research, the way we perceive complex objects is similar to how we perceive simple letters—viewing them in terms of their **component** elements."

Components are parts, or ingredients.

Page 114 "**Subliminal** perception refers to the perception of messages about which we have no awareness."

Subliminal messages are brief auditory or visual messages that are presented below the absolute threshold, so that their chance of perception is less than fifty percent.

■ CHAPTER 3: ANSWER KEY

GUIDED REVIEW			
Section 1:	Section 2:	Section 3:	Section 4:
[a] sensation	[a] visual spectrum	[a] Sound	[a] gestalt laws of organization
[b] perception	[b] cornea	[b] eardrum	[b] feature analysis
[c] stimulus	[c] pupil	[c] middle ear	[c] top-down processing
[d] Psychophysics	[d] iris	[d] oval window	[d] Bottom-up processing
[e] Absolute threshold	[e] retina	[e] cochlea	[e] perceptual constancy
[f] Signal detection theory	[f] rods	[f] basilar membrane	[f] depth perception
[g] difference threshold	[g] cones	[g] hair cells	

| [h] just noticeable difference
[i] Weber's law
[j] adaptation

Evaluate
1. c
2. a
3. d
4. e
5. b | [h] dark adaptation
[i] rhodopsin
[j] optic nerve
[k] optic chiasm
[l] right field of vision
[m] feature detection

Evaluate
1. c
2. d
3. a
4. e
5. b | [h] place theory of hearing
[i] frequency theory of hearing
[j] semicircular canals
[k] otoliths
[l] Pheromones
[m] skin senses
[n] gate-control theory of pain

Evaluate | [g] binocular disparity
[h] monocular cues
[i] Visual illusions
[j] Müller-Lyer illusion
[k] Subliminal perception

Evaluate
1. b
2. e
3. d
4. a
5. c |

Test A	Test B
1. a	1. c
2. e	2. b
3. c	3. e
4. b	4. a
5. d	5. d

Selected Rethink Answers

2. Sensory adaptation, an adjustment in sensory capacity following prolonged exposure to stimuli. Decline in sensitivity is due to the inability of nerve receptors to constantly fire messages to the brain. Receptor cells are most responsive to changes in stimulation and constant stimulation is not effective in producing a reaction. Adaptation to the context of one stimulus alters responses to another. If our senses were constantly bombarded by stimuli that was intense, we would have a constant high rate of stimulation.

5. Benefits of increased sensory capacity might allow us to see great distance. We may also be able to hear sounds from far away. Our sense of touch could cause us to have increased pain from cuts and burns. Science already has invented equipment that allows these things: "Sonic Ear" advertised to hear long distances, new surgery that improves eyesight, etc. These could be great scientific achievements but, to have our senses bombarded by increased stimuli doesn't seem to have overall advantages—how would we distinguish necessary/ unnecessary stimuli?

6. Sensitivity to pheromones may have developed differently for humans because as the culture has evolved, sending out messages that you were available for sexual activity could have been dangerous (sent to others who were not potential partners). Also, societies now set up rules for sexual activity and partnerships (different from that in the animal world).

Practise Test 1:
1. a   obj. 1   p. 80
*a. Correct. Sensory psychology focuses on sensation.
b. Incorrect. Perceptual psychology focuses on sensation and perception
c. Incorrect. Gestalt psychology focuses primarily on perception.
d. Incorrect. Do not know of any such field.

2. d   obj. 2   p. 81
a. Incorrect. This defines a difference threshold.
b. Incorrect. This is referred to as the range of stimulation.
c. Incorrect. This would be some kind of maximum threshold.
*d. Correct. The absolute threshold is the smallest magnitude of a physical stimulus a sensory organ can detect.

3. d   obj. 2   p. 82
a. Incorrect. The difference threshold would account for the initial detection of the new stimulus.
b. Incorrect. Sexual experience may alter his cognitive understanding of the ring, but not his sensory attention to it.
c. Incorrect. Actually, if this applies, it would be the top-down processing of ignoring the stimulus as described in answer d.
*d. Correct. This phenomenon is called sensory adaptation.

4. d   obj. 4   p. 87
a. Incorrect. This kind of recognition of details occurs in other processing areas.
b. Incorrect. The fovea is responsible for this capability.

c.   Incorrect. The discrimination of faces occurs in the association areas of the brain.

*d.   Correct. Feature detection is responsible for pattern recognition.

5.   b   obj. 5   p. 89
a.   Incorrect. Gate control relates to pain perception.

*b.   Correct. Trichromatic accounts for the three different colour spectrum to which the cones are responsive; while the opponent-process theory explains how four colours can be perceived with only three types of cones.

c.   Incorrect. Place relates to hearing, and gate control to pain perception.

d.   Incorrect. These are reversed.

6.   c   obj. 6   p. 93
a.   Incorrect. They are not connected to the basilar membrane.

b.   Incorrect. Otoliths are found in the semicircular canal, not the middle ear.

*c.   Correct. The bones transfer, focus, and amplify mechanical sound from the eardrum to the oval window.

d.   Incorrect. Nothing can minimize these effects.

7.   b   obj. 6   p. 94
a.   Incorrect. This describes high-frequency, not low-frequency sound.

*b.   Correct. Our perception of low frequency is low sound.

c.   Incorrect. The decibel value applies to all sound, regardless of frequency.

d.   Incorrect. Many pets can hear both higher and lower frequencies than their human attendants.

8.   d   obj. 10   p. 101
a.   Incorrect. Endorphins are neurotransmitters involved in reduction of the perception of pain.

b.   Incorrect. Opiates are like endorphins and have similar effects on the neural pain messages.

c.   Incorrect. Opponent processes are related to pain in the release of endorphins, and the persistence of their effects after the pain stimulus has subsided.

*d.   Correct. This is the name of the theory of pain.

9.   b   obj. 12   p. 104
a.   Incorrect. This refers to feature detection.

*b.   Correct. The gestalt psychologists suggested that people organize their perceptions according to consistent principles of organization based on figure/ground relationships and simplicity.

c.   Incorrect. Though some of these neural networks may work in this fashion, this is not the foundation of neural networks.

d.   Incorrect. This shall remain a mystery for some time.

10.   c   obj. 12   p. 105

a.   Incorrect. In a figure/ground relationship, one instrument would stand out against the others.

b.   Incorrect. The law of similarity applies to the similarity of items leading to their being grouped together.

*c.   Correct. The fact that the orchestra creates a sound that is more complex than merely the sum of the sounds made by the individual instruments illustrates this concept.

d.   Incorrect. Perceptual constancy applies to other phenomena altogether.

11.   a   obj. 13   p. 107
*a.   Correct. Top-down processing refers to processing that begins with a broad, general perspective and then completes details from this context.

b.   Incorrect. Bottom-up processing builds the final picture from the details.

c.   Incorrect. Perceptual constancy refers to our tendency to view an object as having a constant size, shape, colour, or brightness even when we see it in different environments or from different points of view.

d.   Incorrect. Feature analysis refers to detection of patterns in an array of neural activity.

12.   d   obj. 13   pp. 107, 108
a.   Incorrect. See answer d.

b.   Incorrect. See answer d.

c.   Incorrect. See answer d.

*d.   Correct. But this applies more to social perception than sensation and perception.

13.   c   obj. 14   p. 109
a.   Incorrect. This describes bifocal disparity.

b.   Incorrect. This is retinal size.

*c.   Correct. Since the eyes are a small distance apart, the images on the eyes vary slightly, and the disparity can be used to determine distance and depth.

d.   Incorrect. This is called linear perspective, and it is a monocular cue.

14.   b   obj. 16   pp 114, 115
a.   Incorrect. ESP typically involves message about which only the perceiver is aware.

*b.   Correct. Perceiving messages below the threshold of awareness is called subliminal perception.

c.   Incorrect. Sounds good, but what is it?

d.   Incorrect. Being tiny crystals, otoliths do not process anything.

15.   c   obj. 14   p. 110
a.   Incorrect. The gestalt principle of figure/ground suggests that we see an object in context of its background.

b.   Incorrect. Binocular disparity works on the basis of the slight disparity between the two images of the retinas since they have slightly different points of view.

*c. Correct. Monocular cues, by definition, come from only one eye.
d. Incorrect. Motion parallax arises when distant objects appear to move less than close objects when the observer moves by them.

16. d   obj. 14   p. 108
17. a   obj. 14   p. 109
18. e   obj. 14   p. 109
19. b   obj. 14   p. 110
20. c   obj. 14   p. 110
21. pupil obj. 3   p. 85
22. Accommodation   obj. 3   p. 85
23. fovea obj. 3   p. 86
24. rod   obj. 3   p. 85
25. chemical molecules obj. 9   pp. 98, 99

26. The major points that should be included in your answer:
▪ Discuss the importance of sensory selectivity—of sense organs being sensitive to limited ranges of physical stimuli.
▪ Though we would probably adjust to the differences, additional information might create duplications.
▪ Describe the things we would be able to hear, smell, taste, and feel if our sensory ranges were broader.
▪ Reflect on the possibility that our ability at sensory adaptation might have to increase.

Practise Test 2:
1.   d   obj. 2   p. 81
a. Incorrect. See answer d.
b. Incorrect. See answer d.
c. Incorrect. See answer d.
*d. Correct. Actually, the organ is the nasal epithelium, and the more area it has, the fewer odorant molecules required to detect an odor.

2.   c   obj. 3   p. 86
a. Incorrect. The lens turns the image upside down.
b. Incorrect. The light energy in the image is not redistributed, but it is converted to neural messages.
*c. Correct. This is the role of the retina, and the rods and the cones of the retina initiate the process.
d. Incorrect. The size of the pupil is controlled by the muscles of the iris.

3.   d   obj. 3   p. 86
a. Incorrect. Buds occur on branches of dendrites, axons, and trees, and in the tongue, but they are not the name of visual receptors.
b. Incorrect. Cones are more responsive to bright light.
c. Incorrect. Ossicles are another pronunciation of the word "icicles."
*d. Correct. Rods are capable of detecting small amounts of light.

4.   c   obj. 3   p. 86

a. Incorrect. This is due to the low number of rods in the fovea, our typical focal point in the eye in normal light.
b. Incorrect. This results from the low levels of light making the operation of the cones less effective.
*c. Correct. Sensitivity changes in low levels of illumination, and coming into bright light can be painful.
d. Incorrect. These people have what is known as night blindness due to problems related to the rods or to processing information from the rods.

5.   a   obj. 5   p. 89
*a. Correct. The opponent colour is activated to balance, or adapt to the intensity of the initial colour. When the initial colour is removed, the opponent colour is seen (the afterimage).
b. Incorrect. Trichromatic theory could not account for negative afterimages.
c. Incorrect. There is not a place theory of colour vision, only one for hearing.
d. Incorrect. The receptive-field theory of colour vision is yet to be developed.

6.   a   obj. 6   p. 94
*a. Correct. The bone conducts sound differently from the air, and the only voice we hear through bone is our own, and no one else hears it through your bone.
b. Incorrect. Everyone hears through tympanic vibrations.
c. Incorrect. Bone conduction is the reason we hear our voices differently from how others hear them.
d. Incorrect. But your voice changes too.

7.   d   obj. 9   p. 99
a. Incorrect. Most receptors respond to only one taste.
b. Incorrect. Only four types are known.
c. Incorrect. Taste receptors are only on the tongue.
*d. Correct. The four basic tastes are sweet, sour, bitter, and salty.

8.   b   obj. 12   p. 105
a. Incorrect. Indeed they are similar, but they are not selected from a larger set of dissimilar objects.
*b. Correct. Objects that are close together tend to be grouped together.
c. Incorrect. Closure would lead to filling in the missing p's in the sequence.
d. Incorrect. Constancy refers to the fact that we view P and p as the same object.

9.   b   obj. 12   p. 105
a. Incorrect. Proximity applies to objects that are close to each other.
*b. Correct. Similar objects do tend to be grouped together.
c. Incorrect. Figure/ground refers to the tendency to see objects in contrast to their background.
d. Incorrect. Closure refers to our tendency to fill in missing or hidden parts of an object.

10. b   obj. 13   p. 108
a.   Incorrect. Top-down processing would begin by understanding the sentence and then finding the missing words.
*b. Correct. Bottom-up processing identifies each part and then builds the larger picture.
c.   Incorrect. Selective attention refers to our ability to ignore irrelevant information or sensory inputs and concentrate on a selected set of data.
d.   Incorrect. Constancy refers to a principle of perception that concerns the tendency to view an object as if it is unchanged even when viewed from different points of view.

11. d   obj. 14   p. 108
a.   Incorrect. This refers to the habituation to a sensory stimulus.
b.   Incorrect. In bottom-up processing, each new view would generate a new image and identity.
c.   Incorrect. Subliminal perception may occur at the limits of conscious perception, but it does not influence perceptual constancy.
*d. Correct. When an object is perceived as not changing even though its visual image changes, than perceptual constancy is at work.

12. b   obj. 14   p. 109
a.   Incorrect. The gestalt principle of figure/ground suggests that we see an object in context of its background.
*b. Correct. Binocular disparity works on the basis of the slight disparity between the two images of the retinas since they have slightly different points of view.
c.   Incorrect. Monocular cues, by definition, come from only one eye.
d.   Incorrect. Motion parallax arises when distant objects appear to move less than close objects when the observer moves by them.

13. b   obj. 15   p. 111
a.   Incorrect. Unseen bulges in the middle of the columns make it look more perfectly square and taller.
*b. Correct. Unseen bulges in the middle of the columns make it look more perfectly square and taller
c.   Incorrect. Unseen bulges in the middle of the columns make it look more perfectly square and taller.
d.   Incorrect. Unseen bulges in the middle of the columns make it look more perfectly square and taller.

14. b   obj. 12   p. 104
a.   Incorrect. There is no gestalt principle of "figure/group."
*b. Correct. Closure involves completing an incomplete figure by filling in missing components.
c.   Incorrect. Proximity involves grouping elements that are close together.

d.   Incorrect. This activity involves grouping according to similar features.

15. c   obj. 14   p. 110
16. d   obj. 15   p. 111
17. e   obj. 6   p. 95
18. b   obj. 8   p. 97
19. a   obj. 11   p. 103
20. Gate-control of pain theory   obj. 10   p. 101
21. top-down processing   obj. 13   p. 107
22. Linear   obj. 14   p. 110
23. Psychophysics   obj. 1   p. 81
24. Iris   obj. 3   p. 85

25.
•   The major point is perception of wholes versus perception of parts. Top-down processing and bottom-up processing may also be used to distinguish the two approaches.
•   Phenomena such as perception of objects when parts are hidden from view and the reading of words without having to identify each letter are better explained by the gestalt approach. Identification of unusual objects by identifying and analyzing parts of the object is better accounted for by feature analysis.

Practise Test 3:
1.   b   obj. 1   p. 81
a.   Incorrect. Just noticeable difference is inappropriate here.
*b. Correct. The pinprick is the stimulus and the pain is the sensation.
c.   Incorrect. The pinprick does not represent a difference threshold.
d.   Incorrect. Quite a few pinpricks would be needed to develop a sensory adaptation, especially if the pain is short in duration.

2.   b   obj. 3   p. 86
a.   Incorrect. This is reversed.
*b. Correct. Rods need little light to be activated, cones require much more.
c.   Incorrect. The amount of rhodopsin is the relevant factor in dark adaptation, not the rod and cone differences.
d.   Incorrect. This is the opposite as well.

3.   d   obj. 6   p. 94
b.   Incorrect. See answer d
b.   Incorrect. See answer d
c.   Incorrect. See answer d.
*d. Correct. Sound IS the movement of air molecules.

4.   d   obj. 6   pp. 93, 94
a.   Incorrect. If you could hear your own voice, then you could be hearing through bone conduction, and the

cochlea, basilar membrane, and auditory cortex would be functioning properly.
b.   Incorrect. If you could hear your own voice, then you could be hearing through bone conduction, and the cochlea, basilar membrane, and auditory cortex would be functioning properly.
c.   Incorrect. If you could hear your own voice, then you could be hearing through bone conduction, and the cochlea, basilar membrane, and auditory cortex would be functioning properly.
*d. Correct. Some blockage would have had to occur in the middle ear, because you would be hearing through bone conduction, and the cochlea, basilar membrane, and auditory cortex would be functioning properly.

5. b   obj. 6   pp. 94, 95
a.   Incorrect. Pitch does not depend on how hard the keys are struck on a piano.
*b. Correct. The keys on the left side would have a lower frequency, and thus lower pitch, than the keys on the right side.
c.   Incorrect. The keys on the left side would have a lower frequency, and thus lower pitch, than the keys on the right side.
d.   Incorrect. Pitch is a function of frequency.

6. b   obj. 6   pp. 94, 95
a.   Incorrect. Intensity may affect resonance, but frequency does not relate to loudness.
*b. Correct. The greater the intensity, the louder the sound; and the higher the frequency, the higher the pitch.
c.   Incorrect. These do not have a match at all.
d.   Incorrect. Intensity will affect all the ear, though the external ear will be affected least, yet consonance will be unaffected by frequency.

7. d   obj. 6   pp. 94, 95
a.   Incorrect. However, pitch is how we perceive the differences between different frequencies.
b.   Incorrect. Intensity refers to loudness, or how tall the crests would be.
c.   Incorrect. This is intensity, or how tall the crests would be.
*d. Correct. The count of the number of crests per second is the frequency of the sound.

8. a   obj. 6   p. 93, 94
*a. Correct. Loudness is measured in decibels and frequency is measured in cycles per second.
b.   Incorrect. See answer a.
c.   Incorrect. See answer a.
d.   Incorrect. See answer a.

9. c   obj. 8   p. 97
a.   Incorrect. This symptom is associated with something eaten, not vertigo.
b.   Incorrect. This symptom is more likely to be found in schizophrenia.

*c. Correct. Vertigo is a disorder or disruption of the sense of balance, and it results in motion sickness and dizziness.
d.   Incorrect. This results from too many illegal drugs.

10. a   obj. 12   p. 98
*a. Correct. This principle is central to the gestalt approach
b.   Incorrect. Only in illusions.
c.   Incorrect. This is the principle of proximity.
d.   Incorrect. That is the physical attraction principle.

11. d   obj. 11   pp. 103, 104
a.   Incorrect. The less predominant the ground, the easier it is to alternate figure and ground.
b.   Incorrect. The less predominant the figure, the easier it is to alternate figure and ground.
c.   Incorrect. Often the images are quite different, causing a dramatic effect.
*d. Correct. If they can alternate, then the reversibility is possible.

12. d   obj. 12   p.104
a.   Incorrect. There is no gestalt principle of "figure/group."
b.   Incorrect. Closure involves completing an incomplete figure by filling in missing components.
c.   Incorrect. Proximity involves grouping elements that are close together.
*d. Correct. This activity involves grouping according to similar features.

13. a   obj. 13   p. 107
*a. Correct. In top-down processing, incomplete information is completed by drawing upon context and memory.
b.   Incorrect. Bottom-up processing would require all the parts of the image.
c.   Incorrect. While selective attention may be involved (the car may have actually been a snowmobile), this example does not illustrate selective attention.
d.   Incorrect. Feature analysis helped you detect the word "mobile," but it was not used in completing the word.

14. a   obj. 14   p. 109
*a. Correct. There are many monocular, or single eye, cues for depth.
b.   Incorrect. They appear smaller because of the physics involved.
c.   Incorrect. Actually, the greater discrepancy makes the depth determination easier.
d.   Incorrect. This is backward.

15. b   obj. 14   p. 108
a.   Incorrect. Right, and it's about to explode.
*b. Correct. Right, so you better take cover—the image is getting larger on your retina.
c.   Incorrect. No, it would have to be moving toward you.
d.   Incorrect. It could have started out sideways, if it is then turning sideways, it would be getting smaller.

16. c   obj. 14   p. 110
a.   Incorrect. The ball moves to quickly for the player to track the ball all the way to the plate.
b.   Incorrect. Focusing is less of a problem than tracking, and if the player cannot track the ball, he certainly cannot focus on it.
*c. Correct. The player must anticipate the location of the ball when it reaches the plate, because it approaches too quickly to be tracked all the way, and he must begin his swing before the ball reaches the plate.
d.   Incorrect. Eye coordination is critical, but he would not be a major league player if he did not already have good coordination.

17. d   obj. 16   p. 114
a.   Incorrect. Try subliminal perception and no it probably will not work.
b.   Incorrect. Try subliminal perception and no it probably will not work.
c.   Incorrect. It is called subliminal perception, but it probably will not work.

*d. Correct. However, there is little evidence supporting the use of subliminal tapes for complex learning.

18. a   obj. 16   p. 114
*a. Correct. Educational level has no impact on the perception of illusions.
b.   Incorrect. Culture does appear to influence the perception of illusions, especially illusions involving objects or situations unfamiliar to members of the culture.
c.   Incorrect. The structure of the eye is one of the factors influencing how illusions work.
d.   Incorrect. Some illusions arise from incorrect interpretations at the level of the brain.

19. rods obj. 3   p. 85
20. Optic nerve   obj. 4   p. 86
21. gestalts   obj. 12   p. 104
22. closure   obj. 12   p. 104
23. Pheromones   obj. 9   p. 99
24. Sensation obj. 1   p. 80
25. Perception   obj. 1   p. 80

States of Consciousness

4

Chapter Overview

Chapter 4 focuses on the states of consciousness. While some psychologists prefer to exclude studying the topic because of its reliance on "unscientific" introspections of experimental participants, contemporary psychologists support the view that several approaches permit the scientific study of consciousness. We can study brain wave patterns under conditions of consciousness ranging from sleep to waking to hypnotic trances. Also, understanding the chemistry of drugs such as marijuana and alcohol has provided insights into the way they provide pleasurable—as well as adverse—effects.

Another reason for the study of consciousness is the realization that people in many different cultures routinely seek ways to alter their states of consciousness.

Consciousness may alter thinking. It may alter people's sense of time and perceptions about oneself or the world.

This chapter considers several states of consciousness, such as sleeping and dreaming, the states of hypnosis and meditation and finally drug-induced states of consciousness.

To further investigate the topics covered in this chapter, you can access the related websites by visiting the following link: http://www.mcgrawhill.ca/college/feldman.

Prologue: The Last Summer Party
Looking Ahead
Sleep and Dreams
The Stages of Sleep
REM Sleep: The Paradox of Sleep
Why Do We Sleep, and How Much Sleep Is Necessary?
The Function and Meaning of Dreaming
Sleep Disturbances: Slumbering Problems
Circadian Rhythms: Life Cycles
Daydreams: Dreams Without Sleep

Becoming an Informed Consumer of Psychology:
Sleeping Better

Hypnosis and Meditation

Hypnosis: A Trance-Forming Experience?
Meditation: Regulating Our Own State of Consciousness

Exploring Diversity: Cross-Cultural Routes to Altered States of Consciousness

Drug Use: The Highs and Lows of Consciousness

Stimulants: Drug Highs

Applying Psychology in the 21st Century: Just Say No—to DARE? Finding Antidrug Programs That Work

Depressants: Drug Lows
Narcotics: Relieving Pain and Anxiety
Hallucinogens: Psychedelic Drugs

Becoming an Informed Consumer of Psychology: Identifying Drug and Alcohol Problems

Learning Objectives

These are the concepts and the learning objectives for Chapter 4. Read them carefully as part of your preliminary survey of the chapter.

Sleep and Dreams

1. Discuss what is meant by consciousness and altered states of consciousness. (p. 122)

2. Explain the cycles of sleep, including REM sleep. (pp. 123–127)

3. Identify the various theories of dreaming and daydreaming, and differentiate among them concerning the functions and meanings of dreams. (pp. 128–131)

4. Describe the sleep disturbances of insomnia, sleep apnea, and narcolepsy. (pp. 131–132)

5. Discuss the roles of circadian rhythms and daydreams in our lives and discuss ways of improving sleep. (pp. 132–134).

Hypnosis and Meditation

6. Discuss hypnosis, including its definition, therapeutic value, and the ongoing controversy regarding whether it represents an altered state of consciousness. (pp. 135–136)

7. Describe how meditation works and the changes that occur during meditation. (p. 137)

Drug Use: The Highs and Lows of Consciousness

8. Describe the characteristics, addictive properties, and psychological reactions to stimulants and depressants, as well as representative drugs from each category. (pp. 139–147)

9. Describe the characteristics, addictive properties, and psychological reactions to narcotics and hallucinogens, as well as representative drugs from each category. (pp. 147–149)

10. Identify the symptoms of drug abuse, and discuss current approaches to drug prevention. (p. 149–150)

SECTION 1: Sleep and Dreams

Prepare

- *What are the different states of consciousness?*
- *What happens when we sleep, and what are the meaning and function of dreams?*
- *What are the major sleep disorders and how can they be treated?*
- *How much do we daydream?*

Organize

- *The Stages of Sleep*
- *REM Sleep*
- *Why Do We Sleep, and how Much Sleep Is Necessary?*
- *The Function and Meaning of Dreaming*
- *Sleep Disturbances*
- *Circadian Rhythms*
- *Daydreams*

Work

[a] _____ is defined as our awareness of the sensations, thoughts, and feelings being experienced at any given moment. Consciousness can range from the perceptions during wakefulness to dreams. The variation in how we experience stimuli can be wide as well, and consciousness varies from active to passive states.

Much of our knowledge of sleep itself comes from the use of the **[b]** _____ to record brain activity throughout the cycles of sleep. The amplitude and frequency of the wavelike patterns formed by the EEG during sleep show regular and systematic patterns of sleep.

These patterns identify four stages of sleep. The first stage, called **[c]** _____, is the stage of transition to sleep, and the brain waves are rapid, low-voltage waves.

[d] _____ is characterized by slower, more regular waves and by occasional sharply pointed waves called spindles. In **[e]** _____ brain waves become even slower with higher peaks and lower valleys. **[f]** _____ has even slower wave patterns. Stage 4 is experienced soon after falling to sleep, and through the night sleep becomes lighter and is characterized by more dreams.

The period of sleep associated with most of our dreaming is identified by the rapid back and forth movement of the eyes called **[g]** _____. REM sleep, which occupies about 20 percent of the total sleep time, is paradoxical because the body is in a state of paralysis even as the eyes are moving about rapidly.

People deprived of sleep over long periods of time, up to 200 hours in some experiments, do not experience any long-term effects.

[h] _____ are the daily rhythms of the body, including the sleep and waking cycle, as well as the cycles of sleepiness throughout the day. Other functions, like body temperature, also follow circadian rhythms. *Seasonal affective disorder* and premenstrual syndrome (PMS) are two examples of rhythmic changes that have cycles longer than twenty-four hours.

[i] _____ are unusually frightening dreams. They appear to occur frequently, perhaps about twenty-four times a year on average. Most dreams, however, involve daily, mundane events. According to Freud's **[j]** _____, dreams are guides into the unconscious. The true meaning of these wishes was disguised, and Freud used the label of **[k]** _____ because the meanings were too threatening. Freud called the story line of the dream the **[l]** _____. Freud sought to uncover the latent content by interpreting the symbols of the dream. Many psychologists reject this theory of dreams, instead preferring to interpret the content in terms of its more obvious references to everyday concerns. Another theory of dreams is called the **[m]** _____. This theory suggests that dreams flush away unnecessary information accumulated through the day. Dreams then have little meaning. Another theory is the **[n]** _____, which suggests that dreams involve a reconsideration and reprocessing of critical information from the day. Dreams in this theory have meaning as they represent important concerns drawn from daily experiences. Currently, the most influential theory is the **[o]** _____, which claims that dreams are by-products of biological processes. These processes are random firings related to changes in neurotransmitter production. Because these activities revive important memories, what begins randomly becomes meaningful.

Evaluate

Test A

_____ 1. stage 1 sleep

_____ 2. stage 2 sleep

_____ 3. stage 3 sleep

_____ 4. stage 4 sleep

_____ 5. rapid eye movement (REM) sleep

a. The deepest stage of sleep, during which we are least responsive to outside stimulation.

b. Sleep characterized by increased heart rate, blood pressure, and breathing rate, erections; and the experience of dreaming.

c. Characterized by sleep spindles.

d. The state of transition between wakefulness and sleep, characterized by relatively rapid, low-voltage brain waves.

e. A sleep characterized by slow brain waves, with greater peaks and valleys in the wave pattern.

Test B

_____ 1. latent content of dreams

_____ 2. manifest content of dreams

_____ 3. reverse learning theory

_____ 4. dreams-for-survival theory

_____ 5. activation-synthesis theory

a. According to Freud, the "disguised" meaning of dreams, concealed by more mundane, everyday material.

b. Hobson's view that dreams are a result of random electrical energy stimulating memories lodged in various parts of the brain. The brain then weaves these memories into a logical story line.

c. The view that dreams have no meaning in themselves, but instead function to rid us of unnecessary information that we have accumulated during the day.

d. The proposal that dreams permit information critical for our daily survival to be reconsidered and reprocessed during sleep.

e. According to Freud, the overt story line of dreams.

Rethink

1. How would studying the sleep patterns of nonhuman species potentially help us figure out

which of the theories of dreaming provides the best account of the functions of dreaming?

2. Suppose that a new "miracle pill" is developed that will allow a person to function with only one hour of sleep per night. However, because a night's sleep is so short, a person who takes the pill will never dream again. Knowing what you do about the functions of sleep and dreaming, what would be some advantages and drawbacks of such a pill from a personal standpoint? Would you take such a pill?

SECTION 2:   Hypnosis and Meditation

Prepare

- *Are hypnotized people in a different state of consciousness?*
- *What are the effects of meditation?*

Organize

- *Hypnosis*
- *Meditation*

Work

[a] _____ is a state of heightened susceptibility to the suggestions of others. When people are hypnotized, they will not perform antisocial behaviours, they will not carry out self-destructive acts, they will not reveal hidden truths about themselves, yet they are capable of lying. Between 5 and 20 percent of the population cannot be hypnotized at all, and about 15 percent are highly susceptible. Ernest Hilgard has argued that hypnosis does represent a state of consciousness that is significantly different from other states. The increased suggestibility, greater ability to recall and construct images, increased memories from childhood, lack of initiative, and ability to accept suggestions that contradict reality suggest that hypnotic states are different from other states. Some researchers have established that some people do pretend to be hypnotized. Moreover, adults do not have special ability to recall childhood events while hypnotized. Hypnotism has been used successfully for the following: 1) controlling pain; 2) ending tobacco addiction; 3) treating psychological disorders; 4) assisting in law enforcement; and 5) improving athletic performance.

[b] _____ is a learned technique for refocusing attention that brings about the altered state. Transcendental meditation (TM), brought to the United States by the Maharishi Mahesh Yogi, is perhaps the best-known form of meditation. TM uses a *mantra*, a sound, word, or syllable, that is said over and over. In other forms, the meditator focuses on a picture, flame, or body part. In all forms the key is to concentrate intensely. Following meditation, people are relaxed, they may have new insights, and in the long term, they may have improved health. The physiological changes that accompany meditation are similar to relaxation: heart rate declines, oxygen intake declines, and brain-wave patterns change. The simple procedures of sitting in a quiet room, breathing deeply and rhythmically, and repeating a word will achieve the same effects as trained meditation techniques.

The cross-cultural aspects of altered states of consciousness are examined in the Exploring Diversity section. The search for experiences beyond normal consciousness is found in many cultures, and it may reflect a universal need to alter moods and consciousness.

Evaluate

_____1. hypnosis

_____2. meditation

_____3. Mesmer

_____4. hypnotic state

_____5. mantra

a. May be a continuum that is neither a totally different state of consciousness nor totally similar to total waking consciousness.

b. A sound, word, or syllable repeated over and over.

c. Argued that a form of "animal magnetism" could influence people and cure illness.

d. Altered state of consciousness brought about by refocusing attention.

e. A trance-like state of heightened susceptibility to suggestions of others.

Rethink

3. What sorts of mental functioning does hypnosis appear to affect most strongly? Do you think it might have more effect on the left or right hemisphere of the brain, or would it affect both equally? Why?

4. Meditation produces several physical and psychological benefits. Does this suggest that we are physically and mentally burdened in our normal state of waking consciousness? Why?

SECTION 3: Drug Use: The Highs and Lows of Consciousness

Prepare

- **What are the major classifications of drugs, and what are their effects?**

Organize

- **Stimulants**
- **Depressants**
- **Narcotics**
- **Hallucinogens**

Work

[a] _____ affect consciousness by influencing a person's emotions, perceptions, and behaviour. Drug use among high school students has declined, as today about

half of the seniors have used an illegal drug in their lives. The most dangerous drugs are those that are addictive. **[b]** _____ produce psychological or biological dependence in the user, and the withdrawal of the drug leads to cravings for it.

Any drug that affects the central nervous system by increasing its activity and by increasing heart rate, blood pressure, and muscle tension is called a **[c]** _____. An example of this kind of drug is *caffeine*, which is found in coffee, soft drinks, and chocolate. Caffeine increases attentiveness and decreases reaction time. Too much caffeine leads to nervousness and insomnia. *Nicotine* is the stimulant found in tobacco products.

[d] _____ and its derivative crack are illegal stimulants. This drug produces feelings of well-being, confidence, and alertness when taken in small quantities. Cocaine blocks the reuptake of excess dopamine, which in turn produces pleasurable sensations. Cocaine abuse makes the abusers crave the drug and go on binges of use.

[e] _____ are a group of very strong stimulants that bring about a sense of energy and alertness, talkativeness, confidence, and a mood "high." The amphetamines, Dexedrine and Benzedrine are commonly known as speed, and excessive amounts of the drugs can lead to overstimulation of the central nervous system, convulsions, and death.

Drugs that slow the central nervous system are called **[f]** _____.

Feelings of *intoxication* come from taking small doses. **[g]** _____ is the most common depressant.

[h] _____ are a form of depressant drug used to induce sleep and reduce stress. They are addictive and can be deadly when combined with alcohol. Quaalude is an illegal drug similar to barbiturates.

[i] _____ increase relaxation and relieve pain and anxiety. *Morphine* and *heroin* are two powerful narcotics. Morphine is used to reduce pain, but heroin is illegal. Heroin effects include an initial rush followed by a sense of well-being. When the sense of well-being ends, the heroin user feels anxiety and the desire to use the drug again. With each use, more heroin is needed to have any effect. A successful treatment for heroin addiction is the use of *methadone*, a drug that satisfies the cravings but does not produce the high. Methadone is biologically addicting.

Evaluate

_____ 1. caffeine

_____ 2. nicotine

_____ 3. cocaine

_____ 4. amphetamines

_____ 5. alcohol

a. An addictive stimulant present in cigarettes.

b. Strong stimulants that cause a temporary felling of confidence and alertness but may increase anxiety and appetite loss and, taken over a period of time, suspiciousness and feeling of persecution.

c. An addictive stimulant that, when taken in small doses, initially creates feelings of

_____ 6. intoxication

confidence, alertness, and well-being, but eventually causes mental and physical deterioration.

d. The most common depressant, which in small doses causes release of tension and feelings of happiness, but in larger amounts can cause emotional and physical instability, memory impairment, and stupor.

e. An addictive stimulant found most abundantly in coffee, tea, soft drinks, and chocolate.

f. A state of drunkenness.

Rethink

5. Why do you think people in almost every culture use psychoactive drugs and search for altered states of consciousness?

6. People often use the word *addiction* loosely, speaking of an addiction to candy or a television show. Can you explain the difference between this type of "addiction" and a true physiological addiction? Is there a difference between this type of "addiction" and a psychological addiction?

Practise Questions

Test your knowledge of the chapter material by answering these questions. These questions have been placed in three Practise Tests. The first two tests are composed of questions that will test your recall of factual knowledge. The third test contains questions that are challenging and primarily test for conceptual knowledge and your ability to apply that knowledge. Check your answers and review the feedback using the Answer Key on the following pages of the *Study Guide*.

PRACTISE TEST 1:

1.   Our experience of consciousness is mainly:
     a.   our awareness of nervous system activity.
     b.   actions observable by others.
     c.   the deeply hidden motives and urges that influence our behaviour in subtle ways but of which, for the most part, we are unaware.
     d.   our own subjective mental activity of which we are aware.

2. Which stage represents the transition from wakefulness to sleep?
   a. stage 1
   b. stage 2
   c. stage 3
   d. rapid eye movement (REM)

3. Which sleep stage is characterized by electrical signals with the slowest frequency, by waveforms that are very regular, and by a sleeper who is very unresponsive to external stimuli?
   a. rapid eye movement (REM)
   b. stage 2
   c. stage 3
   d. stage 4

4. Sleep is considered to be as essential as:
   a. rest and relaxation.
   b. meditation.
   c. food and water.
   d. a drug to which a person has become addicted.

5. The increase in REM sleep during periods after a person has been deprived of it is called:
   a. paradoxical sleep.
   b. the rebound effect.
   c. latent dreaming.
   d. somnambulism.

6. According to Freud, dreams:
   a. are reflections of day-to-day activities.
   b. are reflections of conscious activity.
   c. are reflections of unconscious wish fulfilment.
   d. are remnants of our evolutionary heritage.

7. According to studies, the average person daydreams about:
   a. 10 percent of the time.
   b. 20 percent of the time.
   c. 30 percent of the time.
   d. 40 percent of the time.

8. Insomnia is a condition in which a person:
   a. uncontrollably falls asleep.
   b. sleeps more than twelve hours per night on a routine basis.
   c. has difficulty sleeping.
   d. exhibits abnormal brain wave patterns during rapid eye movement (REM) sleep.

9. Maria is having difficulty sleeping and breathing simultaneously. Her problem is called:
   a. narcolepsy.
   b. sleep apnea.
   c. hypersomnia.
   d. insomnia.

10. Which of the following may account for sudden infant death syndrome according to research discussed in the text?
    a. narcolepsy
    b. sleep apnea
    c. somnambulism
    d. insomnia

11. People who are easily hypnotized tend to:
    a. enroll in general psychology.
    b. be very aware of the outdoors.
    c. spend a lot of time daydreaming.
    d. be very good at biofeedback.

12. A person repeats _____ over and over again during transcendental meditation.
    a. a mantra
    c. a banta

    b.   an allegory   d.   an analogy

13.   A psychoactive drug:
    a.   affects a person's behaviour only if he or she is receptive to "mind expanding" experiences.
    b.   influences thoughts and perceptions and is usually physically addictive.
    c.   affects a person's emotions, perceptions, and behaviour.
    d.   acts primarily on biological functions such as heart rate and intestinal mobility.

14.   The most common central nervous system depressant is:
    a.   phenobarbital.   c.   Valium.
    b.   alcohol.   d.   Quaalude.

_____ 15. rebound effect   a.   An inability to get to sleep or stay asleep.

_____ 16. nightmares   b.   Fantasies people construct while awake.

                                           c.   Unusually frightening dreams.
_____ 17. daydreams

                                           d.   A sleep disorder characterized by difficulty in
_____ 18. insomnia   breathing and sleeping simultaneously.

                                         e.   An increase in REM sleep after one has been
_____ 19. sleep apnea   deprived of it.

20.   People deprived of REM sleep experience a _____ , spending more time in the REM stage when allowed to rest undisturbed.

21.   There is wide _____ in the amount of sleep people need; some needing seven or eight hours and others needing only three hours per night.

22.   As far as we know most people suffer no permanent consequences from temporary

        _____.

23.   A biological rhythm with a period (from peak to peak) of about 24 hours is called

        _____.

24.   Sleep periods characterized by eye movement, loss of muscle tone, and dreaming are called

        _____.

25.   Discuss the competing theories of dreams. Are the theories actually incompatible? Which appears most convincing? Defend your answer.

Practise Test 2:

1.   The deepest stages of sleep are generally experienced:
    a.   during the first half of the sleep interval.
    b.   during the second half of the sleep interval.
    c.   during continuous periods averaging two hours each.
    d.   while the sleeper dreams.

2. As we progress through the stages of sleep toward deepest sleep, within a single sleep cycle the EEG pattern gets:
   a. faster and more regular.
   b. faster and more irregular.
   c. slower and lower in amplitude.
   d. slower and more regular.

3. Which of the following stages of sleep is characterized by irregular breathing, increased blood pressure, and increased respiration?
   a. stage 1
   b. stage 2
   c. rapid eye movement (REM)
   d. non-rapid eye movement (NREM)

4. The major muscles of the body act as if they are paralyzed during:
   a. stage 1 sleep.
   b. stage 3 sleep.
   c. stage 4 sleep.
   d. rapid eye movement (REM).

5. The viewpoint that dreams are the outcome of the random exercising of neural circuits in the brain is called the:
   a. unconscious wish fulfilment theory.
   b. dreams-for-survival theory.
   c. activation-synthesis theory.
   d. reverse learning theory.

6. Freud referred to the story line of a dream as its:
   a. libidinal content.
   b. unconscious content.
   c. manifest content.
   d. latent content.

7. Which of the following does **not** describe a common characteristic of daydreams?
   a. fantastic and creative
   b. mundane, ordinary topics
   c. a part of normal consciousness
   d. a predomination of sexual imagery

8. People pass directly from a conscious, wakeful state to REM sleep if they suffer from:
   a. narcolepsy.
   b. insomnia.
   c. somnambulism.
   d. rapid eye movement (REM) showers.

9. The uncontrollable need to sleep for short periods that can happen at any time during the day is called:
   a. narcolepsy.
   b. sleep apnea.
   c. hypersomnia.
   d. insomnia.

10. The most common hallucinogen in use in the United States is:
    a. PCP
    b. LSD
    c. cocaine
    d. marijuana

11. Generalizing from the text, all of the following are typical suggestions for overcoming insomnia **except**:
    a. choose regular bedtimes.
    b. don't try to go to sleep.
    c. avoid drinks with caffeine.
    d. watch TV in bed.

12. _____ is the procedure, introduced in the United States by Maharishi Mahesh Yogi, in which a person focuses on a mantra to reach a different state of consciousness.
    a. Transactional analysis
    b. Zen Buddhism
    c. Exorcism
    d. Transcendental meditation

13. The problem doctors face with using methadone in drug therapy is that:
    a. the patient is likely to become addicted to methadone.
    b. methadone eventually causes mental retardation in the patient.
    c. methadone patients are at risk of becoming alcoholics.
    d. methadone users find the marijuana high to be very appealing.

14. Caffeine, nicotine, cocaine, and amphetamines are considered:
    a. anesthetic agents.   c. anti-anxiety drugs.
    b. central nervous system stimulants.   d. hallucinogens.

15. Nembutal, Seconal, and Phenobarbital are all depressants and forms of:
    a. opiates.   c. hallucinogens.
    b. barbiturates.   d. hypnotics.

_____ 16. sudden infant death syndrome

_____ 17. narcolepsy

_____ 18. marijuana

_____ 19. lysergic acid diethylamide (LSD)

a. An uncontrollable need to sleep for short periods during the day.

b. A disorder in which seemingly healthy infants die in their sleep.

c. A common hallucinogen, usually smoked.

d. One of the most powerful hallucinogens, affecting the operation of neurotransmitters in the brain and causing brain cell activity to be altered.

20. Despite compliance when hypnotized, people will not perform anti-social behaviours or
    _____.

21. People _____ be hypnotized against their will.

22. People who are readily hypnotized often spend an unusual amount of time _____.

23. Doctors working with seriously ill patients may use hypnosis to control _____.

24. Because hypnotic recollections are sometimes inaccurate, the legal status of information gathered from a person in a hypnotic state is _____.

25. Debates regarding the legalization of drugs, especially marijuana, seem to come and go. If that debate were to arise today, what should psychology contribute? What are your feelings? Should some drugs be legalized or given through prescription? Defend your answer.

Practise Test 3: Conceptual, Applied, and Challenging Questions

1. Sleep involves four different stages. What is the basis for differentiating these stages of sleep?
    a. They are defined according to the electrical properties recorded by an electroencephalogram (EEG) attached to the sleeper.
    b. They are defined by the amount of time elapsed from the onset of sleep.

c. They are based on the mental experiences described when sleepers are awakened and asked what they are thinking.

d. They are characterized by patterns of overt body movements recorded with a video camera that is positioned over the sleeper.

2. Your friend Sandro comes to you concerned about his health after having stayed up for thirty-six hours straight studying. The most valid thing you could tell him is that:
   a. if he is going to stay up for so long, he should see a doctor regularly.
   b. if he continues to stay up for so long, he will probably get sick.
   c. there will probably be severe long-term consequences for not sleeping for that amount of time.
   d. research has demonstrated that lack of sleep will affect his ability to study.

3. Sharon dreams that Drew climbs a stairway and meets her at the top. According to Freudian dream symbols described in the text, this would probably suggest:
   a. that Sharon would like to start a friendship with Drew.
   b. that Sharon is really afraid to talk to Drew, though she would like to start a friendship.
   c. that Drew and Sharon probably work together in a building where there are stairs.
   d. that Sharon is dreaming of sexual intercourse with Drew.

4. If you had a dream about carrying grapefruits down a long tunnel, Freud would interpret the grapefruit as a dream symbol suggesting a wish to:
   a. take a trip to the tropics.
   b. caress a woman's body.
   c. caress a man's genitals.
   d. return to the womb.

5. Suppose that a study were done to show that people who are in new surroundings and involved in major unfamiliar activities have more dreams per night than others whose lives have been stable through the same intervals of the study. This study aims to test:
   a. the unconscious wish fulfilment dream theory.
   b. the dreams-for-survival dream theory.
   c. the activation-synthesis dream theory.
   d. the reverse learning dream theory.

6. During the movie Patty fantasized about making love to Harrison Ford, She was experiencing a:
   a. nervous breakdown.
   b. daydream.
   c. diurnal emission.
   d. mantra.

7. Which of the following statements about sleepwalking is **not** true?
   a. Sleepwalkers should not be awakened.
   b. Sleepwalking occurs in stage 4 sleep.
   c. Sleepwalkers are somewhat aware of their surroundings.
   d. Sleepwalking occurs most frequently in children.

8. In what way is meditation and hypnosis similar?
   a. They are both accompanied by changes in brain activity.
   b. They both result in a decrease in blood pressure.
   c. They are both based on Eastern religious practices.
   d. They both result in total relaxation.

9. Which of the following statements about addiction to drugs is **not** true?
   a. Addiction may be biologically based.

    b.   Addictions are primarily caused by an inherited biological liability.

    c.   All people, with few exceptions, have used one or more "addictive" drugs in their lifetime.

    d.   Addictions may be psychological.

10. You have just taken a tablet someone gave you. You feel a rise in heart rate, a tremor in the hands, and a loss of appetite. You have taken:

    a.   a megavitamin.   c.   a depressant.

    b.   a stimulant.   d.   a hallucinogen.

11. Which of the following is a hallucinogen?

    a.   heroin   c.   marijuana

    b.   cocaine   d.   morphine

12. Meghan dreams about wearing a man's leather jacket and parading around town. In Freud's view, the leather jacket and showing off are:

    a.   latent content.   c.   irrelevant to the meaning.

    b.   manifest content.   d.   day residues.

13. Meghan dreams about wearing a man's leather jacket and parading around town. If the leather jacket is seen as a sexual encounter and the parade as a form of exhibitionism, then in Freud's view, they would have provided insight into:

    a.   latent content.   c.   activation processes.

    b.   manifest content.   d.   day residues.

14. Betsy has just been hypnotized. Which of the following acts is she **least** likely to commit?

    a.   Completely undress.   c.   Recall a past life.

    b.   Flirt with her escort.   d.   Stand on a chair and crow like a rooster.

15. Which of the following are narcotic drugs?

    a.   LSD and marijuana   c.   barbiturates and alcohol

    b.   morphine and heroin   d.   amphetamines and cocaine

_____ 16. barbiturates

_____ 17. morphine

_____ 18. heroin

_____ 19. methadone

_____ 20. hallucinogen

    a.   A powerful narcotic, usually injected, that gives an initial rush of good feeling but leads eventually to anxiety and depression; extremely addictive.

    b.   Addictive depressants used to induce sleep and reduce stress, the abuse of which, especially when combined with alcohol, can be deadly.

    c.   A drug that is capable of producing changes in the perceptual process, or hallucinations.

    d.   A chemical used to detoxify heroin addicts.

    e.   Derived from the poppy flower, a powerful narcotic that reduces pain and induces sleep.

21.   Psychoactive drugs work primarily by affecting _____.

22. After six months of using drugs, Matt developed a _____ and needed more and more to achieve the same effect.

23. Amphetamines, cocaine, caffeine, and nicotine are all examples of _____.

24. The effects of drugs are often the result of their influence on the brain's _____ levels.

25. Physical factors and _____ factors influence the way a particular individual react to the use of a drug.

26. While some consider hypnosis a result of dissociative processes, others believe it is a function of normal sociocognitive processes. Describe the nature of hypnosis and then explain each theory.

Spotlight on Terminology and Language— Cultural Idioms

Page 122 "They argued that because consciousness could be understood only by relying on the 'unscientific' **introspections** of experimental participants about what they were experiencing at a given moment, its study was best left to disciplines such as philosophy."

Introspection is a reflective looking inward. The experimental participants were examining their own thoughts and feelings.

Sleep and Dreams

Page 123 "People with the **malady** have been known to hit others, smash windows, punch holes—in walls—all while fast asleep."

A **malady** is a disease or disorder.

Page 124 "Much of our knowledge of what happens during sleep comes from the **electroencephalogram**, or EEG, a measurement of electrical activity within the brain."

An EEG (**electroencephalogram**) is a recording of brain waves produced by an **electroencephalograph** machine.

Page 124 "People progress through four distinct stages of sleep during a night's rest, moving

through the stages in **cycles** lasting about 90 minutes."

A **cycle** is an interval of time during which a sequence or a recurring chain of events or phenomena is completed.

Page 129 "Because these wishes are threatening to the dreamer's conscious awareness, the actual wishes—called the **latent** content of dreams—are disguised.

The true subject and meaning of a dream, then, may have little to do with its **overt** story line, which Freud called the **manifest** content of dreams."

Latent content is something that is hidden, but is present and capable of becoming visible and obvious. A **latent** fingerprint at the scene of a crime would be one that is scarcely visible but could be developed for study. **Overt** means open to view or **manifest**. The **manifest** story line of dreams is obvious, and easily understood by the mind.

Hypnosis and Meditation

Page 135 "People under hypnosis are in a **trancelike** state of heightened susceptibility to the suggestions of others."

A **trance** is a state of profound absorption, different than both sleeping states and waking states.

Page 135 "Despite their **compliance** when hypnotized, people do not lose all will of their own."

Compliance involves conforming to the statements of the hypnosis operator; it is a disposition to follow suggestions.

Page 136 "The question of whether hypnosis is a state of consciousness that is **qualitatively** different from normal waking consciousness is controversial."

When something is **qualitatively** different, it means it is different in its essential character. This is not to be confused with quantitative, which involves measurements of quantity or amount.

Page 136 "Hypnosis may be employed to heighten relaxation, reduce anxiety, increase expectations of success, or modify **self-defeating** thoughts."

Self-defeating thoughts are negative suggestions you give to yourself.

Page 137 "The **fundamentals** include sitting in a quiet room with eyes closed, breathing deeply and rhythmically, and repeating a word or sound—such as the word *one*—over and over."

The **fundamentals** are the essential and basic steps for experiencing a meditative state.

Drug Use: The Highs and Lows of Consciousness

Page 140 "**Addictive** drugs produce a biological or psychological dependence in the user, and withdrawal from them leads to a **craving** for the drug that, in some cases, can be nearly irresistible."

An **addiction** is a compulsive need for and use of a habit-forming substance, such as caffeine, nicotine, and alcohol. A **craving** is an intense, and sometimes urgent or abnormal desire or longing.

Page 141 "Caffeine can also bring about an improvement in mood, most likely by **mimicking** the effects of a natural brain chemical, adenosine."

To **mimic** is to simulate and produce the same feelings.

Page 141 "Smokers develop a **dependence** on nicotine, and those who suddenly stop smoking develop strong cravings for the drug."

When you develop a **dependence** you develop a reliance on something. When this **dependence** is on drugs or caffeine, this may now constitute an addiction.

Page 142 "Cocaine is inhaled or '**snorted**' through the nose, smoked, or injected directly into the bloodstream."

Snorting is when you are forcing the drug into your system by inhalation.

Page 144 "If taken in too large a quantity, amphetamines overstimulate the central nervous system to such an extent that **convulsions** and death can occur."
Convulsions are abnormally violent and involuntary contractions of the muscles.

Page 146 "The **discrepancy** between the actual and perceived effects of alcohol lies in the initial effects it produces in the majority of individuals who use it."
When two facts, figures or claims are expected to agree, but instead are in disagreement, they are said to be discrepant. The actual effect of alcohol is as a depressant. Yet, often people drink it to become lively, happy, and sociable. Explanation: in low doses alcohol suppresses inhibitions or shyness, and enables drinkers to become more

sociable and outgoing than they would be normally.

Page 147 "Moreover their memories are impaired, brain processing of spatial information is diminished, and speech becomes **slurred** and **incoherent**".
Slurred speech means ones words are unclear or pronounced indistinctly.
Incoherent speech means that ones words lack organization or clarity.
Page 149 "In addition, marijuana smoked during pregnancy has lasting effects on children who are exposed **prenatally**."

When children are exposed to drugs **prenatally,** they are exposed before their birth. **Pre** is a prefix that means before, or earlier than.

Page 149 "Perceptions of colours, sounds, and shapes are altered so much that even the most **mundane** experience—such as looking at the knots in a wooden table—can seem moving and exciting."

Mundane is commonplace, like the **mundane** concerns of day-to-day life. What are some of the mundane activities of your daily existence?

Page 149 "People can experience **flashbacks**— hallucinations that start suddenly, long after they stopped using the drug."

Flashbacks are when past incidents recur vividly in the mind.

■ CHAPTER 4: ANSWER KEY

GUIDED REVIEW			
Section 1: [a] Consciousness [b] electroencephalogram (EEG) [c] stage 1 sleep [d] Stage 2 sleep [e] Stage 3 sleep [f] Stage 4 sleep [g] rapid eye movement (REM) sleep [h] Circadian rhythms [i] Nightmares [j] unconscious wish fulfilment theory [k] latent content of dreams [l] manifest content of dreams [m] reverse learning theory [n] dreams-for-survival theory [o] activation-synthesis theory	Evaluate Test A 1. d 2. c 3. e 4. a 5. b Test B 1. a 2. e 3. c 4. d 5. b	Section 2: [a] Hypnosis [b] Meditation Evaluate 1. a 2. d 3. c 4. e 5. b	Section 3: [a] Psychoactive drugs [b] Addictive drugs [c] stimulant [d] Cocaine [e] Amphetamines [f] depressants [g] Alcohol [h] Barbiturates [i] Narcotics Evaluate 1. e 2. a 3. c 4. b 5. d 6. f

Selected Rethink Answers
2.   List: (1) Wish Fulfilment Theory (Freud) states that our dreams are one way our unconscious gets messages to us that our conscious state can't realize.
         (2) Reverse Learning Theory—dreams flush out unnecessary information.
         (3) Dreams for Survival Theory—permit information needed for survival to be reconsidered and reprocessed; may help us to remember.
         (4) Activation-Synthesis Theory—(Hobson) brain makes sense of chaotic memories, could also be reflection of unconscious wishes.
      Since all theories suggest purposes that help organize information and help us reflect on information, it might be dangerous to eliminate dreaming altogether. For society, if many people made the choice and took the pill and theories held true about

dreams providing time for the organization of information and dreams being an avenue to our unconscious, not dreaming could cause a real deficit in the way we function as a society.

4. Physical and Psychological Effects of Meditation
    Studies show long-term meditation may improve health and longevity.
    Oxygen use decreases, heart and blood pressure decline.
Psychological Effects—although we feel relaxed when we meditate it does not suggest we are overburdened physically or psychologically but it may suggest that there is a stronger mind-body connection than we previously realized.
Meditation may allow us greater opportunities to relax and take time out from our day.

Practise Test 1:

1. d   obj. 1   p. 122
a. Incorrect. We are not aware of the functioning of our nervous system.
b. Incorrect. Our individual consciousness is not observable by others
c. Incorrect. These are unconscious forces.
*d. Correct. This is the definition of our personal conscious experience.

2. a   obj. 2   p. 124
*a. Correct. The transition to sleep occurs in stage 1.
b. Incorrect. See answer a.
c. Incorrect. See answer a.
d. Incorrect. The occurrence of REM is associated with dreaming, while the transition to sleep normally occurs in stage 1.

3. d   obj. 2   p. 125
a. Incorrect. REM sleep has very irregular waveforms, this describes stage 4 sleep.
b. Incorrect. Stage 2 is characterized by electrical signals that are faster than stage 3 or 4.
c. Incorrect. Stage 3 is characterized by electrical signals that are faster than stage 4.
*d. Correct. This is an accurate description of stage 4 sleep.

4. c   obj. 2   p. 126, 127
a. Incorrect. Rest and relaxation normally occur at the same time as sleep. However, they cannot be used as substitutes for sleep.
b. Incorrect. Meditation is a choice but sleep is a necessity in life.
*c. Correct. We could only live without either for a few days at most.
d. Incorrect. We may be able to cure our addition to drugs. There is no "cure" for sleep. In fact, as a society we need to sleep more.

5. b   obj. 2   p. 126
a. Incorrect. Paradoxical sleep refers to the period of REM during which the brain is active and the body is paralyzed.
*b. Correct. After sleep deprivation, the sleeper recovers lost REM time by having extra REM sleep for several nights.
c. Incorrect. Latent dreaming would be hidden dreaming, and this is not associated with REM rebound

d. Incorrect. Somnambulism occurs most often in stage 4 sleep, and it is not a result of sleep deprivation.

6. c   obj. 3   p. 129
a. Incorrect. They include daily activities, but this is not what interested Freud.
b. Incorrect. They tend to reflect unconscious activity.
*c. Correct. Unconscious and repressed wishes often find their way into the content of dreams.
d. Incorrect. Freud might accept this view, but he was interested in the content of current dreams.

7. a   obj. 5   p. 133
*a. Correct. This includes during work, school, and any other activity.
b. Incorrect. People daydream at work, at school, and during any other activity about 10 percent of the time.
c. Incorrect. People daydream at work, at school, and during any other activity about 10 percent of the time.
d. Incorrect. You might want to reappraise what you do with your time. People, on average, daydream at work, at school, and during any other activity about 10 percent of the time.

8. c   obj. 4   p. 131
a. Incorrect. Falling asleep uncontrollably is called narcolepsy.
b. Incorrect. This is an unusual amount of sleep for an adult, but infants and small children sleep this much.
*c. Correct. Insomnia simply refers to having difficulty falling asleep or returning to sleep once awakened during the night.
d. Incorrect. This is not a condition associated with insomnia.

9. b   obj. 4   p. 131
a. Incorrect. The symptom of narcolepsy is falling into REM sleep uncontrollably.
*b. Correct. Associated with snoring, the gasping for breath often awakens the person suffering from sleep apnea.
c. Incorrect. This refers to excessive sleep.
d. Incorrect. Insomnia is difficulty falling asleep and staying asleep.

10. b   obj. 4   p. 131
a. Incorrect. Narcolepsy has not been associated with infant death syndrome.

*b. Correct. Sleep apnea is thought to be the cause of infant death syndrome—in effect, the child forgets to breath.

c. Incorrect. Somnambulism refers to sleep walking.

d. Incorrect. Insomnia involves difficulties falling asleep.

11. c   obj. 6   pp. 135, 136

a. Incorrect. "You will encourage your friends to enroll in this class."

b. Incorrect. Most of us are aware of the outdoors.

*c. Correct. Frequent daydreamers do appear to be more easily hypnotized than infrequent daydreamers.

d. Incorrect. This correlation has not been studied.

12. a   obj. 7   p. 137

*a. Correct. The repeated word is called a mantra.

b. Incorrect. The repeated word is called a mantra.

c. Incorrect. The repeated word is called a mantra.

d. Incorrect. The repeated word is called a mantra.

13. c   obj. 8   p. 140

a. Incorrect. The drug works without regard to the person's willingness to be affected.

b. Incorrect. Not all psychoactive drugs are addictive.

*c. Correct. Psychoactive drugs affect all three.

d. Incorrect. Psychoactive drugs affect emotions, perceptions, and behaviour.

14. b   obj. 8   p. 144

a. Incorrect. The barbiturate phenobarbital is not as common as other depressants.

*b. Correct. Alcohol is indeed the most common depressant.

c. Incorrect. Valium is an antianxiety drug that is quite commonly prescribed.

d. Incorrect. This is a common depressant, but not the most common.

15. e   obj. 2   p. 126
16. c   obj. 3   p. 128
17. b   obj. 5   p. 133
18. a   obj. 4   p. 131
19. d   obj. 4   p. 131
20. rebound effect   obj. 2   p. 126
21. variety   obj. 2   p. 127
22. sleep deprivation   obj. 2   p. 127
23. circadian rhythm   obj. 5   p. 132
24. REM sleep   obj. 2   p. 126

25. The major positions that should be considered in your answer:

- The psychoanalytic view argues that the symbols of dreams reflect deep meanings, many of which are unfulfiled wishes or repressed conflicts.

- The opposing views hold that dreaming is a natural process of cleaning excess material from the day, a survival mechanism, or a by-product of random electrical activity in the brain. These views may not necessarily be incompatible.

Practise Test 2:

1. a   obj. 2   p. 124

*a. Correct. Later in the night's sleep cycle, sleep is less deep.

b. Incorrect. Later in the night's sleep cycle, sleep is less deep.

c. Incorrect. Later in the night's sleep cycle, sleep is less deep.

d. Incorrect. Dreams occur at the least deep levels of sleep.

2. d   obj. 2   pp. 124, 125

a. Incorrect. It gets slower and more regular.

b. Incorrect. It gets slower and more regular.

c. Incorrect. It gets slower and more regular.

*d. Correct. The waveforms during the slowest phase are called delta waves.

3. c   obj. 2   p. 126

a. Incorrect. During stage 1, breathing becomes more regular, blood pressure drops, and respiration slows.

b. Incorrect. During stage 2, breathing continues to become more regular, blood pressure continues to drop, and respiration continues to slow.

*c. Correct. And this happens while the voluntary muscles are inhibited to the point of paralysis.

d. Incorrect. During non-REM sleep, breathing becomes more regular, blood pressure drops, and respiration slows.

4. d   obj. 2   p. 126

a. Incorrect. Paralysis occurs during REM sleep.

b. Incorrect. Paralysis occurs during REM sleep.

c. Incorrect. Paralysis occurs during REM sleep.

*d. Correct. Ironically, REM sleep is also characterized by irregular breathing, increased blood pressure, and increased respiration.

5. c   obj. 3   p. 130

a. Incorrect. This view sees dreams as a means for repressed desires to be expressed.

b. Incorrect. This approach understands dreams as a means of making sense of the information gathered through the day.

*c. Correct. This view accepts the notion of random activity as the source for dreams.

d. Incorrect. Reverse-learning implies undoing, or "cleaning," unnecessary information.

6. c   obj. 3   p. 129

a. Incorrect. Libidinal content would be sexual and may or may not be the obvious story line of the dream.

b. Incorrect. The unconscious content of dreams is most often the hidden, or latent content.

*c. Correct. This is the term he used for the story line of the dream.

d. Incorrect. The latent content is the hidden content of the dream.

7.   d   obj. 5   pp. 133, 134
a.   Incorrect. Daydreams are often a source of creative inspiration for the dreamer.
b.   Incorrect. We often daydream about the most mundane things, like doing laundry or writing answer explanations.
c.   Incorrect. Daydreams are very much part of our normal conscious experiences.
*d. Correct. Few daydreams are sexual in nature (surprised?).

8.   a   obj. 4   p. 131, 132
*a. Correct. A narcoleptic can fall asleep at any time, though stress does seem to contribute to the narcoleptic's symptoms.
b.   Incorrect. Insomnia involves difficulty getting to sleep or staying asleep.
c.   Incorrect. Somnambulism is also known as sleepwalking.
d.   Incorrect. This concept is from some sci-fi movie, no doubt.

9.   a   obj. 4   pp. 131, 132
*a. Correct. Narcolepsy is uncontrollable.
b.   Incorrect. Sleep apnea will make one tired throughout the next day due to the frequent awakening through the night.
c.   Incorrect. Hypersomnia is excessive sleep at night.
d.   Incorrect. Insomnia involves difficulty getting to sleep or staying asleep.

10. d   obj. 9   p. 148
a.   Incorrect. PCP is common, but not the most common.
b.   Incorrect. LSD is common, but not the most common.
c.   Incorrect. Cocaine is a stimulant, not a hallucinogen.
*d. Correct. Marijuana is by far the most commonly used hallucinogen.

11. d   obj. 4   p. 134
a.   Incorrect. A regular bedtime makes for a habit of falling asleep.
b.   Incorrect. Here we apply "reverse" psychology on ourselves.
c.   Incorrect. Caffeine contributes to sleeplessness.
*d. Correct. The TV belongs in the den or living room, not in the bedroom. TV is usually stimulating and not restful.

12. d   obj. 7   p. 137
a.   Incorrect. Transactional analysis comes from Berne's *I'm O.K., You're O.K.*
b.   Incorrect. Zen Buddhists practise meditation, though.
c.   Incorrect. Not quite.
*d. Correct. The name for this process is "transcendental meditation," and research has shown that the effects can be achieved through practised relaxation methods as well.

13. a   obj. 9   p. 148

*a. Correct. Methadone produces an addiction, but it does not have the psychoactive properties of heroin.
b.   Incorrect. Methadone does not cause mental retardation.
c.   Incorrect. Everyone is at risk, methadone does not increase the risk.
d.   Incorrect. Most drug users find the marijuana high to be appealing, nothing about the methadone causes this.

14. b   obj. 8   p. 140
a.   Incorrect. Since they stimulate the nervous system, they do not have an anesthetic effect.
*b. Correct. Each of these is considered a stimulant.
c.   Incorrect. In some cases, even small doses of these drugs can cause anxiety.
d.   Incorrect. With extreme doses, hallucinations are possible, but they do not occur in typical doses.

15. b   obj. 8   pp. 147, 148
a.   Incorrect. An opiate is a narcotic.
*b. Correct. These are all classes of the depressant group known as barbiturates.
c.   Incorrect. These drugs do not cause hallucinations under normal circumstances.
d.   Incorrect. These drugs do not cause hypnosis.

16. b   obj. 4   p. 131
17. a   obj. 4   pp. 131, 132
18. c   obj. 9   p. 148
19. d   obj. 9   p. 149
20. self-destructive acts obj. 6   pp. 135, 136
21. cannot   obj. 6   p. 135
23. daydreaming   obj. 6   pp. 135, 136
23. pain obj. 6   p. 136
24. Unresolved   obj. 6   p. 136

25.
■   Identify the drugs that have been involved in this issue, including marijuana. Some have also argued that drug use should be completely legalized and viewed as a medical or psychological problem.
■   State your view, identifying which drug(s) should be decriminalized and which should not. Many people suggest that the medical benefits of some drugs cannot be explored and used because of their status. Other reasons should be offered as well. For instance, the use of some drugs can be considered victimless, though the drug trade has many victims.
■   If you believe that all drugs should remain illegal, then support your reasoning. Harm to society and to individuals is a common argument. Provide examples.

Practise Test 3:
1.   a   obj. 2   p. 124
*a. Correct. The electrical properties are recorded as waveforms by the EEG, and thus are referred to as brain waves.

b. Incorrect. The time from sleep to stage is not a factor in defining the stages, and people go through several cycles of the stages each night.
c. Incorrect. Stage 4 and REM sleep have specific sleep events associated with them, but these are not used to define the stages.
d. Incorrect. With the exception of REM sleep, when the sleeper is quite still, the body movements are generally the same from one stage to another.

2. d   obj. 2   p. 127
a. Incorrect. There are no long-term effects from sleep deprivation.
b. Incorrect. He is unlikely to get sick, though he might make mistakes at work and be prone to accidents elsewhere.
c. Incorrect. There are no long-term consequences for staying awake thirty-six hours.
*d. Correct. If he is staying awake to study, then he might be jeopardizing his grade—he would be more effective to break the study into smaller parts and get some rest.

3. d   obj. 3   p. 129
a. Incorrect. Probably more than a friendship.
b. Incorrect. Nothing in the dream suggests any anxiety about talking to Jim.
c. Incorrect. This is a possible reading of the manifest content of the dream, but Freudian approach would not differ from any other approach on this view.
*d. Correct. Climbing stairs is indeed an act symbolic of sexual intercourse.

4. b   obj. 3   p. 129
a. Incorrect. This may be what it means, but it is a strange way of making the image clear, and besides, this is not what a Freudian would see.
*b. Correct. Grapefruits can generally be viewed as feminine bodies, but more specifically as breasts.
c. Incorrect. This is not a likely interpretation.
d. Incorrect. The trip down the tunnel may have a quality of a wish to return to the womb, but the grapefruits do not fit the image.

5. b   obj. 3   p. 129
a. Incorrect. Though, the increase in anxiety would lead to additional wish-fulfilment types of dreams.
*b. Correct. The need to make sense of environmental, survival-oriented information makes this choice the better candidate.
c. Incorrect. The random activity would be just as random in either circumstance.
d. Incorrect. Would they not dream less since more of the information from the day was important and relevant?

6. b   obj. 5   p. 133
a. Incorrect. This is not a common fantasy during nervous breakdowns.
*b. Correct. Fantasies about escape are common in daydreams.

c. Incorrect. Since she was in class, and probably not asleep, a nighttime emission is unlikely.
d. Incorrect. A mantra is a word repeated during meditation.

7. a   obj. 4   p. 132
*a. Correct. Sleepwalkers can be awakened, but they will probably be confused and disoriented.
b. Incorrect. Sleepwalking most often occurs in stage 4.
c. Incorrect. If awakened, the sleepwalker can have a vague sense of where they are and what they were doing.
d. Incorrect. Sleepwalking is common throughout age groups.

8. a   obj. 6   pp. 136, 137
*a. Correct. The changes in brain activity can be recorded on an EEG.
b. Incorrect. They both may result in a decrease in blood pressure, but they may not.
c. Incorrect. Hypnosis is an invention of European origin.
d. Incorrect. "Total relaxation" is a bit overstated.

9. b   obj. 8   p. 140
a. Incorrect. Addiction may be either or both biologically and psychologically based.
*b. Correct. This may be true in cases of alcoholism, but other addictions arise from the nature of the body-drug interaction.
c. Incorrect. There simply is no foundation for this statement.
d. Incorrect. Addiction may be either or both biologically and psychologically based.

10. b   obj. 8   p. 141
a. Incorrect. However, that must be some vitamin!
*b. Correct. This is what stimulants do.
c. Incorrect. Depressants slow the heart rate.
d. Incorrect. Among other things, a hallucinogen could cause these symptoms (among many others), but not necessarily.

11. c   obj. 9   p. 148
a. Incorrect. Heroin is a narcotic.
b. Incorrect. Cocaine is a stimulant.
*c. Correct. Marijuana is a hallucinogen.
d. Incorrect. Morphine is a narcotic.

12. b   obj. 3   p. 129
a. Incorrect. The latent content would be what the jacket and showing off might symbolize.
*b. Correct. This is what she actually did in her dream.
c. Incorrect. The manifest content can be quite relevant to the meaning, as it contains the symbols.
d. Incorrect. These would be day residues only if this is what she did the day before.

13. a   obj. 3   p. 129

*a. Correct. As symbols, they hold keys to the repressed or hidden latent content of the dream.
b. Incorrect. The wearing of the jacket and the parading were the manifest content.
c. Incorrect. Activation process is not relevant to the dream interpretation.
d. Incorrect. He would only need to ask Meghan about the daytime activities to make this determination.

14. a   obj. 6   p. 135
*a. Correct. Unless she is an exhibitionist, she would not undress.
b. Incorrect. With slightly lowered inhibitions, she could easily flirt.
c. Incorrect. She is likely to recall a past life, even if she does not have one.
d. Incorrect. Making people do stupid animal tricks is a common hypnotic activity.

15. b   obj. 9   p. 147
a. Incorrect. These are hallucinogens.
*b. Correct. These are the two primary examples of narcotics given in the text.
c. Incorrect. These are depressants.

d.   Incorrect. These are stimulants.

16. b   obj. 8   p. 147
17. e   obj. 9   p. 147
18. a   obj. 9   p. 147
19. d   obj. 9   p. 148
20. c   obj. 9   p. 148
21. consciousness   obj. 8   p. 140
22. tolerance   obj. 8   p. 140
23. stimulants   obj. 8   pp. 141, 144
24. neurotransmitter   obj. 8   p. 140
25. psychological   obj. 8   p. 140

26. Hypnosis is a state of heightened susceptibility to the suggestions of others.
▪ Dissociative processes involve a split in consciousness in which one part of the brain operates independently of another.
▪ Sociocognitive processes regard hypnotic behaviour as falling on a continuum of normal and social and cognitive processes. It is the result of an interaction between the personal abilities and beliefs of the subject and the social influence of the hypnotist.

Learning

5

Chapter 5 defines learning as a relatively permanent change in behaviour brought about by experience. To understand what learning is you must distinguish between performance changes due to maturation and changes brought about by experience. Similarly you must distinguish short-term changes in behaviour due to factors other than learning, such as declines in performance resulting from fatigue or lack of effort, from performance changes due to actual learning.

Some psychologists have approached learning by considering learning as simply any change in behaviour.

This chapter first examines the type of learning that explains responses ranging from a dog salivating when it hears the can opener to the emotions we feel when our national anthem is played. Then theories that consider how learning is a consequence of rewarding circumstances are examined. Finally, approaches that focus on the cognitive aspects of learning are reviewed.

To further investigate the topics covered in this chapter, you can access the related websites by visiting the following link: http://www.mcgrawhill.ca/college/feldman.

Prologue: A Friend Named Pippa
Looking Ahead

Section 1: Classical Conditioning
The Basics of Classical Conditioning
Applying Conditioning Principles to Human Behaviour
Extinction
Generalization and Discrimination
Beyond Traditional Classical Conditioning: Challenging Basic Assumptions

Section 2: Operant Conditioning
Thorndike's Law of Effect
The Basics of Operant Conditioning
Positive Reinforcers, Negative Reinforcers, and Punishment

Psychology at Work: Lynne Calero,
Dolphin Researcher

The Pros and Cons of Punishment: Why Reinforcement Beats Punishment
Schedules of Reinforcement: Timing Life's Rewards
Discrimination and Generalization in Operant Conditioning
Superstitious Behaviour
Shaping: Reinforcing What Doesn't Come Naturally
Biological Constraints on Learning: You Can't Teach an Old Dog Just Any Trick

Pathways Through Psychology: Catherine Rankin
Biopsychologist

Section 3: Cognitive-Social Approaches to Learning
Latent Learning
Observational Learning: Learning Through Imitation
Violence on Television and in Movies: Does the Media's Message Matter?

Applying Psychology in the 21st Century: Does
Virtual Aggression Lead to Actual Aggression?

Exploring Diversity: Does Culture Influence How We
Learn?

The Unresolved Controversy of Cognitive Learning Theory

Becoming an Informed Consumer of Psychology: Using
Behaviour Analysis and Behaviour Modification

Learning Objectives

These are the learning objectives for Chapter 5. Read them carefully as part of your preliminary survey of the chapter.

1. Define learning and distinguish it from performance. (p. 156)

Classical Conditioning

2. Define and describe the major principles of classical conditioning, including neutral stimulus, UCS, UCR, CS, and CS. (pp. 156–157)

3. Apply the concepts of classical conditioning to human behaviour, and define the terms extinction, spontaneous recovery, generalization, and discrimination. (pp. 159–160)

4. Identify the challenges that have been made to the traditional views of classical conditioning. (pp. 160–161)

Operant Conditioning

5. Define and describe the major principles of operant conditioning, including primary and secondary reinforcers, positive and negative reinforcement, and punishment. (pp. 162–168)

6. Outline the schedules of reinforcement and define the operant view of generalization and discrimination, superstitious behaviour, and shaping. (pp. 168–171)

7. Identify the limits of conditioning, such as biological constraints. (p. 171–172)

Cognitive Approaches to Learning

8. Describe the cognitive-social learning concepts of latent learning, cognitive maps, and observational learning. (pp. 173–176)

9. Discuss current learning topics such as the influence of television violence, cultural influences, and behaviour modification. (pp. 176–179)

SECTION 1: Classical Conditioning

Prepare

- *What is learning?*
- *How do we learn to form associations between stimuli and responses?*

Organize

- *The Basics of Classical Conditioning*
- *Applying Conditioning Principles to Human Behaviour*
- *Extinction*
- *Generalization and Discrimination*
- *Beyond Traditional Classical Conditioning*

Work

[a] _____ is distinguished from *maturation* on the basis of whether the resulting change in behaviour is a consequence of experience (learning) or of growth (maturation). Short-term changes in performance, the key measure of learning, can also result

from fatigue, lack of effort, and other factors that are not reflections of learning. According to some, learning can only be inferred indirectly.

Ivan Pavlov's studies concerning the physiology of digestive processes led him to discover the basic principles of [b] _____, a process in which an organism learns to respond to a stimulus that did not bring about the response earlier. An original study involved Pavlov's training a dog to salivate when a tuning fork was sounded. In this process, the tuning fork's sound is considered the [c] _____ because it does not bring about the response of interest. The meat powder, which does cause salivation, is called the

[d] _____. The salivation, when it occurs due to the presence of the meat powder (UCS), is called the [e] _____. The conditioning process requires repeated pairing of the UCS and the neutral stimulus. After training is complete, the neutral stimulus—now called the [f] _____—will bring about the UCR, now called the [g] _____. Pavlov noted that the neutral stimulus had to precede the UCS by no more than several seconds for the conditioning to be the most effective.

One of the more famous applications of classical conditioning techniques to humans is the case of the 11-month-old infant, Albert. Albert was taught a fear of a laboratory rat, to which he had shown no fear initially, by striking a bar behind him whenever he approached the rat.

The process of ending the association of the UCS and the CS is called [h] _____, which occurs when a previously learned response decreases and disappears. If the tuning fork is repeatedly sounded without the meat powder being presented, the dog will eventually stop salivating. Extinction is the basis for the treatment principle called [i] _____, which is used to treat phobias. Systematic desensitization requires the repeated presentation of the frightening stimulus (a CS) without the presentation of the occurrence of the negative consequences.

When a CR has been extinguished, and a period of time has passed without the presentation of the CS, a phenomenon called [j] _____ can occur. The CS is presented and the previously extinguished response recurs, though it is usually weaker than in the original training and can be extinguished again more easily.

[k] _____ takes place when a conditioned response occurs in the presence of a stimulus that is similar to the original conditioned stimulus. In the case of baby Albert, the fear response was generalized to white furry things, including a white-bearded Santa Claus mask. [l] _____ occurs when an organism learns to differentiate (discriminate) one stimulus from another and responds only to one stimulus and not the others.

[ED: No longer in text.] One of the fundamental assumptions of classical conditioning that has been challenged is the importance of the length of the interval between the neutral stimulus and the unconditioned stimulus. Garcia found that nausea caused by radiation, a state that occurred hours after exposure, could be associated with water drunk that has unusual characteristics or with water drunk in a particular place. Garcia's findings that the association could be made with delays as long as eight hours is a direct challenge to the idea that the pairing must be made within several seconds to be effective.

Evaluate

_____ 1.	classical conditioning	a.	A stimulus that brings about a response without having been learned.
_____ 2.	neutral stimulus	b.	A stimulus that, before conditioning, has no effect on the desired response.
_____ 3.	unconditioned stimulus (UCS)	c.	A once-neutral stimulus that has been paired with an unconditioned stimulus to bring about a response formerly caused only by the unconditioned stimulus.
_____ 4.	unconditioned response (UCR)	d.	A response that, after conditioning, follows a previously neutral stimulus (e.g., salivation at the sound of a tuning fork).
_____ 5.	conditioned stimulus (CS)	e.	A response that is natural and needs no training (e.g., salivation at the smell of food).
_____ 6.	conditioned response (CR)	f.	A previously neutral stimulus comes to elicit a response through its association with a stimulus that naturally brings about the response.

Rethink

1. Can you think of ways that classical conditioning is used by politicians? advertisers? moviemakers? Do ethical issues arise from any of these uses?

2. Is it likely that Albert, Watson's experimental subject, went through life afraid of Santa Claus? Describe what probably happened to prevent this.

SECTION 2:   Operant Conditioning

Prepare

- ***What is the role of reward and punishment in learning?***

Organize

- ***Thorndike's Law of Effect***
- ***The Basics of Operant Conditioning***
- ***Positive Reinforcers, Negative Reinforcers, and Punishment***
- ***The Pros and Cons of Punishment***
- ***Schedules of Reinforcement***
- ***Discrimination and Generalization in Operant Conditioning***
- ***Superstitious Behaviour***
- ***Shaping***
- ***Biological Constraints on Learning***

Work

[a] _____ is learning in which the response is strengthened or weakened according to whether it has positive or negative consequences. The term "operant" suggests that the organism *operates* on the environment in a deliberate manner to gain a desired result.

Edward L. Thorndike found that a cat would learn to escape from a cage by performing specific actions in order to open a door that allows it access to food, a positive consequence of the behaviour. Thorndike formulated the [b] _____, stating that responses with satisfying results would be repeated, those with less satisfying results would be less likely to be repeated.

[c] _____ is the process by which a stimulus increases the probability that a preceding behaviour will be repeated. Releasing the food by pecking is a reinforcement, and the food itself is called a [d] _____, which is any stimulus that increases the probability that a preceding behaviour will be repeated. A [e] _____ satisfies a biological need without regard to prior experience. A [f] _____ is a stimulus that reinforces because of its association with a primary reinforcer.

Reinforcers are also distinguished as positive or negative. [g] _____ bring about an increase in the preceding response. [h] _____ lead to an increase in a desired response when they are *removed*. Negative reinforcement requires that an individual take an action to remove an undesirable condition. Negative reinforcement is used in [i] _____, where an organism learns to escape from an aversive situation, and in [j] _____, where the organism learns to act to avoid the aversive situation. [k] _____ refers to the use of an aversive stimulus, by adding it to the environment, in order to *decrease* the probability that a behaviour will be repeated. Punishment includes the removal of something positive, such as the loss of a privilege.

The frequency and timing of reinforcement depends upon the use of [l] _____. With [m] _____, the behaviour is reinforced every time it occurs. [n] _____ describes the technique of using reinforcement some of the time but not for every response. Partial reinforcement schedules maintain behaviour longer than continuous reinforcement before extinction occurs.

A [o] _____ delivers a reinforcement after a certain number of responses. A [p] _____ delivers reinforcement on the basis of a varying number of responses. The number of responses often remains close to an average. The fixed- and variable-ratio schedules depend upon a *number* of responses, and the fixed- and variable-interval schedules depend upon an *amount of time*. **[q]** _____ deliver reinforcements to the first behaviour occurring after a set interval, or period, of time.

[r] _____ deliver reinforcement after a varying interval of time. Fixed intervals are like weekly paychecks, variable intervals are like pop quizzes.

Discrimination and generalization are achieved in operant conditioning through

[s] _____ . In stimulus control training, a behaviour is reinforced only in the presence of specific stimuli. The specific stimulus is called a *discriminative stimulus*, a stimulus that signals the likelihood of a particular behaviour being reinforced.

[t] _____ refers to a behaviour that involves the repetition of elaborate rituals. Learning theory accounts for superstitious behaviour as behaviour that occurs prior to a reinforcement but is coincidental to the behaviour that leads to the reinforcement.

When a complex behaviour is desired, a trainer may shape the desired behaviour by rewarding closer and closer approximations of the behaviour. Many complex human and animal skills are acquired through **[u]** _____ .

Sometimes learning is constrained by behaviours that are biologically innate, or inborn. Not all behaviours can be taught to all animals equally well because of these *biological constraints*. Pigs might root a disk around their cages and raccoons might hoard and then clean similar disks.

Evaluate

_____ 1. operant conditioning

_____ 2. primary reinforcer

_____ 3. secondary reinforcer

_____ 4. positive reinforcer

_____ 5. negative reinforcer

_____ 6. punishment

_____ 7. aversive stimuli

a. An unpleasant or painful stimulus that is added to the environment after a certain behaviour occurs, decreasing the likelihood that the behaviour will occur again.

b. Unpleasant or painful stimuli.

c. A reward that satisfies a biological need (e.g., hunger or thirst) and works naturally.

d. A stimulus added to the environment that brings about an increase in the response that preceded it.

e. A stimulus that becomes reinforcing by its association with a primary reinforcer (e.g., money, which allows us to obtain food, a primary reinforcer).

f. A stimulus whose removal is reinforcing, leading to a greater probability that the response bringing about this removal will occur again.

g. A voluntary response is strengthened or weakened, depending on its positive or negative consequences.

Rethink

3. How might operant conditioning be used to address serious personal concerns, such as smoking and unhealthy eating?

4. How might you go about "curing" superstitious behaviour, such as the rituals people engage in before examinations or athletic competitions? Should we try to extinguish such behaviour?

SECTION 3: Cognitive-Social Approaches to Learning

Prepare

- *What is the role of cognition and thought in learning?*
- *What are some practical methods for bringing about behaviour change, both in ourselves and in others?*

Organize

- *Latent Learning*
- *Observational Learning*
- *Violence on Television and in Movies*
- *The Unresolved Controversy of Cognitive-Social Learning Theory*

Work

The approach that views learning in terms of thought processes is called

[a] _____. This approach does not deny the importance of classical and operant conditioning. It includes the consideration of unseen mental processes as well.

[b] _____ is behaviour that is learned but not demonstrated until reinforcement is provided for demonstrating the behaviour. Latent learning occurs when rats are allowed to wander about a maze without any reward at the end, but once they learn that a reinforcement is available, they will quickly find their way through the maze even though they had not been reinforced for doing so in the past. The wandering around apparently leads them to

develop a [c] _____ of the maze. Humans apparently develop cognitive maps of their surroundings based on landmarks.

Accounting for a large portion of learning in humans, [d] _____ is learning that occurs by observing the behaviour of another person, called the [e]

_____. The classic experiment involved children observing a model strike a Bobo doll, and then later those who had seen the behaviour were more prone to act aggressively. Four processes are necessary for observational learning: (1) paying attention to critical features; (2) remembering the behaviour; (3) reproducing the action; and (4) being motivated to repeat the behaviour. We also observe the kinds of reinforcement that the model receives for the behaviour. Observational learning has been related to how violence on television affects aggression and violence in children.

The Exploring Diversity section examines *learning styles* and how cultural differences are reflected in these different ways of approaching materials. Learning styles are characterized by cultural background and individual abilities.

[f] _____ refers to the formalized use of basic principles of learning theory to change behaviour by eliminating undesirable behaviours and encouraging desirable ones. Behaviour modification can be used to train mentally retarded individuals, to help people lose weight or quit smoking, and to teach people to behave safely. The steps of a typical behaviour program include: 1) identifying goals and target behaviours; 2) designing a data recording system and recording preliminary data; 3) selecting a behaviour change strategy; 4) implementing the program; 5) keeping careful records after the program has been implemented; and 6) evaluating and altering the ongoing program.

Evaluate

_____ 1.   continuous reinforcement schedule

_____ 2.   partial reinforcement schedule

_____ 3.   schedules of reinforcement

_____ 4.   stimulus control training

_____ 5.   model

_____ 6.   behaviour modification

a.   A formalized technique for promoting the frequency of desirable behaviours and decreasing the incidence of unwanted ones.

b.   A person serving as an example to an observer; the observer may imitate that person's behaviour.

c.   Reinforcing of a behaviour every time it occurs.

d.   Reinforcing of a behaviour some, but not all, of the time.

e.   The frequency and timing of reinforcement following desired behaviour.

f.   Training in which an organism is reinforced in the presence of a certain specific stimulus, but not in its absence.

Rethink

5.   What is the relationship between a model (in Bandura's sense) and a role model (as the term is used popularly)? Celebrities often complain that their actions should not be scrutinized closely because they do not want to be role models. How would you respond?

6.   The relational style of learning sometimes conflicts with the traditional school environment. Could a school be created that takes advantage of the characteristics of the relational style? How? Are there types of learning for which the analytical style is clearly superior?

Practise Questions

Test your knowledge of the chapter material by answering these questions. These questions have been placed in three Practise Tests. The first two tests are composed of questions that will test your recall of factual knowledge. The third test contains questions that are challenging and primarily test for conceptual knowledge and your ability to apply that knowledge. Check your answers and review the feedback using the Answer Key on the following pages of the *Study Guide*.

PRACTISE TEST 1:

1. Which of the following statements concerning the relationship between learning and performance is correct?
   a. Learning refers to cognitive gains, whereas performance refers to gains in motor skills.
   b. Performance refers to permanent changes, whereas learning refers to temporary changes.
   c. Performance is synonymous with learning.
   d. Performance is measurable, whereas learning must be inferred.

2. The changes in behaviour brought about by learning:
   a. are hard to measure.
   b. are easily extinguished.
   c. must be measured indirectly.
   d. are generally maturational.

3. The meat powder in Pavlov's experiment was the:
   a. unconditioned stimulus.
   b. conditioned stimulus.
   c. unconditioned response.
   d. conditioned response.

4. Over time, when the conditioned stimulus is presented repeatedly without being paired with the unconditioned stimulus, the result will be:
   a. learning.
   b. perception.
   c. systematic desensitization.
   d. extinction.

5. Systematic desensitization is most closely associated with:
   a. operant conditioning.
   b. token economy.
   c. spontaneous recovery.
   d. extinction.

6. A classically conditioned response can be extinguished by:
   a. adding another conditioned stimulus to the pairing.
   b. no longer presenting the unconditioned stimulus after the conditioned response.
   c. using stimulus substitution.
   d. reintroducing the unconditioned stimulus.

7. Garcia's behavioural investigations of rats that were treated with doses of radiation illustrate that:
   a. rats obey slightly different principles of classical conditioning than humans do.
   b. some research findings involving classical conditioning do not appear to obey Pavlov's conditioning principles.
   c. classical conditioning is a very robust form of learning, since it is not weakened even by large doses of medication.

    d.   changes in classical conditioning are highly sensitive indicators of radiation effects.

8.   We behave according to the _____ when we continue to act in a manner that will lead to pleasing consequences.
    a.   law of frequency.
    b.   principle of similarity.
    c.   law of effect.
    d.   principle of contiguity.

9.   The distinction between primary reinforcers and secondary reinforcers is that:
    a.   primary reinforcers satisfy some biological need; secondary reinforcers are effective because of their association with primary reinforcers.
    b.   organisms prefer primary reinforcers to secondary reinforcers.
    c.   primary reinforcers are not effective with all organisms.
    d.   primary reinforcers depend upon the past conditioning of the organism; secondary reinforcers have a biological basis.

10.   Any stimulus that increases the likelihood that a preceding behaviour be repeated is called:
    a.   a punisher.
    b.   a reinforcer.
    c.   a response.
    d.   an operant.

11.   Negative reinforcement:
    a.   is a special form of punishment.
    b.   is a phenomenon that results when reward is withheld.
    c.   involves the decrease or removal of an aversive stimulus.
    d.   occurs in both classical and instrumental conditioning.

12.   Under variable schedules of reinforcement, the response rate is:
    a.   always high.
    b.   always constant and low.
    c.   easily extinguished.
    d.   highly resistant to extinction.

13.   Since the number of lottery tickets a person must purchase before reinforcement in the form of a winning ticket is not certain, he or she is working on a _____ schedule.
    a.   variable-ratio
    b.   fixed-ratio
    c.   variable-interval
    d.   fixed-interval

14.   Superstitious behaviour is thought to arise because of:
    a.   continuously reinforced patterns of behaviour that have led to results related to the behaviour.
    b.   universal biological constraints that guide specific kinds of behaviour.
    c.   religious dogma.
    d.   partial reinforcement of the connection of incidental events to a specific consequence.

15.   Given the opportunity to explore a maze with no explicit reward available, rats will develop:
    a.   a cognitive map of the maze.
    b.   an aversion to the maze.
    c.   an increased interest in the maze.
    d.   a superstitious fear of the maze.

____	16.	cognitive-social learning theory	a.	The study of the thought processes that underlie learning.
____	17.	latent learning	b.	Learning that involves the imitation of a model.
____	18.	observational learning	c.	A new behaviour is acquired but not readily demonstrated until reinforcement is provided.
____	19.	classical conditioning	d.	A stimulus that, before conditioning, does not naturally bring about the response of interest.
____	20.	neutral stimulus	e.	a type of learning in which a neutral stimulus comes to bring about a response after it is paired with a stimulus that naturally brings about that response.

21.   _____ is the process of teaching a complex behaviour by rewarding closer and closer approximations of the desired behaviour.

22.   A(n) _____ stimulus is one that brings about a response without having been learned.

23.   A(n) _____ stimulus is a once-neutral stimulus that has been paired with an unconditioned stimulus to bring about a response formerly caused only by the unconditioned stimulus.

24.   A(n) _____ response is a response that is natural and needs no training.

25.   The use of physical punishment has become quite controversial. Most school systems now outlaw its use, and many parents try to find alternatives to it. Define the issues related to the use of punishment, and answer the question, "Is it wrong to use physical punishment to discipline children?" As you answer, consider whether there are circumstances that may require routine use, or should it be rare. Describe alternatives for use in normal disciplining of children.

PRACTISE TEST 2:

1.   Learning is best defined as:
   a.   a change in behaviour brought about by growth and maturity of the nervous system.
   b.   a measurable change in behaviour brought about by conditions such as drugs, sleep, and fatigue.
   c.   a behavioural response that occurs each time a critical stimulus is presented.
   d.   a relatively permanent change in behaviour brought about by experience.

2. In classical conditioning, the stimulus that comes to elicit a response that it would not previously have elicited is called the:
   a. classical stimulus.
   b. unconditioned stimulus.
   c. conditioned stimulus.
   d. discriminative stimulus.

3. Prior to the conditioning trials in which Watson planned to condition fear of a rat in Baby Albert, the rat—which Albert was known not to fear—would have been considered:
   a. an unconditioned stimulus.
   b. an adaptive stimulus.
   c. a discriminative stimulus.
   d. a neutral stimulus.

4. Systematic desensitization is achieved by:
   a. no longer allowing the conditioned stimulus and the unconditioned stimulus to be paired in real-life situations.
   b. constructing a hierarchy of situations that produce fear and then gradually pairing less stressful situations with strategies to relax.
   c. identifying the situations that produce fear in order to modify or eliminate them.
   d. gaining exposure to the most fearful situations so that the unpleasant reactions can be extinguished quickly.

5. When the conditioned stimulus is presented repeatedly without being accompanied by the unconditioned stimulus, _____ occurs.
   a. escape conditioning
   b. extinction
   c. stimulus generalization
   d. negative reinforcement

6. Pavlov's assumption that stimuli and responses were linked in a mechanistic, unthinking way has been challenged by:
   a. cognitive learning theorists.
   b. the animal trainers, the Brelands.
   c. Edward Thorndike's law of effect.
   d. operant conditioning.

7. A reinforcement given for the first correct or desired response to occur after a set period of time is called a _____ reinforcement schedule.
   a. fixed-ratio
   b. continuous
   c. fixed-interval
   d. variable-interval

8. Which alternative below is **not** an example of operant conditioning?
   a. A cat pushes against a lever to open a door on its cage.
   b. A student drives within the speed limit to avoid getting another speeding ticket.
   c. A dog rolls over for a dog biscuit.
   d. A student's blood pressure increases when she anticipates speaking with her chemistry professor.

9. Which name below is **not** associated with classical conditioning or operant conditioning?
   a. Pavlov
   b. Skinner
   c. Wertheimer
   d. Thorndike

10. Typically, food is a _____, whereas money is a _____.
    a. discriminative stimulus; conditioned reinforcer

    b.   need; motive

    c.   primary reinforcer; secondary reinforcer

    d.   drive reducer; natural reinforcer

11.   According to the definition given in the text, which of the following is most likely to be considered a primary reinforcer?

    a.   money   c.   good grades

    b.   water   d.   a hammer

12.   According to the text, in which of the following situations would the use of punishment be most effective in reducing the undesired behaviour?

    a.   An employee is demoted for misfiling a report.

    b.   A child is spanked for hitting her sister.

    c.   A teenager is denied the opportunity to attend the Friday dance for staying out late on Monday.

    d.   A child is spanked for running into the street.

13.   Piecework in a factory, where a worker is paid for three pieces made, is an example of a _____ schedule of reinforcement.

    a.   fixed-interval

    b.   variable-interval

    c.   variable-ratio

    d.   fixed-ratio

14.   With a fixed-interval schedule, especially in the period just after reinforcement, response rates are:

    a.   speeded up.   c.   relatively unchanged.

    b.   extinguished.   d.   relatively low.

15.   Rewarding each step toward a desired behaviour _____ the new response pattern.

    a.   inhibits   c.   disrupts

    b.   shapes   d.   eliminates

____ 16.   extinction

____ 17.   systematic desensitization

____ 18.   spontaneous recovery

____ 19.   stimulus generalization

____ 20.   stimulus discrimination

    a.   The weakening and eventual disappearance of a conditioned response.

    b.   The reappearance of a previously extinguished response after a period of time during which the conditioned stimulus has been absent.

    c.   Response to a stimulus that is similar to but different from a conditioned stimulus; the more similar the two stimuli, the more likely generalization is to occur.

    d.   The process by which an organism learns to differentiate among stimuli, restricting its response to one in particular.

    e.   A form of therapy in which fears are minimized through gradual exposure to the source of fear.

21. Stimulus _____ is a response to a stimulus that is similar to but different from a conditioned stimulus.

22. The ability to differentiate between stimuli is stimulus _____.

23. _____ is learning in which a voluntary response is strengthened or weakened, depending on its favourable or unfavourable consequences.

24. _____ is the process by which a stimulus increases the probability that a preceding behaviour will be repeated.

25. Three approaches to learning are described in the text. Classical and operant conditioning rely on external determinants of behaviour, and cognitive learning depends in part on internal, mental activity. How can the differences between these three approaches be reconciled?

PRACTISE TEST 3: Conceptual, Applied, and Challenging Questions

1. Through conditioning, a dog learns to salivate at the sound of a bell because the bell signals that food is coming. In subsequent learning trials, a buzzer is sounded just prior to the bell. Soon the dog salivates at the sound of the buzzer. In this case, the bell acts as the:
   a. unconditioned stimulus.
   b. conditioned stimulus.
   c. unconditioned response.
   d. conditioned response.

2. In preparing food for her daughter, Betsy uses a juicer. Soon the baby knows that the sound of the juicer signals that food is on the way. In this case, the food acts as:
   a. an unconditioned stimulus.
   b. a conditioned stimulus.
   c. an unconditioned response.
   d. a conditioned response.

3. In preparing food for his young son, Daniel uses a blender. Soon the baby knows that the sound of the blender signals that food is on the way. In this case, the blender acts as:
   a. an unconditioned stimulus.
   b. a conditioned stimulus.
   c. an unconditioned response.
   d. a conditioned response.

4. Rats are sometimes sickened by poisoned bait that resembles their favourite foods. Afterwards, the rats avoid eating food that resembles the poisoned bait. The sickness caused by the poisoned bait is _____ in classical conditioning.
   a. an unconditioned response
   b. an unconditioned stimulus
   c. a conditioned response
   d. a conditioned stimulus

5. Joseph looks at his puppy; the puppy barks, and Joseph gently hugs the puppy. In this case, the puppy's bark is:
   a. evidence of stimulus generalization.
   b. an operant response, likely to be repeated.
   c. a reinforcer for the boy's subsequent hug of the puppy.
   d. an aversive response established via classical conditioning.

6. Katie is being taught colours and their names. When shown a red, pink, or yellow rose, the child correctly identifies the colour of each flower. This is an example of:

    a.   stimulus discrimination.   c.   spontaneous generalization.
    b.   stimulus generalization.   d.   spontaneous recovery.

7. High schools have sometimes used dogs to search student lockers. Typically, the dogs are trained to sniff out a specific drug such as cocaine, and to ignore all other drugs. The ability of the dogs to respond only to the specific drug they were trained to detect is an example of:

    a.   stimulus discrimination.   c.   partial reinforcement.
    b.   response generalization.   d.   spontaneous recovery.

8. Students generally study very hard before midterms and then slack off immediately afterward, which is characteristic of behaviour reinforced on a _____ schedule.

    a.   fixed-ratio   c.   fixed-interval
    b.   variable-ratio   d.   variable-interval

9. Professor Watt has been conducting studies in which children are given an opportunity to explore a complicated play area for a time, and then they are asked to locate a specific item in the room. She claims that their speed and accuracy results from unseen mental processes that intervene in learning the area. Which of the following labels best describes Dr. Watt?

    a.   personality psychologist   c.   cognitive psychologist
    b.   sensory psychologist   d.   biopsychologist

10. The existence of _____ supports the idea that learning may occur even though it is not yet evident in performance.

    a.   partial reinforcement   c.   shaping
    b.   classical conditioning   d.   latent learning

11. Kachtia's roommate is playing her stereo with the volume turned almost all the way up. In order to study, Kachtia puts on her own headphones and plays softer music to block out the loud music. Since the headphones result in the removal of the aggravating sound, the action would be called:

    a.   punishment by application.   c.   negative reinforcement.
    b.   positive reinforcement.   d.   punishment by removal.

12. Research studies that show a positive relationship between hours of viewed TV violence and viewers' personal aggressiveness show a methodological weakness in the sense that:

    a.   only a few hundred persons serve as subjects in the study.
    b.   the researchers interpret the results with bias favouring their own theoretical viewpoints.
    c.   people lie habitually on surveys regarding their viewing habits.
    d.   correlational data cannot prove that the TV viewing caused the violent behaviour.

13. In Inuit culture, the formal model of education, *ilisayuq,*

    a.   is based on abstraction, verbal ability, and preparation for some future endeavour
    b.   Includes knowledge based on the real world, such as fishing and hunting
    c.   Could probably serve as a model in observational learning processes.
    d.   Has a tendency toward promoting implicit learning.

14. Which of the following options should Kent select **first** if he wants to improve his study skills?

    a.   He should determine how effective his strategies have been so far.
    b.   He should identify specific tests and class projects on which he wants to improve.
    c.   He should implement the program of skill improvement.

    d.   He should select a study skill to change.

____ 15.   fixed-ratio schedule

    a. Reinforcement occurs after a varying number of responses rather than after a fixed number.

____ 16.   variable-ratio schedule

    b. Any stimulus that increases the probability that a preceding behaviour will be repeated.

____ 17.   fixed-interval schedule

    c. Reinforcement is given at various times, usually causing a behaviour to be maintained more consistently.

____ 18.   variable-interval schedule

____ 19.   reinforcer

    d. A stimulus to which an organism learns to respond as a part of stimulus control training.

____ 20.   discriminative stimulus

    e. Reinforcement is given at established time intervals.

    f. Reinforcement is given only after a certain number of responses is made.

21.   A _____ is any stimulus that increases the probability that a preceding behaviour will occur again.

22.   A _____ reinforcer is a stimulus added to the environment that brings about an increase in a preceding response.

23.   _____ is a stimulus that decreases the probability that a previous behaviour will occur again.

24.   Using the theory of Operant Conditioning, list the steps you might take to get a fifth grader to stop leaving his seat, being disruptive, and acting out in class.

Spotlight on Terminology and Language—
Cultural Idioms

Page 156 "The expertise developed by both Pippa and Jean Little is the result of **painstaking** training procedures…"

Painstaking work is work that has required great effort and care.

Page 156 "Although psychologist have identified a number of different types of learning, a general definition **encompasses** them all: Learning is a relatively permanent change in behaviour brought about by experience."

Encompass is to include. This is an inclusive definition for the many types of learning.

Classical Conditioning

Page 157 "**Classical conditioning** is a type of learning in which a neutral stimulus (such as the experimenter's footsteps) comes to bring about a response after it is paired with a stimulus (such as food) that naturally brings about that response."

Classical conditioning is also called Pavlovian conditioning. It is a type of learning in which an organism comes to associate one stimulus with another.

Page 159 "To produce **extinction**, one needs to end the association between conditioned and unconditioned stimuli."

In classical conditioning, **extinction** is the elimination of the learned response by removal of the unconditioned stimulus. In operant conditioning, **extinction** occurs following the elimination of reinforcement.

Page 160 "If two stimuli are sufficiently distinct from one another so that one **evokes** a conditioned response but the other does not, we can say that stimulus discrimination has occurred."

To **evoke** is to elicit a response.

Operant Conditioning

Page 163 "Thorndike's early research served as the foundation for the work of one of the century's most **influential** psychologists, B. F. Skinner. You may have heard of the Skinner box, a **chamber** with a highly controlled environment used to study operant conditioning processes with laboratory animals."

An **influential** person is a leader. A **chamber** is an enclosed space designed for experimental purposes.

Page 164 " A reinforcer is any stimulus that increases the **probability** that a preceding behaviour will occur again."

When the **probability** of an act is increased, this means that the occurrence or circumstance is likely to occur again.

Page 166 "When a teenager is told she is 'grounded' and will no longer be able to use the family car because of her poor grades, or when an employee is informed that he has been **demoted** with a cut in pay because of poor job evaluations, negative punishment is being administered."

When adolescents are **grounded**, their activities are confined to a limited area, often their home or their room. **Demoted** is reducing to a lower status or less important position.

Page 167 "A parent might not have a second chance to warn a child not to run into a busy street, so punishing the first **incidence** of this behaviour might prove to be wise. Moreover, the use of punishment to **suppress** behaviour, even temporarily, provides the opportunity to reinforce a person for **subsequently** behaving in a more desirable way."

An **incidence** is an occurrence of an action or situation. **Suppress** is to stop behaviour. **Subsequently** is following in time, coming later.

Page 167 "Several disadvantages make the routine use of punishment **questionable**."

When something is **questionable** it is doubted and challenged.

Page 170 "Students' study habits often **exemplify** this reality."

Students study habits are an example of this behaviour.

Page 172 "Biological **constraints** will act to prevent or inhibit an organism from learning a behaviour…. It is clear that animals have specialized learning mechanisms that influence how readily both classical and operant conditioning influence their behaviour, and each species is biologically **primed** to develop particular kinds of associations and to have a difficult time in learning others."

A **constraint** is something that restricts you from a given course of action. A biological **constraint** is a built-in restriction. To be **primed** for something is to be ready and prepared. What are some of the behaviours infants are biologically **primed** to develop?

Page 165 "Our facility is a research education facility in which we do training to educate the public, as well as **monitoring** individual animals' health."

Monitoring is to check systematically, usually for the purpose of collecting data. Do you see a purpose for public or governmental **monitoring** of any specific behaviours?

Page 165 "Overall, my impression is that dolphins are incredibly intelligent, as well as being intensely **intuitive**."

When you know something through **intuition**, you seem to know it without the use of rational processes.

Cognitive-Social Approaches to Learning

Page 174 "In **latent** learning, a new behaviour is learned but not demonstrated until reinforcement is provided for displaying it."

Latent is something present but not evident or active. A fingerprint that is difficult to see but can be made visible for examination is a **latent** fingerprint.

Page 175 "On the eleventh day a critical experimental **manipulation** was introduced."

Manipulation is an activity by a research experimenter intended to influence the research variables and results.

Page 176 "The daughter of a judge from a politically **prominent** family runs off with her **ne'er-do-well** boyfriend."

Prominent here refers to important, or political renowned family. A **ne'er-do-well** is an individual who **never does well**. This type of person is often referred to as good-for-nothing.

Page 178 "A continual diet of aggression can leave us **desensitized** to violence, and what previously would have **repelled** us now produces little emotional response."

When we are **desensitized**, we become insensitive. Researchers are concerned that observing too much violence on television will **desensitize** us to physical aggression. When something **repels** us, we find it disgusts us. Something that **repels** people causes an aversion. Is there any activity that previously would have **repelled** you, but now you have become **desensitized** to?

■ CHAPTER 5: ANSWER KEY

GUIDED REVIEW		
Section 1:	Section 2:	Section 3:
[a] Learning	[a] Operant conditioning	[a] cognitive-social learning theory
[b] classical conditioning	[b] law of effect	[b] Latent learning
[c] neutral stimulus	[c] Reinforcement	[c] cognitive map
[d] unconditioned stimulus (UCS)	[d] reinforcer	[d] observational learning
[e] unconditioned response (UCR)	[e] primary reinforcer	[e] model
[f] conditioned stimulus (CS)	[f] secondary reinforcer	[f] Behaviour modification
[g] conditioned response (CR)	[g] Positive reinforcers	

[h] extinction	[h] Negative reinforcers	Evaluate
[i] systematic desensitization	[i] escape conditioning	1. c
[j] spontaneous recovery	[j] avoidance conditioning	2. d
[k] Stimulus generalization	[k] Punishment	3. e
[l] Stimulus discrimination	[l] schedules of reinforcement	4. f
	[m] continuous reinforcement schedule	5. b
	[n] Partial reinforcement schedule	6. a
Evaluate	[o] fixed-ratio schedule	
1. f	[p] variable-ratio schedule	
2. b	[q] Fixed-interval schedules	
3. a	[r] Variable-interval schedules	
4. e	[s] stimulus control training	
5. c	[t] Superstitious behaviour	
6. d	[u] shaping	
	Evaluate	
	1. g	
	2. c	
	3. e	
	4. d	
	5. f	
	6. a	
	7. b	

Selected Rethink Answers

2. It is unlikely that Watson's subject went through life afraid of Santa Claus. After the experiment:
   -the conditioned response was no longer reinforced.
   -the subject probably had future experiences that involved white furry objects that were not fearful.
   -the longer the CR was present without the CS the less likely would be the conditioning; this is called extinction.

3. The habits of smoking and unhealthy eating can be changed by operant conditioning that would require:
   -First identifying the specific behaviour to be changed.
   -Next, a reward has to be identified that will reinforce the new behaviour (not smoking, healthy eating).
   -Finally, reinforcement schedules must be designed to increase the probability that the new behaviour will occur.

4. Superstitious behaviour could be "cured" by helping the subject (cognitively) become aware that there was no connection between two events or by demonstration that there is no cause-effect pattern to their behaviour.
   Unless the behaviour interferes with a person's ability to function in a given situation it may continue. It may even be beneficial to continue because it gives the student or athlete a sense of confidence and may reduce the stress of the performance; therefore giving them the extra edge in a demanding situation.

Practise Test 1:

1. d   obj. 1   p. 156
a. Incorrect. Learning refers to performance changes as well.
b. Incorrect. Learning refers to permanent changes.
c. Incorrect. Performance changes can result from fatigue.
*d. Correct. Performance is the means of measuring learning.

2. c   obj. 1   p. 156
a. Incorrect. If learning has occurred, then there must be a way to measure it.
b. Incorrect. Learning should result in relatively permanent change.

*c. Correct. Since learning is an internal change, it must be observed indirectly through the changes in behaviour.
d. Incorrect. Learning differs from maturational changes.

3. a   obj. 2   p. 157
*a. Correct. Meat powder caused salivation to occur without any training and thus is "unconditioned."
b. Incorrect. The conditioned stimulus originally did not cause any salivation.
c. Incorrect. The response was salivation.
d. Incorrect. The response was salivation.

4. d   obj. 3   p. 159

a. Incorrect. Learning has already occurred in this scenario.
b. Incorrect. Perception is a mental event related to understanding sensory stimuli.
c. Incorrect. Systematic desensitization is a specialized technique for eliminating a learned response.
*d. Correct. When the CS is repeatedly presented without the UCS being paired with it, then the CS-CR connection becomes extinguished.

5. d   obj. 3   p. 159
a. Incorrect. Operant conditioning does not engage in systematic desensitization.
b. Incorrect. A token economy is a method that applies operant conditioning to discipline.
c. Incorrect. Spontaneous recovery occurs after extinction and may occur after systematic desensitization has occurred.
*d. Correct. Systematic desensitization is a means of achieving extinction of a CS-CR relationship.

6. b   obj. 3   p. 159
a. Incorrect. This method is unlikely to extinguish the initial response.
*b. Correct. This is the standard method of extinction.
c. Incorrect. This refers to the process of acquiring a UCS-CS connection initially.
d. Incorrect. This will actually strengthen the CS.

7. b   obj. 4   p. 161
a. Incorrect. The principles of classical conditioning are meant to apply uniformly to all organisms with the capacity to learn.
*b. Correct. Garcia found that animals could be conditioned in open trial and that the time between the UCS and the CS could be quite long.
c. Incorrect. This is not quite the point of Garcia's research.
d. Incorrect. The effects can be achieved by spinning the rats, so this claim is not true.

8. c   obj. 5   p. 163
a. Incorrect. The law of frequency suggests that conditioning requires frequent pairings.
b. Incorrect. This is the gestalt principle of perception, not a rule for classical or operant conditioning.
*c. Correct. The law of effect says that if a behaviour has pleasing consequences, then it is more likely to be repeated.
d. Incorrect. The principle of contiguity in classical conditioning suggests that the CS and the UCS should be close together in time and space.

9. a   obj. 5   p. 164
*a. Correct. Indeed, primary reinforcers are items like food and water; secondary are like praise and money.
b. Incorrect. Organisms may differ in their preferences but not in any uniform manner.

c. Incorrect. For organisms that respond to operant conditioning, secondary reinforcers have an effect.
d. Incorrect. This statement is reversed.

10. b   obj. 5   p. 164
a. Incorrect. Punishers decrease the likelihood of a response being repeated.
*b. Correct. This defines reinforcers.
c. Incorrect. A response is the behaviour, not the consequence.
d. Incorrect. An operant is a kind of response.

11. c   obj. 5   p. 166
a. Incorrect. It is a form of reinforcement, and it results in the increase of the desired behaviour.
b. Incorrect. Rewards are not withheld in negative reinforcement, in fact, the removal of the aversive stimulus is considered to be a reward.
*c. Correct. The removal of the aversive stimulus is a pleasing consequence and will lead to the repetition of the behaviour.
d. Incorrect. Only instrumental conditioning utilizes reinforcement.

12. d   obj. 6   p. 170
a. Incorrect. The rate depends upon the schedule of reinforcement that has been chosen.
b. Incorrect. The rate depends upon the schedule of reinforcement that has been chosen.
c. Incorrect. The response is actually difficult to extinguish.
*d. Correct. The variability and the partial nature of the reinforcement results in behaviours that are highly resistant to extinction.

13. a   obj. 6   p. 170
*a. Correct. The ratio of successful sales to attempts made varies from sale to sale.
b. Incorrect. This would mean that the frequency of making a sale would be fixed at every fourth, or every fifth attempt (or some number).
c. Incorrect. A variable interval would mean that another sale would not take place until a set amount of time had passed.
d. Incorrect. A fixed interval would mean that a sale would take place on a time schedule, say every hour or every two hours.

14. d   obj. 6   p. 168
a. Incorrect. Superstitious behaviours are rarely reinforced.
b. Incorrect. This results in some other behaviours, not superstitious ones.
c. Incorrect. This probably arises for other reasons.
*d. Correct. The superstitious behaviour of a major-league batter might arise because once he hit a home run after tapping the back of his foot with the bat and then touching his hat. Now he repeats this pattern every time he goes to bat.

15. a   obj. 8   p. 175
*a. Correct. Quicker learning in later trials with reinforcement present suggest that some form of map or learning had developed in the unrewarded exploration.
b. Incorrect. No aversion would occur unless the maze were filled with traps.
c. Incorrect. Rat interest in mazes cannot yet be judged.
d. Incorrect. Since rats are very superstitious, the maze would have little effect on their beliefs.

16. a   obj. 8   p. 173
17. c   obj. 8   p. 174
18. b   obj. 8   p. 175
19. e   obj. 2   p. 156
20. d   obj. 2   p. 157
21. Shaping   obj. 6   p. 168
22. unconditioned   obj. 2   p. 157
23. conditioned   obj. 2   p. 157
24. unconditioned   obj. 2   p. 157

25.
■ Cite examples of the use of physical punishment. Describe alternatives for each use.
■ Identify the conditions under which physical punishment may be necessary. These could include the need for swift and attention-getting action to prevent physical harm. Some parents use corporal punishment when children hit one another, some do so to establish control when alternatives have failed.

Practise Test 2:
1. d   obj. 1   p. 156
a. Incorrect. This definition fits maturation better.
b. Incorrect. This definition applies to circumstantial changes.
c. Incorrect. This definition applies to reflex.
*d. Correct. This is the definition given in the text.

2. c   obj. 2   p. 157
a. Incorrect. No such term is used in learning theory.
b. Incorrect. The unconditioned stimulus elicits the unconditioned stimulus without any conditioning.
*c. Correct. The term applied to this stimulus is the conditioned stimulus.
d. Incorrect. This stimulus helps an organism in instrumental conditioning discriminate between times when a reinforcement would be given and times when a reinforcement is not available.

3. d   obj. 2   p. 157
a. Incorrect. Since the rat did not give rise to fear response, then it could not have been considered an unconditioned stimulus for this study.
b. Incorrect. This has another meaning in some other area of science.
c. Incorrect. The discriminative stimulus helps an organism in instrumental conditioning discriminate

between times when a reinforcement would be given and times when a reinforcement is not available.
*d. Correct. Because it would not give rise to the fear response, it would be considered neutral.

4. b   obj. 3   p. 159
a. Incorrect. This situation sounds more like extinction or avoidance.
*b. Correct. This hierarchy allows the learner to extinguish the fear gradually.
c. Incorrect. This sounds like avoidance.
d. Incorrect. This reverses the graduated approach used in systematic desensitization.

5. b   obj. 3   p. 159
a. Incorrect. This does not describe escape conditioning.
*b. Correct. The conditioned stimulus loses its value as a predictor of the unconditioned stimulus.
c. Incorrect. This does not describe stimulus generalization.
d. Incorrect. Negative reinforcement actually is intended to increase a desired behaviour.

6. a   obj. 4   p. 160
*a. Correct. The cognitive learning theorists have demonstrated that learning can occur as the transformation of mental processes, like the construction of a cognitive map, that later guides behaviour.
b. Incorrect. The Brelands primarily utilized operant conditioning and are concerned with other issues.
c. Incorrect. Thorndike's law of effect does not repudiate classical ideas so much as add to them.
d. Incorrect. Operant conditioning does not repudiate the ideas of classical conditioning, and in fact, is subject to the same challenges.

7. c   obj. 6   p. 170
a. Incorrect. See answer c.
b. Incorrect. See answer c.
*c. Correct. The period f time (interval) is set (fixed).
d. Incorrect. See answer c.

8. d   obj. 5   p. 162
a. Incorrect. The consequence of the behaviour is escape.
b. Incorrect. The consequence of the behaviour is the avoided speeding ticket.
c. Incorrect. The consequence of the behaviour is the biscuit reward.
*d. Correct. The chemistry professor is a conditioned stimulus to which high blood pressure is the response.

9. c   obj. 4, 5 p. 156, 162
a. Incorrect. Pavlov developed classical conditioning.
b. Incorrect. Skinner developed operant conditioning.
*c. Correct. Wertheimer was one of the gestalt psychologists.

d. Incorrect. Thorndike developed the law of effect, a cornerstone of operant conditioning.

10. c   obj. 5   p. 164
a. Incorrect. Food is not considered to be a discriminative stimulus unless an organism has been trained to view it as such.
b. Incorrect. Food satisfies a need; but it may also be a motive (as is true with money).
*c. Correct. Since food satisfies a basic need, it is considered primary; since money must be conditioned to have any reinforcing value, it is a secondary reinforcer.
d. Incorrect. Food may be a drive reducer, but money is not a natural reinforcer.

11. b   obj. 5   p. 164
a. Incorrect. Money requires conditioning to become a reinforcer.
*b. Correct. Water satisfies a basic need, thus it is a primary reinforcer.
c. Incorrect. Good grades require conditioning to become reinforcers.
d. Incorrect. To be a reinforcer, the hammer would require some, though not much, conditioning.

12. d   obj. 5   p. 166
a. Incorrect. The employee would probably become angry for being punished for such a minor offence.
b. Incorrect. The physical spanking reinforces the idea that violence is a way to make others cooperate.
c. Incorrect. Punishment for a teenager can often become an opportunity for reinforcement through attention from friends.
*d. Correct. When self-endangerment occurs, quick and angerless punishment can make the child become attentive to the danger.

13. d   obj. 6   p. 169
a. Incorrect. The time interval for making each piece can change, but the rate is one payment for every three pieces.
b. Incorrect. Variable interval would suggest that the worker would not know when payment would come.
c. Incorrect. In this pattern, the payment would come after five, then three, then four, etc., pieces were made—not every three.
*d. Correct. This is a fixed-ratio schedule.

14. d   obj. 6   p. 168
a. Incorrect. They may speed up just before the interval has ended.
b. Incorrect. They do not become extinguished.
c. Incorrect. They slow down just after the reinforcement.
*d. Correct. The predictability of the interval leads the organism to pause just after the reinforcement.

15. b   obj. 6   p. 168

a. Incorrect. Reinforcement does not inhibit the desired behaviour.
*b. Correct. Shaping is the technique of rewarding each successive behaviour that gets closer to the desired behaviour.
c. Incorrect. Reinforcement would not disrupt the targeted behaviour.
d. Incorrect. Reinforcement would not eliminate the target behaviour.

16. a   obj. 3   p. 159
17. e   obj. 3   p. 159
18. b   obj. 3   p. 160
19. c   obj. 3   p. 160
20. d   obj. 3   p. 160
21. generalization   obj. 3   p. 160
22. discrimination   obj. 3   p. 160
23. Operant conditioning   obj. 5   162
24. Reinforcement   obj. 5   p. 164

25.
▪ Describe each of the three approaches in such a way that they are clearly distinguished.
▪ Identify points of contradiction with each. In classical conditioning, the stimuli must precede the responses; in operant conditioning, the reinforcing stimuli comes after the response; in observational learning, the behaviour does not need to be practised. Mental processes are also involved in observational learning.
▪ Observational learning may actually be reconciled with the other two once mental processes and reinforcement of the model (rather than the learner) are allowed.

Practise Test 3:
1. a   obj. 2   p. 157
*a. Correct. The bell is being used just as the unconditioned stimulus had been in the earlier training.
b. Incorrect. While the bell is a conditioned stimulus, for the purpose of the second training event, it is unconditioned stimulus.
c. Incorrect. The bell is not a response.
d. Incorrect. The bell is not a response.

2. a   obj. 2   p. 157
*a. Correct. The food elicits a response that has not been conditioned.
b. Incorrect. The juicer is the unconditioned response.
c. Incorrect. Food is not a response.
d. Incorrect. Food is not a response.

3. b   obj. 2   p. 157
a. Incorrect. The food is the unconditioned stimulus.
*b. Correct. The child has become conditioned to the blender as the signal for food.
c. Incorrect. The blender is not a response.
d. Incorrect. The blender is not a response.

4.   a   obj. 2   p. 157

*a.   Correct. The sickness occurs without any training, and should thus be considered the "unconditioned" response.

b.   Incorrect. Sickness is a response, not a stimulus in this scenario.

c.   Incorrect. As a response to the poison, the sickness is unconditioned.

d.   Incorrect. If the response of sickness were to the sight of the bait, then it would be "conditioned."

5.   b   obj. 5   p. 163

a.   Incorrect. Generalization would imply the dog barking at any little boy.

*b.   Correct. The bark may have occurred freely, without association and without reinforcement, and would thus be "operant."

c.   Incorrect. Typically, a reinforcer follows the reinforced behaviour.

d.   Incorrect. Barking may accompany aversive responses, but the pattern requires something to be avoided.

6.   a   obj. 3   p. 160

*a.   Correct. Of these choices, this best fits; the child learns to discriminate among different qualities of roses.

b.   Incorrect. With generalization, the discrimination of colours would decline.

c.   Incorrect. There is no such concept as spontaneous generalization.

d.   Incorrect. Spontaneous recovery occurs after extinction has been followed by a period of rest.

7.   a   obj. 3   p. 160

*a.   Correct. This is very discrete training and requires that the dog not respond to similar odours.

b.   Incorrect. If response generalization existed, this would not be it.

c.   Incorrect. Partial reinforcement may have been used in the training, but the ability indicates stimulus generalization.

d.   Incorrect. Spontaneous recovery requires extinction to occur.

8.   c   obj. 6   p. 170

a.   Incorrect. See answer c.

b.   Incorrect. See answer c.

*c.   Correct. The learner quickly identifies the apparent "wait time" that follows a reinforcement in a fixed interval training schedule and thus does not respond for a period of time as no reinforcement will be forthcoming.

d.   Incorrect. See answer c.

9.   c   obj. 8   p. 173

a.   Incorrect. A personality psychologist would be more interested in traits than learned maps.

b.   Incorrect. A sensory psychologist would measure the sensory responses of the children.

*c.   Correct. He was demonstrating how children form cognitive maps and then demonstrate their knowledge at a later point in time.

d.   Incorrect. A biopsychologist might be interested in the underlying processes that account for the learning.

10.   d   obj. 8   p. 174

a.   Incorrect. Partial reinforcement supports the idea that not all performance needs to be reinforced.

b.   Incorrect. Classical conditioning depends upon performance for evidence of learning.

c.   Incorrect. Shaping involves the gradual modification of behaviour toward a desired form.

*d.   Correct. While performance is a measure of learning, the possibility of unmeasured learning is not ruled out.

11.   c   obj. 5   p. 166

a.   Incorrect. Playing the music loud in the first place was a form of punishment.

b.   Incorrect. Positive reinforcement refers to pleasant consequences for a target behaviour (studying is the target behaviour, not finding peace and quiet).

*c.   Correct. "Negative" in this case is the removal of an unwanted stimulus in order to increase a desired behaviour (studying).

d.   Incorrect. She is being rewarded by removal, not punished.

12.   d   obj. 9   p p. 170, 171

a.   Incorrect. Some scientists make stronger claims with only twenty or thirty subjects.

b.   Incorrect. This cannot be determined from this statement.

c.   Incorrect. The study does not indicate how the viewing data was gathered.

*d.   Correct. This is correct only if the researchers claim or imply a causal relationship.

13.   a   obj. 9   p. 178

*a.   Correct. These abstract skills are qualities in the formal Inuit system of education.

b.   Incorrect. These practical skills appertain to the *isumaqsayuq* model in the Inuit system of education.

c.   Incorrect. It could possibly, but this is a wild guess, and it is unclear how it could. It's better to rely on the facts in choice a.

d.   Incorrect. Another wild guess. It's better to rely on the facts in choice a.

14.   b   obj. 9   p. 180

a.   Incorrect. Identifying which area to work on first should precede this step.

*b.   Correct. Identifying objective goals is the first step in making a realistic attempt to improve learning.

c.   Incorrect. This is a later step of the program.

d.   Incorrect. After identifying which classes to work on, he could then identify a specific study skill.

15. f   obj. 6   p. 169

16. a obj. 6 p. 169
17. e obj. 6 p. 170
18. c obj. 6 p. 170
19. b obj. 5 p. 164
20. d obj. 6 p. 170
21. reinforcer obj. 5 p. 164
22. positive obj. 5 p. 165
23. Punishment obj. 5 p. 167

24.
- Establish what behaviours need to be changed.
- Use the concept of Skinner's "shaping" to reward successive approximations of the desired behaviour.
- Decide what reward will be used to reinforce the change.
- Explain the type of reinforcement schedule that would be most effective.

Memory

6

Chapter 6 looks at the nature of memory. First, the several ways that information is encoded, stored and then later retrieved is discussed. Following this, a discussion that suggests that there are several separate types of memory is presented. Each of these approaches functions in a somewhat different way. Next, we examine the problems of retrieving information from memory. We look at the accuracy of memories and the reason that we sometimes forget information. The biological foundations of memory is addressed also. Finally, we discuss some practical methods one can use to increase his or her memory.

To further investigate the topics covered in this chapter, you can access the related websites by visiting the following link: http://www.mcgrawhill.ca/college/feldman

> **Applying Psychology in the 21st Century:** Repressed Memories: Truth or Fiction?

Autobiographical Memory: Where Past Meets Present

> **Exploring Diversity:** Are There Cross-Cultural Differences in Memory?

Section 3: Forgetting: When Memory Fails

Proactive and Retroactive Interference: The Before and After of Forgetting
Memory Dysfunctions: Afflictions of Forgetting

> **Pathways Through Psychology: Holly Tuokko, Associaye Director**
> Centre on Aging: Associate Professor of Psychology

> **Becoming an Informed Consumer of Psychology:**
> Improving Your Memory

Learning Objectives

These are the concepts and the learning objectives for Chapter 6. Read them carefully as part of your preliminary survey of the chapter.

Encoding, Storage, and Retrieval of Memory

1. Define memory and the basic processes of encoding, storing, and retrieving information. (p. 188)

2. Describe sensory memory, discuss the characteristics of short-term memory, and summarize the evidence for the existence of long-term memory as distinct from short-term memory. (pp. 189–193)

3. Describe the four contemporary approaches to memory, discussing levels of processing theory and distinguishing between declarative and procedural memories, semantic and episodic memories, priming, and implicit and explicit memories. (pp. 193-198)

4. Describe the biological basis of memory. (pp. 198-199).

Recalling Long-Term Memories

5. Distinguish between recall and recognition and discuss the levels of processing theory of memory. (pp. 200–201)

6. Describe the concept of flashbulb memories. (pp. 202)

7. Define constructive processes. Consider issues regarding the accuracy of constructed memories, including autobiographical memory. (pp. 203–206)

Forgetting: When Memory Fails

8. Discuss how memories are forgotten, especially the roles of proactive and retroactive interference. (pp. 207–208)

9. Describe the biological bases of memory and distinguish between the common memory disorders. (pp. 209–211)

10. Describe techniques for improving memory skills. (pp. 211–212)

SECTION 1: Encoding, Storage, and Retrieval of Memory

Prepare

- *What is memory?*
- *Are there different kinds of memory?*

Organize

- *The Three Systems of Memory*
- *Contemporary Approaches to Memory*

Work

Three processes comprise memory. **[a]** _____ is the process of placing information in a form that can be used by memory. **[b]** _____ is the process of retaining information for later use. **[c]** _____ is the process of recovering information from storage. By definition, then, **[d]** _____ is the sum of these three processes. Forgetting is an important part of memory because it allows us to make generalizations and abstractions from daily life.

The memory system is typically divided into three storage components or stages. The initial storage system is that of **[e]** _____, where momentary storage of sensory information occurs. **[f]** _____ includes information that has been given some form of meaning, and it lasts for 15 to 25 seconds. **[g]** _____ is the relatively permanent storage of memory. While there are no locations in the brain of these memory stages, they are considered abstract memory systems with different characteristics.

Sensory memories differ according to the kind of sensory information, and the sensory memory is thought of as several types of sensory memories based on the source of the sensory messages. Visual sensory memory is called **[h]** _____, and its source is the visual sensory system; and auditory sensory memory is called **[i]** _____, and its source is the auditory sensory system. Sensory memory stores information for a very short time. Iconic memory may last no more than a second, and echoic memory may last for three to four seconds. The duration of iconic memory was established by George Sperling's classic experiment in which subjects were unable to recall an entire array of letters but could, on a cue after the array was shown for one-twentieth of a second, recall any part of the array. Unless the information taken into the sensory memories is somehow transferred to another memory system, the sensory memories are quickly lost.

Sensory memories are raw information without meaning. In order to be transferred to the long-term memory, these sensory memories must be given meaning and placed in short-term memory. One view of this process suggests that the short-term memory is composed of verbal representations that have a very short duration. George Miller has identified the capacity of short-term memory as seven plus or minus two **[j]** _____, or meaningful groups of stimuli that are stored as a unit in the short-term memory. They can be several letters or numbers or can be complicated patterns, like the patterns of pieces on a chessboard. However, to be placed in a chunk, the board must represent a real or possible game even for chess masters to be able to make a chunk.

Information can be held in short-term memory longer by **[k]** _____, the repetition of information already in the short-term memory. Rehearsal also begins the transferal of information from short-term memory to long-term memory. The rehearsal technique used influences the effectiveness of the transfer to long-term memory. **[l]** _____ occurs whenever the material is associated with other information through placement in a logical framework, connection with another memory, the formation of an image, or some other transformation. The strategies for organizing memories are called **[m]** _____. Mnemonics are formal techniques for organizing information so that recall is more likely.

[n] _____ comes from Baddeley's theory that short-term memory has three components: the *central executive*, the *visuospatial sketch pad*, and the *phonological loop*.

Two kinds of long-term memory have been identified, **[o]** _____ and **[p]** _____. Procedural memory includes the memory for skills and habits, like walking, riding a bicycle, and other physical activity. Declarative memory includes **[q]** _____, memories of specific events related to individual experiences, and **[r]** _____, those that consist of abstract knowledge and facts about the world. Psychologists use [s] _____ to suggest that semantic memories represent the associations between mental representations of various pieces of information. When we think about a particular thing, related ideas are activated because of the association.

[t]_____ refers to the activation of one item, thereby making recall of

related items easier. [u] _____ refers to intentional or conscious

recollection of information. [v] _____ refers to memories of which people are not consciously aware but which nevertheless can affect later behaviour.

An alternative to the three-stage view of memory is the [v] _____. This theory suggests that the difference in memories depends on the depth to which particular information is processed, that is, the degree to which information is analyzed and considered. The more attention information is given, the deeper it is stored and the less likely it is to be forgotten. Superficial aspects of information are given shallow processing, and when meaning is given, the processing is at its deepest level. This approach suggests that memory requires more active mental processing than does the three-stage approach.

Evaluate

_____ 1. storage

_____ 2. retrieval

_____ 3. sensory memory

_____ 4. short-term memory

_____ 5. long-term memory

a. Locating and using information stored in memory.

b. Relatively permanent memory.

c. Information recorded as a replica of the stimulus and typically lasting only an instant

d. Working memory that lasts about 15 to 25 seconds.

e. The retention of information that was placed into memory systems

Rethink

1. It is a truism that "you never forget how to ride a bicycle." Why might this be so? Where is information about bicycle riding stored? What happens when a person has to retrieve that information after not using it for a long time?

2. Priming often occurs without conscious awareness. How might this effect be used by advertisers and others to promote their products? What ethical principals are involved? Can you think of a way to protect yourself from unethical advertisers?

Section 2: Recalling Long-Term Memories

Prepare

- **What causes difficulties and failures in remembering?**

Organize

- *Retrieval Cues*
- *Levels of Processing*
- *Flashbulb Memories*
- *Constructive Processes in Memory*
- *Memory in the Courtroom*
- *Autobiographical Memory*

Work

Retrieving information from long-term memory may be influenced by many factors. The

[a] _____, where one is certain of knowing something but cannot recall it, represents one difficulty. The simple number of items of information that has been stored may

influence recall. We sort through this quantity with the help of [b] _____. These are stimuli that allow recall from long-term memory. *Recall* consists of a series of processes—a search through memory, retrieval of potentially relevant information, then a decision whether the information is accurate, and a continuation of these steps until the right information is found. In contrast, *recognition* involves determining whether a stimulus that has been presented is correct, such as the selection of the stimulus from a list or determining whether the stimulus has been seen before.

In particularly intense events, we may develop [c] _____. A specific, important or surprising event creates memories so vivid that they appear as if a snapshot of the event. Research regarding flashbulb memories concerning President Kennedy's assassination has revealed common details, such as where the person was, who told the person, the person's own emotions, and some personal detail of the event. Harsh and Neisser asked students the day after the *Challenger* accident how they had heard about it, and then asked the same question three years later. One-third were wrong, a result suggesting that flashbulb memories may be inaccurate. Memories that are exceptional may be more easily retrieved than commonplace information.

Our memories represent [d] _____, processes because they are influenced by the meanings we attach to them. Guesses and inferences thus influence memory. Sir Frederic Bartlett first suggested that people remember in terms of

[e] _____, which are general themes without specific details. Schemas were based on an understanding of the event, expectations, and an understanding of the motivation of others. The process of *serial reproduction*, in which people pass on a story from one to another in a sequence, has shown the effect of schemas. The final version of the story is much changed in comparison to the original version, and it reflects the expectations of those retelling the story. Apparently, prior knowledge and expectations influence how we initially store the information. How we understand peoples' motivation also influences memory. In the

[f] _____, knowledge about a person's motivation leads to an elaboration of past events involving that person.

The imperfection of memory has led to research into the accuracy of eye-witness testimony. The mistaken identification of individuals can lead to imprisonment. When a weapon is involved, the weapon draws attention away from other details. In research involving staged crimes, witnesses vary significantly in their judgment of the height of the perpetrator, with judgments differing by as much as two feet. The wording of questions can influence testimony. Children are especially prone to unreliable recollections.

The case of George Franklin illustrates the impact recovered memories can have (he was found guilty on the basis of these memories alone). While childhood recollections can be forgotten and then recovered, the evidence does suggest that much distortion can take place as well, even to the point of fabricating false memories from childhood.

[g] _____ are our collections of information about our lives. People tend to forget information about the past that is incongruent with the way they currently see themselves. Depressed people tend to recall sad events more readily than happy ones from their past. More recent information also appears to be more effected than recollections from earlier times.

Evaluate

_____ 1.   recall

_____ 2.   recognition

_____ 3.   flashbulb memories

_____ 4.   serial reproduction

_____ 5.   soap opera effect

a. Drawing from memory a specific piece of information for a specific purpose.

b. The phenomena by which memory of a prior event involving a person is more reliable when we understand that person's motivations.

c. Memories of a specific event that are so clear they seem like "snapshots" of the event.

d. Acknowledging prior exposure to a given stimulus, rather than recalling the information from memory.

e. The passage of interpretive information from person to person, often resulting in inaccuracy through personal bias and misinterpretation.

Rethink

3.   How do schemas help people process information during encoding, storage, and retrieval? In what ways are they helpful? Can they contribute to inaccurate autobiographical memories?

4.   How might courtroom procedure be improved, based on what you've learned about memory errors and biases?

SECTION 3: Forgetting: When Memory Fails

Prepare

- *Why do we forget information?*
- *What are the biological bases of memory?*

- **What are the major memory impairments?**

Organize

- **Proactive and Retroactive Interference**
- **The Biological Bases of Memory**
- **Memory Dysfunctions**

Work

Herman Ebbinghaus studied forgetting by learning a list of nonsense syllables and then timing how long it took him, at a later trial, to relearn the list. The most rapid forgetting occurs in the first nine hours. Two views concerning the forgetting of information have been developed.

One theory explains forgetting by **[a]** _____, or the loss of information

through non-use. When a memory is formed, a **[b]** _____, or

[c] _____, is formed. An engram is an actual physical change in the brain. The decay theory assumes that memories become more decayed with time, but the evidence does not support this happening, though there is support for the existence of decay. The other theory

proposes that **[d]** _____ between bits of information leads to forgetting. In interference, information blocks or displaces other information, preventing recall. Most forgetting appears to be the result of interference.

There are two kinds of interference. One is called **[e]** _____ *interference* that occurs when previously learned information blocks the recall of newer

information. **[f]** _____ *interference* is when recent information blocks the recall of previous information. Most research suggests that information that has been blocked by interference can eventually be recalled if appropriate stimuli are used.

The biological bases of memory at the level of the neuron point to the underlying process of

[g] _____, or the change in the excitability of a neuron at the synapse. As

these changes occur, the process of **[h]** _____, or transfer of short-term memories to long-term memories, takes place. It was originally thought that memories were evenly distributed throughout the brain. However, the current view suggests that the areas of the brain that are responsible for processing information about the world also store that information.

[i] _____ *disease* includes severe memory problems as one of its many symptoms. Initially, the symptoms appear as simple forgetfulness, progressing to more profound loss of memory, even failure to recognize one's own name and the loss of language abilities. The protein beta amyloid, important for maintaining neural connections, has been implicated in the

progress of the disease. **[j]** _____ is another memory problem. Amnesia is a loss of memory occurring without apparent loss of mental function.

[k] _____ is memory loss for memories that preceded a traumatic event.

[l] _____ is a loss of memories that follow a traumatic event. Long-term alcoholics who develop *Korsakoff's syndrome* also have amnesia. Korsakoff's syndrome is related to thiamine deficiency. A perfect memory, one with total recall, might actually be very discomforting. A case studied by Luria of a man with total recall reveals that the inability to forget becomes debilitating.

The Informed Consumer of Psychology section outlines several mnemonic techniques and how they can be applied to taking tests. They include the *keyword technique*, in which one pairs a word with a mental image, or in the case of learning a foreign language, the foreign word with a similar sounding English word. The *method of loci* requires that one imagine items to be remembered as being placed in particular locations. Another phenomenon that affects memory is

called **[m]** _____ . Recall is best when it is attempted in conditions that are similar to the conditions under which the information was originally learned. The organization of text and lecture material may enhance memory of it. Practise and rehearsal also improve long-term recall. Rehearsal to the point of mastery is called *overlearning*. It should be noted that cramming for exams is an ineffective technique, and the better approach is to distribute practise over many sessions.

Evaluate

_____ 1. Alzheimer's disease

_____ 2. amnesia

_____ 3. retrograde amnesia

_____ 4. anterograde amnesia

_____ 5. Korsakoff's syndrome

a. An illness associated with aging that includes severe memory loss and loss of language abilities.

b. A memory impairment disease among alcoholics.

c. Memory loss unaccompanied by other mental difficulties.

d. Memory loss of the events following an injury.

e. Memory loss of occurrences prior to some event.

Rethink

5. Does the phenomenon of interference help explain the unreliability of autobiographical memory? Why?

6. How might findings on the biological mechanisms of memory aid in the treatment of memory disorders such as amnesia?

Practise Questions

Test your knowledge of the chapter material by answering these questions. These questions have been placed in three Practise Tests. The first two tests are composed of questions that will test your recall of factual knowledge. The third test contains questions that are challenging and primarily test for conceptual knowledge and your ability to apply that knowledge. Check your answers and review the feedback using the Answer Key on the following pages of the *Study Guide*.

PRACTISE TEST 1:

1. The process of identifying and using information stored in memory is referred to as:
   a. storage.
   b. retrieval.
   c. recording.
   d. learning.

2. The process of recording information in a form that can be recalled is:
   a. encoding.
   b. storage.
   c. decoding.
   d. retrieval.

3. _____ memory stores information for approximately 15 to 25 seconds.
   a. Sensory
   b. Short-term
   c. Iconic
   d. Long-term

4. Short-term memory can hold approximately _____ items.
   a. five
   b. seven
   c. ten
   d. eighteen

5. Recalling what we have done and the kinds of experiences we have had best illustrates _____ memory.
   a. periodic
   b. episodic
   c. semantic
   d. serial production

6. Rehearsal:
   a. facilitates neither short-term memory nor long-term memory.
   b. has no effect on short-term memory duration, yet it facilitates the transfer of material into long-term memory.
   c. helps to prolong information in short-term memory but has no effect on the transfer of material into long-term memory.
   d. extends the duration of information in short-term memory and also assists its transfer into long-term memory.

7. If your episodic long-term memory were disabled, you would be unable to:
   a. remember details of your own personal life.
   b. recall simple facts such as the name of the U.S. president.
   c. speak, although you could still comprehend language through listening.
   d. maintain information in short-term memory via rehearsal.

8. Information from long-term memory is easier to access with the aid of:
   a. a retrieval cue.
   b. distractors.
   c. interpolated material.
   d. a sensory code.

9. Constructive processes are associated with all of the following **except**:
   a. episodic memory.
   b. motivation.
   c. procedural memory.
   d. organization.

10. The tip-of-the-tongue phenomenon exemplifies difficulties in:

a. encoding.
b. decoding.

c. storage.
d. retrieval.

11. After memorizing a series of nonsense syllables, Ebbinghaus discovered that forgetting was most dramatic _____ following learning.
   a. two days
   b. an hour

   c. ten days
   d. one day

12. Repeatedly reciting a verbal sequence of words:
   a. minimizes the effects of proactive interference.
   b. prevents trace decay from occurring.
   c. activates different brain areas than when the word sequence is spoken the first time.
   d. is a characteristic symptom of the disorder known as Korsakoff's syndrome; this symptom can, in most cases, be treated with drugs.

13. Which situation below is characteristic of anterograde amnesia?
   a. A person has loss of memory for events prior to some critical event.
   b. A person receives a physical trauma to the head and has difficulty remembering things after the accident.
   c. A person forgets simple skills such as how to dial a telephone.
   d. A person begins to experience difficulties in remembering appointments and relevant dates such as birthdays.

14. Memories lost under retrograde amnesia sometimes are recovered later; this implies that the amnesia interfered with the process of:
   a. encoding.
   b. storage.

   c. retrieval.
   d. association.

15. The keyword technique is a memory aid that can be helpful in learning a foreign language. The first step is to identify:
   a. a word that has similar meaning in a familiar language and pair it with the foreign word to be learned.
   b. a word that has a similar sound in a familiar language to at least part of the foreign word and pair it with the foreign word to be learned.
   c. a word that suggests similar imagery in a familiar language and pair it with the foreign word to be learned.
   d. the first word to come to mind in a familiar language and pair it with the foreign word to be learned.

a. Memory for skills and habits.

____ 16.   echoic memory

b. Stored information relating to personal experiences.

____ 17.   episodic memories

c. Stored, organized facts about the world (e.g., mathematical and historical data).

____ 18.   semantic memories

____ 19.   declarative memory

d. The storage of information obtained from the sense of hearing.

____ 20.   procedural memory

e. Memory for facts and knowledge.

21.   Recording information in a form usable to memory is _____.

22.   _____ memory is the storage of visual information.

23.   A stimulus such as a word, smell, or sound that aids recall of information located in long-term memory is a _____.

24.   Rehearsing material beyond the point of mastery to improve long-term recall is _____.

25.   _____ is a technique of recalling information by thinking about related information.

26.   What role should psychologists play in helping the courts deal with repressed memories of abuse that have been recovered? Consider both the advantages and disadvantages of the answer you give.

PRACTISE TEST 2:

1.   Information deteriorates most quickly from _____ memory.
   a.   explicit
   b.   short-term
   c.   sensory
   d.   episodic declarative

2.   Recording information in the memory system is referred to as:
   a.   encoding.
   b.   storage.
   c.   decoding.
   d.   retrieval.

3.   Information in short-term memory is stored according to its:
   a.   meaning.
   b.   intensity.
   c.   length.
   d.   sense.

4.   The process of grouping information into units for storage in short-term memory is called:
   a.   similarity.
   b.   priming.
   c.   chunking.
   d.   closure.

5. Knowledge about grammar, spelling, historical dates, and other knowledge about the world best illustrates _____ memory.:
    a. periodic
    b. episodic
    c. semantic
    d. interpolation

6. _____ may be necessary while information is in the short-term stage, in order to enhance consolidation of long-term memory.
    a. Massed practice
    b. Elaborative rehearsal
    c. Interpolation
    d. Interference

7. According to the levels-of-processing model, what determines how well specific information is remembered?
    a. the stage attained
    b. the meaning of the information
    c. the quality of the information
    d. the depth of information processing

8. Finding the correct answer on a multiple choice test depends on:
    a. serial search.
    b. recall.
    c. mnemonics.
    d. recognition.

9. Your memory of how to skate is probably based on:
    a. procedural memory.
    b. semantic memory.
    c. elaborative rehearsal.
    d. declarative memory.

10. The detailed, vivid account of what you were doing when you learned of the *Challenger* disaster represents a:
    a. cognitive map.
    b. schema.
    c. flashbulb memory.
    d. seizure.

11. Which explanation has **not** been offered to account for how we forget information that was learned?
    a. decay
    b. interference
    c. spontaneous inhibition
    d. inadequate processing during learning

12. All of the following have been associated with the biological basis of memory **except**:
    a. the hippocampus.
    b. sulci.
    c. neurotransmitters.
    d. long-term potentiation.

13. Which of the following syndromes is the **least** common?
    a. retrograde amnesia
    b. anterograde amnesia
    c. Alzheimer's disease
    d. Korsakoff's syndrome

14. The fundamental issue surrounding the controversy about repressed memories is whether the memories:
    a. are retrieved from long-term memory or from other type of memory.
    b. can be counteracted by therapy.
    c. have any noticeable effect on mental activities or behaviour.
    d. are genuine recollections from the past.

15. Which alternative below is **least** likely to help you do well on your next psychology quiz?

a. Use a prioritized strategy by studying the material only the day before the quiz and avoiding any other subjects that might interfere.
b. Overlearn the material.
c. Take brief lecture notes that focus on major points and that emphasize organization.
d. Ask yourself questions about the material as you study.

_____ 16. memory trace

_____ 17. proactive interference

_____ 18. retroactive interference

_____ 19. keyword technique

_____ 20. memory

a. The pairing of a foreign word with a common, similar sounding English word to aid in remembering the new word.

b. A physical change in the brain corresponding to the memory of material.

c. New information interferes with the recall of information learned earlier.

d. The system used to store the results of learning.

e. Information stored in memory interferes with recall of material learned later.

21. The ability to retrieve and reproduce previously encountered material is called _____.

22. _____ is the ability to identify previously encountered material.

23. _____ is the loss of ability to remember events or experiences that occurred before some particular point in time.

24. Breaking information into meaningful units of information is called _____.

25. Much of our knowledge about memory comes from strictly laboratory studies. Consider how the lack of "real-life" memory studies may bias the kinds of results about how memory works in our daily lives. Do you have any suggestions for how psychologists might study memory in daily life?

PRACTISE TEST 3: Conceptual, Applied, and Challenging Questions

1. While Nick was watching a movie, his young son talked excitedly about the new bike his friend was getting. Somewhat frustrated, the boy exclaimed, "You're not paying attention to me!" At this point, Nick diverted his attention to his son and recited the last few things the boy had said. Which memory system is responsible for this ability?
   a. episodic memory
   b. echoic memory
   c. iconic memory
   d. short-term memory

2. Sensory memory is the information that is:
   a. held until it is replaced by new information.
   b. an accurate representation of the stimulus.
   c. an incomplete representation of the stimulus.

    d.   lost if it is not meaningful.

3.   A story is likely to be transformed when it has been told over and over and:
    a.   ambiguous details become regularized to fit the person's expectations.
    b.   distinctive features of the story are dropped out.
    c.   engrams that were located will become lost.
    d.   the original story will become a "flashbulb," with excellent recall even after several serial reproductions.

4.   Older computer monitor screens sometimes have a brief persistence of the old image when the image is changed. This persistence of the monitor image is analogous to _____ memory.
    a.   flashbulb   c.   echoic
    b.   iconic   d.   declarative

5.   Beth's basketball coach instructs her to practise a basic foul shot for about thirty minutes each day in order to improve her shot. After she does what the coach has suggested, she discovers that she can make a shot without any thought and with complete confidence. This is a demonstration of what kind of memory?
    a.   working memory   c.   autobiographical memory
    b.   declarative memory   d.   procedural memory

6.   After twenty years of not having been on a bicycle, the cycle-shop manager will allow Daniel's son to test a cycle only if Daniel rides one beside him. Within ten seconds, Daniel has adjusted to the bicycle and is even more confident than his son, who has just learned to ride. This is a demonstration of which kind of memory?
    a.   working memory   c.   recovered, repressed memories
    b.   procedural memory   d.   autobiographical memory

7.   Who was responsible for the concept of schemas?
    a.   Sigmund Freud   c.   Frederic Bartlett
    b.   Jean Piaget   d.   Robert Feldman

8.   "The strength of a memory relates directly to the kind of attention given to it when the information was experienced." This statement supports most directly the _____ model of memory.
    a.   three-stage
    b.   mental imagery
    c.   levels-of-processing
    d.   cultural diversity

9.   You are asked to write your new address and phone number on the back of a check. Instead, you write your previous address and number. You are experiencing:
    a.   retroactive interference.   c.   amnesia.
    b.   fugue.   d.   proactive interference.

10.   Lyle learns the word-processing program "Easy Word" on his personal computer. Then he learns a second program, "Perfect Word," at work. He now finds it difficult to remember some of the commands when he uses his word processor at home. This is an example of _____ interference.
    a.   work-induced   c.   proactive
    b.   retroactive   d.   spontaneous

11. A waiter forgets a customer's order because twenty other persons' orders have been completed during the intervening hour. The reduced recall of that customer's order reflects:
    a. Alzheimer's disease.
    b. decay.
    c. proactive interference.
    d. retroactive interference.

12. Alzheimer's disease is associated with deterioration of:
    a. the neurological connection between the spinal cord and muscles.
    b. the connection between the hemispheres.
    c. the manufacture of beta amyloid.
    d. the basal ganglia and lower brain structures.

13. Which situation below is most characteristic of retrograde amnesia?
    a. A person begins to experience difficulties in remembering appointments and relevant dates such as birthdays.
    b. A person receives a physical trauma to the head and has difficulty remembering things after the accident.
    c. A person forgets simple skills such as how to dial a telephone.
    d. A person has loss of memory for events prior to some critical event.

14. Tia, the star of the soap opera *Days and Nights* has found herself without any memory of her past life from a point in time only a few episodes ago. Should her memory failure be real, which of the following types of memory loss best describes her condition?
    a. retrograde amnesia
    b. anterograde amnesia
    c. infantile amnesia
    d. Korsakoff's syndrome

____ 15. rehearsal

____ 16. associative models

____ 17. encoding specificity

____ 18. overlearning

____ 19. retrieval cue

a. A stimulus such as a word, smell, or sound that aids recall of information located in long-term memory.

b. Memory of information is enhanced when recalled under the same conditions as when it was learned.

c. The transfer of material from short- to long-term memory by repetition.

d. Rehearsing material beyond the point of mastery to improve long-term recall.

e. A technique of recalling information by thinking about related information.

20. A technique of recalling information by having been exposed to related information at an earlier time is called _____.

21. We refer to changes in sensitivity at the neuron's synapse as _____.

22. _____ is the process of creating long-term memories.

23. Recollections of the facts about our own lives are referred to as _____.

24. When a person adds meaning to the added information to be remembered, it is called

_____.

25. List the factors that can reduce the accuracy of eyewitness testimony and describe how the misinformation effect works in memory dislocation.

Spotlight on Terminology and Language—
Cultural Idioms

Encoding, Storage, and Retrieving Memory

Page 188 "**Encoding** refers to the process by which information is initially recorded in a form usable to memory."

To **encode** is to transfer information from one system into another. During the **encoding** stage, information is changed into usable form. In the brain, sensory information becomes impulses that the central nervous system reads and codes. On a computer, **encoding** occurs when keyboard entries are transformed into electronic symbols, which are then stored on a computer disk.

Page 188"You can think of these processes as **analogous** to the function of a computer's keyboard (encoding), disk (**storage**), and screen (**retrieval**)."

An **analogy** is a comparison between two situations. During the **storage** stage of memory, information is held in memory. This is the mind's version of a computer hard drive. During the **retrieval** stage, stored memories are recovered from **storage**, just as a saved computer program is called up by name and used again.

Page 188 "Forgetting permits us to form general impressions and **recollections**. For example, the reason our friends consistently look familiar to us is because of our ability to forget their clothing, facial blemishes, and other **transient** features that change from one occasion to the next."
Recollect is to recall, as when you have a memory. **Transient** is something that lasts only a short time. When you daydream you are often having **transient** thoughts.

Page 189 "The **storehouses** vary in terms of their function and the length of time they retain information."

A **storehouse** is a storage area, or a repository. The sea is the world's greatest **storehouse** of raw materials.

Page 189 "Information is recorded by the person's sensory system as an exact **replica** of the stimulus."

A **replica** is a copy or a duplicate. Sensory memory is an exact copy of what you see and hear.

Page 189 "Although the three-part model of memory **dominated** the field of memory research for several decades, recent studies have suggested several newer models."

To **dominate** means to influence and control the field of memory.

Page 190 "It was possible that the information had initially been accurately stored in sensory memory, but during the time it took to **verbalize** the first four or five letters the memory of the other letters faded.

Verbalize is to state in words.

Page 191 "Some theorists suggest that the information is first translated into **graphical** representations or images, and others **hypothesize** that the transfer occurs when the sensory stimuli are changed to words."

Graphical representations are pictorial or symbolic. To **hypothesize** is to assume. A **hypothesis** is a proposition tentatively assumed in order to draw out its logical or empirical consequences and so test its accord with facts that are known or may be determined. A condition of the most genuinely scientific **hypothesis** is that it be developed in such a way that it can be either proved or

disproved by comparison with observed facts.

Page 193 "**Mnemonic**s are formal techniques for organizing information in a way that makes it more likely to be remembered."

Mnemonic devices are memory techniques that involve associating new information with simpler information or information you already know.

Page 197 "Studies have found that people who are anesthetized during surgery can sometimes recall **snippets** of information that they heard during surgery—even though they have no conscious recollection of the information."

A **snippet** is a small part, a little piece.

Page 199 "It is a **truism** that 'you never forget how to ride a bicycle.'"

A **truism** is a self-evident truth. It is undisputed and obvious.

Page 200 "…the **tip-of-the-tongue** phenomenon—exemplifies the difficulties that can occur in retrieving information stored in long-term memory.

Something that is on the **tip of the tongue** is ready to be retrieved from your memory but cannot be brought forth at this time.

Page 200 "…Many psychologists have suggested that the material that makes its way to long-term memory is relatively **permanent**."

Permanent is something that is going to be remaining, something that continues and endures (as in the same state, status, or place) without fundamental or marked change. You think of something permanent as fixed. Can you describe

some of your permanent memories?

Page 200 "If you are like the average college student, your vocabulary includes some 50,000 works, you know hundreds of mathematical "facts," and you are able to **conjure up** images—such as the way your childhood home looked—with no trouble at all."

To **conjure up** is to image. You can **conjure up** many images.

Page 200 "The smell of roasting turkey might **evoke** memories of Thanksgiving or family gatherings."

When you **evoke** a memory, you call it up. You are summoning or eliciting this material.

Page 201 "Levels-of-processing theory has considerable practical **implications**."

To be able to make an **implication** means you are able to make an inference from this theory.

Page 202 "Where were you on September 11, 2001? You may **draw a blank** until this piece of information is added."

To **draw a blank** means to have no results from investing time, effort, money, attention, etc into something. In the present context, it means to have searched one's memory banks and not found the relevant information sought.

Page 203 "As we have seen, although it is clear that we can have detailed recollections of significant and distinctive events, it is difficult to **gauge** the accuracy of such memories."

To **gauge** is to be able to make a measurement of the dimensions or extent of something. It is difficult to gauge the extent of suffering experienced by someone else.

■ CHAPTER 6: ANSWER KEY

GUIDED REVIEW			
Section 1:	Evaluate	**Section 2:**	**Section 3:**
[a] Encoding	1. e	[a] tip-of-the-tongue	[a] decay
[b] Storage	2. a	phenomenon	[b] memory trace
[c] Retrieval	3. c	[b] retrieval cues	[c] engram
[d] memory	4. d	[c] flashbulb memories	[d] interference
[e] sensory memory	5. b	[d] constructive processes	[e] proactive
[f] Short-term memory		[e] schemas	[f] Retroactive
[g] Long-term memory		[f] soap opera effect	[g] long-term
[h] iconic memory		[g] Autobiographical	potentiation
[i] echoic memory		memories	[h] consolidation
[j] chunks			[i] Alzheimer's
[k] rehearsal			[j] Amnesia
[l] Elaborative rehearsal		Evaluate	[k] Retrograde amnesia
[m] mnemonics		1. a	[l] Anterograde amnesia
[n] Working memory		2. d	[m] encoding specificity
[o] declarative memory		3. c	
[p] procedural memory		4. e	
[q] episodic memories		5. b	Evaluate
[r] semantic memories			1. a
[s] associative models			2. c
[t] Priming			3. e
[u] Explicit memory			4. d
[v] implicit memory			5. b
[w] levels-of-processing			
theory			

Selected Rethink Answers

1. Memories for motor skills are extremely long lasting, they may be encoded and stored as kinesthetic (muscular) instructions.

4. Autobiographical memories are our recollections of circumstances and episodes from our lives. Interference means that old memories often interfere with the ability to retrieve new information or new memories interfere with the ability to retrieve old memories. Memories of our past are distorted. We may forget troubled childhoods. Remember passing grades not failing grades.

Practise Test 1:

1. b   obj. 1   p. 188
a. Incorrect. Storage refers to the retention of the encoded memory.
*b. Correct. Retrieval is the recovery of stored, encoded information so that it can be used.
c. Incorrect. Recording is the work of committing information to a record, like taking notes, etc.
d. Incorrect. See Chapter 5.

2. a   obj. 1   p. 188
*a. Correct. Encoding places the information in a manageable form.
b. Incorrect. Storage refers to the retention of the encoded memory.
c. Incorrect. Decoding must mean the removal of the code into which something has been encoded.

d. Incorrect. Retrieval is the recovery of stored, encoded information.

3. b   obj. 2   p. 189
a. Incorrect. Sensory memory has a life of less than a second.
*b. Correct. Unless material is rehearsed, information is quickly lost from the short-term memory.
c. Incorrect. Iconic memory refers to visual sensory memory and has a duration of less than a quarter of a second.
d. Incorrect. The duration of long-term memory is indefinite.

4. b   obj. 2   p. 191
a. Incorrect. It can hold up to nine items, but the average would be seven.
*b. Correct. Psychologists accept the view that we can hold about seven, plus or minus two items in short-term memory.
c. Incorrect. Psychologists accept the view that we can hold about seven, plus or minus two items in short-term memory.
d. Incorrect. Psychologists accept the view that we can hold about seven, plus or minus two items in short-term memory.

5. b   obj. 3   p. 195
a. Incorrect. No such memory concept.
*b. Correct. Memory of life events, or episodes, is one of the types of long-term memory.
c. Incorrect. Semantic memory is memory for declarative knowledge like words and definitions.
d. Incorrect. No concept like this has been used in contemporary psychology.

6. d   obj. 2   p. 191
a. Incorrect. Rehearsal facilitates all memory.
b. Incorrect. It does help short-term memory items persist in short-term memory.
c. Incorrect. It does aid in the transfer of memory to long-tem storage.
*d. Correct. It helps both short-term duration and long-term consolidation.

7. a   obj. 2   p. 195
*a. Correct. Episodic memory is the storage of stories and details about life—that is, episodes.
b. Incorrect. Facts like these are considered semantic.
c. Incorrect. Episodic memory has little to do with speaking.
d. Incorrect. This would not affect short-term memory.

8. a   obj. 5   p. 200
*a. Correct. Retrieval cues are aspects—connections, similarities, etc.—of information that help us recall, or retrieve, the information.
b. Incorrect. Distractors are the stems of multiple choice questions that are designed to distract the test-taker.
c. Incorrect. This is not the answer.
d. Incorrect. The sensory code is relevant to short-term memory and our ability to manipulate that memory.

9. d   obj. 7   p. 203
a. Incorrect. See answer d.
b. Incorrect. See answer d.
c. Incorrect. See answer d.
*d. Correct. In terms of memory phenomena, construction processes apply to episodic memory, motivation, and procedural memory.

10. d   obj. 5   p. 200
a. Incorrect. Difficulties in encoding may make it impossible to retrieve any information.

b. Incorrect. Decoding is not a memory phenomenon.
c. Incorrect. A difficulty with storage would appear in the inability to form new memories.
*d. Correct. We may know that we know something, but not be able to retrieve it.

11. b   obj. 8   p. 207
a. Incorrect. After two days, the memory loss had settled down.
*b. Correct. Within an hour, a significant portion of the list had been forgotten.
c. Incorrect. Only a supermemory could remember the list ten days later.
d. Incorrect. The most dramatic loss occurred within the first hour.

12. c   obj. 4   p. 198
a. Incorrect. May actually magnify if an error is repeated.
b. Incorrect. Trace decay may not occur anyway.
*c. Correct. Different brain areas are at work as the rehearsal begins to influence consolidation.
d. Incorrect. This is not a symptom of this disease.

13. b   obj. 10   p. 211
a. Incorrect. This is retrograde amnesia, covers all the period prior to the trauma.
*b. Correct. This is common for head-injury patients, who lose the time following the accident.
c. Incorrect. This is an apraxia.
d. Incorrect. This is another kind of memory difficulty.

14. c   obj. 1   p. 188
a. Incorrect. Had they been encoded wrong, they could not be recovered.
b. Incorrect. Had they not been stored, they could never be recovered.
*c. Correct. Since they had not been destroyed, they could still be retrieved.
d. Incorrect. Association is not one of the traditional memory processes.

15. b   obj. 10   p. 211
a. Incorrect. The keyword technique suggests that a similar sounding word would help in memory.
*b. Correct. In this description, a similar sounding word is used.
c. Incorrect. One would already need to know the word to make similar imagery.
d. Incorrect. This is a free association technique.

16. d   obj. 2   p. 190
17. b   obj. 3   p. 195
18. c   obj. 3   p. 195
19. e   obj. 3   p. 195
20. a   obj. 3   p. 195
21. encoding   obj. 1   p. 188
22. Iconic   obj. 2   p. 190
23. retrieval cue   obj. 5   p. 200
24. overlearning   obj. 10   p. 212
25. Associative model   obj. 3   p. 196

26.
- State the evidence supporting the existence of repressed memories and describe the problems that can arise from mistaken, recovered memories.
- One might argue that psychologists interfere with and compound the problem further by encouraging clients to "recover " memories that they may not have actually had, something like the demand characteristic in research. Consider whether there are ways to reduce false memories.

Practise Test 2:

1. c   obj. 2   p. 19083
a.   Incorrect. This is a form of long-term memory.
b.   Incorrect. Short-term memory can last about 15 to 25 seconds
*c. Correct. Sensory memory lasts for less than a second.
d.   Incorrect. This is a form of long-term memory.

2. b   obj. 1   p. 188
a.   Incorrect. Encoding involves getting the information in a form that can be stored.
*b. Correct. Storage refers to the process of retaining the information for later use.
c.   Incorrect. Memory has no decoding process.
d.   Incorrect. Retrieval refers to the recovery of memory from storage.

3. a   obj. 2   p. 191
*a. Correct. With meaning, the items in short-term memory have greater duration.
b.   Incorrect. Memory does not have an intensity except in the emotional sense.
c.   Incorrect. Memories cannot be measured in terms of length, though their duration can.
d.   Incorrect. Some visual memory will be coded verbally for easier manipulation.

4. c   obj. 2   p. 191
a.   Incorrect. Similarity is the gestalt organizational principle.
b.   Incorrect. Priming refers to a cognitive theory that suggests memories, thoughts, and other cognitive material can be primed.
*c. Correct. The technical term is chunking, and it refers to grouping information together in any way that can be recalled.
d.   Incorrect. Closure is a gestalt principle of perceptual organization.

5. c   obj. 3   p. 195
a.   Incorrect. There is not a form of memory known as periodic memory.
b.   Incorrect. Episodic memory refers to the personal memories of experiences and life-events.
*c. Correct. This is a definition of the form of declarative memory known as semantic memory.

d.   Incorrect. None of the researchers have suggested a process called interpolation (yet).

6. b   obj. 2   p. 192
a.   Incorrect. Massed practice is not a very effective approach to enhancing long-term memory consolidation.
*b. Correct. Elaborative rehearsal strengthens the memory by providing a rich array of retrieval cues.
c.   Incorrect. None of the researchers have suggested a process called interpolation (yet).
d.   Incorrect. Interference will actually make consolidation more difficult.

7. d   obj. 3   p. 194
a.   Incorrect. The stage of memory?
b.   Incorrect. The meaning can be very important and very significant, but still be forgotten.
c.   Incorrect. Memories do not have qualities in a sense relevant to the levels-of-processing approach.
*d. Correct. The depth of processing is determined by the extent of elaboration and the kinds of information to which the new information was associated.

8. d   obj. 4   p. 193
a.   Incorrect. This is a form of guessing, like your selecting this answer.
b.   Incorrect. Recall refers to the free recall of information without any specific cues.
c.   Incorrect. Mnemonics refers to the techniques or memory aids that can be used to improve memory.
*d. Correct. Since the answer is among the four items presented as alternatives, the test-taker only needs to recognize the right answer.

9. a   obj. 3   p. 195
*a. Correct. Procedural memories are skill-based memories, like riding a bicycle or skating.
b.   Incorrect. A semantic memory is memory of words, definitions, procedures, grammatical rules, and similarly abstract information.
c.   Incorrect. This is a kind of rehearsal that involves making many connections and relationships for an item being remembered.
d.   Incorrect. Declarative memory combines episodic and semantic memory.

10. c   obj. 6   p. 202
a.   Incorrect. A cognitive map is a more mundane memory item created while wandering about.
b.   Incorrect. A schema is an organizational unit that gives structure or organization to a set of information.
*c. Correct. Significant events are often remembered in great detail and apparent specificity, as if a photograph were taken of the event (thus flashbulb memory).
d.   Incorrect. A seizure is a very traumatic experience, and probably would not have this kind of memory associated with it.

11. d   obj .8   pp. 207-208

a. Incorrect. Decay theory says that we lose memories because they fade away.
b. Incorrect. Interference accounts for memory by the displacement of one memory by another.
c. Incorrect. This is not a theory of forgetting.
*d. Correct. We may not have lost the memory, but with inadequate cues, we cannot recall it.

12. b   obj. 9   p. 198
a. Incorrect. The hippocampus is thought to play a role in the consolidation of short-term memories into long-term memories.
*b. Correct. The sulci have yet to be implicated in memory.
c. Incorrect. Neurotransmitters support the memory consolidation process.
d. Incorrect. Changes at the synapse that are relatively permanent are called long-term potentiation.

13. a   obj. 9   pp. 209-211
*a. Correct. The loss of all memories prior to an accident is very uncommon, though it is the most popularized form of amnesia.
b. Incorrect. Retrograde amnesia, the loss of all memories prior to an accident or trauma, is very uncommon, though it is the most popularized form.
c. Incorrect. Retrograde amnesia, the loss of all memories prior to an accident or trauma, is very uncommon, though it is the most popularized form.
d. Incorrect. Retrograde amnesia, the loss of all memories prior to an accident or trauma is very uncommon, though it is the most popularized form of amnesia.

14. d   obj. 7   pp. 203-206
a. Incorrect. True only if "other type" refers to fabrication.
b. Incorrect. Usually they are recovered in therapy, not treated.
c. Incorrect. They do have a noticeable effect, but this is not an identifying feature.
*d. Correct. The problem faced by all is the ability to verify the genuineness of the memories.

15. a   obj. 10   p. 211
*a. Correct. This is called massed practice, and it is not very effective.
b. Incorrect. Overlearning is an effective form of study.
c. Incorrect. Organization helps memory by providing a meaningful scheme for the information.
d. Incorrect. This helps elaborate the material—putting it in your own words.

16. b   obj. 7   p. 200
17. e   obj. 7   p. 201
18. c   obj. 7   p. 201
19. a   obj. 9   p. 204
20. d   obj. 1   p. 182
21. recall   obj. 1   p. 182
22. Recognition   obj. 4   p. 193

23. Retrograde amnesia obj. 8   p. 203
24. Chunking obj. 2   p. 185

25.
▪ Give several examples of laboratory research. The advantages include control over the experiment and the ability to document that prior memories do not influence the outcome.
▪ Identify experiences that are best examined in an everyday context. Much case study and archival research is based on reports that are made when an event occurs or on reports from several points of view and are thus a form of everyday memory research. Other examples should be given.
▪ As stated in the text, both of these techniques are needed to understand memory fully.

Practise Test 3:
1.   d   obj. 2   p. 189
a. Incorrect. Episodic memory would mean that the items had been committed to long-term memory.
b. Incorrect. This is the sensory memory for hearing, and it only lasts about a second.
c. Incorrect. This is the sensory memory for vision, and it only lasts about a quarter of a second.
*d. Correct. Short-term memory would account for most of this ability of recollection. Some, however, think this is a special skill developed by husbands who watch football too much.

2.   b   obj. 2   p. 183
a. Incorrect. This is difficult to judge, since our sensory receptors are always active.
*b. Correct. The sensory information in the sensory memory has not been processed any further than the sensory register, thus it represents the information as it was taken in.
c. Incorrect. The sensory information in the sensory memory has not been processed any further than the sensory register, thus it represents the information as it was taken in; it is therefore as complete as the sensory system makes it.
d. Incorrect. The information will be lost if it is not processed, but some information can be processed and be meaningless.

3.   a   obj. 7   p. 203
*a. Correct. This constructive process may help give the memory its narrative quality.
b. Incorrect. We tend not to lose the distinctive features.
c. Incorrect. Engrams are not sheep.
d. Incorrect. Ambiguous details are not a hallmark of flashbulb memories.

4.   b   obj. 2   p. 190
a. Incorrect. A flashbulb memory implies a photo-like recollection.
*b. Correct. The visual echo or afterimage of the screen is much like the sensory activation in iconic memory.

c. Incorrect. The parallel here would be the persisting buzz of tube radio for the brief moment following it being turned off.

d. Incorrect. Declarative memory is very long term and does not appear to fade in this manner.

5. d   obj. 3   p. 195

a. Incorrect. Working memory applies to memories that soon become insignificant, like what we ate for lunch yesterday or where we parked our car yesterday (though where we parked it today is very important).

b. Incorrect. Declarative does not account for physical skills like this.

c. Incorrect. This contributes to our personal experiences and episodic memory.

*d. Correct. The basketball shot is a procedural skill and thus would be stored in procedural memory.

6. b   obj. 3   p. 195

a. Incorrect. Working memory is significant for only a few days.

*b. Correct. Procedural memory is just this kind of skill-based memory.

c. Incorrect. Only if he had been in a serious bicycle accident could the possibility of a repressed memory play a role.

d. Incorrect. Indeed this may be an important moment in the lives of Daniel and his son, but it is the procedural memory that contributes to Daniel's ability to recall this old skill.

7. c   obj. 7   p. 203

a. Incorrect. Freud did not introduce this idea.

b. Incorrect. Piaget used it, but it was introduced by someone else.

*c. Correct. This was Bartlett's contribution.

d. Incorrect. This is the author of the textbook.

8. c   obj. 4   p. 194

a. Incorrect. If attention means rehearsal, then this would be true.

b. Incorrect. There is no mental imagery model of memory.

*c. Correct. "Attention" would have an effect on how the memory was elaborated (thus given depth).

d. Incorrect. The is no specific cultural diversity model of memory.

9. d   obj. 8   p. 209

a. Incorrect. Try the opposite, where the first list influences the later list.

b. Incorrect. This is a dissociative state similar to amnesia.

c. Incorrect. This is a type of memory failure.

*d. Correct. In proactive interference, an earlier list interferes with a later list.

10. b   obj. 8   p. 209

a. Incorrect. This is not a recognized form of interference.

*b. Correct. In retroactive interference, a later list interferes with an earlier list.

c. Incorrect. In proactive interference, an earlier list interferes with a later list.

d. Incorrect. This is not a recognized form of interference.

11. d   obj. 8   p. 209

a. Incorrect. Alzheimer's disease would affect all the transactions.b. Incorrect. Decay is not thought to be a significant factor, especially if the waiter would have remembered had the other transactions not intervened.

c. Incorrect. Proactive means the previous interfere with the current.

*d. Correct. Retroactive means that the intervening events interfere with the recall of the earlier event.

12. c   obj. 9   p. 209

a. Incorrect. Try: the manufacture of beta amyloid.

b. Incorrect. Try: the manufacture of beta amyloid.

*c. Correct. Platelets form and constrict brain tissue, causing it to die.

d. Incorrect. Try: the manufacture of beta amyloid.

13. d   obj. 9   p. 210

a. Incorrect. This sounds like Alzheimer's disease.

b. Incorrect. This is anterograde amnesia.

c. Incorrect. This sounds like advanced Alzheimer's disease or a stroke victim.

*d. Correct. Memories are lost from prior to the accident.

14. a   obj. 9   p. 210

*a. Correct. Retrograde amnesia is marked by the loss of ability to recall events from prior to an accident or trauma.

b. Incorrect. Anterograde amnesia involves the loss of memory from the point of an accident or trauma forward.

c. Incorrect. This is a loss of memory from early childhood, usually prior to the development of language skills.

d. Incorrect. This is a memory loss syndrome that results from severe, long-term abuse of alcohol.

15. c   obj. 2   p. 192
16. e   obj. 3   p. 196
17. b   obj. 10   p. 211
18. d   obj. 10   p. 212
19. a   obj. 5   p. 201
20. priming   obj. 3   p. 196
21. long-term potentiation   obj. 4   p. 198
22. Consolidation obj. 4   p. 198
23. autobiographical memory   obj. 7   p. 206
24. elaborative rehearsal obj. 2   p. 192

25. source confusion
•   personal schema of the eyewitness
•   power of the misinformation effect
•   evidence related to the false memory syndrome
•   relevant aspects of the encoding specificity theory.

Thinking, Language, And Intelligence

7

Chapter Overview

Chapter 7 is about cognitive psychology, the branch of psychology that focuses on the study of higher mental processes, including thinking, language, memory, problem solving, knowing, reasoning, judging, and decision making.

This chapter concentrates on three broad topics: thinking, language, and intelligence. First, we consider concepts and various kinds of reasoning. Next, a discussion on how language is developed and acquired is presented. Then, the chapter considers intelligence in many varieties. Intelligence represents a focal point for psychologists' intent on understanding how people adapt to their environment. It also is a key aspect in how individuals differ from one another. Various conceptions of intelligence that have been offered by psychologists and the efforts made to develop standardized tests to measure it are discussed.

Finally, the retarded and the gifted, those two groups who display extremes in individual differences are discussed. Both their challenges and the programs developed to meet these challenges will be presented. Finally, this chapter considers how and to what degree intelligence is influenced by heredity and by the environment and whether traditional intelligence tests are biased toward the dominant cultural groups in society.

To further investigate the topics covered in this chapter, you can access the related websites by visiting the following link: http://www.mcgrawhill.ca/college/feldman

Prologue: Housecalls in Space
Looking Ahead

Section 1: Thinking
Mental Images: Examining the Mind's Eye
Concepts: Categorizing the World
Solving Problems

Becoming an Informed Consumer of Psychology:
Thinking Critically and Creatively: Can We Learn to be Better Thinkers?

Section 2: Language

Grammar: Language's Language
Language Development: Developing a Way With Words
Understanding Language Acquisition: Identifying the Roots of Language

> **Pathways through Psychology:** Fred Genesee:
> Professor of Psychology, McGill University

The Influence of Language on Thinking: Do Inuit Have More Words for Snow Than Texan's Have?
Do Animals use Language?

Section 3: Intelligence

Measuring Intelligence

> **Applying Psychology in the 21st Century:** When High IQ Keeps You from Getting a Job: Are You Too Smart for the Job You Want?

Are There Different Kinds of Intelligence?
Variations in Intellectual Ability
Individual Differences in Intelligence: Hereditary and Environmental Determents

> **Exploring Diversity:** The Relative Influence of Heredity and of Environment: Nature, Nurture, and IQ.

Learning Objectives

These are the concepts and the learning objectives for Chapter 7 Read them carefully as part of your preliminary survey of the chapter.

Thinking

1. Define cognition and the processes of thinking, mental imagery, and conceptualizing. (p. 218–220)

2. Discuss how algorithms and heuristics influence our judgments and decision making. (p. 220)

3. Explain the importance of understanding and diagnosing problems as the first step in effective problem solving. (pp. 221–222)

4.   Describe the heuristics used for generating possible solutions to problems, and explain how solutions should be evaluated. (pp. 223–224)

5.   Illustrate how efforts to develop solutions can be blocked by functional fixedness, mental set, and confirmation bias. (pp. 225–227)

6.   Describe the factors that contribute to creativity, and the role of creativity in problem solving and critical thinking. (pp. 227–228)

Language

7.   Define the basic components of language and grammar. (pp. 230–231)

8.   Discuss the developmental processes of language and the theories of language acquisition. (pp. 231–232)

9.   Identify the issues that arise with the linguistic relativity hypothesis and animal language. (p. 233)

Intelligence

10   Define intelligence and the issues related to its definition. (p. 236)

11   Discuss how intelligence is measured, the definition of intelligence quotient, and how achievement and aptitude tests differ from intelligence tests. (pp. 237–239)

12   Distinguish between reliability and validity with regard to psychological and intelligence testing. (pp. 240–242)

13.   Describe the alternative views of intelligence, including the g-factor, fluid and crystallized intelligence, and Gardner's model of multiple intelligences. (pp. 242–243)

14.   Explain how cognitive psychologists use information processing to describe intelligence, and briefly describe the search for the biological basis of intelligence. (pp. 243–245)

15.   Describe the concepts of practical intelligence and emotional intelligence, and discuss whether performance on achievement tests can be improved with training. (p. 245)

16.   Define mental retardation and describe its various classifications. (p. 247)

17   Discuss the causes of mental retardation and the care and treatment of retarded individuals. (p. 247)

18.   Define and describe intellectual giftedness. (pp. 247–248).

19.   Discuss the problem of cultural bias in intelligence tests and the attempts to produce a culture fair IQ test (pp. 248–250)

SECTION 1: Thinking

Prepare

- **What is thinking?**
- **What processes underlie reasoning and decision making?**
- **How do people approach and solve problems?**
- **What are the major obstacles to problem solving**

Organize

- **Mental Images**
- **Concepts**
- **Solving Problems**

Work

The branch of psychology that studies problem solving and other aspects of thinking is called **[a]** _____. The term **[b]** _____ brings together the higher mental processes of humans, including understanding the world, processing information, making judgments and decisions, and describing knowledge.

[c] _____ is the manipulation of mental representations—words, images, sounds, or data in any other modality—of information. Thinking transforms the representation in order to achieve some goal or solve some problem. The visual, auditory, and tactile representations of objects are called **[d]** _____, and these are a key component of thought. The time required to scan mental images can be measured. Brain scans taken while people are forming and manipulating mental images are being used to study the production and use of them. **[e]** _____ are categorizations of objects, events, or people that share common properties. Because we have concepts, we are able to classify newly encountered material on the basis of our past experiences. Ambiguous concepts are usually represented by **[f]** _____, which are typical, highly representative examples of concepts. Concepts provide an efficient way of understanding events and objects as they occur in the complex world.

An **[g]** _____ is a rule that guarantees a solution if it is properly followed. Applying mathematical rules to equations will give us the answer even when we do not know why it works. A **[h]** _____ is a rule of thumb or some other shortcut that may lead to a solution.

Problem solving typically involves three major steps: preparation, production of solutions, and evaluation of solutions. Problems are distinguished as either well-defined or ill-defined. In a

The creation of solutions may proceed at the simplest level as trial and error, but this approach may be inadequate for problems that have a large number of possible configurations. The use of heuristics aids in the simplification of problems. The heuristic of

[i] _____ proceeds by testing the difference between the current status and the desired outcome, and with each test it tries to reduce the difference. The use of

[j] _____ takes a slightly different approach to problem solving, requiring a reorganization of the entire problem in order to achieve a solution. The reorganization of existing elements requires prior experience with the elements.

The final step of problem solving is to evaluate the adequacy of a solution. If the solution is not clear, criteria to judge the solution must be made clear.

In the progress toward a solution, there are several obstacles that can be met.

[k] _____ refers to the tendency to think of an object according to its given function or typical use. Functional fixedness is an example of a broader phenomenon called

[l] _____ , the tendency for old patterns of solutions to persist.

[m] _____ is usually defined as the combining of responses or ideas in novel ways. [n] _____ refers to the ability to generate unusual yet appropriate responses to problems. [o] _____ produces responses that are based primarily on knowledge or logic. *Cognitive complexity* is the use of elaborate, intricate, and complex stimuli and thinking patterns. Humor can increase creative output as well. Apparently intelligence is not related to creativity, perhaps because the tests for intelligence test convergent thinking rather than divergent thinking.

Evaluate

_____ 1. arrangement problems

_____ 2. problems of inducing structure

_____ 3. transformation problems

_____ 4. means-ends analysis

_____ 5. subgoals

a. Problems to be solved using a series of methods to change an initial state into a goal state.

b. A commonly used heuristic to divide a problem into intermediate steps and to solve each one of them.

c. Problems requiring the identification of existing relationships among elements presented so as to construct a new relationship among them.

d. Problems requiring the rearrangement of a group of elements in order to satisfy a certain criterion.

e. Repeated testing to determine and reduce the distance between the desired outcome and what currently exists in problem solving.

Rethink

1. How might the availability heuristic contribute to prejudices based on race, age, and gender? Can awareness of this heuristic prevent this from happening?

2. Are divergent thinking and convergent thinking mutually exclusive or complementary? Why? Are there situations in which one way of thinking is clearly superior? Can the two ways of thinking be combined? How?

SECTION 2: Language

Prepare

- **How do people use language?**
- **How does language develop?**

Organize

- **Grammar: Language's Language**
- **Language Development**
- **Understanding Language Acquisition**
- **The Influence of Language on Thinking**
- **Do Animals Use Language?**

Work

[a] _____ is the systematic, meaningful arrangement of symbols. It is important for cognition and for communication with others. The basic structure of language is

[b] _____, the framework of rules that determine how thoughts are

expressed. The three components of grammar are: **[c]** _____, the smallest

units of sound, called **[d]** _____, that affect the meaning of speech and how

words are formed; **[e]** _____, the rules that govern how words and phrases

are combined to form sentences; and **[f]** _____, the rules governing
meaning of words and sentences.

Language develops through set stages. At first children **[g]** _____, producing speech-like but meaningless sounds. Babbling gradually sounds like actual speech, and by one year, sounds that are not part of the language disappear. After the first year, children

produce short, two-word combinations followed by short sentences. **[h]** _____ refers to the short sentences that contain a critical message but sound as if written as a telegram, with noncritical words left out. As children begin to learn speech rules, they will apply them

without flexibility, a phenomenon known as **[i]**_____, where an "ed" might be applied to every past tense construction. By the age of 5, most children have acquired the rules of language.

The **[j]** _____ to language acquisition suggests that the reinforcement and conditioning principles are responsible for language development. Praise for saying a word like "mama" reinforces the word and increases the likelihood of its being repeated. Shaping then makes child language become more adultlike. This approach has difficulty explaining the acquisition of language rules, because children are also reinforced when their language is incorrect. An alternative proposed by Noam Chomsky suggests that there exist innate mechanisms responsible for the acquisition of language. All human languages have a similar underlying structure he calls **[k]** _____, and a neural system in the brain, the **[l]** _____, is responsible for the development of language.

Psychologists are also concerned whether the structure of language influences the structure of thought or whether thought influences language. The **[m]** _____ _hypothesis_ suggests that language shapes thought, determining how people of a particular culture perceive and understand the world. In an alternative view, language may reflect the different ways we have of thinking about the world, essentially that thought produces language.

Children who enter school as nonnative speakers of English face a number of hardships. The debate over whether to take a bilingual approach or whether all instruction should be in English is a major controversy. Evidence suggests that bilingual children have cognitive advantages, being more flexible, more aware of the rules of language, and having higher scores on verbal and nonverbal intelligence tests. Bilingual students raise questions of the advantage of

[n] _____, in which a person is a member of two cultures. Some have argued that society should promote an **[o]** _____ in which members of minority cultures are encouraged to learn both cultures.

Evaluate

_____ 1.   grammar

_____ 2.   phonology

_____ 3.   phonemes

_____ 4.   syntax

_____ 5.   semantics

a.   The framework of rules that determine how our thoughts can be expressed.

b.   Rules governing the meaning of words and sentences.

c.   The rules governing how words form sentences.

d.   The study of how we use those sounds to produce meaning by forming them into words.

e.   The smallest units of sound used to form words.

Rethink

3.   Why is overgeneralization seen as an argument against a strict learning-theory approach to explaining language acquisition?

Section 3: Intelligence

Prepare

- *How do psychologists characterize and define intelligence?*
- *What are the major approaches to measuring intelligence?*
- *How can the extremes of intelligence be characterized?*
- *Are traditional IQ tests culturally biased?*
- *To what degree is intelligence influenced by the environment and to what degree is it influenced by heredity?*

Organize

- *Measuring Intelligence*
- *Are There Different Kinds of Intelligence?*
- *Variations in Intellectual Ability*
- *Individual Differences in Intelligence*

Work

In a survey of lay persons, three major components of intelligence were identified: (1) problem-solving ability, (2) verbal ability, and (3) social competence.

[a] _____ has been defined by psychologists as the capacity to understand the world, think rationally, and use resources effectively

Alfred Binet developed the first formal **[b]** _____ to identify the "dullest" students in the Parisian school system. His test was able to distinguish the "bright" from the "dull" and eventually made distinctions between age groups. The tests helped to assign children a **[c]** _____, the average age of children who achieved the same score. In order to compare individuals with different *chronological ages*, the

[d] _____ score, was determined by dividing the mental age by the chronological age and multiplying by a factor of 100. Thus an IQ score is determined by the level at which a person performs on the test in relation to others of the same age.

The SAT is an **[e]** _____ meant to determine the level of achievement of an individual, that is, what the person has actually learned. An **[f]** _____ measures and predicts an individual's ability in a particular area. There is quite a bit of overlap among the IQ, achievement, and aptitude tests.

Psychological tests must have **[g]** _____, that is, they must measure something consistently from time to time. The question of whether or not a test measures the characteristic it is supposed to measure is called **[h]** _____. If a test is reliable, that does not mean that it is valid. However, if a test is unreliable, it cannot be valid. A reliable test will produce similar outcomes in similar conditions. All types of tests in psychology, including intelligence tests, assessments of psychological disorders, and the measurement of attitudes must meet tests of validity and reliability.

More than 7 million people in the United States are classified as mentally retarded, and the populations that comprise the mentally retarded and the exceptionally gifted require special attention in order to reach their potential.

[i] _____ is defined by the American Association on Mental Deficiency (1992) as when there is "significantly sub-average general intellectual functioning existing concurrently with deficits in adaptive behaviour and manifested during the developmental period." This definition includes mild to severe retardation. One-third of the people classified as retarded suffer from biological causes of retardation, mostly from **[j]**_____, a genetic disorder caused by an extra chromosome. **[k]**_____ occurs in cases when there is no biological cause but instead may be linked with a family history of retardation. This may be caused by environmental factors like severe poverty, malnutrition, and possibly a genetic factor that cannot be determined. In 1975, Congress passed a law (Public Law 94–142) that entitles individuals who are mentally retarded to a full education and to education and training in the **[l]** _____. This law leads to a process of returning individuals to regular classrooms, a process called **[m]** _____. The view is that by placing individuals in typical environments, they interact with individuals who are not retarded and benefit from the interaction.

The **[n]**_____ comprise about 2 to 4 percent of the population. This group is generally identified as those individuals with IQ scores higher than 130. Contrary to the stereotype, these individuals are usually outgoing, well-adjusted, popular people who do most things better than the average person. Lewis Terman conducted a well-known longitudinal study following 1,500 gifted children (with IQs above 140). They have an impressive record of accomplishments, though being gifted does not guarantee success.

Evaluate

____ 1. intelligence tests

____ 2. Stanford-Binet Test

____ 3. Wechsler Adult Intelligence Scale-III (WAIS-III)

____ 4. Wechsler Intelligence Scale for Children-III (WISC-III)

a. A test of intelligence consisting of verbal and nonverbal performance sections, providing a relatively precise picture of a person's specific abilities.

b. A test of intelligence that includes a series of items varying in nature according to the age of the person being tested.

c. A battery of measures to determine a person's level of intelligence.

d. An intelligence test for children consisting of verbal and nonverbal performance sections, providing a relatively precise picture of a child's specific abilities.

Rethink

4. Job interviews are really a kind of test. In what ways does a job interview resemble an aptitude test? an achievement test? Do you think job interviews can be shown to have validity? reliability?

5. Why do you think negative stereotypes persist of gifted individuals and people with mental retardation, even in the face of contrary evidence? How can these stereotypes be changed?

6. Why might a test that identifies a disproportionate number of minority group members for special education services and remedial assistance be considered potentially biased? Isn't the purpose of the test to help persons at risk of falling behind academically? How can a test created for a good purpose be biased?

Practise Questions

Test your knowledge of the chapter material by answering these questions. These questions have been placed in three Practise Tests. The first two tests are composed of questions that will test your recall of factual knowledge. The third test contains questions that are challenging and primarily test for conceptual knowledge and your ability to apply that knowledge. Check your answers and review the feedback using the Answer Key on the following pages of the *Study Guide*.

PRACTISE TEST 1:

1. Manipulation of mental images is best shown by subjects' abilities to:
   a. use mental images to represent abstract ideas.
   b. anticipate the exit of a toy train from a tunnel.
   c. understand the subtle meanings of sentences.
   d. rotate mentally one image to compare it with another.

2. A concept is defined as:
   a. an idea or thought about a new procedure or product.
   b. a group of attitudes that define an object, event, or person.
   c. a categorization of people, objects, or events that share certain properties.
   d. one of many facts that collectively define the subject matter for a specific area of knowledge (such as psychology).

3. Failing to use formal reasoning, using inaccurate premises, and coming to erroneous conclusions are all errors related specifically to the use of:
   a. deductive reasoning.   c. availability heuristics.
   b. inductive reasoning.   d. algorithms.

4. According to the text, the most frequently used heuristic technique for solving problems is:
   a. the availability heuristic.   c. the representativeness heuristic.
   b. categorical processing.   d. means-ends analysis.

5. According to the text, which of the following is **not** associated with defining and understanding a problem?
   a. discarding inessential information
   b. simplifying essential information
   c. dividing the problem into parts
   d. clarifying the solution

6. Insight is a:
   a. sudden awareness of the relationships among various elements in a problem that previously appeared to be independent of one another.
   b. sudden awareness of the solution to a problem with which one has had no prior involvement or experience.
   c. sudden awareness of a particular algorithm that can be used to solve a problem.
   d. spontaneous procedure for generating a variety of possible solutions to a problem.

7. A simple computer program will include:
   a. trial-and-error solutions.
   b. a syllogism.
   c. a dozen or more heuristics.
   d. an algorithm.

8. Logic and knowledge are exemplified by _____ thinking.
   a. creative
   b. convergent
   c. divergent
   d. imaginal

9. The syntax of a language is the framework of rules that determine:
   a. the meaning of words and phrases.
   b. how words and phrases are combined to form sentences.
   c. the sounds of letters, phrases, and words.
   d. how thoughts can be translated into words.

10. Children sometimes use telegraphic speech. This refers to:
    a. speech that is very rapid.
    b. seemingly nonessential words omitted from phrases and sentences.
    c. the tonal quality of speech is limited.
    d. speech that may speed up, slow down, or contain pauses.

11. The basic elements of intelligence include:
    a. social competence, assertiveness, and innate knowledge.
    b. algorithmic skill, verbal ability, and thrift.
    c. perceptual speed, focal attention, and problem-solving skill.
    d. verbal skill, problem-solving ability, and social competence.

12. A significantly subaverage level of intellectual functioning accompanied by deficits in adaptive behaviour defines:
    a. savant syndrome.
    b. profound retardation.
    c. mental retardation.
    d. severe retardation.

13. The biological cause of Down syndrome is:

    a.   physical trauma to the fetus during pregnancy.

    b.   poisoning of the mother by toxins during particular intervals of the pregnancy when the fetus is very sensitive to those chemicals.

    c.   poisoning of the fetus by alcohol consumed by the pregnant mother.

    d.   an extra chromosome segment in each cell of the body.

14.   Familial retardation:
    a.   results from hereditary factors.
    b.   results from environmental factors.
    c.   is a paradox, since there are no known hereditary or environmental causes.
    d.   may result from either hereditary or environmental factors, although there are no known biological causes.

15.   For the retarded youngster, mainstreaming means:
    a.   more opportunities to relate to other students who are retarded.
    b.   increased opportunities for education and socialization.
    c.   the exclusion of other students who are retarded from the classroom.
    d.   separating retarded and other students.

____ 16.   mental set

____ 17.   confirmation bias

____ 18.   creativity

____ 19.   divergent thinking

____ 20.   convergent thinking

a.   The tendency for patterns of problem solving to persist.

b.   A type of thinking that produces responses based on knowledge and logic.

c.   The ability to generate unusual but appropriate responses to problems or questions.

d.   A bias favouring an initial hypothesis and disregarding contradictory information suggesting alternative solutions.

e.   The combining of responses or ideas in novel ways.

21.   Using a screwdriver as a knife indicates a lack of _____.

22.   The rules of a language that govern how words are combined to form sentences is _____.

23.   _____ speech is the two-word constructions typical of 2 year olds.

24.   Identify a major challenge that you anticipate facing in the next several years. It can involve choosing a career, getting married, selecting a major, choosing a graduate school, or one of many others. Describe the problem or challenge briefly, then describe how you would apply the problem-solving steps presented in the text to the problem to generate solutions that you might try.

PRACTISE TEST 2:

1.   Cognitive psychologists study all of the following **except**:
    a.   how the sensory system takes in information.
    b.   how people understand the world.
    c.   how people process information.
    d.   how people make judgments.

2. Prototypes of concepts are:
   a. new concepts to describe newly emerging phenomena.
   b. new concepts that emerge within a language spontaneously and then are retained or discarded.
   c. representative examples of concepts.
   d. concepts from other languages that are incorporated into a native language if they appear useful.

3. You have relied on _____ if you fail to solve a problem because you misapply a category or set of categories.
   a. an availability heuristic
   b. a mental set
   c. functional fixedness
   d. a representativeness heuristic

4. According to your text, problems fall into one of three categories. Which of the following is **not** one of them?
   a. arrangement
   b. affability
   c. structure
   d. transformation

5. Identifying existing relationships among elements and constructing a new relationship is an example of a(an) _____ problem.
   a. inducing-structure
   b. organization
   c. arrangement
   d. transformation

6. Problems that are solved by changing an initial state into a goal state are called:
   a. transformation problems
   b. problems of inducing structure.
   c. insight problems.
   d. arrangement problems.

7. A student tells her roommate sardonically, "As a student, I measure success one midterm at a time." Her statement implies that her strategy for achieving a college degree is through:
   a. means-ends analysis.
   b. achieving subgoals.
   c. trial and error.
   d. application of algorithms.

8. Functional fixedness and mental set show that:
   a. the person's first hunches about the problem are typically correct.
   b. one's initial perceptions about the problem can impede the solution.
   c. convergent thinking is needed when the problem is well defined.
   d. the person who poses the problem is the one who solves it best.

9. Which of the following is characteristic of a creative thinker?
   a. convergent thought
   b. divergent thought
   c. high intelligence
   d. recurrent thought

10. The order of the words forming a sentence is generated by:
    a. synthetics.
    b. semantics.
    c. syntax.
    d. systematics.

11. The intelligence quotient was developed to:
    a. increase the reliability of the early intelligence tests.

    b.   provide a way to compare the performance of French and American children on intelligence tests.

    c.   permit meaningful comparisons of intelligence among people of different ages.

    d.   correct a systematic scoring error in the first American intelligence tests.

12. Standardized IQ tests, the full range of scores ascribed to normal intelligence is from:

    a.   50 to 150.   c.   0 to 100.

    b.   85 to 115.   d.   70 to 130.

13. Gardner suggested that we have eight types of intelligence. Which of the following is **not** among them?

    a.   general information intelligence   c.   spatial intelligence

    b.   musical intelligence   d.   interpersonal intelligence

14. Among Gardner's suggested intelligences, which intelligence is described as "skill in interacting with others such as sensitivity to moods"?

    a.   linguistic   c.   interpersonal

    b.   bodily-kinesthetic   d.   intrapersonal

_____ 15.   David Wechsler   a.   Suggested there were eight factors of intelligence called primary mental abilities.

_____ 16.   Spearman   b.   First designed IQ tests with verbal and performance scales.

_____ 17.   Howard Gardner ·

                                c.   Emotional intelligence underlies the accurate assessment, evaluation, and expression of emotions.

_____ 18.   Binet

_____ 19.   Daniel Goleman   d.   Assumed there was a general factor for mental ability, the g-factor.

                                e.   Devised the first formal intelligence test.

20. _____ intelligence reflects information-processing capabilities, reasoning, and memory.

21. _____ intelligence is the accumulation of information, skills, and strategies that people have learned through experience and that they can apply in problem-solving situations.

22. An _____ is a measure of intelligence that takes into account the person's mental and chronological ages.

23. _____ hypothesized that head configuration, being genetically determined, was related to brain size, and therefore related to intelligence.

24. A person who has an IQ score between 40 and 54 would be considered to have _____ retardation.

25. Some consider language to be the capability that uniquely distinguishes us as human. Weigh the arguments for the language skills of specially trained chimpanzees and develop your position on this issue. Is language unique to humans? If so, how would you characterize the communication skills of chimpanzees? If not, then what capability does distinguish us from other animals?

PRACTISE TEST 3: Conceptual, Applied, and Challenging Questions

1. Which alternative below does **not** fit within the text's definition of cognition?
   a. the higher mental processes of humans
   b. how people know and understand the world
   c. how people communicate their knowledge and understanding to others
   d. how people's eyes and ears process the information they receive

2. Concepts are similar to perceptual processes in that:
   a. concepts, like visual illusions, can produce errors in interpretation.
   b. concepts allow us to simplify and manage our world.
   c. concepts are to language what figure-ground relationships are to perception.
   d. some concepts and perceptual processes are innate.

3. You have had a number of troublesome, time-consuming, expensive, and emotionally trying experiences with telemarketers. Then you find out that your roommate for next term is a telemarketer. You are convinced, even without meeting your future roommate, that you should not be paired with this person. You have used the _____ heuristic to arrive at your conclusion.
   a. means-ends
   b. representativeness
   c. availability
   d. personality

4. Thinking of a waffle iron in conventional terms may handicap your efforts to solve a problem when a possible solution involves using the waffle iron for a novel use. This phenomenon is called:
   a. functional fixedness.
   b. insight.
   c. awareness.
   d. preparation.

5. The slight difference in meaning between the sentences "The mouse ate the cheese" and "The cheese was eaten by the mouse" is determined by the rules of:
   a. grammar.
   b. phonology.
   c. syntax.
   d. semantics.

6. Which of the following is the first refinement in the infant's learning of language?
   a. production of short words that begin with a consonant.
   b. disappearance of sounds that are not in the native language.
   c. emergence of sounds that resemble words.
   d. production of two-word combinations.

7. Which statement below is **not** true about the language skills of humans and apes?
   a. Many critics feel that the language skills acquired by chimps and gorillas are no different from a dog learning to sit on command.
   b. The language skills of chimps and gorillas are equal to those of a 5-year-old human child.
   c. Sign language and response panels with different-shaped symbols have been used to teach chimps and gorillas language skills.
   d. Humans are probably better equipped than apes to produce and organize language into meaningful sentences.

8. Navaho have many names for the bluish, aquamarine colour of turquoise. Based on how other, similar facts have been understood, this too could be used to support:

a. the theory that language determines thought.
b. the theory that thought determines language.
c. the existence of the language acquisition device.
d. development of the nativistic position.

9. The notion that language shapes the way that people of a particular culture perceive and think about the world is called the:
   a. semantic-reasoning theory.
   b. cultural-language law.
   c. prototypical hypothesis.
   d. linguistic-relativity hypothesis.

10. Charise participates in a study in which she is asked to imagine a giraffe. After indicating that she has constructed the entire image, she is then asked to focus on the giraffe's tail. What should the experimenter be doing as she completes this task?
    a. observing her reaction
    b. timing each step
    c. recording her respiration
    d. getting the next subject ready

11. In a study concerned with concept formation and categorization, you are asked to think about a table. Which of the following would be considered a prototype if you were to have imagined it?
    a. your grandmother's dining room table
    b. a four-legged, rectangular table
    c. the coffee table in the student lounge
    d. a round, pedestal-style oak table

12. Of these first intelligence test statements, which is **not** correct?
    a. It was designed to identify the "gifted" children in the school system.
    b. It was developed by Alfred Binet in France.
    c. It assumed that performance on certain items and tasks improved with age.
    d. Many items were selected for the test when "bright" and "dull" students scored differently on them.

13. About two-thirds of all people have IQ scores of:
    a. 95–105.
    b. 90–110.
    c. 85–115.
    d. 70–110.

14. Which of the following is **not** one of the verbal subtests on the Wechsler intelligence scale?
    a. information
    b. similarities
    c. block design
    d. vocabulary

15. Which of the following situations best illustrates reliability as a quality of psychological tests?
    a. A prospective Air Force pilot takes a test, passes it, and becomes an excellent pilot.
    b. A college student studies diligently for an important exam and earns an A on it.
    c. A psychiatric patient takes a psychological test that yields the diagnosis that had been suspected.
    d. A mentally retarded patient takes an intelligent test on Monday and again on Tuesday, getting the same result on each administration.

_____ 16. insight

_____ 17. cognitive psychology

_____ 18. prototypes

_____ 19. linguistic relativity

_____ 20. creativity

a. Typical, highly representative examples of a concept.

b. Sudden awareness of the relationships among various elements that had previously appeared to be independent of one another.

c. The branch of psychology that specializes in the study of cognition.

d. "Language determines thought."

e. Associated truth, divergent thinking, and playful thinking.

21. When people repeatedly test for differences between desired outcomes and what currently exists they are using _____.

22. Intermediate steps to reach a goal are called _____.

23. _____ occurs when the initial hypothesis is favoured and alternative hypotheses are ignored.

24. When children apply rules even when doing so creates an error (such as "he walked" and "he runned"), it is called _____.

25. A preference for elaborate, intricate thinking patterns is called _____.

26. Discuss the controversy regarding bilingual education.

Spotlight on Terminology and Language— Cultural Idioms

Page 217 "It was a 1.5 billion dollar mistake—a **blunder** on a grand scale. The **finely** ground mirror of the Hubble space telescope, designed to provide an **unprecedented** glimpse into the vast reaches of the universe, was not so finely ground after all."

A **blunder** is a mistake. A **blunder** is an error usually committed as a result of carelessness or ignorance. Within this context, **finely** refers to the tremendous sensitivity of the Hubble space telescope. The telescope is a very precise and discriminating tool. An **unprecedented** glimpse refers to the fact that this was a new way of gaining access to a view of the universe.

Page 217 "These photos provided spectacular views of **galaxies** millions of light years from earth."

A **galaxy** is one of billions of large star systems.

Page 218 "Their success illustrates how intelligent and thoughtful effort can lead to solutions in the face of **formidable** challenges."

Formidable is generally noteworthy by its size or quantity. Something that is **formidable** often produces fear, dread, or apprehension. Many students face **formidable** challenges of time management, money management, and family management when they are going to school, working, and managing a family. Some texts are so **formidable** in size and substance that they deter many readers.

Thinking

Page 218 "The function of thinking is to **transform** that representation of information into new and different forms for the purposes of answering questions, solving problems, or reaching goals."

To **transform** is to change. Why is it so important to **transform** the knowledge you are gaining?

Page 218 "It might be that every sensory **modality** produces corresponding mental images."

Modality is form. Our sensory modalities include sound, a word, a visual image. Which sensory **modality** do you think you are most responsive to? Which sensory **modality** do you use to enhance your learning skills?
Page 219 "Research has found that our representations of mental images have many of the properties of the actual **perception** of objects being represented."

Our skills of **perception** help us to interpret mental images in the light of experience.

Page 219 "The production of mental images has been **heralded** by some as a way to improve various skills."

When you **herald** something, you signal or convey news. You make an announcement. The text has **heralded** the production of mental images as an effective way to enhance skills. Would you be willing to try the techniques of mental rehearsal to help you to improve in one of your physical skills areas, perhaps in perfecting your swimming strokes?

Page 219 "Concepts are **categorizations** of objects, events, or people that share common properties."

A **categorization** is a way of classifying something.

Language

Page 230 "Semantic rules allow us to use words to convey the subtlest of **nuances**."

A **nuance** is a tiny variation, just a shade of difference. You see a **nuance** as a very subtle distinction.

Page 232 "Two major explanations have been offered, one based on learning theory and the other on **innate** processes."

Innate belongs to the essential nature of something. When a capability is **innate** in humans or other living organisms, these characteristics exist from birth.

Page 227 "But the issue of whether animals are capable of being taught to communicate in a way that resembles human language remains **controversial**."

Controversy is a dispute characterized especially by the expression of opposing views.

Intelligence

Page 236 "Some might say the inability of the Trukese to explain in Western terms how their sailing technique works is a sign of **primitive** or even unintelligent behaviour."

Primitive behaviour relates to an early or original state and is often marked by simplicity or an unsophisticated manner.

Page 237 "The **forerunner** of the modern IQ test was based on the uncomplicated, but completely wrong, assumption that the size and shape of a person's head could be used as an objective measure of intelligence."

A **forerunner** is a precursor of, or something that comes first. The **forerunner** of the IQ test for measuring intelligence was the examination of a person's head to determine intelligence. **Fore** is a prefix that means before, earlier, or in front of.

Page 237 "If performance on certain tasks or test items improved with **chronological**, or physical, age, then performance could be used to distinguish more intelligent people from less intelligent ones within a particular age group. Using this principle, Binet, a French psychologist, devised the first **formal** intelligence test, which was designed to identify the 'dullest' students in the Paris school system in order to provide them with remedial aid."

When something is arranged **chronologically**, it is arranged in order of time of occurrence. **Chrono** or **chron** is a prefix relating to time. **Formal** here relates to the essential shape or design of the intelligence test.

Page 237 "By using mental age alone, for instance, we might assume that a 20-year-old responding at an 18-year-old's level would be as bright as a 5-year-old answering at a 3-year-old's level, when actually the 5-year-old would be displaying a much greater **relative** degree of slowness."

Relative means dependent on or interconnected with something else for significance or intelligibility. The text example expresses why mental age is **relative** to chronological age.

Page 238 "**Remnants** of Binet's original intelligence test are still with us, although it has been revised in significant ways."

Remnants are pieces. Some of the original components of Binet's design have survived.

Page 238 "An examiner begins by finding a mental age level at which the person is able to answer all questions correctly, and then moves on to **successively** more difficult problems."

Successively is to follow in order or sequence.

Page 239 "To test understanding and evaluation of social **norms** and past experience"

Norms are standards that allow you to compare one item to another.

Page 239 "There are, however, **sacrifices** made in group testing which, in some cases, may **outweigh** the benefits."

If you have **outweighed** the benefits, you have **sacrificed** too much. **Outweigh** means to be more significant than, to weigh more than. **Sacrifices** are things that you forfeit for another thing thought to be of greater value. Students frequently **sacrifice** sleep and social activities to study and earn high grades.

Page 239 "In some cases it is simply impossible to **employ** group tests, particularly with young children or people with unusually low IQs."

To **employ** group tests would be to use them.

Page 242 "The basic **scheme** for developing norms is for test designers to calculate the average score achieved by a particular group of people for whom the test is designed."

A **scheme** is a system, an orderly plan of action.

Page 241 "Furthermore, one could argue that it is better to have frequent turnover of intelligent workers, rather than be **saddled** with not-so-intelligent employees for long periods."

When you are **saddled** with something, you are burdened with it. Many students feel **saddled** with too much work.

Page 245 "Other information-processing approaches examine **sheer** speed of processing."

These approaches only examine pure speed, nothing else.

■ CHAPTER 7 ANSWER KEY

GUIDED REVIEW

Section 1:	Section 2:	Section 3:
[a] cognitive psychology	[a] Language	[a] Intelligence
[b] cognition	[b] grammar	[b] intelligence tests
[c] Thinking	[c] phonology	[c] mental age
[d] mental images	[d] phonemes	[d] intelligence quotient
[e] Concepts	[e] syntax	[e] achievement test
[f] prototypes	[f] semantics	[f] aptitude test
[g] algorithm	[g] babble	[g] reliability
[h] heuristic	[h] Telegraphic speech	[h] validity
[i] means-ends analysis	[i] overgeneralization	[i] Mental retardation
[j] insight	[j] learning-theory approach	[j] Down syndrome
[k] Functional fixedness	[k] universal grammar	[k] Familial retardation
[l] mental set	[l] language-acquisition device	[l] least restrictive
[m] Creativity	[m] linguistic-relativity	environment
[n] Divergent thinking	[n] biculturalism	[m] mainstreaming
[o] Convergent thinking	[o] alternation model	[n] intellectually gifted
Evaluate	Evaluate	Evaluate
1. d	1. a	1. c
2. c	2. d	2. b
3. a	3. e	3. a
4. e	4. c	4. d
5. b	5. b	

Selected Rethink Answers

1. Define what is meant by the term availability heuristic. Knowing that we act on thoughts that we believe represent certain groups—negative thoughts about any race, age, or gender could lead to our developing a prejudice about that group. The media draws tragic events to our attention on a daily basis. If we believe these events to be true, we develop availability heuristics and use this information to guide future decision making (i.e., people froze while hiking, I shouldn't hike anymore). Awareness can prevent this by allowing us to assess what the real risks in a situation are and not rely on heuristics.

2. They are complementary. Divergent thinking generates a variety of creative solutions on how to solve a problem that can then be offered as choices. Convergent thinking takes choices and with knowledge and logic selects the best solution.

4. Aptitude is defined as the measure of an individual's ability in a particular area. Achievement is a measure of what a person has learned. Job interviews are designed to address both of these areas. Applicants who are hired because of these interview criteria and then are capable on the job would confirm the validity of the interview methods, the interviews assess what they're intended to. If this arrangement worked repeatedly with job applicants, it would be considered a reliable hiring practice.

Practise Test 1:
1. d   obj. 1   p. 219
a. Incorrect. This is difficult to document.
b. Incorrect. This probably relates to spatial-temporal skills.
c. Incorrect. This has to do with language skills.
*d. Correct. Mental rotation and comparison is one technique used to study how people manipulate mental images.

2. c   obj. 1   p. 219

a. Incorrect. Concepts include more than new procedures and products.
b. Incorrect. The term "attitudes" is too restrictive, and this is a definition of a stereotype.
*c. Correct. Concepts are used to categorize thought.
d. Incorrect. Concepts can include natural objects as well as scientific knowledge.

3. a   obj. 2   p. 220
*a. Correct. Deductive reasoning is only as valid as its premises, and the conclusions can be in error because of faulty use of formal reasoning.

b. Incorrect. Inductive reasoning does not derive from premises, rather from cases and examples.
c. Incorrect. Availability heuristics draw conclusions from the most apparent (available) evidence and may ignore other evidence.
d. Incorrect. Algorithms are themselves rules for problem solution and do not have premises.

4. d obj. 4 p. 223
a. Incorrect. The text names means-ends analysis as the most common.
b. Incorrect. The text names means-ends analysis as the most common.
c. Incorrect. The text names means-ends analysis as the most common.
*d. Correct. Consider how often we turn to the desired outcome and let it shape how we approach the problem.

5. d obj. 3 p. 222
a. Incorrect. Removing the inessential may help make the definition of the problem clearer.
b. Incorrect. Making the information simpler, even putting it in a graphic form like a chart, helps make the problem easier to understand.
c. Incorrect. Often dividing the problem into parts helps define the whole problem more clearly.
*d. Correct. Clarifying the solution applies more to the later stages of solving the problem.

6. a obj. 4 p. 224
*a. Correct. This is the definition of insight, where one becomes aware of a new or different arrangement of elements.
b. Incorrect. Insight does not suggest that an individual has no experience of a problem.
c. Incorrect. While one might discover an algorithm for a problem through insight, it is not a necessary aspect of insight.
d. Incorrect. This refers more to brainstorming than insight.

7. d obj. 2 p. 220
a. Incorrect. This requires very complex programming.
b. Incorrect. This is an example of "d," thus not the best answer.
c. Incorrect. Heuristics require much more complicated programming.
*d. Correct. An algorithm is a set of rules that guarantee an answer.

8   b obj. 6 p. 228
a. Incorrect. Creativity draws upon knowledge and experience, but not necessarily so.
*b. Correct. Convergent thinking is defined as thinking exemplified by the use of logical reasoning and knowledge.
c. Incorrect. Divergent thinking often defies logic and is not dependent upon a knowledge base.

d. Incorrect. The use of the imagination does not exemplify logical processes, and is perhaps the least dependent knowledge.

9. b obj. 7 p. 230
a. Incorrect. Semantics determines the meaning of words and phrases.
*b. Correct. Syntax refers to the meaningful structuring of sentences.
c. Incorrect. Phonology governs the production of sounds.
d. Incorrect. Somewhat broader than syntax, grammar governs the translation of thoughts into language.

10. b obj. 8 p. 231
a. Incorrect. Speed and rate of speech are not factors in telegraphic speech.
*b. Correct. Like sending a telegraph, some words may be omitted but the message is still clear.
c. Incorrect. The sound of the speech is not relevant to telegraphic speech.
d. Incorrect. Speed and rate of speech are not factors in telegraphic speech.

11. d obj. 10 p. 236
a. Incorrect. Few people accept a notion of innate knowledge.
b. Incorrect. Thrift is not associated with intelligence
c. Incorrect. These categories may be more acceptable to scientists trying to define intelligence for a scientific study.
*d. Correct. Most people think of intelligence as an ability to succeed at normal life concerns.

12. c obj. 16 p. 247
a. Incorrect. This refers to the syndrome in which an individual, usually mentally retarded, has an extraordinary ability in one area, like mathematics, music, or art.
b. Incorrect. This defines mental retardation, and profound retardation is a category of mental retardation.
*c. Correct. This is the definition of mental retardation.
d. Incorrect. This defines mental retardation, and profound retardation is a category of mental retardation.

13. d obj. 17 p. 247
a. Incorrect. This causes other forms of retardation.
b. Incorrect. Toxins in the environment have detrimental effects on the fetus, but they are not identified with Down syndrome.
c. Incorrect. Fetal alcohol syndrome has its own special set of symptoms, and is not the same as Down syndrome.
*d. Correct. The extra chromosome is the definitive marker of Down syndrome

14. d   obj. 17   p. 247
a.   Incorrect. It may result from hereditary factors, but these are unknown.
b.   Incorrect. Environmental factors may play a role, but the actual cause is unknown.
c.   Incorrect. It is not a paradox, the causes are simply unknown at this time.
*d.   Correct. Familial retardation is characterized by having more than one retarded person in the immediate family group.

15. b   obj. 17   p. 247
a.   Incorrect. Mainstreaming increases the opportunities to interact with non-retarded students.
*b.   Correct. These opportunities are intended to improve educational access and remove the stigma of special classes.
c.   Incorrect. The intent of mainstreaming is to include all persons in the classroom.
d.   Incorrect. Mainstreaming is intended to end the separation of retarded and non-retarded students.

16. a   obj. 5   p. 226
17. d   obj. 5   p. 227
18. e   obj. 6   p. 227
19. c   obj. 6   p. 228
20. b   obj. 6   p. 228
21. functional fixedness   obj. 5   p. 226
22. syntax   obj. 7   p. 230
23. Telegraphic   obj. 8   p. 231

24.
- Describe your problem or challenge. It would be best to identify both the positive and the negative aspects of the challenge. What is gained and what is given up.
- Define the problem in terms of the steps that must be taken to achieve the solution.
- State several possible solution strategies as they apply to your problem.
- State how you will know when you have effectively solved the problem. Remember, if the problem is long-term, selecting one solution strategy may preclude using another.

Practise Test 2:
1.   a   obj. 1   p. 218
*a.   Correct. Perceptual psychologists focus on how the sensory system takes in information.
b.   Incorrect. Our understanding of the world is a focal point of study for cognitive psychologists.
c.   Incorrect. How we process information is a focal point of study for cognitive psychologists.
d.   Incorrect. Decision making is a focal point of study for cognitive psychologists.

2.   c   obj. 1   p. 220
a.   Incorrect. While "prototype" may refer to a new or first type, it also refers to the template or standard.
b.   Incorrect. Prototypes are neither spontaneous nor discarded quickly.

*c.   Correct. In this sense, the prototype is the template or standard for a concept.
d.   Incorrect. Not this option, the concept described here is known as "cognate" or "loan words."

3.   d   obj. 3   p. 222
a.   Incorrect. In the availability heuristic, one applies the most available category to the situation.
b.   Incorrect. A mental set is a set of expectations and inferences drawn from memory that indeed may cause reasoning errors, but not in this manner.
c.   Incorrect. Functional fixedness refers specifically to applying objects to a problem in the manner of their typical or common function, thus being fixated on a particular approach.
*d.   Correct. The representative heuristic selects a category that may represent the situation but can be erroneously applied (or misapplied).

4.   b   obj. 3   p. 221
a.   Incorrect. Problems of arrangement may include puzzles and similar problems.
*b.   Correct. No such type of problem.
c.   Incorrect. A problem of inducing structure involves finding relationships among existing elements.
d.   Incorrect. Transformation problems involve changing from one state to another (the goal state).

5.   a   obj. 3   p. 221
*a.   Correct. True, this describes a problem of inducing structure.
b.   Incorrect. This is not one of the three types of problems, and thus the definition does not apply.
c.   Incorrect. An arrangement problem is more like a jig-saw puzzle, where elements may be rearranged.
d.   Incorrect. A transformation problem involves moving from one state to another (goal state).

6.   a   obj. .3   p. 222
*a.   Correct. Changing from one state to another is a transformation.
b.   Incorrect. This refers to another kind of problem.
c.   Incorrect. Insight is a means of solving a problem, not a type of problem (unless someone is without any insight).
d.   Incorrect. This refers to another kind of problem.

7.   b   obj. 4   p. 224
a.   Incorrect. A means-ends approach might be more, "I know the steps I need to take, and I am taking them."
*b.   Correct. Each step is a subgoal.
c.   Incorrect. Trial and error might be more: "I think I'll try this major next semester."
d.   Incorrect. Algorithmic approach might be more "I need three course from this group, two from that, etc."

8.   b   obj. 5   p. 226
a.   Incorrect. These hunches may actually make it hard to see alternatives.

*b. Correct. Initial perceptions may include more conventional ways of using the elements of the problem and tools at hand to solve it.
c. Incorrect. While true, it does not apply to these two concepts.
d. Incorrect. Not really sure what this means.

9. b   obj. 6   p. 228
a. Incorrect. Convergent thinking involves logical reasoning and knowledge in the process of thinking.
*b. Correct. Divergent thinking is the only consistently identified characteristic of creative thinking.
c. Incorrect. Many creative thinkers are highly intelligent, but this is not a necessary characteristic.
d. Incorrect. Recurrent thought does not characterize creativity.

10. c   obj. 7   p. 230
a. Incorrect. Synthetics is a science fiction word used to describe synthetically produced biological organisms.
b. Incorrect. Semantics is the study of the meanings of words.
*c. Correct. Syntax governs the order in of words in a sentence.
d. Incorrect. Systematics is a neologism (not really a word, but it sounds like one, and is probably used by a lot of people).

11. c   obj. 11   p. 237
a. Incorrect. Other techniques were used to increase the reliability of earlier tests.
b. Incorrect. It does make this possible, but it was not the purpose of developing the intelligence quotient.
*c. Correct. The IQ is a standardized quotient and it allows for comparisons between chronological ages.
d. Incorrect. This was not the purpose for developing the intelligence quotient.

12. b   obj. 11   pp. 237, 238
a. Incorrect. See answer b.
*b. Correct. These scores represent the average range at one standard deviation from the mean.
c. Incorrect. See answer d.
d. Incorrect. See answer b.

13. a   obj. 13   p. 243
*a. Correct. The list of eight is: musical, bodily kinesthetic, logical-mathematical, linguistic, spatial, interpersonal, intrapersonal intelligence, and naturalist.
b. Incorrect. See answer a.
c. Incorrect. See answer a.
d. Incorrect. See answer a.

14. c   obj. 13   p. 244
a. Incorrect. This refers to linguistic capacity.
b. Incorrect. This refers to physical control skills, such as dancers may have.

*c. Correct. Interpersonal skill is recognized as the skill of interaction with others.
d. Incorrect. Intrapersonal intelligence refers to the individuals self-awareness.

15. b   obj. 11   p. 238
16. d   obj. 13   p. 243
17. a   obj. 13   p. 243
18. e   obj. 11   p. 237
19. c   obj. 14   p. 245
20. Fluid   obj. 13   p. 243
21. Crystallized   obj. 13   p. 243
22. intelligence quotient obj. 11   p. 237
23. Sir Francis Galton   obj. 11   p. 237
24. moderate   obj. 17   p. 247

25.
• Chimpanzees acquire an ability to speak that is comparable to a two-year old child.
• The physical ability in humans to produce language has the greatest production capability.
• You may be familiar with research in dolphin and whale communication or work with other animals. Examples could be used to support your answer.
• What is meant by "unique" must be defined to complete this answer. Indeed human language is unique, but other animals do communicate.

Practise Test 3:
1. d   obj. 1   p. 218
a. Incorrect. This is one of the components of the text's definition.
b. Incorrect. Cognition refers to the processes involved in how people come to know their world.
c. Incorrect. Cognition includes language and the interpretation of language.
*d. Correct. This statement describes the processes of sensation and perception, while not part of cognition, they are companion processes.

2. b   obj. 1   p. 219
a. Incorrect. Concepts may result from errors in some way, but they do not themselves produce errors.
*b. Correct. Like perception, concepts help make the world understandable by simplifying and organizing it.
c. Incorrect. Even if this is true, it does not address the similarity between concepts and perception.
d. Incorrect. We know of no innate concepts.

3. b   obj. 2   p. 220
a. Incorrect. The means ends does not apply here.
*b. Correct. Since your roommate is a member of the category of telemarketers, the representative heuristic suggests that somehow he might be representative of that group of people.
c. Incorrect. The availability heuristic would suggest that you utilized only currently available or the most prominent information about telemarketers and

ignored other more important information that is easily recalled from memory. While true, you had no other information about your roommate.
d. Incorrect. There is no such heuristic.

4. a   obj. 5   p. 226
*a. Correct. Functional fixedness forces us to focus on the waffle iron's traditional function, ignoring that it could be used as a weight or a clamp, or even an electrical conductor.
b. Incorrect. Insight is the restructuring of given elements.
c. Incorrect. Awareness seems to be restricted in this case.
d. Incorrect. Over preparation may lead to functional fixedness by encouraging the habitual use of an object, but it is not the name of the phenomena.

5. d   obj. 7   p. 230
a. Incorrect. Grammar governs how a thought becomes language in a general sense, and a more precise possibility is given in the options.
b. Incorrect. Phonology governs the production of sounds.
c. Incorrect. Syntax refers to the structure of sentences and not their meaning.
*d. Correct. Semantics governs the use of words and sentences to make specific meanings, and would govern how the same words can be rearranged to make different meanings.

6. b   obj. 8   p. 231
a. Incorrect. This occurs shortly after the first major development of dropping sounds that the native language does not contain.
*b. Correct. The first thing that happens occurs when babbling sounds that are not in the native language disappear.
c. Incorrect. This can happen at any time but becomes consistent after dropping sounds that the native language does not contain.
d. Incorrect. This occurs after several other milestones.

7. b   obj. 9   p. 233
a. Incorrect. True, critics have compared the language skills of apes to other trained animals.
*b. Correct. The comparison has been made to a 2-year-old. A 5-year-old has most of the grammar skills of an adult.
c. Incorrect. This describes one of the more common techniques used on training apes to produce communication.
d. Incorrect. This reflects the major problem faced by apes: they do not have the correct physical apparatus for speech.

8. a   obj. 9   p. 233
*a. Correct. By having many names for turquoise, the Navaho may be able to make more refined distinctions about turquoise (thus think about it differently).

b. Incorrect. This is a reverse statement of the linguistic relativity hypothesis and is the general view of how grammar works.
c. Incorrect. The language acquisition device does not address how having many words for an object would influence how we think.
d. Incorrect. While the Navaho are considered native Americans, this example does not support the nativist position.

9. d   obj. 8   233
a. Incorrect. If this theory existed this might be a good definition of it.
b. Incorrect. No such law has ever been stated.
c. Incorrect. No such hypothesis has ever been stated.
*d. Correct. The linguistic-relativity hypothesis states that language determines thought.

10. b   obj. 9   p. 233
a. Incorrect. Reactions might be possible items to observe, but little about cognition could be gained from them in this study.
*b. Correct. Timing the process actually provides evidence of how different images can be formed and how people may produce images.
c. Incorrect. After some study, the experimenter would probably find that respiration does not change much while imagining giraffes.
d. Incorrect. Someone has been the subject of too many experiments!

11 a   obj. 1   p. 220
*a. Correct. This example would probably come to mind more readily than the other options.
b. Incorrect. This is not a specific example, but is instead a definition of one type of table.
c. Incorrect. This specific table would be less familiar to you, but could serve as a prototype for someone else.
d. Incorrect. This is not a specific example, but is instead a definition of one type of table.

12. a   obj. 11   p. 237
*a. Correct. The original design was to distinguish between "bright" and "dull" students. Binet developed the test to help place students according to their tested skill level, and students who performed only as well as younger students were considered "dull."
b. Incorrect. See answer a.
c. Incorrect. See answer a.
d. Incorrect. See answer a.

13 c   obj. 11   p. 237
a. Incorrect. See answer c.
b. Incorrect. See answer c.
*c. Correct. Two-third includes the first standard deviation on either side of the average, which for IQ scores is between 85 and 115.
d. Incorrect. See answer c.

14. c   obj. 11   pp. 238, 239
a. Incorrect. See answer c.

b.   Incorrect. See answer c.
*c   Correct. The subtests are: information, comprehension, arithmetic, similarities, digit symbol, picture completion, and object assembly.
d.   Incorrect. See answer c.

15. d   obj. 12   p. 240
a.   Incorrect. See answer d.
b.   Incorrect. See answer d.
c.   Incorrect. See answer d.
*d. Correct. Each time the test is given, it yields the same scores, suggesting that it is reliable from one situation to another. This example illustrates validity, since this test clearly measured what it was supposed to measure.

16. b   obj. 4   p. 224
17. c   obj. 1   p. 218
18. a   obj. 1   p. 220
19. d   obj. 9   p 233
20. e   obj. 6   p. 227

21. means-end analysis   obj. 4   p. 223
22. subgoals   obj. 4   p. 224
23. Confirmation bias   obj. 5   p. 227
24. overgeneralization   obj. 8   p. 231
25 cognitive complexity obj. 6   p. 222

26. Positive:
Attempts to teach immigrants subject material in their own language and slowly adding English instruction. Respecting their cultural differences by acknowledging their language illustrates value for their cultural heritage.
Supporters quote research that states that maintaining a native language will not interfere with learning English.
Bilingual children score higher on intelligence and achievement tests.
Negative:
Those not in favour say bilingual children will be left behind in school and in the workplace.

Motivation and Emotion

8

Chapter Overview

Chapter 8 focuses on the major conceptions of motivation, discussing how the different motives and needs people experience jointly affect behaviour. The theories of motivation draw upon basic instincts, drives, levels of arousal, expectations, and self-realization as possible sources of motives. Thirst and hunger are two motives that have a physiological basis, and the needs for achievement, affiliation, and power are learned motives. Next, the chapter presents three major theories of emotion: the James-Lange Theory, the Cannon-Bard Theory, and the Schachter-Singer Theory. The chapter concludes with similarities in facial expressions and non-verbal behaviour across cultures.

To further investigate the topics covered in this chapter, you can access the related websites by visiting the following link: http://www.mcgrawhill.ca/college/feldman

Prologue: A Change in Direction
Looking Ahead

Section 1: Explaining Motivation

Instinct Approaches: Born to Be Motivated
Drive-Reduction Approaches: Satisfying Our Needs
Arousal Approaches: Beyond Drive Reduction
Incentive Approaches: Motivation's Pull
Cognitive Approaches: The Thoughts Behind Motivation
Maslow's Hierarchy: Ordering Motivational Needs

Pathways Through Psychology: Tara K. MacDonald: Assistant Professor of Psychology, Queen's University, Kingston, Ontario

Applying the Different Approaches to Motivation

Section 2: Human Needs and Motivation: Eat, Drink, and Be Daring

The Motivation Behind Hunger and Eating

> **Becoming an Informed Consumer of Psychology:** Dieting and Losing Weight Successfully

Sexual Motivation: The Facts of Life

> **Exploring Diversity:** Female Circumcision: A Celebration of Culture - or Genital Mutilation?

The Need for Achievement: Striving for Success
The Need for Affiliation: Striving for Friendship
The Need for Power: Striving for Impact on Others

Section 3: Understanding Emotional Experiences

The Functions of Emotions
Determining the Range of Emotions: Labeling Our Feelings

The Roots of Emotions

The James-Lange Theory: Do Gut Reactions Equal Emotions?
The Cannon-Bard Theory: Physiological Reactions as the Result of Emotions
The Schachter-Singer Theory: Emotions as Labels
Contemporary Perspectives on Emotion

> **Applying Psychology in the 21st Century:** The Truth About Lies: Do Lie Detectors Work?

Learning Objectives

These are the concepts and the learning objectives for Chapter 8. Read them carefully as part of your preliminary survey of the chapter.

Explaining Motivation

1. Define motivation and emotion, and discuss the role of each in human behaviour. (p. 258)

2. Describe and distinguish among instinct, drive-reduction, arousal, incentive, and cognitive theories of motivation. (pp. 259–265)

3.   Explain Maslow's hierarchy of motivation. (pp. 262–263)

Human Needs and Motivation: Eat, Drink, and Be Daring

4.   Define obesity, differentiate between biological and social factors associated with hunger, and discuss the roots of obesity. (pp. 265–268)

5.   Describe the eating disorders anorexia nervosa and bulimia nervosa, and discuss possible causes for these disorders. (pp. 268–269)

6.   Indicate the most effective behaviours associated with weight loss. (pp. 269–270)

7.   Describe the biological and psychological aspects of sexual behaviour (pp. 270–271)

8.   Describe patterns of heterosexual behaviour, including premarital, and extramarital sex (pp. 271–272

9.   Define homosexuality and bisexuality, and discuss theories that have been proposed regarding the development of sexual orientation. (pp. 272–274)

10. Discuss the secondary motivations of achievement, affiliation, and power. (pp. 275–276)

Understanding Emotional Experiences

11. Describe the functions of emotions and the range of emotional expression. (pp. 277–279)

The Roots of Emotions

12. Identify the key points of the James-Lange, the Cannon-Bard, and the Schachter-Singer theories of emotion, and distinguish each theory from the others. (pp. 280–283)

13. Describe how emotional responses can be used in lie detection, and discuss the validity of traditional lie detection devices. (p. 284)

SECTION 1: Explaining Motivation

Prepare

- *How does motivation direct and energize behaviour?*

Organize

- *Instinct Approaches*
- *Drive-Reduction Approaches*
- *Arousal Approaches*

- *Incentive Approaches*
- *Cognitive Approaches*
- *Maslow's Hierarchy*
- *Applying the Different Approaches to Motivation*

Work

The factors that direct and energize behaviour comprise the major focus of the study of

[a] _____ . [b] _____ are the desired goals that underlie behaviour. Psychologists who study motivation seek to understand why people do the things they do. The study of emotions includes the internal experience at any given moment.

There are a number of approaches to understanding motivation. An early approach focused

on [c] _____ as inborn, biologically determined patterns of behaviour. Proponents of this view argue that there exist preprogrammed patterns of behaviour.

[d] _____ **approaches to motivation** focus on behaviour as an attempt to remedy the shortage of some basic biological requirement. In this view, a

[e] _____ is a motivational tension, or arousal, that energizes a behaviour to fulfil a need. [f] _____ meet biological requirements, while

[g] _____ have no obvious biological basis. Primary drives are resolved by reducing the need that underlies it. Primary drives are also governed by a basic motivational

phenomena of [h] _____, the goal of maintaining optimal biological functioning. Drive-reduction theories have difficulty explaining behaviour that is not directed at reducing a drive but may be directed instead at maintaining or increasing arousal. Also, behaviour appears to be motivated occasionally by curiosity as well.

The theory that explains motivation as being directed toward maintaining or increasing

excitement is the [i] _____ *approaches to motivation.* If the levels of stimulation are too low, arousal theory says that we will try to increase the levels.

In motivational terms, the reward is the [j] _____ .

[k] _____ *approaches to motivation* explain why behaviour may be motivated by external stimuli.

[l] _____ *approaches to motivation* focus on our thoughts,

expectations, and understanding of the world. [mm] _____ refers to the

value an activity has in the enjoyment of participating in it, and [n] _____ refers to behaviour that is done for a tangible reward. We work harder for a task that has intrinsic motivation. Also, as tangible rewards become available, intrinsic motivation declines and extrinsic motivation increases.

Evaluate

_____ 1.   motives

_____ 2.   emotions

_____ 3.   instinct

_____ 4.   drive

_____ 5.   primary drives

a. An inborn pattern of behaviour that is biologically determined.

b. Desired goals that prompt behaviour.

c. The internal feelings experienced at any given moment.

d. Biological needs such as hunger, thirst, fatigue, and sex.

e. A tension or arousal that energizes behaviour in order to fulfil a need.

Rethink

1. Which approaches to motivation are most commonly used in the workplace? How might each approach be used to design employment policies that can sustain or increase motivation?

2. A writer who works all day composing copy for an advertising firm has a hard time keeping her mind on her work and continually watches the clock. After work she turns to a collection of stories she is creating and writes long into the night, completely forgetful of the clock. What ideas from your reading on motivation help to explain this phenomenon?

SECTION 2:   Human Needs and Motivation: Eat, Drink, and Be Daring

Prepare

- *What biological and social factors underlie hunger?*
- *What are the varieties of sexual behaviour?*
- *How are needs relating to achievement, affiliation, and power motivation exhibited?*

Organize

- *The Motivation Behind Hunger and Eating*
- *Sexual Motivation*
- *The Need for Achievement*
- *The Need for Affiliation*
- *The Need for Power*

Work

One-third of Americans are considered more than 20 percent overweight and thus suffering from [a] _____. Most nonhumans will regulate their intake of food even when it is abundant. Hunger is apparently quite complex, consisting of a number of mechanisms that signal changes in the body. One is the level of the sugar glucose in the blood. The higher the level of glucose, the less hunger is experienced. The [b] _____ monitors the blood chemistry. A rat with its [c] _____ damaged will starve itself to death, and one with the [d] _____ damaged will experience extreme overeating.

One theory suggests that the body maintains a [e] _____ . This set point controls whether the hypothalamus calls for more or less food intake. Differences in people's metabolism may also account for being overweight. [f] _____ is the rate at which energy is produced and expended. People with high metabolic rates can eat as much food as they want and not gain weight. People with low metabolism eat little and still gain. As an alternative to the set-point explanation, the [g] _____ proposes a combination of genetic and environmental factors.

[h] _____ is a disease that afflicts primarily females. Sufferers refuse to eat and may actually starve themselves to death. [i] _____ is a condition in which individuals will binge on large quantities of food and then purge themselves with vomiting or laxatives. People suffering from bulimia are treated by being taught to eat foods they enjoy and to have control over their eating. Anorexia is treated by reinforcing weight gain, that is, giving privileges for success.

Sexual behaviour in humans is filled with meaning, values, and feelings. The basic biology of the sexual response helps us understand the importance of sexual behaviour. Human sexual behaviour is not governed by the genetic control that other animals experience. In males, the testes, part of the male [j] _____, secrete [k] _____, beginning at puberty. Androgens increase the sex drive and produce secondary sex characteristics like body hair and voice change. When women reach puberty, the ovaries, the female reproductive organs, produce [l] _____ and [m] _____, the female sex hormone. Estrogen reaches its highest levels during [n] _____, the release of eggs from the ovary.

Sexual behaviour is influenced by expectations, attitudes, beliefs, and the state of medical and biological knowledge. Defining what is normal can be approached by determining the deviation for an average or typical behaviour, though there are many behaviours that are unusual statistically but not abnormal. Another approach is to compare behaviour against a standard or ideal.

[o] _____ is sexual self-stimulation, and its practise is quite common. Males masturbate more often than females, with males beginning in early teens, though females start later and reach maximum frequency later. Negative attitudes about masturbation continue, though it is perfectly healthy and harmless.

[p] _____ refers to sexual behaviour between men and women. It includes all aspects of sexual contact—kissing, caressing, sex play, and intercourse. Premarital sex continues to be viewed through a [q] _____, as something acceptable for males but unacceptable for females.

The **[r]** _____ is a learned characteristic involving the sustained striving for and attainment of a level of excellence. People with high needs for achievement seek out opportunities to compete and succeed. People with low needs for achievement are motivated by the desire to avoid failure.

The **[s]** _____ is used to test achievement motivation. It requires that the person look at a series of ambiguous pictures and then write a story that tells what is going on and what will happen next.

The **[t]** _____ refers to the needs we have of establishing and maintaining relationships with others. People high in affiliation needs tend to be more concerned with relationships and to be with their friends more. The **[u]** _____ is a tendency to seek impact, control, or influence over others. People with a strong need for power tend to seek office more often than people with a weak need for power. Men tend to display their need for power through aggression, drinking, sexual exploitation, and competitive sports, while women who have high need for power are more restrained.

Evaluate

_____ 1. self-actualization

_____ 2. need for achievement

_____ 3. need for affiliation

_____ 4. need for power

a. A tendency to want to seek impact, control, or influence on others in order to be seen as a powerful individual.

b. A need to establish and maintain relationships with other people.

c. A stable, learned characteristic, in which satisfaction comes from striving for and achieving a level of excellence.

d. A state of self-fulfilment in which people realize their highest potential.

Rethink

3. In what ways do societal expectations, expressed by television shows and commercials, contribute to both obesity and excessive concern about weight loss? How could television contribute to better eating habits and attitudes toward weight? Should it be required to do so?

4. Can traits such as need for achievement, need for power, and need for affiliation be used to select workers for jobs? What other criteria, both motivational and personal, would have to be considered when making such a selection?

Section 3: Understanding Emotional Experiences

Prepare

- **What are emotions, and how do we experience them?**
- **What are the functions of emotions?**

Organize

- **The Functions of Emotions**
- **Determining the Range of Emotions**
- **The James-Lange Theory**
- **The Cannon-Bard Theory**
- **The Schacter-Singer Theory**
- **Contemporary Perspectives on Emotion**

Work

Though difficult to define, **[a]** _____ are understood to be the feelings that have both physiological and cognitive aspects and that influence behaviour. Physical changes occur whenever we experience an emotion, and we identify these changes as emotions.

A number of important functions of emotions have been identified.

- *Preparing us for action.* Emotions prepare us for action by preparing effective responses to a variety of situations.
- *Shaping our future behaviour.* Emotions shape our future behaviour by promoting learning that will influence making appropriate responses in the future by leading to the repetition of responses that lead to satisfying emotional feelings.
- *Helping us to interact more effectively with others.* Emotions also help regulate interactions with others.

Psychologists have been attempting to identify the most important fundamental emotions. Many have suggested that emotions should be understood through their component parts. There may be cultural differences as well, though these differences may reflect different linguistic categories for the emotions.

We have many ways to describe the experiences of emotion that we have. The physiological reactions that accompany fear are associated with the activation of the autonomic nervous system. They include: 1) an increase in breathing rate; 2) an increase in heart rate, 3) a widening of the pupils; 4) a cessation of the functions of the digestive system; and 5) a contraction of the muscles below the surface of the skin.

Though these changes occur without awareness, the emotional experience of fear can be felt intensely. Whether these physiological responses are the cause of the experience or the result of the experience of emotion remains unclear.

The **[b]** _____ *theory of emotion* states that emotions are the perceived physiological reactions that occur in the internal organs. They called this *visceral experience*.

The **[c]** _____ *theory of emotion* rejects the view that physiological arousal alone leads to the perception of emotion. In this theory, the emotion-producing stimuli is first perceived, then the thalamus activates the viscera, and at the same time a message is sent to the cortex.

The **[d]** _____ *theory of emotion* emphasizes that the emotion experienced depends on the environment and on comparing ourselves with others.

For each of the three major theories, there is some contradictory evidence. Emotions are a complex phenomena that no single theory can yet explain adequately.

Evaluate

_____ 1.   James-Lange theory of emotion

_____ 2.   Cannon-Bard theory of emotion

_____ 3.   Schachter-Singer theory of emotion

_____ 4.   emotions

a.   The belief that emotions are determined jointly by a nonspecific kind of physiological arousal and its interpretation, based on environmental cues.

b.   The belief that emotions are determined jointly by a nonspecific kind of physiological arousal and its interpretation, based on environmental cues.

c.   The belief that emotional experience is a reaction to bodily events occurring as a result of an external situation.

d.   Feelings that generally have both physiological and cognitive elements and that influence behaviour.

Rethink

5.   Many people enjoy watching movies, sporting events, and music performances in crowded theatres and arenas more than they like watching them at home alone. Which theory of emotions may help explain this? How?

6.   If researchers learned how to control emotional responses so that targeted emotions could be caused or prevented, what ethical concerns might arise? Under what circumstances, if any, should such techniques be used?

Practise Questions

Test your knowledge of the chapter material by answering these questions. These questions have been placed in three Practise Tests. The first two tests are composed of questions that will test your recall of factual knowledge. The third test contains questions that are challenging and primarily test for conceptual knowledge and your ability to apply that knowledge. Check your answers and review the feedback using the Answer Key in the following pages of the *Study Guide*.

PRACTISE TEST 1:

1.   Primary drives are motives that:
   a.   people rate as being most important to them.
   b.   seem to motivate an organism the most.

    c.   are least likely to be satisfied before self-actualization can occur.

    d.   have a biological basis and are universal.

2.   _____ activate behaviour and orient it toward achieving goals.

    a.   Instincts   c.   Emotions

    b.   Motives   d.   Homeostatic energizers

3.   The process by which an organism tries to maintain an optimal level of internal biological functioning is called:

    a.   primary drive equilibrium.   c.   drive reduction.

    b.   homeostasis.   d.   opponent-process theory.

4.   A motivation behind behaviour in which no obvious biological need is being fulfilled is the definition of:

    a.   a primary drive.   c.   a secondary drive.

    b.   an achievement.   d.   instinct.

5.   The desirable qualities of the external stimulus are the focus of:

    a.   the incentive motivational approach.

    b.   the drive-reduction motivational approach.

    c.   the instinctive motivational approach.

    d.   the cognitive motivational approach.

6.   The incentive theory of motivation focuses on:

    a.   instincts.

    b.   the characteristics of external stimuli.

    c.   drive reduction.

    d.   the rewarding quality of various behaviours that are motivated by arousal.

7.   The expectancy-value theory states that the two types of cognitions that control motivation are:

    a.   drive reductions and positive incentives.

    b.   rewards and punishments.

    c.   intrinsic motivation and extrinsic motivation.

    d.   hopes and disappointments.

8.   According to Maslow, which of the following must be met before people can fulfil any higher-order motivations?

    a.   extrinsic needs   c.   primary needs

    b.   intrinsic needs   d.   secondary needs

9.   A college woman has experienced a major weight loss and has begun refusing to eat. She denies that she has an eating problem and does not recognize that she suffers from:

    a.   hyperphagia.   c.   rolfing.

    b.   bulimia.   d.   anorexia nervosa.

10.   According to the text, which of the following is thought to be primarily involved in the physiological regulation of eating behaviour?

    a.   cortex   c.   hypothalamus

    b.   amygdala   d.   hippocampus

11. According to the text, which alternative below is **not** good advice for a person trying to lose weight?
    a. Exercise regularly.
    b. Reduce the influence of external cues and social behaviour on your eating.
    c. Choose a diet program that gives rather rapid weight losses so that you will stay motivated.
    d. Remember, when you reach your desired goal, you're not finished!

12. The _____ is used to measure an individual's need for achievement.
    a. Scholastic Assessment Test
    b. Intelligence Quotient Test
    c. Yerkes-Dodson Achievement Analysis
    d. Thematic Apperception Test

13. Which theory postulates that emotions are identified by observing the environment and comparing ourselves with others?
    a. Schachter-Singer theory   c. James-Lange theory
    b. Cannon-Bard theory   d. Ekman's theory

14. William James and Walter Lange suggested that major emotions correlate with particular "gut reactions" of internal organs. They called this internal response:
    a. a physiological pattern.   c. an autonomic response.
    b. a psychological experience.   d. a visceral experience.

15. Which theory assumes that both physiological arousal and emotional experiences are produced simultaneously?
    a. Schachter-Singer theory   c. James-Lange theory
    b. Cannon-Bard theory   d. Ekman's theory

_____ 16. drive-reduction theory

a. Motivation by focusing on the role of an individual's thoughts, expectations, and understanding of the world.

_____ 17. arousal approach to motivation

b. The theory that claims that drives are produced to obtain our basic biological requirements.

_____ 18. homeostasis

c. The belief that we try to maintain certain levels of stimulation and activity, changing them as necessary.

_____ 19. incentive approach to motivation

d. The theory explaining motivation in terms of external stimuli.

_____ 20. cognitive approaches to motivation

e. The process by which an organism tries to maintain an internal biological balance.

21. An internal motivational state that is created by a physiological need is called a _____.

22. The _____ model views motivated behaviour as directed toward the reduction of a physiological need.

23. _____ is the body's mechanism for maintaining an optimum, balanced range of physiological processes.

24. Theories that stress the active processing of information are _____ of motivation.

25. Describe each of the main theories of motivation and attempt to explain a single behaviour from the point of view of each theory.

PRACTISE TEST 2:

1. According to the text, the main function of motivation is to:
   a. create tension.
   b. provide feeling.
   c. promote learning of survival behaviours.
   d. provide direction to behaviour.

2. Which of the following is the best example of a drive that is common to both humans and animals?
   a. power
   b. hunger
   c. cognition
   d. achievement

3. The compensatory activity of the autonomic nervous system, which returns the body to normal levels of functioning after a trauma, is called:
   a. homeostasis.
   b. biorhythmicity.
   c. biofeedback.
   d. transference.

4. In the drive-reduction motivation model, _____ is the drive related to the need for water.
   a. the drinking instinct
   b. thirst
   c. repetitive water-intake behaviour
   d. water-balance in body tissues

5. According to the text, some psychologists feel that the incentive theory of motivation is strengthened when combined with complementary concepts drawn from:
   a. instinct theory.
   b. drive-reduction theory.
   c. arousal theory.
   d. cognitive theory.

6. Our hopes that a behaviour will cause us to reach a certain goal and our understanding that the goal will be meaningful or important to us are combined in:
   a. the expectancy-value theory of motivation.
   b. the drive-reduction theory of motivation.
   c. Maslow's hierarchy of motivation.
   d. arousal theory of motivation.

7. Which theory is **least** tied to biological mechanisms?
   a. instinct theory
   b. cognitive theory
   c. drive-reduction theory
   d. arousal theory

8. In Maslow's hierarchal pyramid of motivation, self-actualizers:
   a. are notably self-sufficient at all levels: growing their own food, finding their own friends, creating their own artwork, etc.
   b. are dependent upon others but are inwardly focused.
   c. have achieved their major goals in life.
   d. encourage others to do their best while remaining modest themselves.

9. Approximately how many obese individuals can correctly attribute their obesity to their body set point?

a. none
b. all
c. not all, but a high number
d. some, but a low number

10. Which of the following is an eating disorder usually affecting attractive, successful females between the ages of 12 and 40 who refuse to eat and sometimes literally starve themselves to death?
   a. metabolic malfunction
   b. bulimia
   c. anorexia nervosa
   d. obesity

11. Which alternative below is **not** true of the need for achievement?
   a. Individuals with a high need for achievement choose situations in which they are likely to succeed easily.
   b. It is a learned motive.
   c. Satisfaction is obtained by striving for and attaining a level of excellence.
   d. High need for achievement is related to economic and occupational success.

12. According to the text, women, as opposed to men, tend to channel their need for power through:
   a. socially responsible ways.
   b. questionable means.
   c. quietly aggressive ways.
   d. uncharted, high-risk opportunities.

13. According to the James-Lange theory of emotion, _____ determines the emotional experience.
   a. physiological change
   b. a cognitive process
   c. an instinctive process
   d. the environment

14. _____suggests that when people lack some biological requirement such as water a drive is produced.
   a. The expectancy-value theory of motivation.
   b. The drive-reduction theory of motivation.
   c. Maslow's hierarchy of motivation.
   d. The arousal theory of motivation

_____ 15. hypothalamus

_____ 16. lateral hypothalamus

_____ 17. ventromedial hypothalamus

_____ 18. metabolism

_____ 19. weight set point

a. The part of the brain that, when damaged, results in an organism's starving to death.

b. The particular level of weight that the body strives to maintain.

c. The part of the brain that, when injured, results in extreme overeating.

d. The structure in the brain that is primarily responsible for regulating food intake.

e. The rate at which energy is produced and expended by the body.

20. The view that basic needs must be met before an individual can move on to higher levels of satisfaction is illustrated by _____.

21. A range of weight that the body seems to maintain over time is referred to as the
_____.

22. _____ is the need to be with others and avoid being alone.

23. According to your text, Eleanor Roosevelt, Abraham Lincoln, and Albert Einstein all fulfilled the highest levels of motivational needs, Maslow's level of _____.

24. The _____ is the tiny brain structure primarily responsible for food intake.

25. Under what conditions might a polygraph test be considered fair? Outline the possible ethical and scientific concerns that arise from the use of the polygraph in support of your answer. In contrast, discuss the same concerns regarding the use of honesty, or integrity tests, by employers who attempt to discover the likelihood that job applicants would steal.

PRACTISE TEST 3: Conceptual, Applied, and Challenging Questions

1. Advertisements for a job boast that it offers $5 more than minimum wage, a guaranteed cash bonus after thirty days, and a paid vacation. This advertisement emphasizes the concept of:
   a. opponent-process motivation.
   b. arousal motivation.
   c. drive-reduction motivation.
   d. extrinsic motivation.

2. Brothers Patrick, the thin one, and Jerome, the obese one, had lunch just before boarding their plane. When flight attendants serve lunch, what will the two brothers be expected to do, according to the external-cue theory?
   a. Neither will eat the lunch on the plane.
   b. The obese man will eat a second lunch, while the thin man may skip it.
   c. The thin man will eat a second lunch, but the obese man will skip it.
   d. Both men will eat a second lunch.

3. What percentage of Canadiian children are seriously overweight and face possible health problems?
   a. 5 percent
   b. 25 percent
   c. 50 percent
   d. 65 percent

4. Abby developed a cycle of binge eating, during which she consumed enormous quantities of high calorie foods and then induced vomiting afterward. Dr. Slocum told Abby that she could do permanent damage to her health if she continued the behaviour and that if she continued she could become:
   a. ischemic.
   b. depressed.
   c. volumetric.
   d. bulimic.

5. Katherine finished her college degree with honours and received a variety of excellent job offers. Instead, she decided to enter graduate school to acquire more advanced skills and get even better job offers. Katherine is demonstrating her:
   a. need for affiliation.
   b. need for achievement.
   c. fear of failure.
   d. need for power.

6. Emotions play an important role in all of the following **except**:
   a. making life interesting.

b. helping us to regulate social interaction.

c. informing us of internal bodily needs.

d. preparing us for action in response to the external environment.

7. Shannon, who devotes her efforts to maintaining her standing on the Dean's List, is highly motivated in her need for:

a. affiliation.

c. power.

b. cognition.

d. achievement.

8. The notion that the same nerve impulse triggers simultaneously the physiological arousal and the emotional experience is a hallmark of the:

a. Cannon-Bard theory of emotion.

c. Schachter-Singer theory of emotion.

b. facial-affect theory of emotion.

d. James-Lange theory of emotion.

9. A polygraph is an electronic device that detects lying by measuring:

a. brain waves.

c. breathing patterns and sweating.

b. brain waves and sweating.

d. breathing patterns and brain waves.

10. Jason feels unprepared after finishing four years of schooling that qualified him as an accountant. Instead of applying for and taking a position after graduation, as he had planned to do, he decides to take more time and go to graduate school instead. Jason is demonstrating his:

a. need for affiliation.

c. fear of failure.

b. need for achievement.

d. need for power

11. The notion that emotion resulted from the interpretation of the perception of bodily change is the:

a. Cannon-Bard theory of emotion

c. Schachter-Singer theory of emotion

b. facial-affect theory of emotion

d. James-Lange theory of emotion

12. Which of the following is most typical of an individual high in the need for power?

a. Tina, who is aggressive and flamboyant

b. Daniel, who has joined the local chapter of a political party

c. Barbara, who shows concern for others and is highly nurturant

d. Mary, who enjoys competitive sports

13. Which of the following is most typical of an individual high in the need for affiliation?

a. Marie, who appears sensitive to others and prefers to spend all her free time with friends

b. Nicolas, who joins a local political group

c. Therese, who enjoys team sports and likes to attend parties

d. Michael, who is aggressive and controlling whenever he is in groups

14. A job opportunity that encourages individual initiative, a competitive salary, and a paid vacation emphasizes the concept of:

a. opponent-process motivation.

c. drive-reduction motivation.

b. arousal motivation.

d. extrinsic motivation.

15. At first, Jose is quite excited about keeping his new car cleaned and serviced, and he does it without being asked. His father then begins a system of rewarding his efforts with an additional allowance. According to the cognitive approach to motivation, what is the most likely response that Jose will have?

a. His tendency to clean his car will be increased.

b. He will probably be less eager to clean his car.

c. He will be even more enthusiastic, but he will not clean his car any more frequently.

d. He will be unwilling to clean his car at all.

_____ 16. secondary drives

_____ 17. intrinsic motivation

_____ 18. extrinsic motivation

_____ 19. incentive

_____ 20. obesity

a. Anticipated rewards in motivation.

b. Participating in an activity for a tangible reward.

c. Participating in an activity for its own enjoyment, not for a reward.

d. Having weight that is more than 20 percent above the average weight for a person of a given height.

e. Drives in which no biological need is fulfilled.

21. In order to increase your _____, the rate at which food is converted to energy, you need to increase exercise.

22. Parents who are demanding and overcontrolling may increase the likelihood that their daughters will develop _____.

23. The tendency to seek impact, control, and influence over others is called the

_____.

24. Preparing us for action, shaping future behaviour, and helping us act more effectively with others are all functions of _____.

25. Explain how parents can attempt to minimize the negative affects of a culture that demands an unreasonable focus on thinness for its youth, especially females.

Spotlight on Terminology and Language—
Cultural Idioms

Explaining Motivation

Page 259 "As a result of these **shortcomings**, newer explanations have replaced conceptions of motivation based on instincts."

Shortcomings are deficiencies or flaws. What were some of the **shortcomings** of the early explanations defining motivation?

Page 259 "We usually try to satisfy a primary drive by reducing the need **underlying** it."

Underlying means lying under or beneath. To satisfy the primary drive, we would identify the need.

Page 259 "The reason for such behaviour is **homeostasis**, a basic motivational phenomenon underlying primary drives."

Homeostasis is the steady state of physiological equilibrium. It is the ability of a cell or an organism to maintain internal equilibrium by adjusting its internal processes.

Page 260 "**Incentive** approaches to motivation suggest that motivation stems from the desire to obtain valued external goals, or incentives."

An **incentive** is something that stimulates. Can both the fear or punishment and the expectation of rewards be **incentives**? What **incentives** do you find are most effective in motivating you to study?

Page 260 "Although the theory explains why we might **succumb** to an incentive (like a mouth-watering dessert) even though internal cues (like hunger) are lacking, it does not provide a complete explanation of **motivation**, since organisms seek to fulfil needs even when incentives are not apparent."

When you succumb, you yield to an overwhelming desire or overpowering force. **Motivation** is an inner state that energizes people toward the fulfilment of a goal. This would be the psychological process that arouses, directs, and maintains behaviour toward a goal.

Page 262 "**Intrinsic motivation** causes us to participate in an activity for our own enjoyment, rather than for any concrete, **tangible** reward that it will bring us. In contrast, **extrinsic motivation** causes us to do something for money, a grade, or some other concrete, tangible reward."

Intrinsic motivation is the inner drive that motivates people in the absence of external reward or punishment. What are some of your activities that are intrinsically motivated? A **tangible** reward is something able to be perceived as materially existent. When you receive money for your efforts, you receive a **tangible** reward. **Extrinsic** motivation is the desire to engage in an activity for money, recognition, or other tangible benefits. Describe some examples of how your work site motivates you both **intrinsically** and **extrinsically**.

Page 263 "**Self-actualization** is a state of self-fulfilment in which people realize their highest **potential** in their own unique way."

In Maslow's theory, **self-actualization** is the individual's predisposition to try to fulfil his or her potential. **Potential** is the inherent ability or capacity for growth or development.

Page 263 " In a sense, achieving self-actualization produces a decline in the striving and **yearning** for greater fulfilment that marks most people's lives and instead provides a sense of satisfaction with the current state of affairs."

When you **yearn** for something, you experience a strong desire. You want something very badly. Are their goals you **yearn** to obtain?

Human Needs and Motivation: Eat, Drink, and Be Daring

Page 265 "We'll begin with hunger and sex, the primary drives that have received the most attention from researchers, and then turn to secondary drives— those uniquely human strivings, based on learned needs and past experience, that help explain why people strive to achieve, to **affiliate** with others, and to seek power over others."

Affiliate means to associate with. Have you noticed that you choose to **affiliate** with particular people?

Page 266 "It's not just a matter of an empty stomach causing hunger pangs and a full one **alleviating** hunger."

To **alleviate** is to relieve. We may work to **alleviate** mental suffering through the use of psychotherapy.

Page 270 "In light of how difficult it can be to lose weight, psychologists Janet Polivy and C. Peter Herman suggest—**paradoxically**—that the best approach might be to avoid dieting in the first place."

A **paradox** is a seemingly contradictory statement that may nevertheless be true.

■ CHAPTER 8: ANSWER KEY

GUIDED REVIEW

Section 1:	Section 2:	Evaluate	Section 3:
[a] motivation	[a] obesity	1. d	[a] emotions
[b] Motives	[b] hypothalamus	2. c	[b] James-Lange
[c] instincts	[c] lateral hypothalamus	3. b	[c] Cannon-Bard
[d] Drive-reduction	[d] ventromedial	4. a	[d] Schachter-Singer
[e] drive	hypothalamus		
[f] Primary drives	[e] weight set point		Evaluate
[g] secondary drives	[f] Metabolism		1. c
[h] homeostasis	[g] settling point		2. b
[i] arousal	[h] Anorexia nervosa		3. a
[j] incentive	[i] Bulimia		4. d
[k] Incentive	[j] genitals		
[l] Cognitive	[k] androgens		
[m] intrinsic motivation	[l] estrogen		
[n] extrinsic motivation	[m] progesterone		
	[n] ovulation		
	[o] masturbation		
Evaluate	[p] heterosexuality		
1. b	[q] double standard		
2. c	[r] need for achievement		
3. a	[s] Thematic Apperception		
4. e	Test (TAT)		
5. d	[t] need for affiliation		
	[u] need for power		

Selected Rethink Answers

1. The arousal approach might be seen in the workplace by employees who seek either a very high or a very low level of stimulation and activity. Individuals may self-select into jobs that meet this need. Employees should look for "goodness of fit" in employee-job matching. The incentive approach, the desire to obtain valued external goals would encourage employers to find out what they can provide for employees to work toward. In the cognitive approach employees should encourage the development of intrinsic motivation by employees for the job they do.

5. Schachter-Singer Theory: Attending group events allows an individual to identify his or her own emotions by experiencing, observing, and comparing his or her emotions with the emotional experience of others in the group.

Practise Test 1:
1. d   obj. 2   p. 259
a. Incorrect. Since we may satisfy our primary drives without much difficulty, they may not hold much importance when compared with other types of drives.
b. Incorrect. Other types of drives may motivate an organism more.
c. Incorrect. They must be satisfied for self-actualization to occur.
*d. Correct. By definition, primary drives are those that have a biological basis.

2. b   obj. 1   p. 258
a. Incorrect. True, but "motives" is a more comprehensive choice.
*b. Correct. This defines "motives."

c. Incorrect. This is true also, but "motives" is a more comprehensive choice.
d. Incorrect. These are currently unknown to earthling science.

3. b   obj. 2   p. 259
a. Incorrect. There is no concept called "primary drive equilibrium."
*b. Correct. "Homeostasis" is the term used to describe a biological balance or equilibrium.
c. Incorrect. Though, drive reduction might be used to achieve a state of homeostasis.
d. Incorrect. Opponent-process theory is one of the theories that depends upon the tendency toward homeostasis to account for many phenomena.

4. c   obj. 2   p. 259

a. Incorrect. A primary drive has a clear biological need that it satisfies.
b. Incorrect. An achievement may or may not have a biological drive.
*c. Correct. By definition, secondary drives are not based on biological needs.
d. Incorrect. An instinct is a species specific behaviour governed by genetics and is thus biological.

5. a   obj. 2   p. 260
*a. Correct. External stimuli provide for "incentives" to act in a certain way.
b. Incorrect. The drive-reduction model focuses upon internal stimuli.
c. Incorrect. Desirableness would be irrelevant to instincts.
d. Incorrect. While important for this theory, external stimuli would not be the focus.

6. b   obj. 2   p. 260
a. Incorrect. Instinct theory, not incentive theory, focuses on instincts.
*b. Correct. The characteristics of external stimuli provide the incentive, or promise of reinforcement, that governs incentive theory.
c. Incorrect. Drive reduction is a core concept of drive theory.
d. Incorrect. This refers to arousal theory.

7. c   obj. 2   pp. 260, 262
a. Incorrect. These two factors are taken from two other approaches to motivation.
b. Incorrect. Both of these are typically extrinsic.
*c. Correct. Actually, motivations can only be one or the other of these two types.
d. Incorrect. These would have more to do with expectancy-value motivation.

8. c   obj. 3   p. 262
a. Incorrect. Some higher-order motivations may involve extrinsic motivations.
b. Incorrect. Higher-order motivations would include quite a few intrinsic needs.
*c. Correct. Primary needs must be satisfied before the individual can move on to higher-order motivation.
d. Incorrect. Higher-order motivation includes many secondary drives.

9. d   obj. 5   p. 268
a. Incorrect. Hyperphagia would not account for the refusal to admit to the eating problem.
b. Incorrect. Unlike the anorexic, the bulimic eats—and then regurgitates the meal.
c. Incorrect. This is a deep massage technique.
*d. Correct. Someone suffering anorexia refuses to eat and claims that she is overweight.

10. c   obj. 4   p. 266
a. Incorrect. The cortex plays a role, but it is not central; try the hypothalamus.

b. Incorrect. In the limbic system, but try the hypothalamus.
*c. Correct. The hypothalamus monitors blood sugar and other body chemistry to regulate eating behaviour.
d. Incorrect. In the limbic system, but try the hypothalamus.

11. c   obj. 6   pp. 269, 270
a. Incorrect. This is very good advice.
b. Incorrect. A regular, internally driven eating behaviour will minimize the effects of external cues.
*c. Correct. A slow diet will be more effective than a fast diet.
d. Incorrect. This is good advice because weight management is a lifelong endeavor.

12. d   obj. 10   p. 276
a. Incorrect. The SAT measures achievement.
b. Incorrect. IQ tests measure IQ.
c. Incorrect. This test is yet to be developed.
*d. Correct. The thematic Apperception Test, or TAT, was used by McClelland to determine levels of achievement motivation in his research subjects.

13. a   obj. 12   p. 282
*a. Correct. Schachter and Singer proposed a theory of emotions that includes the cognitive element of interpretation of surroundings.
b. Incorrect. Cannon and Bard were critical of the James-Lange theory and proposed that exciting information went to the thalamus and then to the cortex and the physiological systems simultaneously.
c. Incorrect. The James-Lange theory is based on the perception of visceral changes.
d. Incorrect. Ekman's theory states that nonverbal responses to emotion-evoking stories seems to be universal.

14. d   obj. 12   p. 280
a. Incorrect. Try "visceral experience."
b. Incorrect. Try "visceral experience."
c. Incorrect. Try "visceral experience."
*d. Correct. Visceral refers to the internal organs.

15. b   obj. 12   p. 281
a. Incorrect. Schachter and Singer proposed a theory of emotions that includes the cognitive element of interpretation of surroundings.
*b. Correct. Cannon and Bard were critical of the James-Lange theory and proposed that exciting information went to the thalamus and then to the cortex and the physiological systems simultaneously.
c. Incorrect. The James-Lange theory is based on the perception of visceral changes.
d. Incorrect. Ekman's theory states that nonverbal responses to emotion-evoking stories seems to be universal.

16. b   obj. 2   p. 259
17. c   obj. 2   p. 259

18. e   obj. 2   p. 259
19. d   obj. 2   p. 260
20. a   obj. 2   p. 260
21. drive   obj. 2   p. 259
22. drive-reduction   obj. 2   p. 259
23. Homeostasis   obj. 2   p. 259
24. cognitive theories   obj. 2   p. 260

25.
- Describe each of the main theories: instinct, drive reduction, arousal, incentive, opponent process, cognitive, and need theories.
- Select an activity—it could be anything from watching television to playing a sport—and describe the behaviour involved from the point of view of the motivation theories (no more than one sentence each).
- Remember, some behaviours, like those satisfying basic needs, will be easier to describe from the points of view of some theories while others will be easier to describe from other theories.

Practise Test 2:
1.   d   obj. 1   p. 258
a.   Incorrect. It may be focused on alleviating tension.
b.   Incorrect. Feelings come from other aspects of behaviour, though feelings and motivation may both be processed at least in part in the limbic system.
c.   Incorrect. Many survival behaviours do not have to be learned, and many motivations are not survival oriented.
*d. Correct. Motivation guides and energizes behaviour.

2.   b   obj. 2   p. 259
a.   Incorrect. Some animals and some humans may not be interested in power.
*b. Correct. Hunger appears to be a rather universal drive among humans, animals, and insects.
c.   Incorrect. Cognition is not considered a drive.
d.   Incorrect. Achievement is a particularly human drive.

3.   a   obj. 2   p. 259
*a. Correct. This is the activity of the parasympathetic system.
b.   Incorrect. This new term may soon find its way into scientology.
c.   Incorrect. Biofeedback requires intentional activity to control body processes.
d.   Incorrect. This is a technical, psychoanalytic term that is not relevant to homeostasis.

4.   b   obj. 2   p. 259
a.   Incorrect. No such instinct.
*b. Correct. Actually, this is true in all approaches to motivation.
c.   Incorrect. Sounds good, though.
d.   Incorrect. The need for fluid in body tissues is important information for the brain's regulation of fluid in the body.

5.   b   obj. 2   p. 260

a.   Incorrect. Instinct theory focuses on innate drives and thus would not complement incentive theory.
*b. Correct. Incentives account for external factors while drive reduction would account for internal factors.
c.   Incorrect. Arousal theory says that we actually seek ways to increase stimulation (in contrast to drive reduction).
d.   Incorrect. Cognitive theory suggests motivation is a product of people's thoughts, expectations, and goals.

6.   a   obj. 2   p. 260
*a. Correct. Expectancy-value motivation is one of the cognitive approaches, and thus it includes our understanding.
b.   Incorrect. Drive reduction is not goal-oriented in this way, and may occur without our awareness.
c.   Incorrect. Maslow's approach does not necessarily involve goals and awareness of goals.
d.   Incorrect. Arousal theory says that we seek ways to increase stimulation.

7.   b   obj. 2   p. 260
a.   Incorrect. Instinct theory requires the innate mechanisms known as instincts.
*b. Correct. Cognitive theory applies to understanding of goals, their consequences, and our abilities to reach them.
c.   Incorrect. Drive reduction depends upon the biological concept of drives.
d.   Incorrect. Arousal is biological.

8.   c   obj. 3   p. 263
a.   Incorrect. This is a gross overstatement of the idea of self-actualization.
b.   Incorrect. Everyone is dependent upon others for some aspect of living.
*c. Correct. Self-actualizers are striving toward goals and seeking to express their potential.
d.   Incorrect. Often self-actualizers are not as concerned with the successes of others.

9.   d   obj. 4   p. 268
a.   Incorrect. See answer d.
b.   Incorrect. See answer d.
c.   Incorrect. See answer d.
*d. Correct. The obesity of only a few individuals can be explained by the weight-set-point hypothesis.

10. c   obj. 5   p. 268
a.   Incorrect. Try anorexia nervosa.
b.   Incorrect. Bulimia is a similar disorder, but it involves binging and purging behaviour to maintain or lose weight.
*c. Correct. Often sufferers of this disorder will not eat or will develop the disorder known as bulimia and then binge and purge.
d.   Incorrect. But these females appear to have an extreme fear of obesity, and will perceive themselves as obese even when they are dramatically underweight.

11.　a　obj. 10　p. 275
*a. Correct. They are more likely to chose situations that are moderately challenging, not easy.
b. Incorrect. It is learned, or acquired.
c. Incorrect. Individuals with a high need for achievement do find satisfaction from attainment.
d. Incorrect. This is true as well.

12.　a　obj. 10　p. 276
*a. Correct. Women tend to find power through socially acceptable ways more often than do men.
b. Incorrect. The means are rarely questionable and do tend to be socially acceptable.
c. Incorrect. The quality of aggression is not necessarily a matter of power.
d. Incorrect. This is much more likely with men than women.

13.　a　obj. 12　p. 280
*a. Correct. The perception of a physiological change is the emotion for James and Lange.
b. Incorrect. However, since they argued that it was the perception of the physiological change that was the emotion, this answer is partially correct.
c. Incorrect. They did not turn to instinctive process.
d. Incorrect. The environment does not play a very big role in their theory.

14.　b　obj. 2　p. 259
a. Incorrect. Expectancy-value motivation is one of the cognitive approaches, and thus it includes our understanding.
*b. Correct. Drive reduction is biological and may occur without our awareness.
c. Incorrect. Maslow's approach does not necessarily involve goals and awareness of goals.
d. Incorrect. Arousal theory says that we seek ways to increase stimulation.

15. d　obj. 4　p. 266
16. a　obj. 4　p. 266
17. c　obj. 4　p. 266
18. e　obj. 4　p. 267
19. b　obj. 4　p. 267
20. Maslow's hierarchy　obj. 3　p. 262
21. weight set point　obj. 4　p. 267
22. Affiliation obj. 10　p. 276
23. self-actualization　obj. 3　p. 263
24. Hypothalamus obj. 4　p. 266

25.
▪ State the conditions for which you consider polygraph use to be appropriate. Give an example from your own experience if you have one.
▪ Indicate the rational that makes its use fair or appropriate. Are the rights of the test taker protected? Would incrimination lead to damage to the individual?
▪ Is it fair to use a technique that has established scientific validity in specific areas in applications that go beyond the established validity?

▪ Integrity tests have now replaced the polygraph, and the issues now include concern for prejudging someone as "likely to steal." Like the polygraph, these honesty tests are considered of questionable validity.

Practise Test 3:
1.　d　obj. 3　p. 262
a. Incorrect. No opponent processes are indicated here.
b. Incorrect. Arousal motivation suggests that we would seek an exciting job, not necessarily a high-paying one.
c. Incorrect. However, the money may eventually lead to a reduction drive.
*d. Correct. The extrinsic rewards are quite evident.

2.　b　obj. 4　p. 267
a. Incorrect. See answer b.
*b. Correct. Due to food being an external cue, the obese man is more likely to experience "hunger" as a result of the food, even though he already had lunch.
c. Incorrect. The thin man is probably not so easily influenced by the external cue of another meal.
d. Incorrect. Only if the thin man is one of those people who can eat all the time and gain no excess weight.

3.　b　obj. 4　p. 266
a. Incorrect. See answer b.
*b. Correct.
c. Incorrect. See answer b.
d. Incorrect. See answer b.

4.　d　obj. 5　p. 269
a. Incorrect. Interesting word, though.
b. Incorrect. Depression is not the cause.
c. Incorrect. Any type of measurement having to do with volume.
*d. Correct. The disorder is known as bulimia.

5.　b　obj. 10　p. 275
a. Incorrect. A need for affiliation could be at work here if she thought she would be isolated from friends once she began work.
*b. Correct. This sounds most like a need for achievement.
c. Incorrect. A fear of failure could be operative here, if she is avoiding beginning her career for fear of failure.
d. Incorrect. Power can be achieved without education.

6.　c　obj. 11　p. 277
a. Incorrect. Life would probably be interesting without emotions, but far less so.
b. Incorrect. Emotion plays a major role in regulating social interaction.
*c. Correct. We are informed of our bodily needs through other mechanisms, mainly those related to motivation.
d. Incorrect. Emotions are crucial for our preparation for actions, especially emergencies.

7.　d　obj. 10　p. 275

a. Incorrect. A need for affiliation would explain joining a sorority.
b. Incorrect. The need for cognition might better explain a desire to know and solve problems.
c. Incorrect. A need for power would account for a student running for student government offices.
*d. Correct. If the effort is aimed at retaining the recognition of the Dean's List, then this describes a need for achievement.

8. a   obj. 12   p. 281
*a. Correct. Their position differed from that of James and Lange, who thought it was our perception of the bodily changes that was the emotion.
b. Incorrect. This suggests that the facial changes result in emotional feelings.
c. Incorrect. Schachter and Singer thought that the emotion resulted from the interpretation of the perception of a bodily change.
d. Incorrect. James and Lange thought it was our perception of the bodily changes that was the emotion.

9. c   obj. 13   p. 284
a. Incorrect. The polygraph does not measure brain waves.
b. Incorrect. The polygraph does not measure brain waves.
*c. Correct. The polygraph measures breathing rate, heart rate, blood pressure, and sweating.
d. Incorrect. The polygraph does not measure brain waves.

10. c   obj. 10   p. 275
a. Incorrect. A need for affiliation could be at work here, if he thought he would be isolated from friends once he began work.
b. Incorrect. This is not a need for achievement.
*c. Correct. A fear of failure is operative here; he is avoiding beginning his career for fear of failure.
d. Incorrect. Power can be achieved without education.

11. c   obj. 12   p. 282
a. Incorrect. Their position differed from that of James and Lange, who thought it was our perception of the bodily changes that was the emotion.
b. Incorrect. This suggests that the facial changes result in emotional feelings.
*c. Correct. Schachter and Singer thought that the emotion resulted from the interpretation of the perception of a bodily change.
d. Incorrect. James and Lange thought it was our perception of the bodily changes that was the emotion.

12. c   obj10   p. 276
a. Incorrect. Being aggressive and flamboyant is not a typical approach for women who are high in the need for power.

b. Incorrect. Belonging to a political party in itself is not a sign of a need for power.
*c. Correct. Women tend to display their need for power through socially acceptable methods, like concern for others and nurturing behaviour.
d. Incorrect. Competitive sports are not themselves related to individual need for power.

13. a   obj. 10   p. 276
*a. Correct. Sensitivity to others and desires to spend time with friends are reflective of a need for affiliation.
b. Incorrect. Membership in a political group is not in itself sufficient to indicate a need for affiliation.
c. Incorrect. Partying and sports are not themselves signs of high need for affiliation.
d. Incorrect. Aggressive behaviour does not signal a need for affiliation.

14. d   obj. 2   p. 262
a. Incorrect. No opponent processes are indicated here.
b. Incorrect. Arousal motivation suggests that we would seek an exciting job, not necessarily a high-paying one.
c. Incorrect. However, the money may eventually lead to a reduction drive.
*d. Correct. The extrinsic rewards are quite evident.

15. b   obj. 2   p. 265
a. Incorrect. See answer b.
*b. Correct. The shift from intrinsic to extrinsic rewards can undermine the behaviour.
c. Incorrect. See answer b.
d. Incorrect. The shift from intrinsic to extrinsic rewards can undermine the behaviour, but it will not necessarily destroy it.

16. e   obj. 2   p. 259
17. c   obj. 2   p. 262
18. b   obj. 2   p. 262
19. a   obj. 2   p. 260
20. d   obj. 4   p. 268
21. metabolism   obj. 4   p. 267
22. anorexia   obj. 5   p. 268
23. need for power   obj. 10   p. 276
24. Emotions   obj. 11   p. 278

25.
▪ Discuss the biological and socioculture viewpoints about weight control. Suggest behavioural alternatives.
▪ Allow children to select food and only eat until thy are full—not until they clean their plate—don't use food as a reward, escape, or for consolation.
▪ Increase opportunities for exercise.
▪ Encourage individuals to focus on what they can do, not how they look.

Development

9

The fundamental issue for developmental psychology is the interaction between nature and nurture in human development. Development from conception to birth illustrates the nature/nurture interaction. This chapter first discusses various topics of study within the field and distinguishes among several research methods. Genetic abnormalities and environmental influences that affect prenatal development are listed. Stages of development starting with the newborn and following through to middle childhood are presented. A description of the developmental theories that address the physical, psychosocial, and cognitive development at each stage is discussed.

The chapter then examines development from adolescence through to late adulthood. The section on adolescence covers the physical, emotional, and cognitive changes that occur during the transition to adulthood. Next, early and middle adulthood is discussed. They are marked by the formation of a family, the establishment and success (or failure) in work, and the gradual progress toward old age. Finally, the chapter shows how old age does not conform to our myths about it. Many elderly people are still quite capable of leading active and happy lives. An examination of the physical, intellectual, and social changes that occur at this time of life show both improvements and declines in various types of functioning.

To further investigate the topics covered in this chapter, you can visit the related websites by visiting the following link: : http://www.mcgrawhill.ca/college/feldman

Prologue: The Brave New World of Childhood
Looking Ahead

Section 1: Nature and Nurture: The Enduring Developmental Issue
Determining the Relative Influences of Nature and Nurture
Specific Research Approaches

Section 2: Prenatal Development: From Conception to Birth
The Basics of Genetics
Development from Zygote to Birth

Applying Psychology in the 21st Century:
Cloning, Gene Therapy, and the Coming Medical Revolution

Section 3: The Extraordinary Newborn
Reflexes
Development of the Senses: Taking in the World

The Growing Child: Infancy Through Middle Childhood
Physical Development
Development of Social Behaviour: Taking on the World
Cognitive Development: Children's Thinking About the World

Section 4: Adolescence: Becoming an Adult
Physical Development: The Changing Adolescent
Moral and Cognitive Development: Distinguishing Right from Wrong
Social Development: Finding Oneself in a Social World

Pathways Through Psychology: Lorrie Sippola,
Developmental Psychologist

Exploring Diversity: Rites of Passage: Coming of
Age Around the World

Section 5: Early and Middle Adulthood: The Middle Years of Life
Physical Development: The Peak of Health
Social Development: Working at Life
Marriage, Children, and Divorce: Family Ties

Section 6: The Later Years of Life: Growing Old
Physical Changes in Late Adulthood: The Aging Body
Cognitive Changes: Thinking About—and During—Late Adulthood

Psychology at Work: Kevin J. Sweryd, Funeral Director,
Manager

The Social World of Late Adulthood: Old but Not Alone

> ### Becoming an Informed Consumer of Psychology:
> Adjusting to Death

Learning Objectives

These are the concepts and the learning objectives for Chapter 9. Read them carefully as part of your preliminary survey of the chapter.

Nature and Nurture: The Enduring Developmental Issue

1. Define developmental psychology and discuss various topics of study within the field, especially the influence of nature and nurture on human development. (pp. 290–292)

2. Distinguish among cross-sectional, longitudinal, and cross-sequential research methods. (p. 293)

Prenatal Development: From Conception to Birth

3. Describe the major events that occur from conception to birth. (pp. 293–296)

4. Discuss genetic abnormalities and environmental influences that affect prenatal development. (pp. 297–298)

The Extraordinary Newborn

5. Describe the appearance and behaviour of the neonate. (p. 299)

6. Discuss the sensory and perceptual capacities of newborn infants and their typical course of development. (pp. 299–302)

The Growing Child: Infancy Through Middle Childhood

7. Describe the physical and social development of the infant and child, including attachment issues, the role of the father, peer social relationships, and the influence of day care. (pp. 302–306)

8. Describe the four parenting styles and their effect on children's social development. (pp. 306–307)

9. Outline and describe the first four psychosocial stages of development as identified by Erik Erikson. (pp. 307–308)

10. Outline and describe the cognitive developmental stages identified by Jean Piaget, including criticisms of the stage approach. (pp. 308–312)

11. Explain the information-processing approach to cognitive development, as well as Lev Vygotsky's sociocultural approach. (pp. 312–314)

Adolescence: Becoming an Adult

12. Define adolescence, and describe the physical changes that mark its beginning. (pp. 315–316)

13. Describe the moral and cognitive development that occurs during adolescence. (pp. 316-318)

14. Identify and discuss Erikson's psychosocial stages relevant to adolescence and adulthood. (pp. 318-319)

15. Identify the major problems of adolescence. (pp. 319–321)

Early and Middle Adulthood: The Middle Years of Life

16. Define early and middle adulthood, and describe the physical changes that accompany it. (pp. 322–323)

17. Discuss the concerns of adulthood that result from demands of society and the pressures of work, marriage, and family. (pp. 323–324)

18. Describe the roles of males and females in marriage and in the family, specifically as they relate to the course of adult development. (pp. 324–325)

The Later Years of Life: Growing Old

19. Define old age, the physical changes that accompany it, and the theories that attempt to account for it. (pp. 325–326)

20   Identify the changes that occur in cognitive ability, intelligence, and memory during old age. (pp. 326–329)

21. Describe the challenges and changes faced by the elderly in regard to their social involvement. (pp. 329–330)

22. List and define Kübler-Ross's five stages of adjustment to death. (p. 331)

SECTION 1: Nature and Nurture: The Enduring Developmental Issue

Prepare

- *How do psychologists study the influences of hereditary and environmental factors in development?*
- *What is the nature of development prior to birth?*
- *What factors affect a child during the mother's pregnancy?*

Organize

- *Determining the Relative Influences of Nature and Nurture*
- *Specific Research Approaches*
- *The Basics of Genetics*
- *Development from Zygote to Birth*

Work

[a] _____ is the branch of psychology focused on explaining the similarities and differences among people that result from the growth and change of individuals throughout life.

Developmental psychologists are interested in a fundamental question of distinguishing the causes of behaviour that are *environmental* from the causes that result from *heredity*. This question is identified as the [b] _____. However, both nature and nurture are involved, and it is not a question of nature or nurture. Some theories focus on learning and the role of the environment, and other theories focus on the role of growth and

[c] _____, or the development of biologically predetermined patterns, in causing developmental change. Environment plays a role in enabling individuals to reach the potential allowed by their genetic background. Developmental psychologists take an

[d] _____ position, arguing that behaviour and development are determined by genetic and environmental influences.

One approach used by developmental psychologists is the study of [e] _____. Different behaviours displayed by identical twins must have some environmental component. Many studies seek to find identical twins who were separated at birth by adoption. Nontwin siblings who are raised apart also make contributions to these kinds of studies. The opposite approach takes people of different genetic backgrounds and examines their development and behaviour in similar environments.

Development begins at the point of [f] _____ when the male's sperm penetrates the female's egg. The fertilized egg is at this point called a [g] _____.

It contains twenty-three pairs of [h] _____, one-half from the father the other half from the mother. Each chromosome contains thousands of [i] _____, the individual units that carry genetic information. Genes are responsible for the development of the systems of the body, heart, circulatory, brain, lungs, and so on. At four weeks, the zygote becomes a structure called the **[j]** _____. It has a rudimentary heart, brain, intestinal tract, and other organs. By the eighth week, the embryo has arms and legs. Beginning at the eighth week, the embryo faces a **[k]** _____ of development—a period during which specific growth must occur if the individual is to develop normally. Eyes and ears must form, and environmental influences can have significant effects. At the ninth week the individual is called a **[l]** _____. At sixteen to eighteen weeks the movement of the fetus can be felt by the mother. At the twenty-fourth week, the fetus has the characteristics of a newborn, though it cannot survive outside the mother if born prematurely. At twenty-eight weeks, the fetus can survive if born prematurely, and this is called the

[m] _____. At twenty-eight weeks the fetus will weigh about three pounds.

Evaluate

____ 1. conception

____ 2. zygote

____ 3. chromosomes

____ 4. genes

____ 5. embryo

____ 6. fetus

a. A zygote that has a heart, a brain, and other organs.

b. The one-celled product of fertilization.

c. A developing child, from nine weeks after conception until birth.

d. Structures that contain basic hereditary information.

e. The parts of a chromosome through which genetic information is transmitted.

f. The process by which an egg cell is fertilized by a sperm.

Rethink

1. What sort of policy might you create for notifying persons who have genetically based disorders that can be identified by genetic testing? Would your policy treat potentially fatal disorders differently from less serious ones? Would it make a distinction between treatable and nontreatable disorders?

2. Given the possible effects of the environment on the developing child, do you think expectant mothers should be subject to legal prosecution for their use of alcohol and other drugs that can seriously harm their unborn children? Defend your position.

SECTION 2: The Extraordinary Newborn
The Growing Child: Infancy Through Middle Childhood

Prepare

- *What are the major competencies of newborns?*
- *What are the milestones of physical and social development during childhood?*

Organize

- ### *Reflexes*
- ### *Development of the Senses*
- ### *Physical Development*
- ### *Development of Social Behaviour*

Work

At birth, the newborn baby is called a **[a]** _____ . The neonate looks strange because the journey through the birth canal squeezes and shapes the skull. The neonate is covered with **[b]** _____ , a white, greasy material that protects the skin prior to birth, and a soft hair called **[c]** _____ . The neonate is born with a number of **[d]** _____ , unlearned, involuntary responses. Most are necessary for survival and maturation. The **[e]** _____ fans out the toes when the edge of the foot is touched. These reflexes are lost within a few months and replaced by more complex behaviours.

In the first year of life, children triple their birth weight and their height increases by 50 percent. From 3 to 13 years of age, the child adds an average of 5 pounds and 3 inches per year. The proportion of body and body parts changes through the time period as well.

In addition to physical and perceptual growth, infants grow socially as well.

[f] _____ refers to the positive emotional bond between a child and a particular individual. Harry Harlow demonstrated the importance of attachment by showing that baby monkeys preferred a terry-cloth "mother" to a wire "mother," even though the wire version provided food and the terry cloth one did not. Infants play an active role in the development of the bond.

Recently the father's role in children's development has been researched. Fathers spend less time caring for their children, but the attachments can be just as strong.

[g] _____ with peers are crucial for a preschooler's social development. Play serves to increase social competence, provide a perspective on the thoughts and feelings of others, and helps to teach children self-control.

Diana Baumrind has proposed that there are three main categories of child-rearing patterns. The **[h]** _____ are rigid and punitive and expect unquestioning obedience.

[i] _____ are lax and inconsistent though warm. **[j]** _____ set limits and are firm, but as their children get older, they reason and explain things to them. Children of authoritarian parents tend to be unsociable, unfriendly, and withdrawn. Children of permissive parents are immature, moody, and dependent with low self-esteem. Children of authoritative parents are likable, self-reliant, independent, and cooperative.

Children are born with **[k]** _____ , or basic, innate dispositions. The temperament can elicit a certain child-rearing style. The child-rearing styles may be applicable to

American culture, where independence is highly valued. For instance, Japanese parents encourage dependence to promote values of community and cooperation.

Erik Erikson has proposed an eight-stage theory of social development. Each stage of

[l] _____ involves a basic crisis or conflict. Though each crisis is resolved as we pass through the stages, the basic conflict remains throughout life.

Evaluate

_____ 1.   neonate

_____ 2.   vernix

_____ 3.   lanugo

_____ 4.   reflexes

_____ 5.   Babinski reflex

a.   A white lubricant that covers a fetus, protecting it during birth.

b.   Unlearned, involuntary responses to certain stimuli.

c.   A soft fuzz covering the body of a newborn.

d.   The reflex where an infant's toes fan out in response to a stroke on the outside of its foot.

e.   A newborn child.

Rethink

3.   In what ways might the infant's major reflexes—the rooting, sucking, gagging, and Babinski reflexes—have had survival value, from an evolutionary perspective? Does the infant's ability to mimic the facial expressions of adults have a similar value?

4.   Do you think the growing trend toward greater parental involvement by fathers will have effects on the child-rearing styles to which children are exposed? Will it affect attachment? Psychosocial development? Why or why not?

SECTION 3:   Cognitive Development: Children's Thinking About the World

Prepare

- *How does cognitive development proceed during childhood?*

Organize

- *Cognitive Development*

Work

[a] _____ refers to the developmental changes in the understanding of the world. Theories of cognitive development attempt to explain the intellectual changes that occur throughout life. Jean Piaget proposed that children passed through four distinct stages of

cognitive development and that these stages differed in both the quantity of information acquired and the quality of knowledge and understanding. Maturation and relevant experiences are needed for children to pass through the stages.

Piaget's first stage is called the **[b]** _____ stage, and it is from birth to 2 years. This stage is marked by the child's lack of ability to use images, language, and symbols. Things not immediately present are not within the child's awareness until the development of

[c] _____, the awareness that objects continue to exist when they are out of sight.

The **[d]** _____ stage is from 2 to 7 years of age. Children gain the ability to represent objects internally and can use symbols for objects.

The **[e]** _____ stage is from 7 to 12 years of age. Children master conservation, reversibility, and thinking in a logical manner.

The **[f]** _____ stage, from 12 years to adulthood, is marked by the use of abstract, formal, and logical thought. Though it emerges at this time, formal thought is used infrequently. Studies show that only 40 to 60 percent of college students reach this stage and only 25 percent of the general population do so.

An alternative to Piaget's theory is **[g]** _____, which examines how people take in, use, and store information.

According to the Russian developmental psychologist Lev Vygotsky's view, children's cognitive abilities increase when they are exposed to information that falls into their

[h] _____, which he describes as the level at which a child can almost, but not fully, comprehend or perform a task on his or her own. Parents, teachers, and peers provide supportive information that serves as **[i]** _____ for the child's development.

Evaluate

_____ 1. sensorimotor stage

_____ 2. object permanence

_____ 3. preoperational stage

_____ 4. principle of conservation

_____ 5. concrete operational stage

a. Objects do not cease to exist when they are out of sight.

b. Little competence in representing the environment.

c. Characterized by language development.

d. Characterized by logical thought.

e. Quantity is unrelated to physical appearance.

Rethink

5. According to Piaget's theory, children must reach a certain level of maturity before they can learn particular kinds of information. What might be the pros and cons of exposing a child to more complex material at an early age? What might information-processing theory have to say about this?

6. Do you think the widespread use of IQ testing in the United States contributes to parents' views that their children's academic success is largely due to their children's innate intelligence? Why? Would it be possible (or desirable) to change this view?

SECTION 4: Adolescence: Becoming an Adult

Prepare

- *What major physical, social, and cognitive transitions characterize adolescence?*

Organize

- *Physical Development*
- *Moral and Cognitive Development*
- *Social Development*

Work

Development continues throughout life, from adolescence to adulthood and old age. The major biological changes that begin with the attainment of physical and sexual maturity and the changes in social, emotional, and cognitive function that lead to adulthood mark the period called

[a] _____.

The dramatic physical changes of adolescence include a growth in height, the development of breasts in females, the deepening of the male voice, the development of body hair, and intense sexual feelings. The growth spurt begins around age 10 for girls and age 12 for boys. The development of the sexual organs begins about a year later. There are wide individual variations, however. Better nutrition and medical care in Western cultures is probably the cause of the

decreasing age of onset of [b] _____. Early-maturing boys have an advantage over later-maturing boys, doing better in athletics and being more popular, though they do have more difficulties in school. Early-maturing girls are more popular and have higher self-concepts than those who mature late, but the obvious changes in breasts can cause separation from peers and ridicule. Late-maturers suffer because of the delay, with boys being ridiculed for their lack of coordination and girls holding lower social status in junior high and high school.

Erikson's theory of psychosocial development identifies the beginning of adolescence with

his fifth stage, called the [c] _____ *stage.* During this stage, individuals

seek to discover their abilities, skills, and [d] _____. If one resolves this stage with confusion, then a stable identity will not be formed and the individual may become a social deviant or have trouble with close personal relationships later. The stage is marked by a shift from dependence on adults for information and the turn toward the peer group for support.

During college, the [e] _____ *stage* describes the basic conflict. This stage focuses on developing relationships with others. Middle adulthood finds people in the [f]

_____ *stage.* The contribution to family, community, work, and society comprise generativity; and feelings of triviality about one's activities indicate the difficulties of the stage and lead to stagnation. The final stage is the **[g]** _____ *stage*, and it is marked by a sense of accomplishment if successful in life or a sense of despair if one regrets what might have been.

Evaluate

_____ 1. identity-versus-role-confusion stage

_____ 2. intimacy-versus-isolation stage

_____ 3. generativity-versus-stagnation stage

_____ 4. ego-integrity-versus-despair stage

a. A period from late adulthood until death during which we review life's accomplishments and failures.

b. A period in middle adulthood during which we take stock of our contributions to family and society.

c. A period during early adulthood that focuses on developing close relationships with others.

d. A time in adolescence of testing to determine one's own unique qualities.

Rethink

7. In what ways do school cultures help or hurt teenage students who are going through adolescence? What school policies might benefit early-maturing girls and late-maturing boys? Would same-sex schools help, as some have argued?

8. Many cultures have "rites of passage" that officially recognize young people as adults. Do you think such rites can be beneficial? Does the United States have any such rites? Would setting up an official designation that one has achieved "adult" status have benefits?

SECTION 5:Early and Middle Adulthood: The Middle Years of Life

Prepare

  - *What are the principal kinds of physical, social, and intellectual changes that occur in early and middle adulthood, and what are their causes?*

Organize

  - *Physical Development*
  - *Social Development*
  - *Marriage, Children, and Divorce*

Work

Early adulthood is generally considered to begin at about 20 years of age and to last until about 40 to 45 years, and middle adulthood lasts from 40 to 45 to about 65 years of age. These ages have been studied less than any other. Fewer significant physical changes occur, and the social changes are diverse.

The peak of physical health is reached in early adulthood, and quantitative changes begin at about 25 years as the body becomes less efficient and more prone to disease through time. The major physical development is the female experience of **[a]** _____, the cessation of menstruation and the end of fertility. The loss of estrogen may lead to hot flashes, a condition that is successfully treated with artificial estrogen. Problems that were once blamed on menopause are now seen as resulting from the perceptions of coming old age and society's view of it. Though men remain fertile, the gradual decline of physical abilities has similar effects to menopause, causing the man to focus on the social expectations of youthfulness.

Daniel Levinson's model of adult development identifies six stages from beginning adulthood through the end of middle adulthood. At the beginning, the individual formulates a "dream" that guides career choices and the vision the person has of the future. At about 40 or 45, people enter a period called the **[b]** _____, during which past accomplishments are assessed, and in some cases, the assessment leads to a

[c] _____, in which the signs of physical aging and a sense that the career will not progress combine to force a reevaluation of and an effort to remedy their dissatisfaction. Most people go through the midlife transition without any difficulties. During their fifties, people become more accepting of others and of their own lives. They realize that death is inevitable and seek to understand their accomplishments in terms of how they understand life. Since Levinson's research was based on males, the difference in roles and socialization has raised questions about whether women go through the same stages.

Evaluate

_____ 1.   Erik Erikson

_____ 2.   Lawrence Kohlberg

_____ 3.   Jean Piaget

_____ 4.   Elisabeth Kübler-Ross

_____ 5.   Daniel Levinson

a.   Moral development.

b.   Death and dying.

c.   Psychosocial development.

d.   Cognitive development.

e.   Adult social development.

Rethink

9.   How do you think popular culture contributes to the midlife crisis experienced by some people as they reach their forties? What sorts of cultural changes might ease the midlife crisis or make the phenomenon less prevalent?

10. Given the current divorce rate and the number of households in which both parents work, do you think it is reasonable to still think in terms of a "traditional" household in which the father is the breadwinner and the wife is a homemaker? What problems might such a definition cause for children whose homes do not match this definition?

SECTION 6:   The Later Years of Life: Growing Old

Prepare

- *How does the reality of old age differ from the stereotypes about*

> *the period?*
> - *How can we adjust to death?*

Organize

> - *Physical Changes in Late Adulthood*
> - *Cognitive Changes*
> - *The Social World of Late Adulthood*

Work

   [a] _____ study development and the aging process from the age of about 65. Gerontologists reexamine our understanding of aging, suggesting that the stereotype of aging is inaccurate. Napping, eating, walking, and conversing are the typical activities of both the elderly and college students. The obvious physical changes that appear in old age include thinning and greying hair, wrinkling and folding skin, and a loss of height. Vision and hearing become less sharp, smell and taste are less sensitive, reaction time slows, and oxygen intake and heart-pumping abilities decrease. Two types of theories have been offered to account for these changes. One group includes the **[b]** _____ *theories of aging*, which suggest that there are preset time limits on the reproduction of human cells governed by genetics. The other group includes the **[c]** _____ *of aging*, which suggest that the body simply stops working efficiently. By-products of energy production accumulate, and cells make mistakes in their reproduction.

   The view that the elderly are forgetful and confused is no longer considered an accurate assessment. Tests show declines in **[d]** _____ in old age but **[e]** _____ actually increases. Fluid intelligence may be more sensitive to changes in the nervous system than crystallized intelligence.

   One assumption about the elderly is that they are more forgetful. Evidence suggests that forgetfulness is not inevitable. The decline in cognitive function associated with old age is called **[f]** _____, but this is now viewed as a symptom caused by other factors, like **[g]** _____, anxiety, depression, or even overmedication.

   Loneliness is a problem for only a small portion of the elderly, though social patterns do change in old age. Two theories account for how people approach old age. The **[h]** _____ *theory of aging* views aging as a gradual withdrawal from the world on physical, psychological, and social levels. Energy is lower and interaction lessens. This view sees aging as an automatic process. The **[i]** _____ *theory of aging* suggests that the happiest people are ones who remain active and that people should attempt to maintain the activities and interests they develop during middle age. The nature of the activity is the most important factor, not the quantity.

   Death requires major adjustments, as the death of those near you causes changes in life and makes you consider the possibility of your own death. Elisabeth Kübler-Ross outlined five stages of the death process: 1) **[j]** _____, the person denies the fact that he or she is dying; 2) **[k]** _____, the person becomes angry at people who are healthy, angry at the medical profession for not being able to help, and angry at God; 3)

[l] _____, after anger, the person may try to postpone death through a

bargain in exchange for extended life; 4) [m] _____, once bargaining fails,
the person experiences depression, realizing that death is inevitable; and 5)

[n] _____, which is signaled by the end of mourning one's own life,
becoming unemotional and noncommunicative as if at peace with oneself.

Evaluate

____ 1. genetic preprogramming theories of aging

____ 2. wear-and-tear theories of aging

____ 3. disengagement theory of aging

____ 4. activity theory of aging

a. Theories that suggest that the body's mechanical functions cease efficient activity and, in effect, wear out.

b. A theory that suggests that the elderly who age most successfully are those who maintain the interests and activities they had during middle age.

c. Theories that suggest a built-in time limit to the reproduction of human cells.

d. A theory that suggests that aging is a gradual withdrawal from the world on physical, psychological, and social levels.

Rethink

11. Is the possibility that life might be extended for several decades a mixed blessing? What societal consequences might an extended life span bring about?

12. It has been found that people in late adulthood require intellectual stimulation. Does this have implications for the societies in which older people live? In what way might stereotypes about older individuals contribute to their isolation and lack of intellectual stimulation?

Practise Questions

Test your knowledge of the chapter material by answering these questions. These questions have been placed in three Practise Tests. The first two tests are composed of questions that will test your recall of factual knowledge. The third test contains questions that are challenging and primarily test for conceptual knowledge and your ability to apply that knowledge. Check your answers and review the feedback using the Answer Key in the following pages of the *Study Guide*.

PRACTISE TEST 1:

1. The belief that a combination of genetic and environmental factors determines the course of development is the central point of view for:

a. all psychologists.
b. neuropsychologists.
c. interactionists.
d. social psychologists.

2. When theories stress the role of heredity in their explanations of change in individual development, the focus of their accounts would be on:
a. maturation.
b. nurture.
c. environmental factors.
d. social growth.

3. Which set of subjects would provide the **least** information for a study regarding the nature-nurture question in humans?
a. identical twins reared apart
b. children adopted from different families reared together
c. siblings reared apart
d. siblings reared together

4. A study in which several different ages groups are examined over different points in time is called:
a. cross-sectional.
b. maturational.
c. longitudinal.
d. cross-sequential.

5. Certain events must take place in a specific timeframe; otherwise, the entire sequence of fetal growth is thrown off and the result will be either no development or abnormal development. This timeframe is called:
a. longitudinal development.
b. cross-section maturation.
c. the resolution phase.
d. the critical period.

6. Hereditary information is represented in thousands of _____, which are tiny segments of stringy material called _____.
a. zygotes; embryos.
b. chromosomes; zygotes.
c. genes; neonates.
d. genes; chromosomes.

7. In prenatal development, the age of viability is a developmental stage in which:
a. the eyes and other sense organs are functional.
b. the fetus can survive if born prematurely.
c. development has advanced sufficiently so that the fetus is capable of learning from environmental cues.
d. the sexual organs of the fetus are differentiated.

8. Which of the following is caused by genetic birth defects?
a. phenylketonuria (PKU)
b. AIDS
c. diethylstilbestrol (DES)
d. fetal alcohol syndrome

9. At birth, the neonate is covered with a white, greasy substance that protects the skin prior to birth, called:
a. veridical.
b. vernix.
c. fornix.
d. lanugo.

10. The infant's later temperament is known to be affected by the mother's:
a. consumption of "junk foods" during pregnancy.
b. sleep patterns during early fetal development.
c. attitude about whether the baby is wanted or unwanted.

    d.   emotional state during the late fetal period.

11.   Which reflex below helps the newborn infant position its mouth onto its mother's breast when it feeds?
    a.   rooting reflex   c.   gag reflex
    b.   startle reflex   d.   surprise reflex

12.   Dramatic physical and psychological change and attainment of sexual maturity is called:
    a.   adulthood.   c.   puberty.
    b.   adolescence.   d.   childhood.

13.   If a person's behaviour reflected the desire to please other members of society, he or she would be considered to be at Kohlberg's _____ level of moral reasoning.:
    a.   preconventional.   c.   conventional.
    b.   postconventional.   d.   nonconventional.

14.   Developmentalist Lawrence Kohlberg's approach to the study of moral reasoning is:
    a.   to check the person's criminal record to see whether he or she is a convict.
    b.   to collect survey data in which subjects rate their own moral reasoning.
    c.   to ask spouses to talk freely and confidentially about their partners.
    d.   to study the person's thinking in response to moral dilemma.

15.   The most noteworthy feature of Erikson's theory of psychosocial development is that:
    a.   both men and women are included in its descriptions of developmental changes.
    b.   it accurately describes developmental changes that people in other cultures also experience.
    c.   it has greatly increased understanding of infant development.
    d.   it suggests that development is a lifelong process.

16.   Which of these is typical of adolescent development?
    a.   preconventional morality   c.   ego-integrity versus despair
    b.   infertility   d.   striving for identity

_____ 17.   trust-versus-mistrust stage   a.   The stage of psychosocial development where children can experience self-doubt if they are restricted and overprotected.

_____ 18.   autonomy-versus-shame-and-doubt stage

                                         b.   The first stage of psychosocial development, occurring from birth to 18 months of age.

_____ 19.   initiative-versus-guilt stage

                                         c.   The period during which children may develop positive social interactions with others or may feel inadequate and become less sociable.

_____ 20.   industry-versus-inferiority stage

                                         d.   The period during which children experience conflict between independence of action and the sometimes negative results of that action.

21.   The reflex that causes neonates to turn toward anything that touches their cheek is called the

    _____.

22. The reflex that makes neonates suck on anything that touches their lips is called the
_____.

23. The _____ causes a number of movements when a loud noise is sounded.

24. _____ is marked by the development of independence and exploration at about 18 months of age.

25. The conflict that arises when the desire to initiate independent activities conflicts with the guilt that arises from the consequences is called _____.

26. Considering the discussion of the nature-nurture issue at the beginning of the chapter, what is your assessment of the role of child-rearing practices in the development of the person as a unique individual? Are certain styles more likely to help individuals reach their potential?

PRACTISE TEST 2:

1. The philosophical view that infants are born with a blank slate favours which of the following as a dominant influence upon development?
   a. interactionism
   b. nature
   c. nurture
   d. dualism

2. Identical twins are especially interesting subjects for developmental studies because they:
   a. communicate via telepathy, i.e., direct mental transfer of ideas.
   b. have typically shared their lives together in their parents' home.
   c. have identical genetic makeup since they developed from one zygote.
   d. are very highly cooperative in their dealings with psychologists.

3. A study in which particular individuals are followed as they age is called:
   a. cross-sectional.
   b. maturational.
   c. longitudinal.
   d. cross-sequential.

4. The units that produce particular characteristics in an individual are called:
   a. chromosomes.
   b. genes.
   c. spores.
   d. somes.

5. At conception a zygote is formed. What is the next stage the organism progresses through after the zygote has developed?
   a. embryo
   b. neonate
   c. fetus
   d. fertilization

6. An individual who is described as having "vernix and lanugo":
   a. may be attending a drug abuse rehabilitation program.
   b. suffers the after-effects of infantile malnutrition.
   c. has parents who continued to have intercourse during pregnancy.
   d. is a neonate.

7. The unborn fetus has many of the features and characteristics of a newborn as early as:

a. 8 weeks.   c. 16 weeks.
b. 12 weeks.   d. 24 weeks.

8. A genetic defect that leads to a very short life due to a breakdown in strategic metabolic processes and occurs most frequently among Jews of Eastern European descent is called:
   a. Tay-Sachs disease.   c. meningitis.
   b. Down syndrome.   d. phenylketonuria (PKU).

9. Which developmental disorder results from the presence of an extra chromosome?
   a. Down syndrome   c. Tay-Sachs disease
   b. sickle-cell anemia   d. phenylketonuria (PKU)

10. Rubella is also known as:
    a. Down syndrome.   c. phenylketonuria (PKU).
    b. German measles.   d. sickle-cell anemia.

11. A neonate is:
    a. a prenatal infant in its thirtieth to thirty-eighth week of development.
    b. a newborn infant.
    c. an infant born with deformities because of chromosomal abnormalities.
    d. a premature baby up to the time at which the normal due date passes.

12. A researcher compares visual abilities in four groups of infants of ages 1 month, 3 months, 5 months, and 7 months. This is an application of the _____ research method.
    a. longitudinal   c. cross-sectional
    b. critical period   d. cross-sequential

13. The theory of aging that is based on the notion that mechanical functions of the body stop working efficiently is called:
    a. genetic preprogramming.   c. wear-and-tear.
    b. genetic breakdown.   d. failure of function.

14. The _____ theory of aging states that aging involves a gradual withdrawal from the world on multiple levels.
    a. wear-and-tear   c. disengagement
    b. genetic preprogramming   d. activity

15. Which type of intelligence actually increases with age?
    a. fluid intelligence   c. basic intelligence
    b. verbal intelligence   d. crystallized intelligence

_____ 16. egocentrism	a. Piaget's stage of cognitive development where the individual is able to think abstractly and see things from another point of view.
_____ 17. personal fables	
_____ 18. sexual attraction	b. A state of self-absorption in which the world is viewed from one's own point of view.
_____ 19. formal operations	
	c. Gilligan's theory of morality suggests that

_____ 20. caring	women display a morality of more _____. d. An adolescent's view that what happens to him or her is unique, exceptional, and shared by no one else. e. Begins early in adolescence as sexual organs mature.

21. Kneeling in hot coals, being hit with sticks, and cutting of genitals are all _____ in some cultures.

22 The ages between 20 and 45 are generally considered by psychologists to be _____.

23. People's weight generally _____ during early adulthood.

24 An explanation of why most cultures place greater emphasis on rites of passage into adulthood for _____ relative to _____ is because female transition into adulthood is marked by a single, definite, biological event: menstruation.

25. Apply the disengagement and the activity theories of aging to the question of mandatory retirement. Should there be a mandatory retirement age and, if either "yes" or "no," what are the exceptions and who shall judge?

PRACTISE TEST 3: Conceptual, Applied, and Challenging Questions

1. Of the organs listed below, which is **not** yet formed at the embryonic stage?
    a. heart
    b. brain
    c. intestinal tract
    d. eyes

2. The view of developmental psychologists today is that:
    a. environmental stimulation is necessary to achieve full genetic potential.
    b. genetic factors are most important in individual development.
    c. environmental influences are most important in individual development.
    d. different factors are important for different individuals.

3. One-tenth of the African-American population in the United States has the possibility of passing on _____, which leaves the newborn with a variety of health problems and very short life expectancy.
    a. hypertension
    b. sickle-cell anemia
    c. Tay-Sachs disease
    d. phenylketonuria

4. Which developmental influence below does not belong with the others?
    a. mother's nutrition and stress level
    b. mother's drug and medication intake
    c. hereditary defects
    d. birth complications

5. Which statement about the sensory and perceptual capabilities of infants is **not** true?

    a.   At 4 days of age, they can distinguish between closely related sounds such as "ba" and "pa."

    b.   At 60 days of age, they can recognize their mother's voice.

    c.   After 6 months of age, they are capable of discriminating virtually any difference in sounds that is relevant to the production of language.

    d.   They prefer sweetened liquids to unsweetened liquids.

6. According to the text, if a fetus were exposed to a teratogenic drug that caused subsequent language difficulties, when would exposure to the drug be most likely to have its most devastating effect?

    a.   especially shortly before or during the critical period

    b.   principally during the critical period

    c.   especially shortly during or after the critical period.

    d.   either shortly before, after, or during the critical period

7. Why are there generally differences in the form of attachment between the baby and its mother and father?

    a.   Mothers spend more time directly nurturing their children, whereas fathers spend more time playing with them.

    b.   Mother spend more time playing with their children, whereas fathers spend more time nurturing them.

    c.   Mothers generally are identified as primary caregivers, so the attachment is stronger.

    d.   Fathers spend more time doing things with their children than mothers.

8. Which statement best represents the father's typical attachment to his children?

    a.   It is superior to the mother's attachment in most situations.

    b.   It is aloof and detached.

    c.   It is generous with affection, especially during verbal interaction.

    d.   It is qualitatively different, but comparable to the mother's attachment.

9. Which type of parents would be most likely to explain things to children and try reasoning with them when conflicts or problems arise?

    a.   permissive parents   c.   caretaking parents

    b.   authoritative parents   d.   authoritarian parents

10. Play in young children has many consequences. Which alternative below is **not** one of them?

    a.   They become more competent in their social interactions with other children.

    b.   They learn to take the perspective of other people and to infer others' thoughts and feelings.

    c.   They learn to control emotional displays and facial expressions in situations where this is appropriate.

    d.   They become more independent of other children from ages 2–6.

11. A developmental psychologist is evaluating a young child's cognitive development. The psychologist shows the child two separate arrangements of red disks. Eight disks are laid in a straight line in one arrangement. Another eight disks are arranged in a random "scatter" pattern in the other. The psychologist asks, "Is the amount of disks in each arrangement the same?" The psychologist is testing the child's understanding of:

    a.   spatial reversibility.   c.   spatial inertia.

    b.   conservation   d.   reorganization.

12. Jess and Kelly were playing with two balls of clay. Kelly was moulding a cake and Jess was making a bowl. Jess then suggested they get new balls of clay so that they could make something different. Kelly informed her that no new clay was necessary; the clay could be remoulded to make different objects. What principle was Kelly teaching to Jess?
    a.   the principle of conservation   c.   the principle of egocentric thought
    b.   the principle of reversibility   d.   the principle of logic

13. The last time Stephanie used her personal computer, she observed that several files were not copied onto the floppy disk as she had expected. She carefully checked her sequence of operations and considered the characteristics of the software. After evaluating alternative explanations for what had happened, she correctly deduced why the files were not copied. Stephanie was in Piaget's:
    a.   concrete operational stage of cognitive development.
    b.   preoperational stage of cognitive development.
    c.   sensorimotor stage of cognitive development.
    d.   formal operational stage of cognitive development.

14. According to Piaget, _____ is mastered early in the _____ for most children.
    a.   reversibility; sensorimotor stage   c.   object permanence; formal operational stage
    b.   conservation; concrete operational stage   d.   abstraction; preoperational stage

_____ 15.   phenylketonuria (PKU)   a.   A disease of the blood that affects about 10 percent of America's African-American population.

_____ 16.   sickle-cell anemia

    b.   German measles.

_____ 17.   Tay-Sachs disease

    c.   A disorder caused by the presence of an extra chromosome, resulting in mental retardation.

_____ 18.   Down syndrome

_____ 19.   rubella   d.   An inherited disease that prevents its victims from being able to produce an enzyme that resists certain poisons, resulting in profound mental retardation.

_____ 20.   fetal alcohol syndrome

    e.   A genetic defect preventing the body from breaking down fat and typically causing death by the age of 4.

    f.   An ailment producing mental and physical retardation in a baby as a result of the mother's behaviour.

21.   Women with hot flashes, poor concentration and other symptoms of menopause sometimes find relief from the symptoms with _____.

22.   A phenomenon that is consistent among racial and ethnic groups is that after a divorce children live with the _____.

23.   Kübler-Ross states that _____ is the first stage for those facing impending death.

24.   Kübler-Ross states that _____ is the last stage for those facing impending death.

25. One of the main points of the chapter is that developmental psychologists are interested in finding ways that the individual potential can be maximized. Children can be stimulated through contact with parents, through play, while at day care, and they can be encouraged to explore by having the appropriate attachments. What would the world of a perfectly "enriched" child look like? Is it possible to overstimulate?

Spotlight on Terminology and Language—
Cultural Idioms

Page 289 "Although she said she had faced **taunts** of 'test tube baby' or 'weirdo' a few times at school, she said she had never felt **resentful** about her **conception**."

Taunts are sarcastic insults. When someone expresses **resentment**, they are expressing annoyance or ill will. **Conception** is the circumstances involved in beginning life.

Page 290 "These issues, along with many others, are addressed **by developmental psychology**, the branch of psychology that studies the patterns of growth and change occurring throughout life."

Developmental psychology is the study of moral, social, emotional, and cognitive development throughout a person's entire life. Developmental psychologists study a person's biological, emotional, cognitive, personal, and social development across the life span, from infancy through late adulthood.

Page 291"However, developmental psychologists of different **theoretical** persuasions agree on some points."

A **theorem** is an idea accepted or proposed as a confirmable truth.

Page 293 "A **cohort** is a group of people who grow up at similar times, in similar places, and under similar conditions."

A **cohort** is a group of individuals having a statistical factor, such as age or class

membership, in common in a demographic study.

Page 294 "Each chromosome contains thousands of genes—smaller units through which genetic information is **transmitted**."

Genetic information is sent or conveyed when it is **transmitted**.

Page 294 "To better understand how genes influence human characteristics and behaviour, scientists have mapped the specific location and **sequence** of every human **gene** in the **massive**, multiyear Human Genome Project."

The **sequence** is the order, or the succession of related genes. A **gene** is a specific segment on the strand of DNA (the chromosome) that contains instructions for making proteins, the chemical building blocks from which all parts of the brain and body are constructed. A **genome** is the genetic material of an organism. The Human Genome project was tremendously large in scope and degree; it was **massive**.

Page 295 "At this point it has developed a **rudimentary** beating heart, brain, and intestinal tract, and a number of other rudimentary organs."

Rudimentary means an organ just beginning to develop.

Page 298 "Mothers who take illegal and physically addictive drugs such as cocaine run the risk of giving birth to babies who are similarly **addicted**."

An **addiction** is a compulsive need for and use of a habit-forming substance, such as nicotine, alcohol, or cocaine. An addiction is characterized by tolerance and by distinct physiological symptoms upon withdrawal.

Page 302 "Otherwise a model of **decorum**, Russell had somehow learned how to unzip the Velcro chin strap to his winter hat."

When a child is a model of **decorum**, he or she is well-behaved.

Page 303 "As anyone who has seen an infant smiling at the sight of her or his mother can guess, at the same time as infants are growing physically and **honing** their perceptual abilities, they are also developing socially."

When you **hone** something, you make it more effective.

Page 303 "He labeled this process **imprinting**, behaviour that takes place during a critical period and involves attachment to the first moving object that is observed."

Imprinting is the inherited tendencies or responses that are displayed by newborn animals when they encounter certain stimuli in their environment.

Page 303 "Building on this pioneering work with nonhumans, developmental psychologists have suggested that human **attachment** grows through the responsiveness of infants' caregivers to the signals the babies provide, such as cries, smiles, reaching, and **clinging**."
Attachment is a close, fundamental emotional bond that develops between the infant and his or her caregiver. A baby who is **clinging** is holding on tightly or tenaciously.

Page 305 "Fathers engage in more physical, **rough-and-tumble** sorts of activities, whereas mothers play more verbally oriented and traditional games such as peek-a-boo."

Rough-and-tumble is rough, rowdy, unrestrained fighting.

Page 305 "This play serves purposes other than **mere** enjoyment."

The play is more valuable than pure enjoyment

Page 315 "I went to a National Honour Society **induction**."

An **induction** is an initiation experience. Would you be able to describe the procedure by which a civilian is **inducted** into military service?

Page 315 "It is a time of profound changes and, occasionally, **turmoil**."

Turmoil is a period of extreme confusion, agitation, or commotion.

Page 315 "At the same time, these **physiological** changes are **rivaled** by important social, emotional, and cognitive changes that occur as adolescents strive for independence and move toward adulthood."

Physiology is the branch of biology that deals with the organic processes and phenomena of an organism or any of its parts or of a particular bodily process. When something is **rivaled**, it is in competition with competing forces.

Page 316 "**Puberty**, the period when the sexual organs mature, begins at about age 11 or 12 for girls and 13 or 14 for boys."
Puberty is a developmental period when the individual experiences significant biological changes, and as a result, develops secondary sexual characteristics and reaches sexual maturity.

Page 317 "Adolescents, however, are capable of reasoning on a **higher plane**, having typically reached Piaget's **formal operational stage** of cognitive development.**"**

Reasoning on a **higher plane** refers to a higher level of consciousness or intellectual and moral development. Piaget's fourth cognitive stage is known as the formal operations stage. This stage lasts from about 12 years old through adulthood. During the formal operations stage, adolescents and adults develop the capability to think about abstract or hypothetical concepts, to consider an issue from another person's viewpoint, and to resolve cognitive problems in a logical manner. Cognitive development refers to how a person perceives, thinks and gains an understanding of his or her world through the interaction and influence of genetic and learning factors.

Page 317 "Knowing right from wrong does not mean that we will always act **in accordance with** our judgments."

To act **in accordance with** is to act in agreement with our judgments. Are there times when you may have discarded your judgments and acted in accord with your intuition instead?

Page 318 "Compassion for individuals is a more **salient factor** in moral behaviour for women than it is for men."

A **salient factor** is something that stands out conspicuously. The compassion of women is of notable significance.

Page 318 "Erikson's theory of psychosocial development emphasizes the search for **identity** during the adolescent years."

Identity is how we describe ourselves, including our values, goals, traits, interests, and motivations.
Page 311 "Confusion over the most appropriate role to follow in life can lead to lack of a **stable identity**, adoption of a socially unacceptable role such as that of a social **deviant**, or difficulty in maintaining close personal relationships later in life."

A **stable identity** refers to an identity that is not changing or fluctuating, but is rather permanent and enduring. A **deviant** is a person who differs markedly form the group norm.

Page 318 "During the identity-versus-role-confusion period, pressures to identify what one wants to do with one's life are **acutely** felt."

During this period, people experience these pressures intensely. They provoke **acute** distress.

Page 319 "**Spanning** the period of early adulthood (from postadolescence to the early thirties), the focus is on developing close relationships with others."

Spanning means extending across. The career of some college professors spans four decades.

Page 320 "One reason for the increase in **discord** during adolescence appears to be the **protracted** period in which children stay at home with their parents."

Discord is the lack of agreement or harmony between family members. A **protracted** period is an extended period. Families keep their children home for a longer period of time than was done with previous generations.

Page 321 "Another source of **strife** with parents lies in the way adolescents think. Adolescence fosters adolescent **egocentrism**, a state of self-absorption in which adolescents view the world from their own point of view."

Strife is a bitter and sometimes violent conflict. **Egocentric** thinking is seeing and thinking of the world only from our own viewpoint and having difficulty appreciating someone else's viewpoint. Adolescent egocentric thinking encompasses the difficulties in separating one's own thought and feelings from those of others.

Page 321 "**Rites of Passage**: Coming of Age Around the World."

Rites of passage refer to a ritual associated with a crisis or a change of status for an individual. What are some of the **rites of passage** associated with marriage, illness and death in your culture?

■ CHAPTER 9: ANSWER KEY

Section 1:	Section 2:	Section 3:	Section 4:	Section 6:
[a] Developmental psychology	[a] neonate	[a] Cognitive development	[a] adolescence	[a] Gerontologists
[b] nature-nurture issue	[b] vernix	[b] sensorimotor	[b] puberty	[b] genetic preprogramming
[c] maturation	[c] lanugo	[c] object permanence	[c] identity-versus-role-confusion	[c] wear-and-tear theories
[d] interactionist	[d] reflexes	[d] preoperational	[d] identity	[d] fluid intelligence
[e] identical twins	[e] Babinski reflex	[e] concrete operational	[e] intimacy-versus-isolation	[e] crystallized intelligence
[f] conception	[f] Attachment	[f] formal operational	[f] generativity-versus-stagnation	[f] senility
[g] zygote	[g] Friendships	[g] information processing	[g] ego-integrity-versus-despair	[g] Alzheimer's disease
[h] chromosomes	[h] authoritarian parents	[h] zone of proximal development, or ZPD		[h] disengagement
[i] genes	[i] Permissive parents	[i] scaffolding	Evaluate	[i] activity
[j] embryo	[j] Authoritative parents		1. d	[j] denial
[k] critical period	[k] temperaments		2. c	[k] anger
[l] fetus	[l] psychosocial development		3. b	[l] bargaining
[m] age of viability			4. a	[m] depression
		Evaluate		[n] acceptance
Evaluate	Evaluate	1. b	Section 5:	
1. f	1. e	2. a	[a] menopause	Evaluate
2. b	2. a	3. c	[b] midlife transition	1. c
3. d	3. c	4. e	[c] midlife crisis	2. a
4. e	4. b	5. d		3. d
5. a	5. d		Evaluate	4. b
6. c			1. c	
			2. a	
			3. d	
			4. e	
			5. b	

Selected Rethink Answers

4. Children raised with more influence from fathers may have the opportunity to be exposed to different parent methods, they may also have fathers who have the same style and support and reinforce mother's childrearing styles. This trend's effect on attachment could mean that the child will develop a closer attachment to more than one person and this would appear to be an advantage to a child. Children who can learn from the modeling of both mothers and fathers have the advantage of experiencing the qualities that society has always seen as strongly male or strongly female. For example, with fathers play is different, more physical. Mothers are more verbal. Having more experiences and more choices and role models as they develop should have a positive effect on the development of children.

7. Schools traditionally have a great deal of bullying and teasing that goes on with the kids that are different, maturing early or late would make one different. Gym classes where students have to dress and shower in groups, gym classes where students have to compete, schools that place great emphasis on sports, and schools that perpetuate the "think thin" mentality can all have the potential to hurt teen development. Same sex schools would assume that the problems come because of the new male-female relationships. Many times the competitiveness is strongest in same sex groups.

8. Rights of passage are beneficial because they allow us to be publicly acknowledged for different stages in maturity. It helps adolescents to both expect and accept certain responsibilities that go with the age. In the United States getting a driver's licence, graduating from high school, moving out of parents' homes, and the right to vote are a few rites of passage. In the United States turning 18 years of age does give a person adult status and holds them legally responsible for their actions.

Practise Test 1:

1. c   obj. 1   p. 290
a. Incorrect. Not all psychologists believe in a combination; a few may view the development as primarily genetic, but many view development as primarily a result of environmental factors.
b. Incorrect. Neuropsychologist are probably more focused on the genetic and biological factors of environment than upon the mix between them.
*c. Correct. Interactionists focus upon the interaction of genetic and environmental forces.
d. Incorrect. Social psychologists are primarily interested in the social and environmental factors that influence development.

2. a   obj. 1   p. 291
*a. Correct. Maturation involves, to a large extent, the unfolding of genetic code.
b. Incorrect. Nurture refers to the element of environmental influence, not heredity.
c. Incorrect. Environmental factors are not hereditary.
d. Incorrect. Social growth would reveal environmental, nurturing types of factors and some hereditary factors.

3. d   obj. 1   p. 291
a. Incorrect. Identical twins reared apart would probably provide the most information regarding the roles of nature and nurture.
b. Incorrect. This pattern would shed light on how common environments interact with different genetic factors.
c. Incorrect. Siblings reared apart would indicate some aspects of the extent of genetic influence, though the genetic similarity may not be as strong as in twins.
*d. Correct. Siblings reared together share genes and environment, and the ability to separate which factors were influential in which behaviour or trait would be very limited.

4. d   obj. 2   p. 293
a. Incorrect. A cross-sectional study examines several groups at one given point in time.
b. Incorrect. There is no type of study called "maturational."
c. Incorrect. A longitudinal study follows a single group through a given span of time, taking measurements at points along the way.
*d. Correct. The cross-sequential study combines longitudinal and cross-sectional approaches by studying different groups in a longitudinal fashion, often allowing for a shorter timeframe to complete the study.

5. d   obj. 3   p. 296
a. Incorrect. If longitudinal development referred to a special concept, it would probably mean something like development through time.
b. Incorrect. When people reach middle age, they begin to experience cross-section maturation.

c. Incorrect. This phase occurs in the sexual response cycle but not in human development.
*d. Correct. This phase is called a "critical period" because certain developmental tasks must be achieved during the period or they become very difficult to achieve later.

6. d   obj. 3   p. 294
a. Incorrect. Zygotes and embryos refer to different stages of the fetus.
b. Incorrect. Zygotes are fetuses, not genes.
c. Incorrect. Neonates are newborn, not chromosomes.
*d. Correct. Each of our 46 chromosomes is composed of thousands of genes.

7. b   obj. 3   p. 296
a. Incorrect. Many sense organs are functional long before the fetus reaches a level of physical maturity that would allow it to survive if born.
*b. Correct. This age continues to be earlier and earlier as medical technology evolves.
c. Incorrect. Viability and learning are independent of each other in that viability depends upon the ability of the fetus to function physically independent of the mother, and this may be highly reflexive.
d. Incorrect. Sexual organs are differentiated long before viability.

8. a   obj. 4   p. 297
*a. Correct. This disease is inherited and causes mental retardation through the accumulation of toxins.
b. Incorrect. AIDS results from HIV infection.
c. Incorrect. This is a hormone that was prescribed in the 1960s and has resulted in abnormalities in the cervix and vagina in the daughters of women who took the hormone.
d. Incorrect. This syndrome occurs in children who are exposed to high levels of alcohol as fetuses.

9. b   obj. 5   p. 299
a. Incorrect. This means "true" or "realistic."
*b. Correct. This substance is like a very high-quality skin lotion.
c. Incorrect. This is someone who is for the New York Knicks.
d. Incorrect. The lanugo is the fine hair that covers the fetus.

10. d   obj. 4   p. 297
a. Incorrect. Junk food might affect some other aspect of development, but this link has not been established.
b. Incorrect. This link has not been established.
c. Incorrect. This is more likely to affect the marriage and the child's later behaviour.
*d. Correct. Research suggests that this is true, possibly because the chemicals in the mother's system enter and influence the child's temperament.

11. a   obj. 5   p. 300

*a. Correct. Whenever the baby's cheek is stroked, he will turn his head in the direction of the stroked cheek.
b. Incorrect. The startle reflex is a pattern of actions related to being startled in which the baby flings out his arms, spreads out his fingers, and arches his back.
c. Incorrect. This reflex helps the baby clear his throat.
d. Incorrect. The startle reflex would probably be considered a "surprise" reflex, but there is not a reflex officially named this.

12. b   obj. 12   p. 315
a. Incorrect. Adulthood follows this period, which is called adolescence.
*b. Correct. The developmental period is called adolescence, and this phase of growth and sexual maturation is called puberty.
c. Incorrect. Puberty is the name given the phase of growth and sexual maturation, but the developmental period is known as adolescence.
d. Incorrect. Childhood ends with the onset of this stage.

13. b   obj. 13   p. 317
a. Incorrect. In the preconventional stage, people are more likely to be motivated by rewards and avoidance of punishment.
*b. Correct. The conventional stage is marked by a desire to get along socially.
c. Incorrect. Individuals in the postconventional stage are not likely to be concerned with how others think about them.
d. Incorrect. Kohlberg did not define a nonconventional stage.

14. d   obj. 13   p. 317
a. Incorrect. This is not something he did.
b. Incorrect. He did not collect any survey data of this kind.
c. Incorrect. This was not his thing.
*d. Correct. Kohlberg was interested in how the person reasoned to solve a moral dilemma.

15. d   obj. 14   p. 319
a. Incorrect. Many of the other theories are inclusive of both males and females.
b. Incorrect. Cross-cultural studies have not supported nor rejected a universal application of Erikson's views.
c. Incorrect. Erikson does not place any special emphasis on understanding infant development in comparison to the rest of the life span.
*d. Correct. Erikson has been a leader in placing emphasis on the entire life span.

16. d   obj. 14   p. 318
a. Incorrect. Preconventional morality is more common in children.
b. Incorrect. Usually experienced by women who have reached menopause.
c. Incorrect. Identified with the very elderly.
*d. Correct. Adolescents are very concerned with their self-identity and roles

17. b   obj. 9   p. 307
18. a   obj. 9   p. 307
19. d   obj. 9   p. 308
20. c   obj. 9   p. 308
21. rooting reflex   obj. 5   p. 300
22. sucking reflex   obj. 5   p. 300
23. startle reflex   obj. 5   p. 300
24. Autonomy-versus-shame-and-doubt stage   obj. 9   p. 307
25. initiative versus guilt   obj. 9   p. 309

26.
▪ Identify the relative importance of nature and nurture for your views. Do you see them as equal or is one stronger than the other?
▪ Each of the styles may imply a view of the nature-nurture debate. The authoritarian style, for instance, may see children as naturally unruly and in need of strict discipline to come under control. The permissive parent may expect the child to find his or her own potential, that such exploration is natural.
▪ The view that sees nature and nurture as interacting would suggest that the parenting style is the place that an inherited potential can be realized, so child-rearing practices are crucial.

Practise Test 2:
1. c   obj. 1   p. 291
a. Incorrect. Interactionism admits to genetic (not a blank slate) influences.
b. Incorrect. The "nature" element is that of heredity, suggesting some aspects of development are influenced by one's disposition.
*c. Correct. Nurture implies the forces of the environment, including the caregiving and socializing influences, so nurture would be the dominant influence for someone with such a view.
d. Incorrect. Dualism refers to the philosophical perspective of the duality of the mind and body, not the duality of nature and nurture.

2. c   obj. 1   p. 291
a. Incorrect. Only those born of alien parents.
b. Incorrect. Non-twin siblings have shared their lives just as much.
*c. Correct. Having identical genes makes the difference.
d. Incorrect. Most subjects are very highly cooperative in their dealings with psychologists.

3. c   obj. 2   p. 293
a. Incorrect. Cross-sectional studies look at sets of individuals at different stages of life or in different conditions and compares the groups.
b. Incorrect. No study goes by the name "maturational."
*c. Correct. A longitudinal study examines individuals, usually a large group of individuals, as they grow and change over an extended period of time.
d. Incorrect. A cross-sequential study includes observing individuals through a period of time, but it also includes comparing different groups at the same time,

and it would be described as a combination of longitudinal and cross-sectional study methods.

4. b   obj. 3   p. 294
a. Incorrect. Chromosomes contain genes, and genes are the basic information units.
*b. Correct. Genes are the basic information units in genetics.
c. Incorrect. Spores are released by fungi.
d. Incorrect. Somes is the plural of "some," which would still only be some.

5. a   obj. 3   p. 295
*a. Correct. The next stage is an embryo, and this is followed by the stage known as a fetus.
b. Incorrect. A neonate is a newborn, and an embryo would not survive birth.
c. Incorrect. A fetus is the stage that follows embryo, which follows zygote.
d. Incorrect. Fertilization precedes the zygote phase.

6. d   obj. 5   p. 299
a. Incorrect. It sounds convincing though.
b. Incorrect. See answer d.
c. Incorrect. Intercourse during pregnancy is perfectly healthy as long as it remains comfortable—it has nothing to do with the hairiness of the baby.
*d. Correct. Vernix is a creamy substance that acts as a moisturizer and lanugo is short body hair, both of which are present during pregnancy and remain shortly after birth.

7. d   obj. 3   p. 296
a. Incorrect. At eight weeks, only arms, legs, and face are discernable.
b. Incorrect. At this stage, the face does not have any characteristics of later life to it, and eyes do not open, among many other differences.
c. Incorrect. At this stage, the fetus can move noticeably, the face has characteristics it will have later, and major organs begin to function.
*d. Correct. At 24 weeks, most of the characteristics that will be seen in the newborn are present, eyes will open and close, it can cry, grasp, look in directions.

8. a   obj. 4   p. 297
*a. Correct. Children with Tay-Sachs disease are unable to break down fat, and they die by the age of 4.
b. Incorrect. Down syndrome can occur in any child, but it is more frequent with children of older parents.
c. Incorrect. Meningitis is not a genetic disease.
d. Incorrect. Phenylketonuria, or PKU, is a genetic disease that can afflict anyone, and it does not result in early death, rather it results in retardation if not treated properly.

9. a   obj. 4   p. 297
*a. Correct. Down syndrome children have an extra chromosome, which results in mental retardation and unusual physical features.

b. Incorrect. Sickle-cell anemia is a recessive trait common among people of African descent.
c. Incorrect. Children with Tay-Sachs disease are unable to break down fat, and they die by the age of 4.
d. Incorrect. Phenylketonuria, or PKU, is a genetic disease that results in retardation if not treated properly.

10. b   obj. 4   p. 297
a. Incorrect. Down syndrome children have an extra chromosome, which results in mental retardation and unusual physical features.
*b. Correct. This disease can cause serious malformation and prenatal death.
c. Incorrect. Phenylketonuria, or PKU, is a genetic disease that results in retardation if not treated properly.
d. Incorrect. Sickle-cell anemia is a recessive trait common among people of African descent.

11. b   obj. 5   p. 299
a. Incorrect. A neonate is a newborn.
*b. Correct. This is the official term used to refer to newborns in their first week.
c. Incorrect. A neonate is any newborn.
d. Incorrect. A neonate is a newborn, and can be early, late, or on time.

12. c   obj. 2   p. 293
a. Incorrect. Longitudinal method follows one group through many years.
b. Incorrect. However, the length of funding for the project would probably define the critical period.
*c. Correct. The researcher is comparing different age groups at the same time to compare the different abilities shown by each group.
d. Incorrect. This combines longitudinal and cross-sectional, following several groups for an extended period of time.

13. c   obj. 22   p.331
a. Incorrect. The genetic programming theories suggest that aging results from preprogrammed failures at the cellular level
b. Incorrect the genes do not break down, but may actually program the breakdown of cells.
*c Correct. This is the main thesis of the wear and tear theories.
d. Incorrect. This is not a theory of aging.

14. c   obj. 22   p.331
a. Incorrect. The wear-and-tear theory suggests that the body wears out.
b. Incorrect. The genetic preprogramming theory suggests that the body is programmed to slow and die.
*c Correct. The disengagement theory says that people age because they consciously withdraw.
d. Incorrect. The activity theory of aging suggests that people who remain active have a more successful old age.

15. d   obj. 22   p. 331
a.   Incorrect. Fluid intelligence declines with age.
b.   Incorrect. Verbal Intelligence may increase as crystallized intelligence increases.
c.   Incorrect. Basis intelligence is not defined adequately to suggest that it exists much less changes with age.
*d   Correct. As described, crystallized intelligence increases as the experiences and memories become more important aspects of intelligent behaviour in later adulthood.

16. b   obj.15   p. 321
17. d   obj.15   p. 321
18. e   obj.12   p. 315
19. a   obj 10   p. 312
20. c   obj.13   p. 318
21. rites of passage obj. 13   p. 318
22. middle adulthood   obj. 16   p. 322
23. Increases obj. 22   p. 313
24. males, females obj. 15   p. 321

25.
• First, describe each of these two theories and offer an example of how they differ.
• The activity theory suggests that a successful retirement would require a level of activity that would allow continuity.
• Retirement serves as an important marker of age in the disengagement theory.
• Describe the benefits (such as making room for people entering the job market) or costs (loss of expertise) of mandatory retirement in order to support your yes or no answer.

Practise Test 3:
1.   d   obj. 3   p.295
a.   Incorrect. See answer d.
b.   Incorrect. See answer d.
c.   Incorrect. See answer d.
*d. Correct. A rudimentary heart, brain, and intestinal tract are formed during the embryonic stage.

2.   a   obj. 1   p. 291
*a. Correct. This statement reflects the interactionist views of most developmental psychologists.
b.   Incorrect. Few developmental psychologists take such a strong view of genetics, and most are unwilling to claim genetics or environment as stronger than the other factor.
c.   Incorrect. Few developmental psychologists take such a strong view of the environment, and most are unwilling to claim genetics or environment as stronger than the other factor.
d.   Incorrect. This is a true statement, and it actually supports the contemporary interactionist view, which is best described in another of the alternatives.

3.   b   obj. 4   p. 297
a.   Incorrect. While hypertension has some genetic disposition, it is not identifiable enough to be said to

be directly transmitted, and it does not cause a short life expectancy.
*b. Correct. This disease results from recessive genes (passed on by both parents), and the red blood cells have a deformed, sickle shape.
c.   Incorrect. Children with Tay-Sachs disease are unable to break down fat, and they die by the age of 4, but they are usually of Jewish descent.
d.   Incorrect. Phenylketonuria, or PKU, is a genetic disease that can afflict anyone, and it does not result in early death, rather it results in retardation if not treated properly.

4.   c   obj. 4   p. 297
a.   Incorrect. See answer c.
b.   Incorrect. See answer c.
*c. Correct. The mother contributes to problems arising from 'her nutrition and stress level, the mother's drug and medication, and birth complications and these may all be within her control, while hereditary defects are not in the mother's control and require contributions form the father.
d.   Incorrect. See answer c.

5.   b   obj. 6   p. 302
a.   Incorrect. And the infants production of speech sounds and recognition of sounds continues to grow rapidly.
*b. Correct. Infants can recognize their mother's voice as early as three days.
c.   Incorrect. This too is true.
d.   Incorrect. The sweet tooth must be built in.

6.   b   obj. 4   p. 296
a.   Incorrect. See answer b.
*b. Correct. Beore or after the critical period would most likely cause less or no effect.
c.   Incorrect. See answer b.
d.   Incorrect. See answer b.

7.   a   obj. 7   p. 294
*a. Correct. The style of interaction between mother and child differs from that of father and child.
b.   Incorrect. This is reversed.
c.   Incorrect. The attachment is not stronger or weaker, but of a different style.
d.   Incorrect. Fathers probably spend less time with their children, but this is not universally true.

8.   d   obj. 7   p. 304
a.   Incorrect. Few would describe the difference as one of superiority.
b.   Incorrect. Rather than aloof and detached, fathers are often quite physical and in close contact with their children.
c.   Incorrect. While affectionate, fathers do not express this as verbally as do mothers.
*d. Correct. Due to the differences in how fathers and mothers interact with their children, the best description is that the attachment differs in quality.

9.   b   obj. 8   p. 306

a. Incorrect. Permissive parents are lax and inconsistent with the discipline of their children.
*b. Correct. Authoritative parents set limits and are firm, but not inflexible.
c. Incorrect. This is not a type of parent, but the very definition of being a parent.
d. Incorrect. Authoritarian parents are rigid and punitive.

10. d   obj. 7   p. 305
a. Incorrect. See answer d.
b. Incorrect. See answer d.
c. Incorrect. See answer d.
*d. Correct. Play may actually increase mutual dependence and support. Play builds social competence, encourages taking the perspective of others, and requires emotional control.

11. b   obj. 10   p. 310
a. Incorrect. Reversibility would refer to the ability to reverse an operation.
*b. Correct. This test describes an effort to determine the ability of the child to conserve a number even if the objects are arranged differently.
c. Incorrect. A developmental psychologist would not test for spatial inertia.
d. Incorrect. Reorganization is not one of the principles that could be tested by a developmental psychologist.

12. b   obj. 10   p. 310
a. Incorrect. The principle of conservation would be applied to whether a lump of clay was more if it was long or short and fat—even if it was the same ball of clay.
*b. Correct. As simple as it sounds, Jess is learning that he can reverse his bowl back into a ball of clay.
c. Incorrect. If egocentric thought were at work, Jess might simply decide that the cake Kelly made was a pot of soup for his bowl.
d. Incorrect. Logic will come much later.

13. d   obj. 10   p. 312
a. Incorrect. This sequential and systematic problem solving approach is most common of someone in the formal operations stage, not the concrete operations stage.
b. Incorrect. This sequential and systematic problem solving approach is most common of someone in the formal operations stage, not the preoperational stage.
c. Incorrect. This sequential and systematic problem solving approach is most common of someone in the formal operations stage, not the sensorimotor stage.
*d. Correct. This sequential and systematic problem solving approach is most common of someone in the formal operations stage.

14. b   obj. 10   p. 310
a. Incorrect. Reversibility is mastered in the concrete operations stage, not the sensorimotor stage.
*b. Correct. Conservation is one of the major accomplishments of the stage.
c. Incorrect. Object permanence occurs in the sensorimotor stage.
d. Incorrect. Abstraction occurs in the formal stage.

15. d   obj. 4   p. 297
16. a   obj. 4   p. 297
17. e   obj. 4   p. 297
18. c   obj. 4   p. 297
19. b   obj. 4   p. 297
20. f   obj. 4   p. 298
21. estrogen replacement therapy   obj. 16   p. 323
22. mother   obj. 17   p. 324
23. denial   obj. 22   p. 330
24. acceptance   obj. 22   p. 330

25.
- Describe the factors that you consider important for early exposure. Can a child's later learning be enhanced through early exposure to academic skills like spelling and math? Or should the focus be on processes like imagination and creative work?
- What criteria would you use to identify overstimulation? Keep in mind that the child must feel safe and have a secure attachment in order to explore the environment freely.

Personality

10

Chapter 10 introduces both the approaches to the understanding of personality along with methods psychologists use to assess individual personality characteristics. Personality is the sum of the characteristics that differentiate individuals and provide the stability in a person's behaviour across situations and time. First, the psychoanalytic approach to personality is discussed. Psychoanalysis understands personality in terms of how a person manages the unconscious that seeks to dominate behaviour. Next, four major alternatives to the psychoanalytical approach are investigated. These are trait approaches, learning approaches, biological approaches, and humanistic approaches. Finally, the chapter illustrates several ways that personality can be assessed. Psychological tests that demonstrate both reliability and validity and also have standardized norms are studied. The most frequently given assessments include the MMPI, the Rorschach test and the TAT.

To further investigate the topics covered in this chapter, you can visit the related websites by visiting the following link: http://www.mcgrawhill.ca/college/feldman

Prologue: Good Guy or Good Fella?
Looking Ahead

Section 1: Psychoanalytic Approaches to Personality
Freud's Psychoanalytic Theory
The Neo-Freudian Psychoanalysts

Section 2: Other Major Approaches to Personality: In Search of Human Uniqueness
Trait Approaches: Placing Labels on Personality
Learning Approaches: We Are What We've Learned
Biological and Evolutionary Approaches: Are We Born with Personality?

Applying Psychology in the 21st Century: Can Unjustified High Self-Esteem Lead to Violence?

Humanistic Approaches: The Uniqueness of You
Comparing Approaches to Personality

Section 3: Assessing Personality: Determining What Makes Us Special

> **Exploring Diversity:** Should Norms Be Based on Race and Ethnicity?

Self-Report Measures of Personality
Projective Methods
Behavioural Assessment

> **Becoming an Informed Consumer of Psychology:**
> Assessing Personality Assessments

Learning Objectives

These are the concepts and the learning objectives for Chapter 10. Read them carefully as part of your preliminary survey of the chapter.

Psychoanalytic Approaches to Personality

1. Define personality and describe the basic structure of personality according to Sigmund Freud. (pp. 338–339)

2. Outline the five stages of personality development according to Freud. (pp. 339–341)

3. Define and describe the defence mechanisms and their role in psychoanalytic theory. (pp. 341–342)

4. Discuss the contribution made by Freud, the criticisms of the psychoanalytic theory of personality, and the contributions made by the neo-Freudians. (pp. 342–345)

Other Major Approaches to Personality: In Search of Human Uniqueness

5. Describe and evaluate the trait theory approaches to personality development. (pp. 345–348)

6. Describe and evaluate the learning theory approaches to personality development. (pp. 348-

350)

7.   Describe and evaluate the biological and evolutionary approaches to personality development. (pp. 350–353)

8.   Describe and evaluate the humanistic approaches to personality development. (pp. 353–355)

Assessing Personality: Determining What Makes Us Special

9.   Discuss personality assessment and define the concepts of validity, reliability, and norms. (pp. 356–357)

10.   Differentiate between and cite examples of the following methods of personality assessment: self-report, projective, behavioural assessment, and cross-cultural (358–361)

11.   Evaluate the various personality assessment methods. (p. 362)

SECTION 1: Psychoanalytic Approaches to Personality

Prepare

- *How do psychologists define and use the concept of personality?*
- *What do the theories of Freud and his successors tell us about the structure and development of personality?*

Organize

- *Freud's Psychoanalytic Theory*
- *The Neo-Freudian Psychoanalysts*

Work

The field of psychology known as **[a]** _____ studies the characteristics that make a person unique and attempts to explain what makes a person act the same in different situations and through time.

[b] _____ are concerned with understanding the hidden forces that govern people's behaviour and remain outside of awareness. These forces have their roots in childhood experiences. This theory, called **[c]** _____, was developed by Sigmund Freud. Slips of the tongue are examples of how thoughts and emotions are held in the

[d] _____, the part of the personality that remains beyond the person's awareness. Slips reflect these hidden concerns. The unconscious also contains *instinctual drives*, which include infantile wishes, desires, demands, and needs that remain hidden because of the conflicts they can cause. Freud described conscious experience as the top of an iceberg, suggesting that the larger part of our personality was unconscious. In order to understand personality, these unconscious elements must be illuminated. The contents of the unconscious are disguised, thus requiring that slips of the tongue, fantasies, and dreams be interpreted in order to understand how unconscious processes direct behaviour.

Freud described a general model of the personality that contains three interacting structures. The **[e]** _____ is the raw, unorganized, inherited part of the personality aimed at reducing the tension caused by basic drives of hunger, sex, aggression, and irrational impulses. The drives are powered by **[f]** _____, or "psychic energy," and the id operates according to the **[g]** _____, or the desire for immediate gratification of all needs. Reality limits the expression of these id impulses. The

[h] _____ is responsible for constraining the id. It serves as a buffer between reality and the pleasure-seeking demands of the id. The ego operates on the

[i] _____, in which restraint is based on the safety of the individual and an effort to integrate into society. The ego is the seat of the higher cognitive functions. The

[j] _____ represents the rights and wrongs of society as represented by the parents and is composed of two parts. The **[k]** _____ prevents us from

behaving immorally and the **[l]** _____ motivates us to do the morally correct thing. Both the superego and the id make unrealistic demands. The ego must compromise between the moral-perfectionist demands of the superego and the pleasure-seeking gratification sought by the id.

Freud proposed a theory of development that accounted for how the adult personality comes into existence. Difficulties and experiences from a childhood stage may predict adult behaviours, and each stage focuses on a biological function. The first period of development is the

[m] _____ _stage_ during which the baby's mouth is the focus of pleasure. This suggested to Freud that the mouth is the primary site of sexual pleasure.

[n] _____ means that an adult shows personality characteristics that are related to that stage. At about 12 to 18 months until the age of 3, the child is in the

[o] _____ _stage_. The major source of pleasure moves to the anal region, and the child derives pleasure from the retention and expulsion of feces. If toilet training is particularly demanding, fixation can occur. Fixation can lead to unusual rigidity and orderliness or the extreme opposite of disorder or sloppiness. At the age of 3, the

[p] _____ _stage_ begins and the source of pleasure moves to the genitals. Children unconsciously begin to desire the parent of the opposite sex. However, in the end, girls identify with their mothers, and boys with their fathers and repress these feelings. The next phase

is called the **[q]** _____ _period_, beginning around 5 or 6 and lasting to

puberty. Sexual concerns become latent. The final phase, the **[r]** _____ _stage_, begins at puberty. Mature adult sexuality emerges during this period.

Anxiety, an intense, negative emotional experience, arises as a signal of danger to the ego. Though anxiety may arise from realistic fears, the _neurotic anxiety_ arises because of the irrational impulses from the id that threaten to break into consciousness. The ego has developed unconscious strategies to control the impulses called [s] _____. *Regression* involves using behaviour from earlier stages of development to deal with the anxiety. *Displacement* is the process of redirecting the unwanted feeling onto a less threatening person. *Rationalization* occurs when reality is distorted by justifying events with explanations that protect our self-esteem. *Denial* occurs when a person simply refuses to acknowledge the existence of an anxiety-producing piece of information. *Projection* involves protecting oneself by attributing unwanted impulses and feelings to someone else. *Sublimation* is the diversion of unwanted impulses to socially acceptable behaviours. According to Freud, these mechanisms are used to some degree by everyone, though some people devote a large amount of energy to dealing with unacceptable impulses to the extent that daily life becomes hampered. He identified this tendency as neurosis.

Evaluate

_____ 1. unconscious

_____ 2. instinctual drives

_____ 3. id

_____ 4. libido

_____ 5. fixation

a. Behaviour reflecting an earlier stage of development.

b. Infantile wishes, desires, demands, and needs hidden from conscious awareness.

c. A person is unaware of this determinant of behaviour.

d. The raw, unorganized, inherited part of personality created by biological drives and irrational impulses.

e. The sexual energy underlying biological urges.

Rethink

1. Can you think of ways in which Freud's theories of unconscious motivations are commonly used in popular culture? How accurately do you think such popular uses of Freudian theories reflect Freud's ideas?

2. What are some examples of archetypes in addition to those mentioned in this chapter? In what ways are archetypes similar to and different from stereotypes?

SECTION 2:   Other Major Approaches to Personality: In Search of Human Uniqueness

Prepare

- *What are the major aspects of trait, learning, biological and evolutionary, and humanistic approaches to personality?*

Organize

- *Trait Approaches*
- *Learning Approaches*
- *Biological and Evolutionary Approaches*

- *Humanistic Approaches*
- *Comparing Approaches to Personality*

Work

A number of theories take a different approach than that of psychoanalysis. These include

[a] _____, which assumes that individuals respond to different situations in

a fairly consistent manner. [b] _____ are the enduring dimensions of

personality characteristics along which people differ. Trait theories assume that all people have

certain traits, and the degree to which a trait applies to a specific person varies.

Gordon Allport identified 18,000 separate terms that could be used to describe personality,

which he then reduced to 4,500 descriptors. In order to make sense of this number, he defined

three basic categories of traits. A [c] _____ is a single characteristic that

directs most of a person's activities. Most people do not have cardinal traits, instead they have

five to ten [d] _____ that define major characteristics.

[e] _____ are characteristics that affect fewer situations and are less

influential than cardinal or central traits. Preferences would be secondary traits.

The statistical technique called [f] _____, in which relationships among

a large number of variables are summarized into smaller, more general patterns, has been used to

identify fundamental patterns or combinations of traits. Raymond Cattell suggested that there are

forty-six *surface traits*, or clusters of related behaviours. Cattell then reduced this number to

sixteen *source traits* that represent the basic dimensions of personality. He then developed the

Sixteen Personality Factor Questionnaire (16 PF). Hans Eysenck used factor analysis to identify

three major dimensions. [g] _____ is the dimension marked by quiet and

restrained individuals on one end and outgoing and sociable ones on the other.

[h] _____ is the dimension marked by moody and sensitive behaviour

(neuroticism) on the one hand and calm, reliable, and even-tempered behaviour (stability) on the

other. [i] _____ refers to the degree to which reality is distorted. Recent

research has suggested that there are five traits: *surgency, neuroticism, intellect, agreeableness,*

and *conscientiousness.*

According to B. F. Skinner, personality is a collection of learned behaviour patterns.

Similarities across situations are caused by a similarity of reinforcements. Strict learning theorists

are less interested in the consistency issue than they are in finding ways to modify behaviour. In

their view, humans are quite changeable.

[j] _____ *approaches* emphasize the role of a person's cognitions in

determining personality. According to Albert Bandura, people are able to foresee the outcomes of

behaviours prior to carrying them out by using the mechanism of [k] _____.

Bandura considers [l] _____, the expectations of success, to be an

important factor in determining the behaviours a person will display. The key to understanding behaviour, **[m]** _____, refers to the interaction between environment, behaviour, and the individual.

Traditional learning theories have been criticized for ignoring internal processes and reducing behaviour to stimuli and responses.

[n] _____ *approaches* to personality suggest that important components of personality are inherited. The study of **[o]** _____, the basic innate disposition that emerges early in life, is studied through the biological approach. Jerome Kagan's study of inhibited and uninhibited children suggests that *inhibited children* have an inborn characteristic of greater physiological reactivity.

[p] _____ *approaches to personality* emphasize the basic goodness of people and their tendency to grow to higher levels of functioning. Carl Rogers is a major representative of this approach. The positive regard others have for us makes us see and judge ourselves through the eyes of other people. The views others have of us may not match our own *self-concept*. If the difference is great, we may have problems with daily functioning. The discrepancy is overcome by support from another person in the form of

[q] _____, defined as an attitude of acceptance and respect no matter what the person says or does. Rogers and Maslow view the ultimate goal of personality growth to be

[r] _____.

The criticisms of humanistic theory are centred on the difficulty of verifying the basic assumptions of the theory. The assumption that all people are basically "good" is unverifiable and injects nonscientific values into scientific theories.

Evaluate

_____ 1. cardinal trait

_____ 2. central traits

_____ 3. secondary traits

_____ 4. surface traits

_____ 5. source traits

a. A single trait that directs most of a person's activities.

b. The sixteen basic dimensions of personality.

c. Clusters of a person's related behaviours that can be observed in a given situation.

d. Traits less important than central and cardinal traits.

e. A set of major characteristics that compose the core of a person's personality.

Rethink

3. If personality traits are merely descriptive and not explanatory, of what use are they? Can assigning a trait to a person be harmful—or helpful? Why or why not?

4. In what ways are Cattell's 16 source traits, Eysenck's three dimensions, and the "Big Five" factors similar, and in what ways are they different? Which traits seem to appear in all three schemes (under one name or another) and which are unique to one scheme? Is this significant?

SECTION 3: Assessing Personality: Determining What Makes Us Special

Prepare

- *How can we most accurately assess personality?*
- *What are the major types of personality measures?*

Organize

- *Self-Report Measures of Personality*
- *Projective Methods*
- *Behavioural Assessment*

Work

The intentionally vague statements that introduce the topic of assessment suggest that measuring different aspects of personality may require great care and precision. The assessment of personality requires discriminating the behaviour of one person from that of another.

[a] _____ are standard measures that measure aspects of behaviour objectively.

Psychological tests must have [b] _____, that is, they must measure something consistently from time to time. A reliable test will produce similar outcomes in similar conditions. The question of whether or not a test measures the characteristic it is supposed to measure is called [c] _____. If a test is reliable, that does not mean that is valid. [d] _____ are the standards of test performance that allow comparison of the scores of one test taker to others who have taken it. The norm for a test is determined by calculating the average score for a particular group of people for whom the test is designed to be given.

Instead of conducting a comprehensive interview to determine aspects of childhood, social relationships, and success and failures, the use of [e] _____ allows individuals to respond to a small sample of questions. The most frequently used self-report measure is the [f] _____. Originally developed to distinguish people with psychological disturbances from people without disturbances, the MMPI scores have been shown to be good predictors of such things as whether college students will marry within ten years and whether they will get an advanced degree. The test has 567 true-false items covering items like mood, opinions, and physical and psychological health. The interpretation of the responses is important, there are no right or wrong answers. The test is scored on ten scales and includes a lie scale for people trying to falsify their answers. The MMPI has undergone a procedure called

[g] _____ by which the test authors have determined which items best differentiate among groups of people, like differentiating those suffering depression from normal subjects.

[h] _____ *tests* require the subject to describe an ambiguous stimulus. The responses are considered to be projections of what the person is like. The best known is the

[i] _____ *test*, which consists of symmetrical stimuli. The

[j] _____ consists of a series of pictures about which the person is asked to write a story. Inferences about the subject are then based on these stories. These tests are criticized because too much inference depends upon the scorer.

In order to obtain an objective test based on observable behaviour, a

[k] _____ may be conducted either in a natural setting or in a laboratory under controlled conditions. The behavioural assessment requires quantifying behaviour as much as possible.

Evaluate

_____ 1.   Minnesota Multiphasic Personality Inventory-2 (MMPI-2)

_____ 2.   test standardization

_____ 3.   projective personality test

_____ 4.   Rorschach test

_____ 5.   Thematic Apperception Test (TAT)

a.   Used to identify people with psychological difficulties.

b.   Consists of a series of ambiguous pictures about which a person is asked to write a story.

c.   Uses inkblots of indefinite shapes.

d.   Uses ambiguous stimuli to determine personality.

e.   Validates questions in personality tests by studying the responses of people with known diagnoses.

Rethink

5.   What do you think are some of the problems that developers and interpreters of self-report personality tests must deal with in their effort to provide useful information about test-takers? Why is a "lie scale" included on such measures?

6. Should personality tests be used for personnel decisions? Should they be used for other social purposes, such as identifying individuals at risk for certain types of personality disorders? What sorts of policies would you devise to ensure that such tests were used ethically?

Practise Questions

Test your knowledge of the chapter material by answering these questions. These questions have been placed in three Practise Tests. The first two tests are composed of questions that will test your recall of factual knowledge. The third test contains questions that are challenging and primarily test for conceptual knowledge and your ability to apply that knowledge. Check your answers and review the feedback using the Answer Key in the following pages of the *Study Guide*.

PRACTISE TEST 1:

1. According to Sigmund Freud, the _____ harbours repressed emotions and thoughts as well as instinctual drives.
   a. unconscious
   b. collective unconscious
   c. conscience
   d. conscious

2. Which of the following is **least** likely to involve making unrealistic demands on the person?
   a. the id
   b. the ego
   c. the superego
   d. the pleasure principle

3. In Freud's psychoanalytic theory, the most important mental factors were:
   a. those which the person consciously controls or manipulates.
   b. associated with the latency developmental stage.
   c. those about which the person is unaware.
   d. based on social learning and influence.

4. According to the text, Freud's concept of the ego-ideal refers to:
   a. infantile wishes, desires, demands, and needs hidden from conscious awareness.
   b. the part of the superego that motivates us to do what is morally proper.
   c. the part of personality that provides a buffer between the id and the outside world.
   d. the part of the superego that prevents us from doing what is morally wrong.

5. A child who is in the midst of toilet training is probably in the:
   a. genital psychosexual stage.
   b. anal psychosexual stage.
   c. phallic psychosexual stage.
   d. oral psychosexual stage.

6. Which of the following defence mechanisms did Freud find most socially acceptable?
   a. repression
   b. sublimation
   c. rationalization
   d. projection

7. Defence mechanisms are unconscious strategies that people use to:
   a. decrease their reliance on the reality principle.
   b. reduce anxiety.
   c. increase the superego's power to regulate behaviour.
   d. prevent Freudian slips.

8. According to trait theorists, everyone has:
   a. the same traits, but in different amounts.
   b. different traits that do not change with time.
   c. different traits, and they change with time.
   d. different traits, but they cannot be measured.

9. Which of the psychologists listed below is **not** a trait theorist?
   a. Albert Bandura   c. Raymond B. Cattell
   b. Gordon Allport   d. Hans Eysenck

10. From the perspective of learning theorists such as B. F. Skinner, consistencies of behaviour across situations relate to:
    a. stable individual characteristics called personality traits.
    b. the dynamics of unconscious forces.
    c. the rewards or punishments received by the person previously.
    d. any conflict between one's experiences and his or her self-concept.

11. Factor analysis is:
    a. a method of recording data that requires sophisticated equipment.
    b. a method of understanding how the unconscious works.
    c. a statistical method of finding common traits.
    d. a sociometric method of determining personality traits in a group.

12. Humanistic theories of personality assume that:
    a. man's basic goodness is contrasted with an evil unconscious.
    b. man is self-sufficient and that society corrupts the individual.
    c. man is basically good and desires to improve.
    d. man's fundamental depravity may be offset through education.

13. The conscious, self-motivated personal ability to improve is the core of:
    a. the learning theory of personality.
    b. the neo-Freudian psychoanalytic theory of personality.
    c. the humanistic theory of personality.
    d. the trait theory of personality.

14. Which one of the following tests is designed to uncover unconscious content?
    a. MMPI   c. California Psychological Inventory
    b. TAT   d. Edwards Personal Preference Schedule

15. A student retakes the Graduate Record Exam. Despite her claim that she did badly the first time because she was very sleepy that day, her score is within 2 percent of her first score. This outcome supports the notion that the GRE test is:
    a. a standardized type of   c. a reliable assessment tool.

assessment tool.
b.   an academic ability assessment tool.   d.   a valid assessment tool.

____ 16.   pleasure principle   a.   Provides a buffer between the id and the outside world.

____ 17.   ego   b.   The principle by which the id operates.

                               c.   Prevents us from doing what is morally wrong.

____ 18.   reality principle   d.   Represents the morality of society as presented by
                                     parents, teachers, and others.

____ 19.   superego   e.   The principle by which the ego operates.

____ 20.   conscience

21.   The _____ provides a buffer between the id and the outside world.

22.   A phenomenon whereby adults have continuing feelings of weakness and insecurity is referred to
       as having an _____.

23.   _____ is when unpleasant id impulses are pushed back into the unconscious.

24.   The refusal to accept anxiety-producing information is known as _____.

25.   Allport suggests three basic categories of traits: cardinal, central, and _____.

26.   Given that Freud's theory appears to be primarily focused on male development and thus on a male
       personality, identify the areas of Freud's theory that are the weakest with regard to female
       psychological issues. Defend your response with other points of view presented in the text.

PRACTISE TEST 2:

1. Which of the following theories suggests that behaviour is triggered largely by powerful forces found
    in the unconscious?
    a.   humanistic theory   c.   psychoanalytic theory
    b.   learning theory   d.   trait theory

2. Freud's structure of personality has three major parts. Which alternative below is **not** one of them?
    a.   libido   c.   superego
    b.   id   d.   ego

3. Which of the following controls thought, solves problems, and makes decisions?
    a.   id   c.   superego
    b.   ego   d.   conscience

4. According to Freud's theory of psychosexual development, a child who is constantly putting things in its mouth is most likely at the:
   a. genital stage.
   b. anal stage.
   c. phallic stage.
   d. oral stage.

5. Freud's stages theory of mature sexual relationships begin to occur at which psychosexual stage?
   a. phallic
   b. oral
   c. genital
   d. anal

6. According to Sigmund Freud, defence mechanisms are:
   a. unconscious.
   b. instinctive.
   c. learned.
   d. reflexive.

7. Victims of child abuse, rape, or incest attacks might not recall the incident or may remember only scanty details. Freud suggested that the reason for this is that the defence mechanism of _____ was applied.
   a. sublimation
   b. repression
   c. denial
   d. projection

8. For Gordon Allport, _____ traits were so distinct that having only one of these traits will define a person's personality.
   a. general
   b. secondary
   c. central
   d. cardinal

9. According to Gordon Allport, what are the three important categories of personality dimensions?
   a. primary, secondary, and tertiary
   b. factors, traits, and features
   c. source, surface, and circumscript
   d. cardinal, central, and secondary

10. The basic assumption shared by trait personality theorists is that:
    a. the traits are consistent across situations.
    b. the unconscious mind is the underlying source of the traits we have.
    c. traits are learned habits that are modified by reinforcers.
    d. people possess the traits to the same degree but differ in how they choose to apply them.

11. We can modify our own personalities, according to Bandura, through the use of:
    a. defence mechanisms.
    b. drive reduction.
    c. psychoanalysis.
    d. self-reinforcement.

12. Temperament is presumed to originate from the child's:
    a. personally chosen interests and ideas.
    b. source traits.
    c. early learning experiences with the primary caregiver or mother.
    d. genetic predisposition.

13. If a test provides a consistent score for a particular individual over repeated administrations, the test is said to be:
    a. accurate.
    b. valid.
    c. reliable.
    d. statistical.

14. The MMPI was originally developed to:
    a. identify personality disorders.   c. locate traits.
    b. uncover unconscious thoughts.   d. conduct behavioural assessments.

15. Test stimuli are the most ambiguous on the:
    a. TAT.   c. Rorschach.
    b. California Psychological Inventory.   d. MMPI.

_____ 16. oral stage   a. A child's attempt to be similar to the same-sex parent.

_____ 17. anal stage   b. An infant's centre of pleasure is the mouth.

_____ 18. phallic stage   c. A child's interest focuses on the genitals.

_____ 19. identification   d. A child's pleasure is centred on the anus.

_____ 20. penis envy   e. A girl's wish that she had a penis.

21.   According the Freud, children's sexual concerns are temporarily put aside during the

    _____.

22.   A defence mechanism identified by an unwanted feeling directed toward a weaker object is

    _____.

23.   When a person attributes his inadequacies or faults to someone else it is known as

    _____.

24.   _____ is the diversion of unwanted impulses into acceptable thoughts, feelings and behaviours.

25.   _____ is defined as supportive behaviour for another individual.

26.   State one issue or situation that most adolescents tend to deal with during their high school years. Look over Freud's defence mechanisms and describe how three of the mechanisms might be used by the adolescent to "protect one's psyche" from the anxiety produced by the stated situation.

PRACTISE TEST 3: Conceptual, Applied, and Challenging Questions

1. Listed below are four alternatives. Three of the four give pairs of items that are related. Which alternative below contains items that are **not** related?
    a. ego; reality principle   c. superego; "executive" of personality
    b. Sigmund Freud; Viennese physician   d. id; pleasure principle

2. A psychoanalyst most likely would view a thumb-sucking 7 year old as:

    a.   a normal youngster.

    b.   fixated at the oral stage of development.

    c.   having been breastfed as an infant.

    d.   ready to enter the phallic stage of development.

3. According to the psychoanalytic perspective, a rapist would be considered to have:
   a. unconditioned positive regard for his victim.
   b. a well-developed ego-ideal.
   c. a deficient superego.
   d. brain damage.

4. Jerome kept his clothes hung up and neatly pressed, while his roommate Juan rarely laundered or hung up his clothes. Freud might have suggested that both men were fixated at the:
   a. anal stage.   c. phallic stage.
   b. oral stage.   d. genital stage.

5. A colleague at work accepts a date from a young man she greatly admires. At the time of the date, however, the man doesn't show up. In response she exclaims, "I didn't want to go out with him anyway!" This illustrates:
   a. rationalization.   c. regression.
   b. denial.   d. repression.

6. Freud's stages of psychosexual development:
   a. emphasize adolescence as the key interval in personality development.
   b. designate the oral stage as the highest in the sequence.
   c. identify parts of the body that are biological pleasure zones toward which gratification is focused.
   d. relate to the same behaviours described in Piaget's theory.

7. The _____ approach emphasizes voluntary conscious aspects of personality while the _____ approach emphasizes unconscious aspects.
   a. biological; learning   c. humanistic; psychoanalytic
   b. trait; humanistic   d. trait; humanistic

8. Listed below are four alternatives. Three of the four list pairs of items that are related. Which alternative below contains items that are **not** related?
   a. Jung; collective unconscious
   b. Horney; women do not have penis envy
   c. Adler; inferiority complex
   d. Cattell; striving for superiority

9. A trait theorist would most likely make which of the following statements:
   a. He really hurt her feelings, but he's rationalizing it away.
   b. He really could have gone a long way, but his inferiority complex destroyed any confidence.
   c. These are five stages in the process of his development toward fulfilling his highest potential.
   d. He is a sensitive, warm, and considerate person.

10. Various approaches to personality have names and concepts uniquely associated with them. Three of the four alternatives below list pairs of items that are related. Which alternative below contains items that are **not** related?
    a. trait theory; assessment of traits that comprise personality
    b. learning theory; experiences with situations in the environment
    c. learning theory; Skinner
    d. psychoanalytic theory; consistency of behaviour across situations

11. Kate loves art and wants to study it in college. Her boyfriend wants her to be a computer analyst and criticizes her for her love of art. According to Carl Rogers, this conflict will lead to:
    a. Kate learning to love being a computer analyst.
    b. anxiety on the part of Kate.
    c. Kate becoming a fully-functioning person.
    d. unconditional positive regard.

12. Which of the following situations best illustrates reliability as a quality of psychological tests?
    a. A prospective Air Force pilot takes a test, passes it, and becomes an excellent pilot.
    b. A college student studies diligently for an important exam and receives an A on it.
    c. A psychiatric patient takes a psychological test that yields the diagnosis the patient had suspected.
    d. A mentally retarded patient takes an intelligence test on Monday and again on Tuesday, getting the same result on each administration.

13. Which of the following statements about the heritability of traits is most accurate?
    a. The degree of heritability of traits is compromised by the important role of parents in shaping the environment.
    b. Traditionalism and stress reaction were highly heritable, while achievement and social closeness were somewhat lower.
    c. Alienation and absorption were low in heritability and social control is high.
    d. Heritability plays about a 50 percent role in important traits and is lower in less important traits.

14. According to the text, estimates of the influence of genes on personality are only estimates that apply to groups, and not individuals,
    a. because it is impossible to fully control and assess the influence of environmental factors.
    b. because it is impossible to fully control and assess the influence of all the genes.
    c. because genetic influences change continually as children mature.
    d. because the environment changes continually as children mature.

15. Which of the following would be a confounding variable for studies that are attempting to demonstrate which traits parents pass on to their children genetically?
    a. The fact that social traits like religiosity rate high in twin studies, even when this trait is entirely dependent upon traditional cultural practices.
    b. When twins are separated at birth, they always express similar traits.
    c. The role of parents in shaping the environment.
    d. Evidence that some traits appear more heritable than others.

____ 16.   anxiety

____ 17.   neurotic anxiety

____ 18.   defence mechanisms

____ 19.   collective unconscious

____ 20.   archetypes

a.   The concept that we inherit certain personality characteristics from our ancestors and the human race.

b.   Anxiety caused when irrational impulses from the id threaten to become uncontrollable.

c.   Universal, symbolic representations of a particular person, object, or experience.

d.   A feeling of apprehension or tension.

e.   Unconscious strategies used to reduce anxiety by concealing its source from oneself and others.

21.   The _____ is defined by marked mature sexual behaviour.

22.   A defence mechanism identified by the justification of a negative situation to protect one's self-esteem is called _____.

23.   Behaviour that is reminiscent of an earlier stage of development is called _____.

24.   _____ is learning by viewing the actions of others.

25.   Psychologists refer to the realization of one's highest potential as _____.

26.   A major issue that will affect virtually everyone is the creation of norms for different minority and ethnic groups. Describe the issues involved and discuss whether or not the use of different norms will be helpful, harmful, or a mixture of both.

Spotlight on Terminology and Language—
Cultural Idioms

Psychoanalytic Approaches to Personality

Page 339 "The **id** operates according to the **pleasure principle**, in which the goal is the immediate reduction of tension and the maximization of satisfaction."

The **id** is Freud's first division of the mind. The **id's** goal is to pursue pleasure and satisfy the biological drives. The goals of someone operating according to the **pleasure principle** would be the satisfaction of drives and avoidance of pain, without concern for moral restrictions or society's regulations. According to Freudian theory, this is the id's operating principle.

Page 339 "The **ego** strives to balance the desires of the id and the realities of the objective, outside world."

The **ego** is Freud's second division of the mind. The **ego** develops from the id during infancy. The goal of the **ego** is to find safe and socially acceptable ways of satisfying the id's desires and to negotiate between the id's wants and the superego's prohibitions.

Page 339 "The **superego**, the final personality structure to develop, represents social right and wrong as taught and modeled by a person's parents, teachers, and other significant individuals."

The goal of the **superego** is to apply the moral values and standards of one's parents or caregivers and society in satisfying one's wishes.

Page 340 "In the first stage of development, called the **oral stage**, the baby's mouth is the **focal** point of pleasure."
The **oral stage** is the first psychosexual stage identified by Freud. During the **oral stage**, the infant's pleasure seeking is centred on the mouth. The **focal** point is the focus—the centre of activity and attention.

Page 340 "**Fixation** refers to conflicts or concerns that persist beyond the developmental period in which they first occur."

Fixation is the persistent concentration of libidinal energies upon objects characteristic of psychosexual stages of development preceding the genital stage. When a Freudian theorist refers to **fixation**, this is seen as the process through which an individual may be locked into a particular psychosexual stage because his or her wishes were overgratified or undergratified in that stage.

Page 340 "From around 12 to 18 months until 3 years of age—where the emphasis in Western cultures in on toilet training—the child enters the **anal stage**."

In the **anal stage**, the child's pleasure seeking is centred on the anus and its functions of elimination.

Page 340 "At about age 3, the **phallic stage** begins, at which point there is another major shift in the primary source of pleasure for the child."

In the **phallic stage**, the child becomes interested in his or her own sexual organs.

Page 341 "Following the resolution of the Oedipus conflict, typically at around age 5 or 6, children move into the **latency period**, which lasts until puberty."

In the **latency period**, the child represses sexual

thought and engages in nonsexual activities, such as developing social and intellectual skills.

Page 341 "Freud's efforts to describe and theorize about the underlying **dynamics** of personality and its development were motivated by very practical problems that his patients faced in dealing with anxiety, an intense, negative emotional experience."

Dynamics is the pattern or process of change, growth, or activity.

Page 341 "**Defence mechanisms** are unconscious strategies people use to reduce anxiety by concealing its source from themselves and others."

Defences mechanisms operate at unconscious levels to help the ego reduce anxiety through self-deception.
What **defence mechanisms** do you recognize in your family members?

Page 342 "Freud's emphasis on the unconscious has been partially supported by current research on dreams and **implicit memory**…"

Implicit memories are memories of performing motor or perceptual tasks, carrying out habitual behaviours, and responding to stimuli because of classical conditioning. We are not conscious of these memories.

Page 343 "According to Jung, this **collective unconscious** is shared by everyone and is displayed in behaviour that is common across diverse cultures—such as love of mother, belief in a supreme being, and even behaviour as specific as fear of snakes."

According to Jung, the **collective unconscious** is defined as ancient memory traces and symbols that are passed on by birth and are shared by all people in all cultures.

Page 343 "Jung went on to propose that the collective unconscious contains **archetypes**, universal symbolic representations of a particular person, object, or experience."

Archetype is an inherited idea or mode of thought in the psychology of Carl Jung that is derived from the experience of the race and is present in the unconscious of the individual.

Other Major Approaches to Personality: In Search of Human Uniqueness

Page 345 "**Trait theorists** do not assume that some people have a trait and others do not; rather, they propose that all people possess certain traits, but that each person possesses a given trait to a given degree than can be quantified, and that people can differ in the degree to which they have a trait."

Trait theory is an approach for analyzing the structure of personality by measuring, identifying, and classifying similarities and differences in distinguishing qualities or personality characteristics.

Page 345 "When personality psychologist Gordon Allport systematically **pored** over an unabridged dictionary, he came up with some 18,000 separate terms that could be used to describe personality."

Pore is to read studiously or attentively.

Page 346 "**Factor analysis** is a method of summarizing the relationships among a large number of variables into fewer, more general patterns."

Factor analysis is a complicated statistical method that finds relationships among different or diverse items and allows them to be grouped together.

■ CHAPTER 10: ANSWER KEY

GUIDED REVIEW

Section 1:
[a] personality
[b] Psychoanalysts
[c] psychoanalytic theory
[d] unconscious
[e] id
[f] libido
[g] pleasure principle
[h] ego
[i] reality principle
[j] superego
[k] conscience
[l] ego-ideal
[m] oral
[n] Fixation
[o] anal
[p] phallic
[q] latency
[r] genital
[s] defence mechanisms

Evaluate
1. c
2. b
3. d
4. e
5. a

Section 2:
[a] trait theory
[b] Traits
[c] cardinal trait
[d] central traits
[e] Secondary traits
[f] factor analysis
[g] Introversion-extroversion
[h] Neuroticism-stability
[i] Psychoticism
[j] Cognitive-social
[k] observational learning
[l] self-efficacy
[m] reciprocal determinism
[n] Biological and evolutionary
[o] temperament
[p] Humanistic
[q] unconditional positive regard
[r] self-actualization

Evaluate
1. a
2. e
3. d
4. c
5. b

Section 3:
[a] Psychological tests
[b] reliability
[c] validity
[d] Norms
[e] self-report measures
[f] Minnesota Multiphasic Personality Inventory-2 (MMPI-2)
[g] test standardization
[h] Projective personality
[i] Rorschach
[j] Thematic Apperception Test (TAT)
[k] behavioural assessment

Evaluate
1. a
2. e
3. d
4. c
5. b

Selected Rethink Answers

3. Traits are enduring dimensions of personality characteristics along which people differ. Since each person probably possesses certain traits, what makes them different is the degree to which a given trait applies to a single person. Traits allow us to compare one person with another and provide an explanation for a person's behavioural consistency. Assigning certain negative traits to a person may cause a person to be stigmatized by others. Assigning other, more positive traits to a person may raise peoples' expectations of them and cause them undo pressure in many situations.

6. Personality tests might be useful to both the employer and the employee as one more source of information in trying to make employment decisions. Test should be used to find ways to include people and place them in appropriate work situations. In this way both parties would gain. No single test should be used alone to exclude anyone from obtaining a position. Tests are helpful to distinguish personality disorders when they are one of several assessment tools. They are not accurate enough to make conclusive judgments on their own. Anyone who is going to be excluded from a job, placed in or excluded from a program should have a means to appeal the decision and have other means of assessment available to determine if the decision is valid.

Practise Test 1:

1. a obj. 1 p. 338
*a. Correct. Repressed wishes, desires, anxiety, and conflict are found in the realm Freud called the unconscious.
b. Incorrect. This was a concept introduced by Freud's follower, Carl Jung.
c. Incorrect. The conscience is to be found in the superego.
d. Incorrect. The conscious contains our awareness of the world.

2. b obj. 1 p. 339
a. Incorrect. The id is always making demands on the person that are unrealistic, even sometimes dangerous.
*b. Correct. It is the role of the ego to manage the competing demands of the id and the superego, and it responds according to the reality principle.
c. Incorrect. The superego's demands of moral perfection and ego ideal are unrealistic and in conflict with the id.
d. Incorrect. The pleasure principle is the principle that animates the id, making its demands very unrealistic.

3. c obj. 1 p. 338
a. Incorrect. While important, they are not at the centre of his theory.
b. Incorrect. More likely the earlier stages.
*c. Correct. The mental factors of which we are least aware can have the most grave effects on our personality.
d. Incorrect. This theory came long after Freud.

4. b obj. 1 p. 339
a. Incorrect. This describes the id.
*b. Correct. The ego ideal represents the internalized expectations of our parents and others for us to do and be moral.
c. Incorrect. This is the role of the ego.

d. Incorrect. There is no part of the superego that does this.

5. b obj. 2 p. 340
a. Incorrect. The genital stage is the last stage in the sequence and it occurs long after toilet training.
*b. Correct. During the anal stage, the child learns self-control, and one of the manifestations of self-control is toilet training.
c. Incorrect. The phallic stage is marked by the Oedipal conflict and it occurs after the stage that includes toilet training.
d. Incorrect. The oral stage is the first stage, and it is marked by a focus upon pleasure taken from the mouth.

6. b obj. 3 p. 342
a. Incorrect. Repression forces conflict into the unconscious.
*b. Correct. Sublimation converts repressed desire, especially sexual desire, into socially acceptable forms, like work.
c. Incorrect. Rationalization involves creating self-justifying reasons after the fact.
d. Incorrect. Projection places unacceptable impulses onto a safe object.

7. b obj. 3 p. 341
a. Incorrect. Probably just the opposite.
*b. Correct. Anxiety is a great threat to the ego, so the ego's defence mechanisms helps protect it.
c. Incorrect. The ego, at times, needs protection against the superego as well.
d. Incorrect. Sometimes, defence mechanisms themselves cause Freudian slips.

8. a obj. 5 p. 335
*a. Correct. For most trait theorists, everyone has the major traits to some extent, and the amount of these traits tends to be stable through time.

b. Incorrect. For most trait theorists, everyone has the major traits to some extent, and the amount of these traits tends to be stable through time.

c. Incorrect. For most trait theorists, everyone has the major traits to some extent, and the amount of these traits tends to be stable through time.

d. Incorrect. For most trait theorists, everyone has the major traits to some extent, and the amount of these traits tends to be stable through time.

9. a   obj. 5   p. 345, 346, 349
*a. Correct. Albert Bandura is the leading social learning theorist.
b. Incorrect. Allport is known for the cardinal, central, and secondary traits.
c. Incorrect. Cattell is known for the 16 facto theory, distinguishing source from surface traits.
d. Incorrect. Eysenck proposed three main trait characteristics, extroversion, neuroticism, and psychoticism.

10. c   obj. 6   p. 348
a. Incorrect. This terminology is that of the trait theorists.
b. Incorrect. This terminology is from the psychodynamic perspective.
*c. Correct. As Skinner is a behaviourist, "traits" are explained in behavioural terms.
d. Incorrect. This terminology is from the humanistic perspective.

11. c   obj. 5   p. 345
a. Incorrect. It is an analytic technique, and it requires no special equipment.
b. Incorrect. Used by trait theorists, this use is unlikely.
*c. Correct. Factor analysis is a method that identifies common patterns in data and was used by Cattell to identify the source traits in his theory.
d. Incorrect. While it might help identify personality traits in a group (if that is possible), it is only a statistical technique.

12. c   obj. 8   p. 353
a. Incorrect. Humanistic theories tend not to judge the unconscious as evil.
b. Incorrect. Society is not generally viewed by humanistic theories as a corrupting force.
*c. Correct. Humans have within themselves the ability to heal their own psychological disorders and resolve their conflicts.
d. Incorrect. No psychological view holds to this thesis of fundamental depravity.

13. c   obj. 8   p. 353
a. Incorrect. Learning theory depends upon conditioning and reinforcement.
b. Incorrect. The psychodynamic theory focuses upon unconscious forces.

*c. Correct. The humanistic approach focuses upon the abilities of the individual to engage in self-actualization.
d. Incorrect. The trait theory searches for long-term, consistent behaviour patterns.

14. b   obj. 10   p. 360
a. Incorrect. The MMPI asks for the test taker to respond to questions concerning items of which the test taker has an awareness.
*b. Correct. The Thematic Apperception Test (TAT) asks that respondents tell a story about a picture and through that story they may reveal unconscious concerns.
c. Incorrect. The California Psychological Inventory is a self-report test, thus it reveals only items about which the test taker has awareness.
d. Incorrect. This is probably another self-report instrument.

15. c   obj. 9   p. 357
a. Incorrect. It is a standardized test, but the scenario does not support this notion.
b. Incorrect. Indeed, it is supposed to be an academic ability assessment tool, but this scenario does not question that.
*c. Correct. Since it measured her performance and knowledge the same in both circumstances, the assessment is quite reliable.
d. Incorrect. It may be valid, but this story does not support that claim.

16. b   obj. 1   p. 339
17. a   obj. 1   p. 339
18. e   obj. 1   p. 339
19. d   obj. 1   p. 339
20. c   obj. 1   p. 339
21. ego obj. 1   p. 339
22. inferiority complex obj. 4   p. 343
23. Repression   obj. 3   p. 341
24. denial   obj. 3   p. 342
25. secondary obj. 5   p. 345

26.
▪ The weakest area is Freud's developmental stages, particularly with the Oedipus complex. Freud's concept of penis envy is not well accepted by many.
▪ Just as Gilligan contests Kohlberg's views of moral development, one could argue that Freud's concept of a genital stage rests on masculine norms.

Practise Test 2:
1. c   obj. 1   p. 338
a. Incorrect. Humanistic theory is concerned with the person recognizing his or her own potential and finding ways to achieve self-actualization.
b. Incorrect. Learning theory is concerned with the kinds of reinforcements and punishments that have

contributed to the formation of the current patterns of behaviour of an individual.

*c. Correct. Psychoanalytic theory considers the hidden contents of the unconscious to be powerful forces in the shaping of personality.

d. Incorrect. Trait theory seeks to identify and measure the consistent patterns of traits manifested by people.

2. a   obj. 1   p. 339
*a. Correct. The libido is psychic energy and not a part of Freud's structural model of the personality. The three parts of Freud's structural model of the personality are the id, ego, and superego.

b. Incorrect. See answer a.

c. Incorrect. See answer a.

d. Incorrect. See answer a.

3. b   obj. 1   p. 339
a. Incorrect. The id seeks to satisfy the pleasure principle and is not concerned with thought, decisions, or solving problems.

*b. Correct. The ego is responsible for balancing the demands of the id and the superego, and thus must solve problems, think, and make decisions.

c. Incorrect. The superego seeks to present a moralistic, ego ideal and a judgmental conscience to the ego.

d. Incorrect. The conscience is one of the two components of the superego, the other is the ego ideal.

4. d   obj. 2   p. 340
a. Incorrect. See answer d.

b. Incorrect. See answer d.

c. Incorrect. See answer d.

*d. Correct. This child is seeking pleasure from the mouth, and is thus in the oral stage.

5. c   obj. 2   p. 341
a. Incorrect. The child is only about 6 during this stage, and thus unlikely to participate in mature sexual relations.

b. Incorrect. The child is less than 2 years old during this stage, and thus will not be engaging in any mature sexual relations.

*c. Correct. This was the name Freud gave to the stage in which sexual maturity develops.

d. Incorrect. This stage occurs when the child is between 2 and 4 years of age, and thus mature sexual relations are unlikely.

6. a   obj. 3   p. 341
*a. Correct. Defence mechanisms operate below the level of awareness as part of their role in protecting the ego from anxiety and conflict.

b. Incorrect. There are two instincts (drives) in Freud's view, eros and the death drive.

c. Incorrect. Freud did not describe whether or not the defence mechanisms were learned or innate.

d. Incorrect. After they have been utilized, they may become reflexive, but they respond to complex stimuli rather than the simple stimuli typically associated with reflexes.

7. b   obj. 3   p. 341
a. Incorrect. Sublimation does not apply here.

*b. Correct. Repression is a form of intentional forgetting.

c. Incorrect. Denial is one means of dealing with this kind of trauma, but the core mechanism is repression.

d. Incorrect. After repression, the victims of child abuse may project fears onto other people.

8. d   obj. 5   p. 345
a. Incorrect. Allport did not identify any traits as "general."

b. Incorrect. Allport's concept of secondary traits is that people have many of these, and they govern such things as the style and preference of many everyday behaviours.

c. Incorrect. In Allport's view, everyone has several central traits, but these do not dominate the personality.

*d. Correct. Allport called these cardinal traits, and they dominate the personality of the individual.

9. d   obj. 5   p. 345
a. Incorrect. Try again.

b. Incorrect. Try again.

c. Incorrect. Try again.

*d. Correct. The cardinal trait controls and dominates the personality, while at the other end, secondary traits define style and preferences.

10. a   obj. 5   p. 345
*a. Correct. If traits exist, then by definition they need to persist.

b. Incorrect. Trait theories did not commonly offer a theory for the existence of traits.

c. Incorrect. To only a few are traits learned in the traditional operant conditioning approach.

d. Incorrect. People do not chose to apply traits.

11. d   obj. 6   p. 349
a. Incorrect. This is Freud's idea.

b. Incorrect. This belongs to other drive theorists, like Clark Hull.

c. Incorrect. Bandura may agree that psychoanalysis will modify our personality, but not by using any of Bandura's concepts.

*d. Correct. Self-reinforcement is an important component of the social learning theory of Bandura.

12. d   obj. 7   p. 351

a. Incorrect. Since it appears long before the child has an opportunity to form interests, this answer is incorrect.
b. Incorrect. Temperament might itself be considered a source trait.
c. Incorrect. Temperament is present prior to the opportunity to have early learning experience.
*d. Correct. This is the current view of temperament, that it is genetically disposed.

13. c   obj. 9   p. 357
a. Incorrect. If the test does not measure what it should, it would not be very accurate.
b. Incorrect. If the test made the same measure each time, it would still have to measure what it is supposed to measure to be considered valid.
*c. Correct. Even if the test failed to measure what it was supposed to measure, yet it made the same measurement each time, then the test would be reliable.
d. Incorrect. A statistical test would have to measure some kind of statistics, would it not?

14. a   obj. 10   p. 358
*a. Correct. The MMPI measures tendencies toward a number of psychological difficulties, but it can be taken by anyone and it does produce meaningful results for people who do not have psychological problems.
b. Incorrect. The MMPI is a self-report test, and thus unlikely to reveal many thoughts that are not within the awareness of the test taker.
c. Incorrect. The MMPI does not locate "traits" and is not specific to any trait theory.
d. Incorrect. The MMPI is a self-report test, and thus it cannot be used for a behavioural assessment except for the selection of true or false on the test.

15. c   obj. 10   p. 348
a. Incorrect. The TAT uses ambiguous pictures, but they are not as ambiguous as the inkblots used on the Rorschach.
b. Incorrect. The California Psychological Inventory and the MMPI both use statements that require a direct and unambiguous response to a rather unambiguous item.
*c. Correct. The Rorschach inkblots are probably the most ambiguous test stimuli used in this manner.
d. Incorrect. The California Psychological Inventory and the MMPI both use statements that require a direct and unambiguous response to a rather unambiguous item.

16. b   obj. 2   p. 340
17. d   obj. 2   p. 340
18. c   obj. 2   p. 340
19. a   obj. 2   p. 340
20. e   obj. 2   p. 341
21. latency period   obj. 2   p. 341
22. displacement   obj. 3   p. 342

23. projection obj. 3   p. 342
24. Sublimation   obj. 3   p. 342
25. Unconditional positive regard obj. 8   p. 353

26. Adolescents want autonomy and attempt to negotiate with their parents for more freedom to make their own decisions
  ▪ Regression allows them to scream and yell and carry on when they don't get their own way. They act as they did when they were younger in order to avoid the real conflict and get their way.
  ▪ Rationalization would involve creating self-justifying excuses after the fact.
  ▪ Projection places unacceptable impulses onto a safe object.

Practise Test 3:
1. c   obj. 1   p. 339
a. Incorrect. The ego does operate on the reality principle as it tries to balance demands of the id and the superego.
b. Incorrect. Sigmund Freud was a Viennese physician.
*c. Correct. The ego is considered the executive of the personality, not the superego.
d. Incorrect. The id follows the pleasure principle as it seeks to satisfy desires and wishes.

2. b   obj. 2   p. 340
a. Incorrect. This is unusual, yet not abnormal for a child of this age.
*b. Correct. Thumb sucking is an oral behaviour, so the youngster must be fixated in the oral stage.
c. Incorrect. Breast feeding is not relevant to later thumb sucking.
d. Incorrect. The child is probably already in the phallic stage, but the fixation or regression to the oral stage is present.

3. c   obj. 1   p. 339
a. Incorrect. The concept of unconditioned positive regard is from humanistic theory, and the rapist is the last person who would have such regard for another person.
b. Incorrect. Only if the ego-ideal was that of a rapist.
*c. Correct. The superego provides a sense of right and wrong, and a rapist is clearly missing this dimension of morality.
d. Incorrect. A psychoanalyst would not attribute the behaviour of a rapist to brain damage.

4. a   obj. 2   p. 340
*a. Correct. The extremes of neatness and messiness have been associated with the anal stage, with the neat person overdoing anal retention and the messy person rejecting order.
b. Incorrect. The messy person could be fixated in the oral stage, but not the neat one.

c. Incorrect. Fixation in the phallic stage does not result in messiness or neatness.

d. Incorrect. Freud did not describe what fixation would be like for stages in which we are currently occupied.

5. b   obj. 3   p. 342
a. Incorrect. Rationalization would involve making an explanation that would protect the self through after-the-fact justification.
*b. Correct. The young woman is denying that she had any interest in the young man in the first place.
c. Incorrect. Regression would require that she regress to an earlier developmental stage.
d. Incorrect. Repression requires that she force her anxiety and anger into the unconscious.

6. c   obj. 2   p. 340
a. Incorrect. Many researchers in addition to Freud, saw earlier childhood as critical for the development of the personality.
b. Incorrect. The first in the sequence, but highest only if you stand up.
*c. Correct. Infants, children, and adults seek physical pleasure.
d. Incorrect. Piaget's sensorimotor stage is quite similar to Freud's oral stage, but the others differ.

7. c   obj. 8, 2   pp. 353, 338
a. Incorrect. The biological view would not be that interested in conscious decisions.
b. Incorrect. The trait approach does not consider traits within the person's ability to choose, and the humanistic approach certainly focuses upon conscious behaviour.
*c. Correct. The humanistic approach rests on the person's ability to be rational and self-motivated while the psychodynamic approach assumes the power of the irrational and unconscious forces in the person.
d. Incorrect. The biological view would not be that interested in conscious decisions, and the humanistic approach certainly focuses upon conscious behaviour.

8. d   obj. 5   p. 346
a. Incorrect. Jung proposed the idea of a collective unconscious.
b. Incorrect. Horney argued that women do not have penis envy.
c. Incorrect. Adler did develop the idea of an inferiority complex.
*d. Correct. Striving for superiority is Adler's idea, not Cattell's.

9. d   obj. 5   p. 345
a. Incorrect. Sounds psychoanalytic.
b. Incorrect. Sounds like Adler's idea of inferiority complex.

c. Incorrect. Sounds like Maslow's hierarchy of needs.
*d. Correct. A trait theorist wound describe someone in terms of traits, like warm and considerate.

10. d   obj. 1, 5   pp. 338, 355
a. Incorrect. Trait theory does propose that traits can be assessed and a picture of the person be composed.
b. Incorrect. Learning theory does suggest that the environment is a major force in shaping the personality.
c. Incorrect. Skinner is associated with learning theory.
*d. Correct. While psychoanalytic theory would suggest that behaviour would be consistent across situations, this is a major issue for trait theorists.

11. b   obj. 8   p. 353
a. Incorrect. This is unlikely, except if she compromises her own desires.
*b. Correct. The incongruency between Kate and her boyfriend could lead to anxiety.
c. Incorrect. If this incongruency becomes a condition of worth, then Kate cannot become a fully functioning person.
d. Incorrect. Unconditional positive regard requires more acceptance than this.

12. d   obj. 9   p. 357
a. Incorrect. This suggests that the test was a valid measure of pilot potential.
b. Incorrect. This suggests that studying is a valid means of preparing for an exam.
c. Incorrect. The test has validated the suspicion.
*d. Correct. Repeating a test and getting the same or nearly the same score on each administration demonstrates reliability.

13. b   obj. 7   p. 352
a. Incorrect. This statement cannot be made based on the evidence reported in the text.
*b. Correct. Believe it or not, the extent to which a person is traditional and the manner in which the person responds to stress are highly heritable.
c. Incorrect. Alienation and absorption were moderately high.
d. Incorrect. The research did not judge which traits were important and which were not.

14. a   obj. 7   pp. 351, 352.
*a. Correct. It is virtually impossible to isolate the influence of genes from the environment which they need in order to express themselves.
b. Incorrect. The effect of all of the genes need not be controlled to study the influence of one.
c. Incorrect. It is of no consequence that influences change over time if personality is stable. In any case, the genes would not change.

d.   Incorrect. . It is of no consequence that influences change over time if personality is stable. In any case, the genes would not change.

15. c   obj. 7   p. 350
a.   Incorrect. Traditionalism itself has been shown to be heritable.
b.   Incorrect. This would actually indicate something about the dependent variable, not a confounding variable.
*c. Correct. When trying to separate parental genes from environmental forces, one must accept the confounding aspect of the parent's role in shaping the environment.
d.   Incorrect. This is not a confounding element.

16. d   obj. 3   p. 341
17. b   obj. 3   p. 341
18. e   obj. 3   p. 341

19. a   obj. 4   p. 343
20. c   obj. 4   p. 343
21. genital stage   obj. 2   p. 341
22. rationalization obj. 3   p. 342
23. regression obj. 3   p. 342
24. Observational learning   obj. 6   p. 349
25. self-actualization   obj. 8   p. 353

26.
- Some people argue that any kind of separation of a group from the larger society is detrimental.
- One major problem is the use of norms or averages to prepare job "profiles." These are still average and composite pictures of the individual and may unfairly discriminate against those who do not fit the profile. With these kinds of norms, negative reactions can and have occurred by those excluded from the special normed group. Recent court cases will change how this is viewed as well.

Health Psychology: Stress, Coping, and Well-Being

11

Psychological Aspects of Cancer
Smoking

> **Exploring Diversity:** Hucksters of Death: Promoting
> Smoking Throughout the World

Well-Being and Happiness

> **Applying Psychology in the 21st Century:** If You Won the
> Lottery, Would You Be Happier?

Section 3: Psychological Factors Related to Physical Illness: Going to the Doctor

Physician-Patient Communication
Complying with Physicians' Recommendations

Learning Objectives

These are the concepts and the learning objectives for Chapter 11. Read them carefully as part of your preliminary survey of the chapter.

Stress and Coping

1.   Define health psychology and its centrally important concept of stress, including the biological and psychological costs of that stress. (pp. 370–371)

2.   Describe and illustrate Selye's general adaptation syndrome. (pp. 371–373)

3.   Describe how a person's nature and experience influences that individual's perception of stressful events (p. 373)

4.   Identify the major categories of stressors and their consequences, including posttraumatic stress disorder. (pp. 374–375)

5.   Discuss the concept of learned helplessness, how it develops, and its effect on behaviour. (p. 375-376)

6.   Describe coping strategies, including defence mechanisms, social support, hardiness, and related strategies. (pp. 376–379)

Psychological Aspects of Illness and Well-Being

7.   Distinguish Type A and Type B personalities and the major health risks of Type A

behaviour, especially coronary heart disease. (pp. 381–382)

8. Discuss the role of health psychology in the treatment of cancer. (pp. 382–383)

9. Discuss the problem of smoking, how one becomes addicted, and how one attempts to quit. (pp. 384–386)

10. Discuss the characteristics of happy people. (pp. 386–387)

Psychological Factors Related to Physical Illness: Going to the Doctor

11. Outline and describe the various problems that hinder effective communication between the physician and the patient. (pp. 388–389)

12. Discuss the problems associated with patient compliance to physician's orders and the various ways to increase compliance. (pp. 389–390)

SECTION 1: Stress and Coping

Prepare

- *How is health psychology a union between medicine and psychology?*
- *What is stress, how does it affect us, and how can we best cope with it?*

Organize

- *Stress*
- *Coping with Stress*

Work

[a] _____ focuses on the application of psychology to the prevention, diagnosis, and treatment of medical problems. Health psychologists view the mind and the body as closely linked. Good health and the ability to stay healthy are affected by how a person manages stress and the person's health habits. The [b] _____ of the body is affected by attitudes and emotional state. Health psychology has changed the view of disease from a purely biological problem, and it has helped people cope with the problems associated with adjustment to diseases that last for a long time. [c] _____ is the study of the relationship between psychological factors and the immune system.

The response to events that threaten or challenge a person is called [d] _____, and the events themselves are called *stressors*. Stressors can be both pleasant and unpleasant events, though the negative events can be more detrimental. The class of medical problems called [e] _____ disorders, caused by the interaction of psychological, emotional, and physiological problems, are also related to stress. High levels of stress interfere with people's ability to cope with current and new stressors.

Hans Selye proposed that everyone goes through the same set of physiological responses no matter what the cause is, and he called this the [f] _____. The first stage is the [g] _____, during which the presence of a stressor is detected and the sympathetic nervous system is energized. The second stage is the [h] _____, during which the person attempts to cope with the stressor. If coping is inadequate, the person enters the [i] _____. The person's ability to cope with stress declines and the negative consequences appear. These include illness, psychological symptoms like the inability to concentrate, and possibly disorientation and losing touch with reality. The GAS has provided a model that explains how stress leads to illness. The primary criticism has focused on the fact that the model suggests that every stress response is physiologically the same.

If people are to consider an event stressful, they must perceive it to be threatening and must lack the ability to cope with it adequately. The same event may not be stressful for everyone. The perception of stress may depend upon how one attributes the causes for events.

There are three classes of events that are considered stressors. The first is

[j] _____, strong stressors that affect many people at the same time. The stress of these events is usually dealt with well because so many people experience the event and share the problem. Some people experience prolonged problems due to catastrophic events, and

this is called [k] _____. People may experience flashbacks or dreams during which they re-experience the event. The symptoms can include a numbing of emotional experience, sleep difficulties, problems relating to others, and drug problems, among others. The

second class of stressor is [l] _____, which include life events that are of a personal or individual nature, like the death of a parent or spouse, the loss of a job, or a major illness. Typically, personal stressors cause an immediate major reaction that tapers off. Sometimes, though, the effects can last for a long time, such as the effects of being raped. The

third class of stressors is called [m] _____, and they include standing in

long lines, traffic jams, and other [n] _____. Daily hassles can add up, causing unpleasant emotions and moods. A critical factor is the degree of control people have over the daily hassles. When they have control, the stress reactions are less. On the other side of

daily hassles are [o] _____, positive events that lead to pleasant feelings.

In an environment in which control is seen as impossible, one can experience

[p] _____. Victims of learned helplessness have decided that there is no link between the responses they make and the outcomes that occur. When elderly people in nursing homes were given control over simple aspects of their lives, they were less likely to experience an early death. Not everyone experiences helplessness.

Our efforts to control, reduce, or learn to tolerate stress are known as

[q] _____. Many of our responses are habitual. The

[r] _____ are unconscious strategies that help control stress by distorting or denying the actual nature of the situation. Denying the significance of a nearby geological fault is

an example. [s] _____, in which a person does not feel emotions at all, is another example. Another means of dealing with stress is the use of direct and positive means.

These include [t] _____, the conscious regulation of emotions, and

[u] _____, the management of the stressful stimulus. People use both strategies, but they are more likely to use the emotion-focused strategy when they perceive the problem as unchangeable.

People can be described as having preferred coping styles. [v] _____ refers to the style that is associated with a low rate of stress-induced illness. The style consists of three components: commitment, challenge, and control. Commitment is a tendency to be involved in whatever we are doing with a sense that it is important and meaningful. Challenge refers to the view that change is the standard condition of life. Control refers to the sense of being able to influence events. The hardy person is optimistic and approaches the problem directly.

Relationships with others help people cope with stress. The knowledge of a mutual network of concerned, interested people helping individuals experience lower levels of stress is called

[w] _____. Social support demonstrates the value of a person to others and provides a network of information and advice. Also, actual goods and services can be provided through social support networks. Even pets can contribute to this support.

Stress can be dealt with through several steps: Turn stress into a challenge, make the threatening situation less threatening by changing attitudes about it, change goals in order to remove oneself from an uncontrollable situation, and take physical action. The most successful approach requires that the person be prepared for stress. One method of preparation is called

proactive coping. With [x] _____, stress is dealt with through preparation for both the nature of the possible stressors and developing or learning clear strategies for coping.

Evaluate

____ 1.	immune system	a.	Circumstances that produce threats to our well-being.
____ 2.	stressors	b.	A person's initial awareness of the presence of a stressor.
____ 3.	psychophysiological disorders	c.	The second stage of coping with the stressor.
____ 4.	alarm and mobilization	d.	Medical problems caused by an interaction of psychological, emotional, and physical difficulties.
____ 5.	resistance	e.	The body's natural defences that fight disease.

Rethink

1. Why are cataclysmic stressors less stressful in the long run than other types of stressors? Does the reason relate to the coping phenomenon known as social support? How?

2. Given what you know about coping strategies, how would you train people to avoid stress in their everyday lives? How would you use this information with a group of Gulf War veterans suffering from posttraumatic stress disorder?

3. What are the implications of psychophysiological disorders for explaining human behaviour, emotions and physical conditions? What are the advantages of the approach from the viewpoint of health psychology to treat disorders in any of these domains?

SECTION 2:   Psychological Aspects of Illness and Well-Being

Prepare

- *How do psychological factors affect such health-related problems as coronary heart disease, cancer, and smoking?*

Organize

- *The A's and B's of Coronary Heart Disease*
- *Psychological Aspects of Cancer*
- *Smoking*
- *Well-Being and Happiness*

Work

Two characteristic behaviour patterns have been identified that are associated with coronary heart disease. **[a]** _____ is seen in individuals who are competitive, have a sense of urgency about time, are aggressive, and are driven regarding their work.

[b] _____ is seen in individuals who are less competitive, less time-oriented, and not aggressive, driven, or hostile. In an extensive study, people with Type A behaviour developed heart disease twice as frequently as Type B individuals. One theory says that Type A individuals become excessively aroused when they are placed in stressful situations and that this arousal increases the hormones epinephrine and norepinephrine, in turn leading to higher blood pressure and heart rate. Long-term damage then results. The evidence supporting the connection between Type A behaviour and coronary heart disease is not conclusive. One study showed Type A individuals more likely to survive a second heart attack.

Cancer is the second leading cause of death after coronary heart disease. Though its causes remain unknown, the progress of cancer is from altered cell to tumor, and the tumor robs nutrients from healthy tissue, eventually impairing normal function. Evidence is growing that the emotional response to cancer influences the progress of the disease. Fighters appear more likely to recover than pessimists. Survival rates for women with breast cancer were higher among those who fought the disease or even denied it than for those who stoically accepted the illness or who accepted their fate. Evidence suggests that the patient's immune system may be affected by emotional state. Positive emotional responses may help increase the natural "killer" cells. Negative emotions may suppress these kinds of cells. Other studies have found that positive emotional states improve longevity of cancer patients. Social support and cancer have also been linked. One study found that individuals who receive psychotherapy live longer than those who do not.

Though the link between smoking and cancer is well-established, millions of people continue to smoke. Most smokers agree that smoking damages their health, but they continue to smoke.

Mostly caused by environmental factors, the habit of smoking moves through four stages that end in the habit.

- At first, a relatively positive attitude about smoking develops
- The second stage is when smoking a cigarette becomes a rite of passage and is seen as a sign of growing up
- During the third, smoking becomes part of the self-concept and the body becomes tolerant of nicotine
- At the fourth stage, various aspects of smoking become part of the routine

Quitting smoking is very difficult. Only about 15 percent of those trying to stop smoking will have long-term success. Behavioural strategies for quitting view smoking as a learned habit that needs to be unlearned. Social norms will also eventually lead to reduced smoking, as smoking is banned in more and more public places and society begins to change its attitude about those who smoke. Still more than a quarter of the population smokes, and those who begin do so at an earlier age.

Cigarette manufacturers have turned to new markets as the number of smokers in the United States declines. The new markets include targeted campaigns toward teenagers, African-Americans, Chinese people, and people of Latin American countries.

Evaluate

_____ 1.   emotion-focused coping

_____ 2.   problem-focused coping

_____ 3.   hardiness

_____ 4.   Type A behaviour pattern

_____ 5.   Type B behaviour pattern

a. The conscious regulation of emotion as a means of dealing with stress.

b. Characterized by noncompetitiveness, nonaggression, and patience in times of potential stress.

c. Characterized by competitiveness, impatience, a tendency toward frustration, and hostility.

d. Characterized by commitment, challenge, and control.

e. The management of a stressful stimulus as a way of dealing with stress.

Rethink

4.   Do you think Type A or Type B behaviour is more widely encouraged in the United States? Why?

5.   If money doesn't buy happiness, what *can* you do to make yourself happier? As you answer, consider the research findings on stress and coping, as well as our discussion of emotions in Chapter 8

SECTION 3: Psychological Factors Related to Physical Illness: Going to the Doctor

Prepare

- ***How do our interactions with physicians affect our health and compliance with medical treatment?***

Organize

- ***Physician-Patient Communication***
- ***Complying with Physicians' Recommendations***

Work

How the patient and the physician communicate can influence the effectiveness of the diagnosis and medical treatment. Many patients are reluctant to tell their physicians their symptoms. The prestige and power of the physician intimidates many patients. On the other side, physicians have difficulties getting their patients to provide the proper information. The technical nature of their questions does not mesh with the personal nature of the individual's concerns. The reluctance can prevent the health-care giver from understanding the full nature of the problem, and often the patient sees the physician as all-knowing. Patients who do not understand their treatment cannot ask questions about it. Many patients do not know how long they should take their medication and many do not know the purpose of the drug. The use of professional jargon to communicate technical information does not help the patient understand the treatment. Sometimes medical practitioners use "baby talk" and talk down to the patient. The number of patients seen makes it difficult for many physicians to determine how much each patient can understand. Patients often construct their own theories about their illnesses that have little to do with reality. The problem can be dealt with by training patients to ask more direct questions. Physicians who are taught simple rules of courtesy, like saying hello, addressing the patient by name, and saying goodbye, are better perceived by their patients.

One major consequence of the difficulties in communication between the physician and the patient is the lack of compliance with medical advice. Noncompliance can include failing to meet appointments, not following diets, discontinuing medication, and other behaviours. Patients may practise **[a]** _____, in which they adjust their treatments themselves.

Sometimes noncompliance results from **[b]** _____, a disagreeable emotional and cognitive reaction that results from the restriction of one's freedom and can be associated with medical regimens. Compliance is linked to the degree of satisfaction a patient has with the physician. Satisfied patients tend to comply better than dissatisfied patients. Patients with a positive view of the physicians may also have a greater sense of control, and they perceive themselves as in a kind of partnership rather than merely following advice. Physicians may themselves be motivated to keep the patient uninformed. Apparently, physicians avoid telling patients when they are terminally ill. On the other hand, almost every survey shows that people want to be informed about the details of their illnesses. Patients prefer to be well-informed, and their degree of satisfaction is linked to how well the physician is able to convey the nature of the illness. An increase in satisfaction tends to have a positive effect on recuperation.

Evaluate

_____ 1. creative nonadherence

_____ 2. reactance

_____ 3. subjective well-being

_____ 4. noncompliance

_____ 5. increase of compliance

a. Negative emotional and cognitive reaction that results from the restriction of one's freedom.

b. Patient discontinues medication, misses appointments, doesn't follow treatment.

c. Occurs when patient is friendly and satisfied with a physician.

d. Patient adjusts a treatment prescribed by a physician relying on their own medical judgment.

e. People evaluate their lives based on thoughts and emotions.

Rethink

6. Do you think stress plays a role in communication difficulties between physicians and patients? Why?

7. You are given the job of instructing a group of medical school students on "Physician/Patient Interactions." How would you set up your class, and what kind of information would you provide?

Practise Questions

Test your knowledge of the chapter material by answering these questions. These questions have been placed in three Practise Tests. The first two tests are composed of questions that will test your recall of factual knowledge. The third test contains questions that are challenging and primarily test for conceptual knowledge and your ability to apply that knowledge. Check your answers and review the feedback using the Answer Key in the following pages of the *Study Guide*.

PRACTISE TEST 1:

1. The system of organs and glands that form the body's natural defence against disease is called:
   a. the limbic system.
   b. the endocrine system.
   c. the immune system.
   d. the sympathetic system.

2. Which alternative below is **not** a stage of Selye's general adaptation syndrome?
   a. resistance
   b. challenge
   c. alarm and mobilization
   d. exhaustion

3. A circumstance that produces threats to people's well-being is known as:

    a.   a stressor.   c.   a defence mechanism.

    b.   a mobilization state.   d.   an inoculation.

4.   The alarm and mobilization stage of Selye's general adaptation syndrome is characterized by:

    a.   preparing to react to the stressor.   c.   emotional and physical collapse.

    b.   increased resistance to disease.   d.   becoming aware of the presence of a stressor.

5.   According to the text, events that are strong stressors and that occur suddenly and affect many people simultaneously are called:

    a.   cataclysmic events.   c.   uplifts.

    b.   background stressors.   d.   personal stressors.

6.   The textbook defines uplifts to be:

    a.   minor irritations of life that are encountered daily.

    b.   minor positive events that make a person feel good.

    c.   exhilarating experiences that leave a person in a dazed state.

    d.   major positive life events.

7.   High blood pressure, ulcers, or eczema are common:

    a.   defence mechanism disorders.   c.   hardiness disorders.

    b.   life-crisis disorders.   d.   psychophysiological disorders.

8.   The ability to tolerate, control, or reduce threatening events is called:

    a.   defence.   c.   coping.

    b.   arousal.   d.   adaptation.

9.   Someone who is classified as hardy:

    a.   is unable to cope with stress at all.

    b.   is unlikely to develop stress-related disease.

    c.   is unlikely to view stress as a challenge.

    d.   is affected mostly by hard emotional choices.

10.   Which personality type is most highly associated with heart disease, independent of other single factors?

    a.   Type A   c.   hardy personality

    b.   Type B   d.   cataclysmic

11.   Which behaviour or personality type is best described by the following traits: achievement, competitiveness, and commitment to completing a task?

    a.   Type B behaviour   c.   helpless personality

    b.   hardy personality   d.   Type A behaviour

12.   Addiction to nicotine may first emerge as:

    a.   a positive attitude towards smoking.

    b.   a relationship between smoking, nicotine levels and the smoker's emotional state

    c.   a rite of passage and a sign of growing up.

    d.   part of the self-concept and physiological dependence

13.   According to the text, which alternative below is **not** a reason for communication difficulties between doctor and patient?

a. Physicians may ask patients questions that are of a highly technical nature.
b. Physicians have difficulty encouraging patients to give helpful information.
c. Physicians sometimes simplify things too much and talk down to the patient.
d. Patients have the primary responsibility for discussing their medical problems and they are often unskilled in initiating discussions about their problems.

14. According to the text, the accuracy with which physicians present information about the nature of medical problems is related to the degree of patient:
a. suffering.
b. anxiety.
c. discontent.
d. satisfaction.

15. Which of the following might a physician do to enhance a physician-patient relationship?
a. be courteous and supportive toward the patient
b. use very simplistic explanations
c. explain diagnosis in professional jargon
d. encourage the patient to construct a personal theory to account for the reported symptoms

____ 16. cataclysmic events

____ 17. personal stressors

____ 18. background stressors

____ 19. daily hassles

____ 20. uplifts

a. The same as background stressors.

b. Strong stressors that occur suddenly, affecting many people at once (e.g., natural disasters).

c. Events, such as the death of a family member, that have immediate negative consequences that generally fade with time.

d. Minor positive events that make one feel good.

e. Events such as being stuck in traffic that cause minor irritations but have no long-term ill effects unless they continue or are compounded by other stressful events.

21. Commitment, control, and challenge seem to make _____ people more resistant to negative stressors.

22. The fight or flight response is also known as the _____ stage.

23. When the body looses its ability to respond or adjust, we have reached the _____ stage of GAS.

24. _____ are things like lost keys, rude sales clerks, and bad hair days.

25. Calculate the degree of stress in your life using Table 11-1. Interpret the results using the scoring information at the bottom of the table. What do the results say about the cause of illness and the role of stress in your health?

PRACTISE TEST 2:

1. The branch of psychology devoted to exploring psychological factors and principles in treatment, diagnosis, and prevention of physical illness is called:
a. health psychology.
b. physiological psychology.
c. forensic psychology.
d. organizational psychology.

2. Which of the following individuals developed the general adaptation syndrome model?
   a. Martin Seligman
   b. Hans Selye
   c. B. F. Skinner
   d. Sigmund Freud

3. Hans Selye's general adaptation syndrome states that:
   a. stress generates biological responses in animals that differ from those in humans.
   b. stressful situations produce many different responses in individuals.
   c. the same set of physiological reactions to stress occur regardless of the situation.
   d. immobilization happens when the organism confronts a stressor.

4. A man has been coping with the death of his wife. He has been hospitalized for an acute respiratory infection, fatigue, and physical collapse. He is likely experiencing the _____ stage of the general adaptation syndrome.
   a. resistance
   b. alarm and mobilization
   c. exhaustion
   d. challenge

5. The best predictor of breast cancer victims' survival time was a factor of mental resilience and vigour, also labeled as:
   a. acceptance.
   b. hardiness.
   c. fatalism.
   d. joy.

6. Background stressors do not require much coping or response, but continued exposure to them may produce:
   a. an inability to use problem-focused techniques.
   b. as great a toll as a single, more stressful incident.
   c. as great a toll as a cataclysmic event.
   d. psychosomatic illness.

7. According to Seligman, _____ occurs when one concludes that unpleasant or annoying stimuli cannot be controlled.
   a. learned helplessness
   b. hysteria
   c. cataclysmic stress
   d. posttraumatic stress

8. What are the two types of strategies people may use when consciously attempting to regulate a stressful situation?
   a. control-oriented or defensive coping strategies
   b. emotion-focused or problem-focused coping strategies
   c. emotional insulation or denial coping strategies
   d. conscious or unconscious coping strategies

9. Which of the following traits is characteristic of a Type B personality?
   a. relaxed
   b. aggressive
   c. scheduled
   d. competitive

10. Frequently experiencing negative emotions has been linked to _____ and also to the _____ personality.
    a. hypertension; Type B
    b. lowered incidence of heart failure; Type A
    c. eczema; Type B

d.   coronary heart disease; Type A

11. According to the text, there is some evidence suggesting that, rather than focusing on Type A behaviour as the cause of heart disease, a more effective approach should concentrate on:
   a.   Type A behaviours that affect the immune system.
   b.   Type B behaviours that appear critical to the prevention of heart disease.
   c.   Type A behaviours that can be altered instead of eliminated.
   d.   Type B behaviours that work with the immune system.

12. Though about _____ of smokers agree that smoking is bad for your health, only about _____ are able to achieve long-term successes in their efforts to stop smoking.
   a.   95 percent; 40 percent   c.   70 percent; 15 percent
   b.   80 percent; 30 percent   d.   30 percent; 15 percent

13. Which behaviour personality type would best be described as someone who is quite resilient to stress and does not get stress-related diseases?
   a.   type A behaviour   c. helpless personality
   b.   hardy personality   d. type B behaviour

14. Patients' erroneous theories about their own illnesses:
   a.   reinforce their confidence in the physician's wisdom.
   b.   lead them to disobey the doctor's prescribed course of treatment.
   c.   are actually correct in an amazingly large number of cases.
   d.   relate closely to their improvements from prior medical treatment.

15. Which of the following is **not** likely to bring you the best possible health care?
   a.   Choose physicians who communicate well.
   b.   Ask questions until you fully understand your treatment.
   c.   Accept some responsibility for your treatment.
   d.   Do anything necessary to gain the attention of the health-care providers.

_____ 16.   learned helplessness   a.   Preparation for stress before it is encountered.

_____ 17.   coping   b.   The efforts to control, reduce, or learn to tolerate the threats that lead to stress.

_____ 18.   defence mechanisms   c.   A learned belief that one has no control over the environment.

_____ 19.   social support   d.   Unconscious strategies people use to reduce anxiety by concealing its source from themselves and others.

_____ 20.   proactive coping   e.   Knowledge of being part of a mutual network of caring, interested others.

21.   The _____ is the complex of organs, glands, and cells that make up our body's natural line of defence.

22.   A defence mechanism that protects a person from negative experiences, but also blocks out positive experiences is called emotional _____.

23. The tendency to throw ourselves into whatever we are doing with a sense the activity is important is called _____.

24. One characteristic of hardiness is the anticipation of change that serves as an incentive rather than a threat. This is called _____.

25. _____ is comfort provided by other humans as well as pets.

26. Smoking is a serious habit with both psychological and physiological addictions involved. Should smoking be banned in public places? Discuss the problems posed by such a ban and the benefits that should be expected by enforcing it.

PRACTISE TEST 3: Conceptual, Applied, and Challenging Questions

1. Which alternative about health psychology below is **not** correct?
    a. Health psychology uses treatments such as prescription medications, surgery, and radiation therapy when indicated.
    b. Health psychology is concerned with changing people's habits and lifestyles to help them prevent disease.
    c. Health psychology recognizes that health is interwoven with psychological factors.
    d. Health psychology recognizes that psychological factors may affect the immune system and have beneficial or detrimental effects upon health.

2. Health psychologists take the position on the mind-brain problem that:
    a. the mind-brain problem is an eternal mystery that will never be solved.
    b. mind and brain are separate and operate independently.
    c. mind and brain are separate but work with perfect synchrony, like two clocks that are set to give synchronized time readings.
    d. mind and brain interact with each other.

3. Carlos realized that he had failed to reach his sales goals at the end of the year, so he set new goals for the following year. Carlos' behaviour is typical for a person at the _____ stage of the general adaptation syndrome.
    a. resistance
    c. alarm and mobilization
    b. exhaustion
    d. repression

4. For those involved, the terrorist bombing of an office building is which type of stressor?
    a. personal stressor
    c. daily hassle
    b. background stressor
    d. cataclysmic event

5. Upon visiting the doctor's office and going through extensive testing, Michael finds out that he has a lung disease. Which type of stress is Michael likely to experience?
    a. cataclysmic stress
    c. posttraumatic stress
    b. personal stress
    d. background stress

6. A physician uses his assistants to regulate in-patients' every activity. By the end of their time in his clinic, the patients take no initiative. This demonstrates:
    a. the general adaptation syndrome.
    c. the inferiority complex.
    b. daily hassles.
    d. learned helplessness.

7. Your boss learns that he exhibits Type A behaviour pattern, while attending a company-sponsored stress workshop. Which alternative below is correct?
    a. There is nothing that can be done to change your boss's Type A behavioural pattern.
    b. Your boss should remember that the relationship between the Type A behaviour pattern and heart attacks or development of coronary heart disease is correlational.
    c. There is little hope for your boss, since the Type A behaviour pattern has been found to cause heart attacks or development of heart disease.
    d. Your boss is fortunate, since women are at even greater risk with Type A behaviour patterns.

8. In a study that placed patients with advanced breast cancer either in psychotherapy or a control that did not receive psychotherapy, what were the results?
    a. The psychotherapy group felt better, and they lived longer.
    b. The psychotherapy group felt better, but there was no impact on their survival rate.
    c. The psychotherapy group became more depressed because of their increased awareness of the cancer, but they also lived longer.
    d. The study proved that psychotherapy increased the survival rate of cancer patients.

9. Aunt Nina, who is 87 years old, is in the hospital for minor surgery. However, since she is older, she realizes that even minor surgery can be risky. Her surgeon, apparently trying to calm her fears, says "We'll just pop right in there and sneak back out." The problem with his comments appears to be quite common in that:
    a. they treat Nina as if she were either a child or senile.
    b. they don't go far enough in minimizing the risk factors.
    c. when spoken to in this manner, patients get an exaggerated sense of the surgeon's ability.
    d. they reflect techniques taught in medical school.

10. Kiesha, who is 35 years of age, has been smoking for 15 years. She knows it is extremely unhealthy for her and wants to stop but is having a difficult time doing so. What may prove to be the most effective means to help Kiesha to stop smoking?
    a. the "cold-turkey" method
    b. banning smoking in all public places
    c. behaviour strategies that concentrate on changing the smoking response
    d. changing societal norms and attitudes about smoking

11. The malfunction of the Three Mile Island plant in the early 1980s exposed people to a potential nuclear meltdown. This produced emotional, behavioural, and psychological consequences that lasted more than a year. This would be considered a:
    a. cataclysmic event   c. uplift
    b. background stressor   d. personal stressor

12. A patient decides that she will do better by maintaining her exercise and taking the rest of some medication she had been given earlier instead of carefully following the prescribed regimen of rest and antibiotics for an infection. This is an example of:
    a. reactance.   c. preventive medicine.
    b. Type A behaviour.   d. creative nonadherence.

13. In a group therapy session with alcoholics, the counselor describes the range of personal issues that are aggravated by alcohol; this approach is meant to promote:
    a. hardiness.   c. learned helplessness.
    b. problem-focused coping.   d. stress inoculation.

14. Whenever Pablo measures his blood pressure at the drug store where they have free blood-pressure checks, his pressure is always in the normal range. However, whenever he goes to his physician, he gets very nervous and anxious, and his blood pressure usually measures in the high range. This could best be explained by:
    a. reactance.
    b. Type A behaviour.
    c. Type B behaviour.
    d. creative nonadherence.

15. Social support is an effective means of coping with all of the following types of stress. However, based on the descriptions in the text, in which one of the following is social support most likely to occur as a matter of the nature of the stressor?
    a. personal stressors
    b. events leading to posttraumatic stress disorder
    c. cataclysmic events
    d. uplifts

_____ 16. general adaptation syndrome (GAS)

_____ 17. posttraumatic stress disorder (PTSD)

_____ 18. creative nonadherence

_____ 19. reactance

a. When patients modify a physician's treatment.

b. A set of symptoms that occurs after disturbing events; trouble concentrating, anxiety, guilt, and sleep difficulties.

c. Typical series of responses to stressful situations that includes alarm, resistance, and exhaustion.

d. A negative emotional and cognitive reaction to a restriction of one's freedom.

20. Most _____ agree with the statement, "Cigarette smoking frequently causes disease and death."

21. People smoke in an effort to regulate both emotional states and _____ in the blood.

22. Research on well-being shows that happy people have high _____.

23. _____ helps individuals to persevere at tasks and ultimately to achieve more.

24. One explanation for the stability of subjective well-being is that people may have a general _____ for happiness.

25. Define the personality characteristic hardiness. Discuss how parents can encourage the development of hardiness in their children.

Spotlight on Terminology and Language— Cultural Idioms

Page 370 "They have paid particular attention to **the immune system**, the complex of organs, glands, and cells that constitute our body's natural line of defence in fighting disease."

The **immune system** comprises the body's defence and surveillance network of cells and chemicals that fight off bacteria, viruses, and other foreign or toxic substances.

Page 370"Health psychologist's are among the primary investigators in a growing field called **psychoneuroimmunology**."

Psychoneuroimmunology is the study of the connection among the central nervous system, the endocrine system, and psychosocial factors such as cognitive reactions to stressful procedures, the individual's personality traits, and social pressures.

Page 370 "We examine the ways in which patient-physician interactions influence our health, and offer suggestions for increasing people's **adherence** to behaviour that will improve their well-being."

Adherence is conforming or adapting one's actions to follow closely another's wishes, a rule, or instructions.

Page 370 "Feeling **exasperated**, she walked to the computer lab to print out the paper she had completed the night before."

Exasperated is annoyed and aggravated.

Page 371 "Even pleasant events—such as planning a party or beginning a sought-after job—can produce stress, although negative events result in greater **detrimental** consequences than positive ones."

When something is **detrimental**, it is damaging, such as the **detrimental**, or harmful, effects of pollution. What are some **detrimental** events that have occurred in your life?

Page 371 "Exposure to stressors generates a rise in certain hormones secreted by the **adrenal glands**, an increase in heart rate and blood pressure, and changes in how well the skin conducts electrical impulses."

Adrenal glands are structures in the endocrine system. The outer part—the adrenal cortex—secretes hormones that regulate salt and sugar balance and help the body resist stress. The inner part—the adrenal medulla—secretes two

hormones that arouse the body to deal with stress and emergencies.

Page 372 "The **general adaptation syndrome** model has had a substantial impact on our understanding of stress."

According to Selye, the **general adaptation syndrome** consists of a series of three stages: alarm, resistance, and exhaustion. Each stage corresponds to the three different reactions of the body to stressful situations.

Page 374 "Although it might seem that **cataclysmic** events would produce **potent**, **lingering** stress, this is not always true."

A **cataclysm** is a catastrophe, an event that is momentous and violent. **Potent** is powerful. When something like stress **lingers**, it is slow to leave you. It remains in existence although it wanes in strength, importance, and influence.

Page 374 **In the long run** is the eventual outcome at the end an extended or prolonged period of time or of an extensive sequence of

Page 374 "Symptoms of posttraumatic stress disorder include re-experiencing the event, emotional **bluntness**, sleep difficulties, problems relating to others, alcohol and drug abuse, and — in some cases —, suicide."

When one is emotionally **blunt**, he or she may have a reduced ability to feel emotions and diminished interest or participation in previously enjoyed activities.

Page 375 "Typically, personal stressors produce an immediate major reaction that soon **tapers off**."

When something **tapers** off, it gradually decreases.

Page 375 "The flip side of hassles are **uplifts**, those minor positive events that make one feel good—even if only temporarily."

An **uplift** is a bettering of a condition, especially spiritually, socially, or intellectually.

Page 383 "Some findings suggest that cancer patients are less **emotionally reactive**, suppress anger, and lack outlets for emotional release".

Some studies suggest that cancer patients are unable to react in ways that release harmful emotion safely. However, this interpretation of these studies is not universally accepted.

P 390 **Psychological reactance** refers to the negative emotional and cognitive states of patients who react angrily to medical orders that restrict their freedom. Often the things they do end up causing their health situation to worsen.

Page 376 **Defence mechanisms** are unconscious, mental strategies involving the distortion or denial of events or information the person perceives as emotionally threatening.

Page 376 **Emotional insulation** is an example of a defence mechanism that shields the person from both negative and positive experiences. Defence mechanisms are ultimately inadequate means of coping with stress.

Page 377 "You may know people who habitually react to even the smallest amount of stress with hysteria, and others who calmly confront even

the greatest stress in an **unflappable** manner."

A person who is **unflappable** exhibits behaviour that is marked by assurance and self-control.

Page 377 "Among those who cope with stress most successfully are people with the coping style of **hardiness**, a personality characteristic associated with a lower rate of stress-related illness."

The personality trait of **hardiness** protects and buffers people from the potentially harmful effects of stressful situations. **Hardiness** reduces the chances of developing psychosomatic illness.

Page 377 Hardy individuals approach stress **optimistically** and take direct action to learn about and deal with stressors, thereby changing stressful events into less threatening ones."

An **optimist** is someone with an inclination to put the most favourable construction upon actions or events or to anticipate the best possible outcomes.

■ CHAPTER 11: ANSWER KEY

GUIDED REVIEW			
Section 1: [a] Health psychology [b] immune system [c] Psychoneuroimmunology [d] stress [e] psychophysiological disorders [f] general adaptation syndrome (GAS) [g] alarm and mobilization stage [h] resistance stage [i] exhaustion stage [j] cataclysmic events [k] posttraumatic stress disorder, or PTSD [l] personal stressors [m] background stressors [n] daily hassles [o] uplifts	Evaluate 1. e 2. a 3. d 4. b 5. c	Section 2: [a] Type A behaviour pattern [b] Type B behaviour pattern Evaluate 1. a 2. e 3. d 4. c 5. b	Section 3: [a] creative nonadherence [b] reactance Evaluate 1. d 2. a 3. e 4. b 5. c

HEALTH PSYCHOLOGY: STRESS, COPING, AND WELL-BEING

[p] learned helplessness [q] coping [r] defence mechanisms [s] Emotional insulation [t] emotion-focused coping [u] problem-focused coping [v] Hardiness [w] social support [x] proactive coping			

Selected Rethink Answers

1. Cataclysmic stressors are strong stressors that occur suddenly and affect many people. They produce less stress in the long run because they have a clear resolution. Social support, the sharing of the event with others, helps reduce stress because there are others who know how you are feeling.

2. To avoid stress people can be trained to identify and manage their emotions in the face of stress by getting support or reframing the situation to identify any positive aspects of a situation. People can develop strategies or plans of action to deal with stress such as planning, anticipating problems, and having pre-planned solutions.

3. Psychophysiological disorders illustrate the links that exists between a person's emotions, thoughts, behaviour, and physical condition. Health psychology studies show that an immense number of conditions that may exhibit only physical or psychological symptoms superficially, are in fact deeply influenced by both physical and psychological causes.

4. The United States is a highly competitive society. Person's who are aggressive and have drive in their personal and professional life are regarded positively; they can also be aggressive and hostile when things don't go their way. Our democratic society focuses largely on the success of the individual whereas other cultures focus on cooperation and the success of the community.

Practise Test 1:

1. c   obj. 1   p. 370
a. Incorrect. The limbic system is part of the brain.
b. Incorrect. The endocrine system is the system of hormone-secreting organs, and it is part of the larger system that defends against disease.
*c. Correct. The system, which includes the endocrine system, the sympathetic system, and parts of the limbic system, as well as other organs, is called the immune system.
d. Incorrect. The sympathetic system is part of the nervous system, and it is part of the larger immune system.

2. b   obj. 2   p. 371-373
a. Incorrect. See answer b.
*b. Correct. The stages of Selye's general adaptation syndrome are alarm and mobilization, resistance, and exhaustion.
c. Incorrect. See answer b.
d. Incorrect. See answer b.

3. a   obj. 1   p. 371
*a. Correct. Stressors present threats or challenges to a person and require some type of adaptive response.
b. Incorrect. A mobilization state is not a threat to a person's well-being.
c. Incorrect. A defence mechanism is a mechanism used by the ego to protect against unconscious conflict.

d. Incorrect. An inoculation is a medical intervention or a natural event that builds the immune system response.

4. d   obj. 2   p. 371
a. Incorrect. The stage is part of the reaction to a stressor, not just a preparation to react.
b. Incorrect. Increased resistance to the stressor occurs in the next stage, during which the ability to resist disease declines.
c. Incorrect. This describes the final stage of the general adaptation syndrome.
*d. Correct. The "alarm" involves the psychological awareness of the stressor.

5. a   obj. 3   p. 374
*a. Correct. Cataclysmic events include manmade and natural disasters, like earthquakes and terrorist attacks.
b. Incorrect. Background stressors are the ongoing demands made on the individual all the time.
c. Incorrect. Uplifts are the positive challenges that contribute to a sense of accomplishment or completion.
d. Incorrect. Personal stressors are the demands that are unique to the person and typically not shared with others (like being fired from a job).

6. b   obj. 3   p. 375
a. Incorrect. These are described as hassles.

*b. Correct. These minor positive events may be just as demanding and stressful on the individual as are hassles, but they leave the person feeling good rather than drained.
c. Incorrect. Uplifts, by definition, would not be exhilarating.
d. Incorrect. Uplifts, by definition, would not be major.

7. d   obj. 1   p. 371
a. Incorrect. These disorders can appear as a result of the extended operation of the resistance phase of the GAS, and are sometimes called disorders of defence (but not of the psychodynamic ego defence mechanisms).
b. Incorrect. These do not immediately threaten life.
c. Incorrect. Hardy people appear to have fewer of these disorders than the less hardy.
*d. Correct. These disorders often have psychological origins in stress and are thus considered psychophysiological.

8. c   obj. 6   . 376
a. Incorrect. In the psychoanalytic view, "defence" would apply to unconscious events that threaten the ego.
b. Incorrect. Arousal is not the appropriate noun.
*c. Correct. "Coping" is the term used to describe the ability to deal with stress and the techniques used.
d. Incorrect. However, coping is a form of adaptation.

9. b   obj. 5   p. 377
a. Incorrect. Hardy individuals are quite capable of coping with stress.
*b. Correct. The hardy individual is quite resilient to stress and does not get stress-related diseases.
c. Incorrect. The hardy individual does recognize the challenge of stress.
d. Incorrect. Everyone is affected in some way by emotional choices, especially if they are difficult.

10. a   obj. 7   p. 381
*a. Correct. Type A behaviour pattern is most associated with heart disease.
b. Incorrect. Type A, not Type B, is most associated with heart disease.
c. Incorrect. The hardy personality is actually more resistant to stress-related heart disease.
d. Incorrect. There is no personality type known as cataclysmic (though you may know someone who would fit such a description).

11. d   obj. 7   pp 381, 382
a. Incorrect. Type B behaviour is neither competitive nor driven by achievement.
b. Incorrect. The hardy individual is resistant to stress-related diseases.
c. Incorrect. A helpless person would not be competitive or focused upon completion of tasks.
*d. Correct. These traits describe the Type A behaviour pattern.

12. d   obj. 9   p. 384

a. Incorrect. This is the stage in which positive attitudes toward smoking are developed.
b. Incorrect. After becoming a smoker, maintenance of the habit requires making the behaviour part of the routine.
c. Incorrect. This is the stage marked by first experimenting with cigarettes.
*d. Correct. The nicotine addiction marks the ascension to being a smoker.

13. b   obj. 11   p. 389
a. Incorrect. Physicians apparently have difficulty asking questions in such a way that the patient can answer them with information that is useful.
*b. Correct. Patients often begin the discussion, and when they do take responsibility, the communication with the physician often improves.
c. Incorrect. A common response with the elderly is to act as if they are children and condescend to them.
d. Incorrect. Physicians often ask questions that patients have difficulty understanding, or they understand them in other ways.

14. d   obj. 11   pp. 389, 390
a. Incorrect. Suffering results from the disease.
b. Incorrect. See answer d.
c. Incorrect. See answer d.
*d. Correct. The accuracy of the communication seems to improve the satisfaction that the patient has with treatment and lessens anxiety about the disease and discontent with the physician.

15. a   obj. 11   pp. 389, 390
*a. Correct. Simple courtesy goes a long way.
b. Incorrect. Simplistic answers and explanations make the understanding of the problem more difficult.
c. Incorrect. Professional jargon is the greatest barrier to improved communication.
d. Incorrect. Patients will do this if the explanation they receive is not well understood.

16. b   obj. 4   p. 374
17. c   obj. 4   p. 375
18. e   obj. 4   p. 375
19. a   obj. 4   p. 375
20. d   obj. 4   p. 375
21. hardy   obj. 6   p. 377
22. alarm and mobilization   obj. 2   p. 371
23. exhaustion   obj. 2   p. 372
24. Hassles   obj. 4   p. 375

25.
▪ Tabulate your stress score using Table 11-1.
▪ Determine whether you are at risk or normal. Do the events that contribute to your score seem part of the normal course of life, or have your experienced an unusual number of things recently?
▪ Identify any recent illnesses that would have been influenced by the stress.

Practise Test 2:

1. a   obj. 1   p. 370
*a. Correct. Health psychology includes all the psychological aspects of health.
b. Incorrect. Physiological psychology is focused on the various psychological aspects of our biological organism.
c. Incorrect. Forensic psychology is the use of psychology in the legal system.
d. Incorrect. Organizational psychology attends to the study of behaviour in organizations.

2. b   obj. 2   p. 371
a. Incorrect. Seligman is responsible for the concept of learned helplessness.
*b. Correct. A Canadian physician, Hans Selye proposed and researched this universal pattern of stress reaction.
c. Incorrect. Skinner is responsible for operant conditioning.
d. Incorrect. Freud developed psychoanalytic theory.

3. c   obj. 2   p. 371
a. Incorrect. See answer c.
b. Incorrect. The psychological responses vary considerably, but the physiological responses differ only by degree.
*c. Correct. Selye believed and demonstrated through his research that the physiological stress response pattern was pretty much universal.
d. Incorrect. This happens rarely and with extreme stressors.

4. c   obj. 2   p. 372
a. Incorrect. This is the middle stage, during which the individual puts up a fight.
b. Incorrect. This is the earliest stage of initial response, and it does mot have these symptoms.
*c. Correct. The conditions describe suggest that the man has reached the final stage of the GAS.
d. Incorrect. There is no "challenge" stage.

5. d   obj. 8   p. 383
a. Incorrect. Acceptance does not have an influence on survival of cancer.
b. Incorrect. Hardiness does not have an influence on survival of cancer.
c. Incorrect. Fatalism has a negative impact on survival of cancer.
*d. Correct. Researchers defined this as joy, and indeed it was correlated to higher survival rates.

6. b   obj. 4   p. 374
a. Incorrect. This ability depends upon factors other than the presence of background stressors.
*b. Correct. The effect of background stress, and any stress, can accumulate, with the sum of many small stressors having the same effect as one large one.
c. Incorrect. This would be difficult to judge.
d. Incorrect. Background stressors would be unlikely to cause a psychosomatic illness.

7. a   obj. 5   pp. 375, 376

*a. Correct. Seligman applied this term to the perception that a situation was beyond the control of the individual.
b. Incorrect. Hysteria refers to a psychological disorder treated by Freud.
c. Incorrect. Cataclysmic stress refers to major stressful events that affect many people.
d. Incorrect. Posttraumatic stress disorder refers to the long-term effects of highly stressful events.

8. b   obj. 6   pp 376, 377
a. Incorrect. See answer b.
*b. Correct. The two types are emotion-focused and problem-focused coping. Emotion-focused coping is used more in situations in which circumstances appear unchangeable.
c. Incorrect. See answer b.
d. Incorrect. See answer b.

9. a   obj. 7   p. 381
*a. Correct. Of the traits given, relaxed best fits the Type B personality. Aggressive, scheduled, and competitive are Type A characteristics.
b. Incorrect. See answer a.
c. Incorrect. See answer a.
d. Incorrect. See answer a.

10. d   obj. 7   pp. 381, 382
a. Incorrect. Type B personalities tend to have less hypertension than Type A.
b. Incorrect. This may be true only of second heart attacks.
c. Incorrect. Eczema is not associated with Type A or B patterns.
*d. Correct. The Type A behaviour that correlates most with CHD is negative emotions.

11. b   obj. 7   p. 382
a. Incorrect. It appears that all the Type A behaviours have an effect on the immune system.
*b. Correct. Those Type B behaviours that are associated with healthy results can be taught to the Type A person.
c. Incorrect. This approach has not been successful.
d. Incorrect. Rather than those that work with the immune system (if they can be isolated) the approach has been to focus on those that are successful with heart conditions.

12. c   obj. 8   p. 372
a. Incorrect. Try 70 percent and 15 percent.
b. Incorrect. Try 70 percent and 15 percent.
*c. Correct. Smoking is one of the most difficult habits to break.
d. Incorrect. Try 70 percent and 15 percent.

13. b   obj. 6   p. 381
a. Incorrect. The need for achievement, competitiveness and commitment sometimes lead to illness.
*b. Correct. The hardy individual is less affected by stress.

c.   Incorrect. An individual who is neither competitive
     nor driven is still affected by stress.
d.   Incorrect. The person who is neither competitive nor
     driven, may be less likely to get illness than Type A.

14. b   obj. 12   p. 389
a.   Incorrect. They probably did not receive any of their
     physician's wisdom.
*b. Correct. They become their own physicians and
     change their regime of treatment.
c.   Incorrect. Simply not true.
d.   Incorrect. Perhaps one accidental correct guess may
     lead them to think they know better.

15. d   obj. 11   pp. 388, 389
a.   Incorrect. Better communication reduces anxiety and
     improves recovery after surgery.
b.   Incorrect. Never give up, these answers make a
     difference in your health.
c.   Incorrect. The more responsibility you accept, they
     better your chances of recovery.
*d. Correct. This may result in some detrimental effects,
     including being ignored when a true emergency
     occurs.

16. c   obj. 5   p. 363
17. b   obj. 6   p. 377
18. d   obj.6   p. 376
19. e   obj. 6   p. 378
20. a   obj. 6   p. 379
21. immune system   obj. 1   p. 370
22. insulation   obj. 6   p. 376
23. commitment   obj. 6   p. 377
24. challenge obj. 6   p. 377
25. Social support   obj. 6   p. 378, 379

26.
▪   Identify whether you believe that public places should
    ban smoking.
▪   Under which conditions should a person be
    allowed/not allowed to smoke in public?
▪   Describe the difficulties and problems that would be
    involved with enforcing a complete ban.

Practise Test 3:
1.   a   obj. 1   p. 378
*a. Correct. Health psychology may promote the effective
     use of medical treatments, but it is not itself involved
     in using the treatments.
b.   Incorrect. Health psychology can contribute to
     changing habits by implementing behaviour
     modification strategies, among other strategies.
c.   Incorrect. Some health psychologists have taken a
     holistic view of mind and body, suggesting that the
     two are inseparable.
d.   Incorrect. The role of the immune system and the way
     psychological factors can affect it is a major interest
     for health psychology.

2.   d   obj. 1   p. 378

a.   Incorrect. The mind-brain problem is a mystery
     created by modern philosophy.
b.   Incorrect. True only among philosophers.
c.   Incorrect. This is a view reminiscent of the
     philosopher Leibniz.
*d. Correct. Without this basic assumption, attention to
     the physical health of the brain as an organ (and the
     rest of the body as well) would have no impact on the
     mind.

3.   c   obj. 2   p. 371
a.   Incorrect. This is a new stress, so Carlos is probably at
     the alarm and mobilization stage.
b.   Incorrect. Exhaustion would only appear in this
     circumstance after many years of failing to meet goals.
*c. Correct. Since this is a new recognition, Carlos has
     mobilized his energies and already begun to cope with
     the stress of not meeting this year's goals.
d.   Incorrect. In repression, Carlos would probably ignore
     his failure to meet this year's goals and make no effort
     to compensate for next year.

4.   d   obj. 3   p. 374
a.   Incorrect. Personal stressors are major life events like
     marriage or death.
b.   Incorrect. Background stressors include everyday
     annoyances like traffic.
c.   Incorrect. Daily hassles are also known as background
     stressors, and they include everyday annoyances like
     traffic.
*d. Correct. The traumatic experience would be classed as
     cataclysmic.

5.   b   obj. 4   p. 375
a.   Incorrect. Cataclysmic stress involves many people,
     such as during war, earthquakes, and terrorist attacks.
*b. Correct. This is considered a major personal stressor.
c.   Incorrect. Posttraumatic stress disorder actually
     follows a significant period of traumatic stress.
d.   Incorrect. Background stress includes the many small
     and insignificant worries and challenges one faces
     each day.

6.   d   obj. 5   pp. 375, 376
a.   Incorrect. This does not illustrate the GAS.
b.   Incorrect. Daily hassles will not account for their not
     taking any initiative.
c.   Incorrect. If they come to believe that they are inferior,
     then the answer would be "d" anyway.
*d. Correct. They have learned that they are totally under
     the control of the assistant coaches, thus helpless.

7.   b   obj. 7   pp. 381, 382
a.   Incorrect. Certainly, he can change a number of his
     behaviour patterns or he can take measures to improve
     his health practices.
*b. Correct. The correlation does not mean that he will
     definitely develop coronary heart disease.
c.   Incorrect. With precautions, he will have just as good
     an outlook as anyone else.

d. Incorrect. Women are not at greater risk with these patterns.

8. a obj. 8 pp. 382, 383
*a. Correct. They had a more positive outlook, and in early studies, they extended their lives significantly.
b. Incorrect. There apparently was a link between how they felt and their survival rate.
c. Incorrect. They were less depressed.
d. Incorrect. The study did not prove the relationship, it only suggested that more study was necessary.

9. a obj. 11 p. 389
*a. Correct. This condescending approach is extremely common among physicians.
b. Incorrect. They go too far in minimizing the risks involved.
c. Incorrect. If they are not entirely put off, the patient may develop expectations of success that are not realistic.
d. Incorrect. They reflect that for many physicians, techniques for communicating with patients have not been taught at all.

10. c obj. 9 p. 385
a. Incorrect. The cold turkey method is effective in only a small number of cases.
b. Incorrect. Banning smoking in public places helps the non-smokers, but it does not help the smokers.
*c. Correct. Behaviour strategies have proved the most effective, but they still require perseverance.
d. Incorrect. This will help others avoid starting the habit, but it will not help Kiesha.

11. d obj. 4 p. 375
a. Incorrect. Although they occur suddenly and affect many people, they usually have a clear resolution.
b. Incorrect. Minor irritations that are sometimes called daily hassles. Require little coping.
c. Incorrect. Positive events that make one feel good.
*d. Correct. Major life events where the effects produce an immediate major reaction but that can sometimes linger for long periods of time.

12. d obj. 12 p. 390
a. Incorrect. Reactance is the disagreeable emotional and cognitive reaction to being restricted to a medical regimen.
b. Incorrect. Type A behaviour does not predict compliance to medical prescriptions.
c. Incorrect. It may prevent physicians from losing their jobs since she will probably have to visit them again.
*d. Correct. The term for her actions is creative nonadherence.

13. b obj. 6 p. 377

a. Incorrect. Hardiness may be improved by shifting to a problem-focused coping approach.
*b. Correct. Attention to problems that can be addressed and resolved.
c. Incorrect. Therapists should not promote learned helplessness.
d. Incorrect. Stress inoculation would focus more on what is about to happen, not what has already surfaced.

14. a obj. 12 p. 390
*a. Correct. Reactance is the disagreeable emotional and cognitive reaction to being restricted to a medical regimen, and it can cause higher reading on blood pressure due to increased anxiety about the physician.
b. Incorrect. Reactance is independent of Type A or Type B behaviour.
c. Incorrect. Reactance is independent of Type A or Type B behaviour.
d. Incorrect. Creative nonadherence occurs when a patient creates his or her own course of treatment, often ignoring the prescribed treatment.

15. c obj. 4 p. 374
a. Incorrect. Personal stressors are not shared unless someone seeks out support.
b. Incorrect. One element of the posttraumatic stress disorder is the failure of the support systems in the first place.
*c. Correct. Since many others have just experienced the same major stressor, the social support group is already defined.
d. Incorrect. Uplifts are personal, background stressors that result in the person feeling good.

16. c obj. 3 pp. 371, 372
17. b obj. 4 p. 374
18. a obj. 12 p. 390
19. d obj. 12 p. 390
20. smokers obj. 9 p. 384
21. nicotine levels obj. 9 p. 384
22. self-esteem obj. 11 p. 386
23. Optimism obj. 9 p. 387
24. set point obj. 10 p. 387

25.
- Hardiness is the coping style whose characteristics are associated with a lower rate of stress-related illness.
- Parents can encourage their children to be optimistic; to commit themselves to activities that are important and meaningful to them.
- Children should understand that change rather than stability is the standard condition of life.
- Parents can allow children a sense of control over the events in their lives.

Psychological Disorders

12

Chapter Overview

In chapter 12 you see that abnormality is difficult to define, and it is best to consider behaviour as being on a continuum from normal to abnormal. The contemporary perspectives that attempt to explain abnormal behaviour are the medical perspective, the psychoanalytical perspective, the behavioural perspective, the cognitive perspective, the humanistic perspective, and the sociocultural perspective. The system used by most professionals to classify mental disorders is the DSM IV. The major disorders discussed are the anxiety disorders, the somatoform disorders, and the conversion disorders. Lastly, mood disorders, schizophrenia, and personality disorders are presented and discussed.

To further investigate the topics covered in this chapter, you can access the related websites by visiting the following link: http://www.mcgrawhill.ca/college/feldman

> **Applying Psychology in the 21st Century:**
> Erasing the Stigma of Psychological Disorders

Section 3:
Mood Disorders
Schizophrenia

> **Pathways Through Psychology: Sylvia Geist,**
> Community and Clinical Psychologist

Personality Disorders

Section 4: Beyond the Major Disorders: Abnormal Behaviour in Perspective

> **Exploring Diversity:** The *DSM* and Culture—and the Culture
> Of the *DSM*

The Prevalence of Psychological Disorders

> **Becoming an Informed Consumer of Psychology:**
> Deciding When You Need Help

Learning Objectives

These are the concepts and the learning objectives for Chapter 12. Read them carefully as part of your preliminary survey of the chapter.

Normal Versus Abnormal: Making the Distinction

1. Discuss the various approaches to defining abnormal behaviour. (pp. 396–398)

2. Describe and distinguish the various perspectives of abnormality, and apply those perspectives to specific mental disorders. (pp. 398–401)

3. Describe the *DSM-IV* and its use in diagnosing and classifying mental disorders. (pp. 401–403)

Major Disorders

4. Describe the anxiety disorders and their causes. (pp. 404–407)

5. Describe the somatoform disorders and their causes. (p. 408)

6. Describe the dissociative disorders and their causes. (pp. 408–410)

Mood Disorders

7. Describe the mood disorders and their causes. (pp. 411–414)

8. Describe the types of schizophrenia, its main symptoms, and the theories that account for its causes. (pp. 414–418)

9. Describe the personality disorders and their causes. (pp. 419–420)

Beyond the Major Disorders: Abnormal Behaviour in Perspective

10. Discuss the other forms of abnormal behaviour described in the *DSM-IV*, the prevalence of psychological disorders, and issues related to seeking help. (pp. 421–423)

Section 1: Normal Versus Abnormal: Making the Distinction

Prepare

- *How can we distinguish normal from abnormal behaviour?*
- *What are the major perspectives on psychological disorders used by mental health professionals?*
- *What classification system is used to categorize psychological disorders?*

Organize

- *Defining Abnormality*
- *Perspectives on Abnormality*
- *Classifying Abnormal Behaviour*

Work

A passage from James Joyce's *Ulysses* suggests that madness cannot be determined by a small sample of a person's behaviour. The text examines the following approaches to the definition of abnormal behaviour. They are:

- *Abnormality as deviation from the average.* This definition uses the statistical definition of behaviour to define "abnormal" as behaviour that is statistically unusual or rare. The problem with this approach is that simply being unusual or rare does not define abnormal: individuals with high IQs are rare, but they are not considered abnormal.
- *Abnormality as deviation from the ideal.* This definition classifies behaviour as abnormal if it deviates from the ideal or standard behaviour. However, society has very few standards on which everyone agrees.

- *Abnormality as a sense of subjective discomfort.* This approach focuses on the consequences of behaviour that make a person experience discomfort. However, some people who engage in what others would consider abnormal behaviour do not experience discomfort.
- *Abnormality as the inability to function effectively.* People who are unable to adjust to the demands of society and unable to function in daily life are considered abnormal in this view. An unemployed homeless woman would be classified as abnormal in this view even if the choice to live on the streets was her own.
- *Legal definitions of abnormality.* The legal system uses the concept of insanity to distinguish normal from abnormal behaviour. Insanity refers generally to whether the defendant could understand the difference between right and wrong when the act was committed. The precise definition and how it is used varies from one jurisdiction to another.

None of the five approaches is broad enough to include all possibilities of abnormal behaviour, and the line between normal and abnormal remains unclear. The best way to solve the problem is to consider normal and abnormal as on a continuum, or scale, of behaviour rather than to consider them to be absolute states. In the past, abnormal behaviour has been attributed to superstition, to witchcraft, or to demonic possession. The contemporary approach includes six major perspectives on abnormal behaviour:

- The **[a]** _____ of abnormality views the cause of abnormal behaviour to have a physical origin such as a hormone or chemical imbalance or a physical injury.
- The **[b]** _____ of abnormality maintains that abnormal behaviour comes from childhood. The conflicts of childhood that remain unresolved can cause abnormal behaviour in adulthood.
- The **[c]** _____ of abnormality views the behaviour itself as the problem, because it proposes that one's behaviour is a response to stimuli that one finds in one's environment.
- The **[d]** _____ of abnormality assumes that *cognitions* are central to a person's abnormal behaviour, which can then be changed by learning new cognitions.
- The **[e]** _____ of abnormality emphasizes the control and responsibility people have for their own behaviour. This model considers people to be basically rational, oriented to the social world, and motivated to get along with others.
- The **[f]** _____ of abnormality assumes that behaviour is shaped by the family group, society, and culture. The stresses and conflicts people experience promote and maintain abnormal behaviour.

One standard classification system has been accepted by most professionals for classifying mental disorders. Devised by the American Psychiatric Association, the system is known as the

[g] _____ . The manual has more than 200 diagnostic categories. It evaluates behaviour according to five dimensions called *axes*. The first three axes address the primary disorder exhibited, the nature of any personality disorders or developmental problems, and any physical disorders. The fourth and fifth axes address the severity of stressors and the general level of functioning. The *DSM-IV* attempts to be descriptive and to avoid suggestions of cause. The objective is to provide precise description and classification. Criticisms include the fact that it reflects categories that assume a physiological view of causes (arising from the fact that it was developed by physicians) and that the categories are inflexible. In other views, the labeling of an individual as deviant is seen as a lifelong, dehumanizing stigma. A classic study by Rosenhan illustrated how the stigma of being labeled mentally ill can linger. Eight people, including Rosenhan, presented themselves to mental hospitals complaining of only one symptom, hearing voices. Though they did not complain of the symptom again, they stayed for an average of nineteen days and were released with labels like "schizophrenia in remission." None of the impostors was detected by the staff. Despite its drawbacks, the *DSM-IV* does provide a reliable and valid way to classify psychological disorders.

Evaluate

_____ 1.   medical model

_____ 2.   psychoanalytic model

_____ 3.   behavioural model

_____ 4.   cognitive model

_____ 5.   humanistic model

_____ 6.   sociocultural model

a.   Suggests that abnormality stems from childhood conflicts over opposing desires regarding sex and aggression.

b.   Suggests that people's behaviour, both normal and abnormal, is shaped by family, society, and cultural influences.

c.   Suggests that people's thoughts and beliefs are a central component to abnormal behaviour.

d.   Suggests that when an individual displays symptoms of abnormal behaviour, the cause is physiological.

e.   Suggests that abnormal behaviour itself is the problem to be treated, rather than viewing behaviour as a symptom of some underlying medical or psychological problem.

f.   Suggests that abnormal behaviour results from an inability to fulfil human needs and capabilities.

Rethink

1.   Imagine that an acquaintance of yours was recently arrested for shoplifting a $3 pen. What sorts of questions and issues would be raised by proponents of *each* of these perspectives on abnormality: medical, psychoanalytic, behavioural, cognitive, humanistic, and sociocultural?

2. Do you agree or disagree that the *DSM* should be updated every several years? What makes abnormal behaviour so variable? Why can't there be one, unchanging definition of abnormal behaviour?

Section 2: Major Disorders

Prepare

* ***What are the major psychological disorders?***

rganize

* ***Anxiety Disorders***
* ***Somatoform Disorders***
* ***Dissociative Disorders***

Work

Everyone experiences *anxiety*, a feeling of apprehension or tension, at some time. When anxiety occurs without external reason and interferes with daily functioning, the problem is known as **[a]** _____ . **[b]** _____ refers to the disorder in which an individual experiences long-term consistent anxiety without knowing why. The anxiety makes the person unable to concentrate, and life becomes centred on the anxiety.

[c] _____ is distinguished by **[d]** _____ that may last a few seconds or several hours. In a panic attack, the individual feels anxiety rise to a peak and gets a sense of impending doom. Physical symptoms of increased heart rate, shortness of breath, sweating, faintness, and dizziness may be experienced. **[e]** _____ has as its primary symptom, a **[f]** _____ , an irrational fear of specific objects or situations. Exposure to the stimulus may cause a full-blown panic attack. (A list of common phobias is given in Table 12-3.) Phobias may be minor, or they may cause extreme suffering.

[g] _____ is characterized by unwanted thoughts and the impulse to carry out a certain action. **[h]** _____ are thoughts or ideas that keep recurring. Though everyone has some obsessions, when they continue for days and months and include bizarre images, they make it difficult for the individual to function. **[i]** _____ are urges to repeat behaviours that seem strange and unreasonable even to the person who feels compelled to act. If they cannot carry out the action, extreme anxiety can be experienced. The cleaning ritual described in the text is a good example of a compulsion. Carrying out the action usually does not reduce the anxiety.

The causes of anxiety disorders are not fully understood. A tendency for both identical twins to have an anxiety disorder if one of them has the disorder suggests that there may be a biological cause. Some chemical deficiencies in the brain have also been linked to the disorder. The behavioural approach suggests that anxiety is a learned response to stress and that the anxiety is reinforced by subsequent encounters with the stressor. The cognitive approach suggests that anxiety grows out of inappropriate and inaccurate cognitions.

[j] _____ involves a constant fear of illness, and physical sensations are misinterpreted as disease symptoms. The symptoms are not faked—hypochondriacs actually experience the symptoms. Hypochondriasis belongs to a class of disorders known as

[k] _____, which are psychological difficulties that take physical forms. There are no underlying physical problems to account for the symptoms, or if one does exist, the

person's reaction exaggerates it. A major somatoform disorder is [l] _____, a disorder in which actual physical symptoms are caused by psychological problems. These disorders usually have a rapid onset—a person may awaken one morning totally blind or with a numb hand (called "glove anesthesia"). One characteristic is that individuals with conversion disorders seem relatively unconcerned with the symptoms. Generally, conversion disorders occur when an emotional stress can be reduced by having a physical symptom.

[m] _____ have been the most dramatized disorders, including the multiple-personality stories of *The Three Faces of Eve* and *Sybil*. The central factor is the dissociation, or splitting apart, of critical parts of the personality. There are three major

dissociative disorders. [n] _____, or multiple personality, occurs when two or more distinct personalities are present in the same individual. Each personality is a separate person with distinctive desires and reactions to situations. Even vision can change when the personality changes. Since they reside in only one body, they must take turns, causing what

appears to be quite inconsistent behaviour. [o] _____ is a failure or inability to remember past experiences. In psychogenic amnesia, information has not been forgotten, it simply cannot be recalled. In some cases memory loss can be quite total, as illustrated in the case of Jane Doe, who had to go on television to have her identity discovered.

[p] _____ is a state in which people take an impulsive, sudden trip and assume a new identity. After a period of time, they realize that they are in a strange place. They often do not recall what they did while wandering.

Evaluate

_____ 1. generalized anxiety disorder

_____ 2. panic disorder

_____ 3. panic attack

_____ 4. phobic disorder

_____ 5. dissociative disorder

a. Characterized by the splitting apart of critical personality facets that are normally integrated.

b. Sudden anxiety characterized by heart palpitations, shortness of breath, sweating, faintness, and great fear.

c. The experience of long-term anxiety with no explanation.

d. Characterized by unrealistic fears that may keep people from carrying out routine daily behaviours.

e. Anxiety that manifests itself in the form of panic attacks.

Rethink

3. What cultural factors might contribute to the rate of anxiety disorders found in a culture? What perspectives on psychological disorders would best explain cultural contributions to anxiety disorders?

4. Do you think the behavioural perspective would be effective in dealing with dissociative disorders? Why or why not? Which perspective do you think would be most promising for this type of disorder?

Section 3: Mood Disorders

Prepare

- *What are the most severe forms of psychological disorders?*

Organize

- *Schizophrenia*
- *Personality Disorders*

Work

Changes in mood are a part of everyday life. However, mood changes can be extreme enough to cause life-threatening problems and to cause an individual to lose touch with reality. These situations result from **[a]** _____, disturbances in mood severe enough to interfere with daily life. **[b]** _____ is one of the more common mood disorders. As many as 14 to 15 million people experience major depression at any time. Twice as many women as men experience major depression, and one in four females will encounter it at some time. Depression is not merely sadness, but involves feelings of uselessness, worthlessness, loneliness, and despair. Major depression is distinguished by the severity of the symptoms.

[c] _____ refers to an extended state of intense euphoria and elation. Also, people experience a sense of happiness, power, invulnerability, and energy. They may be involved with wild schemes. When mania is paired with bouts of depression, it is called a

[d] _____. The swings between highs and low can occur every several days or can be over a period of years. Typically, the depression lasts longer than the mania.

The psychoanalytic view holds that depression is anger at oneself. Major depression and bipolar disorder may have a biological cause, and heredity may play a role in bipolar disorder.

The cognitive approach draws on the experience of **[e]** _____, a state in which people perceive that they cannot escape from or cope with stress. According to this view, depression is a response brought on by helplessness. Aaron Beck has suggested that depression involves faulty cognitions held by the sufferer about themselves. Theories about the cause of depression have not explained why twice as many women get it as men. One theory suggests that the stress for women is higher at certain times of life. Women are also more subject to physical and sexual abuse, earn less money than men, and report greater unhappiness with marriage.

[f] _____ refers to the class of disorders in which severe distortion of reality occurs. Thinking, perception, and emotion deteriorate, there is a withdrawal from social interaction, and there may be bizarre behaviour. (Classes of schizophrenia are listed in Table 12–5.) The characteristics of schizophrenia include:

- *Decline from a previous level of functioning.*
- *Disturbances of thought and language*, in which logic is peculiar, thoughts do not make sense, and linguistic rules are not followed.
- *Delusions* are unshakable beliefs that have no basis in reality, involving thoughts of control by others, persecution, or the belief that thoughts are being broadcast to others.
- *Perceptual disorders* occur in which schizophrenics do not perceive the world as everyone else does, and they may have **[g]** _____, the experience of perceiving things that do not actually exist.
- *Emotional disturbances* include a lack of emotion or highly inappropriate emotional responses.
- Schizophrenics tend to *withdraw* from contact with others.

The symptoms follow two courses: **[h]** _____ develops symptoms early in life, with a gradual withdrawal from the world; and **[i]** _____ has a sudden and conspicuous onset of symptoms. Reactive schizophrenia responds well to treatment; process schizophrenia is more difficult to treat. Another distinction has been drawn between *positive-symptom schizophrenia* and *negative-symptom schizophrenia*. **[j]** _____ refers to symptoms like withdrawal or loss of ability to function, and **[k]** _____ refers to disordered behaviour like hallucinations, delusions, and extremes of emotionality.

Schizophrenia is recognized to have both biological and psychological components at its root. The biological components are suggested by the fact that schizophrenia is more common in some families than others. This suggests a genetic link to the disease. Another biological explanation suggests the presence of a chemical imbalance or a structural defect. The **[l]** _____ suggests that schizophrenia occurs when there is an excess activity in the areas of the brain that use dopamine to transmit signals across nerve cells. Drugs that block dopamine action are effective in reducing symptoms. These drugs take effect immediately, but the symptoms linger for several weeks, suggesting that there must be other factors at work. Structural differences in the brains of schizophrenics have also been found.

Evaluate

____ 1.	hypochondriasis	a.	Characterized by actual physical disturbances.
____ 2.	somatoform disorder	b.	A failure to remember past experience.
____ 3.	conversion disorder	c.	Characteristics of two or more distinct personalities.
____ 4.	dissociative identity disorder	d.	A misinterpretation of normal aches and pains.
		e.	Psychological difficulties that take on physical form.
____ 5.	dissociative amnesia		

Rethink

5. Do any of the explanations of schizophrenia offer the promise of a treatment or cure of the disorder? Do any of the explanations permit us to predict who will be affected by the disorder? How is explanation different from treatment and prediction?

6. Personality disorders are often not apparent to others, and many people with these problems seem to live basically normal lives without being a threat to others. If these people can function well in society, why should they be considered psychologically disordered?

Section 4: Beyond the Major Disorders: Abnormal Behaviour in Perspective

Prepare

- **What indicators signal a need for the help of a mental health practitioner?**

Organize

- **The Prevalence of Mental Disorders**

Work

Other forms of abnormal behaviour described by the *DSM-IV* include

[a] _____, [b] _____, and

[c] _____. The disorders in the *DSM-IV* reflect late-twentieth-century thinking. There was also significant controversy during its development. One controversial disorder was "self-defeating personality disorder," which referred to people in abusive relationships. This disorder was not placed in the *DSM-IV*. The other disorder was "premenstrual dysphoric disorder," or premenstrual syndrome. This disorder was included. The Exploring Diversity section discusses the differences between cultures in the nature of abnormal behaviour.

Determining the number of people with signs of psychological disorders is a difficult task. A survey of 8,000 Americans found that 30 percent currently had a mental disorder and a total of 48 percent had experienced a disorder at some time in their lives.

The decision concerning if and when to seek help for psychological disorders is difficult, but several guidelines should help. If the following signals are present, help should be considered: long-term feelings of distress that interfere with functioning, occasions when stress is overwhelming, prolonged depression, withdrawal from others, chronic physical problems, a fear or phobia that prevents normal functioning, feelings that other people are talking about the person or are out to get the person, or the inability to interact effectively with others.

Evaluate

_____ 1. premenstrual dysphoric disorder

_____ 2. anxiety disorder

_____ 3. Diagnostic and Statestical Manual IV

_____ 4. depression

_____ 5. self-defeating personality disorder

a. Directory where the specific nature of the disorders is a reflection of twentieth-century Western values.

b. Removed from *DSM-IV*, applied to cause in which individuals in unpleasant or demeaning situations take no action.

c. Controversial inclusion to the *DSM-IV*.

d. One of four categories found in all cultures.ncludes schizophrenia, bipolar disorder, depression.

e. Most common of all psychological disorders.

Rethink

7. Why is inclusion in the *DSM-IV* of "borderline" disorders such as self-defeating personality disorder and premenstrual dysphoric disorder so controversial and political? What disadvantages does inclusion bring? Does inclusion bring any benefits?

8. What societal changes would have to occur for psychological disorders to be regarded as the equivalent of appendicitis or another treatable physical disorder? Do you think a person who has been treated for a psychological disorder could become president of the United States? Should such a person become president?

Practise Questions

Test your knowledge of the chapter material by answering these questions. These questions have been placed in three Practise Tests. The first two tests are composed of questions that will test your recall of factual knowledge. The third test contains questions that are challenging and primarily test for conceptual knowledge and your ability to apply that knowledge. Check your answers and review the feedback using the Answer Key in the following pages of the *Study Guide*.

PRACTISE TEST 1:

1. _____ is the constant fear of illness and the misinterpretation of normal aches and pains.
    a. Conversion disorder   c. Somatoform disorder

b. Hypochondriasis   d. Phobic disorder

2. When the *Titanic* sank in 1912, some male passengers saved themselves at the expense of women and children, contrary to the Victorian standard of manly heroism. This behaviour was abnormal because it was:
   a. very different from average.
   b. insane.
   c. opposed to an ideal.
   d. severely uncomfortable.

3. If someone's abnormal behaviour is related to an endocrine system malfunction, their problem best fits the _____ model of abnormality.
   a. medical.
   b. psychoanalytic.
   c. behavioural
   d. sociocultural

4. The _____ model of abnormality suggests that when an individual displays the symptoms of abnormal behaviour, the diagnosed causes are physiological.
   a. humanistic
   b. medical
   c. psychoanalytic
   d. sociocultural

5. Which of the following models of abnormality is least likely to see the therapist as the expert who cures the patient?
   a. the behavioural model
   b. the humanistic model
   c. the medical model
   d. the psychoanalytic model

6. The sources of one's strange beliefs or actions are hidden conflicts that are carried over from childhood, according to the _____ model.
   a. psychoanalytic
   b. humanistic
   c. cognitive
   d. behavioural

7. Many people with psychological disorders come from broken homes and low-income backgrounds. To understand the effects of these and similar conditions on abnormal behaviour, a comprehensive diagnosis must include insights from the _____ model.
   a. behavioural
   b. psychoanalytic
   c. humanistic
   d. sociocultural

8. In the *DSM-IV* there are approximately _____ different diagnostic categories.
   a. 50
   b. 100
   c. 200
   d. 500

9. The term used to describe nervousness and fear that has no apparent justification and impairs normal daily functioning is the _____ disorder.
   a. psychosomatic
   b. personality
   c. anxiety
   d. neurotic

10. The main character in the book *Sybil* suffered from:
    a. schizophrenia.
    b. psychogenic personality.
    c. disordered personality.
    d. dissociative identity disorder.

11. Feelings of impending doom or even death paired with sudden and overwhelming bodily reactions are typical symptoms of:
   a. obsessive-compulsive disorder.
   b. panic attack.
   c. personality disorder.
   d. generalized anxiety disorder.

12. Unable to account for the past three weeks, Portland native Tony X could recall memories prior to his amnesia, but could not relate how he arrived in Tucson. The above description exemplifies:
   a. dissociative identity disorder.
   b. dissociative fugue.
   c. hypochondriasis.
   d. panic attack.

13. A bipolar disorder is one in which an individual has:
   a. opposing phobias.
   b. alternation of mania and depression.
   c. a split personality.
   d. alternation of phobia and panic.

14. _____ schizophrenia is characterized by gradual onset, general withdrawal from the world, blunted emotions, and poor prognosis.
   a. Paranoid
   b. Catatonic
   c. Process
   d. Reactive

15. The belief that Bigfoot lurks in closets and comes out at night to hide the TV remote would be regarded as a:
   a. compulsion.
   b. hallucination.
   c. delusion.
   d. early sign of narcissism.

_____ 16. dissociative fugue

_____ 17. anxiety

_____ 18. mood disorder

_____ 19. mania

_____ 20. bipolar disorder

a. A disorder in which a person alternates between euphoric feelings of mania and bouts of depression.

b. Affective disturbance severe enough to interfere with normal living.

c. A condition in which people take sudden, impulsive trips, sometimes assuming a new identity.

d. An extended state of intense euphoria and elation.

e. A feeling of apprehension or tension.

21. _____ is a constant fear of illness and the misinterpretation of normal aches and pains.

22. The _____ study illustrated that placing labels on individuals influences how their actions are perceived and interpreted.

23. The intense but real fear Megan felt at just the thought of an airplane flight is known as a _____.

24. People whose lives seem to centre around their worry may suffer from _____.

25. People experiencing _____ feel intense happiness, power, invulnerability, and energy.

26. Discuss the implications of Rosenhan's study, in which he and seven other individuals faked mental illness in order to test the ability of mental hospitals to distinguish abnormal behaviour from normal and the effects of labeling. What are the scientific issues related to his study? Are there any ethical issues?

PRACTISE TEST 2:

1. Use of the expression "mental illness" implies that:
   a. demons and devils exert their evil influence on the body through medical ailments, especially ailments of the nervous system.
   b. the target person suffers a lack of unconditional positive regard.
   c. the person has bizarre thoughts but not bizarre behaviour.
   d. the speaker or writer accepts the medical model.

2. The main difference between panic disorder and generalized anxiety disorder is that generalized anxiety is:
   a. more intense than panic.
   b. continuous while panic is short-term.
   c. triggered by alcohol while panic is triggered by social events.
   d. dissociative while panic is schizophrenic.

3. Which of the following models of abnormality is likely to hold most strongly to the concept that the patient has little control over his or her actions?
   a. the medical model   c. the behavioural model
   b. the sociocultural model   d. the humanistic model

4. According to the psychoanalytic model of abnormality, abnormal behaviour derives from:
   a. failure to develop logical thought processes.
   b. physiological malfunctions.
   c. unresolved childhood conflicts.
   d. confusion in the collective unconscious.

5. Which of the following models of abnormality is most likely to emphasize the patient's responsibility and participation in the treatment?
   a. the medical model   c. the behavioural model
   b. the psychoanalytic model   d. the humanistic model

6. According to the text, proponents of which model are most likely to take the position that there is no such thing as abnormal behaviour?
   a. the sociocultural model   c. the behavioural model
   b. the psychoanalytic model   d. the medical model

7. The *DSM-IV* is used primarily to:
    a. show the causes of and to treat abnormality.
    b. classify and identify causes of abnormality.
    c. classify and describe abnormality.
    d. describe and treat abnormality.

8. The Rosenhan (1973) study in which normal individuals were admitted to mental hospitals showed that:
    a. therapeutic techniques that improve disordered patients can be applied by normal people to make them even better adjusted than they were at first.
    b. mental patients served as models for each others' strange behaviours.
    c. the "mental patient" label affects how ordinary acts are perceived.
    d. the *DSM-IV* categories are prone to stability and change.

9. According to the text, which of the following is **not** a reasonable criticism of the *DSM-IV*?
    a. Mental disorders are classified into a "category" rather than along a continuum.
    b. The *DSM-IV* materials usually do not reflect changing views in society about mental disorders, since the manual is updated only every fifteen years.
    c. The *DSM-IV* system of classification may be too heavily influenced by the medical model.
    d. A diagnosis may become an explanation for a problem.

10. Dissociative disorders all share a common feature, that is:
    a. the hereditary basis is well-known and documented.
    b. an obsessive-compulsive disorder usually precedes the onset of any dissociative disorder.
    c. they tend to occur in persons who are poor and have large families.
    d. they allow the person to escape from anxiety-producing situations.

11. Psychological difficulties that take on a physical form but have no actual physical or physiological abnormality are called _____ disorders.
    a. somatoform
    b. psychological
    c. psychophysical
    d. freeform

12. Together, dissociative identity disorder, amnesia, and dissociative fugue are called:
    a. depressive disorders.
    b. schizophrenic disorders.
    c. somatoform disorders.
    d. dissociative disorders.

13. Mania and bipolar disorder differ mainly in:
    a. the sense that mania applies to both genders but bipolar applies to men.
    b. the fact that mania has a psychological origin but bipolar is biological.
    c. the stability of the emotional state.
    d. the sense that one is a personality disorder while the other is a mood disorder.

14. The polygraph, or lie detector, is used to detect lies based on the assumption that the autonomic system of people who are not being truthful becomes aroused as their emotionality increases. The polygraph is able to detect the physiological changes that are indicative of this arousal. This suggests that sociopaths can fool the lie detector test because they:
    a. feel stress or anxiety more or less continuously.
    b. are psychologically sophisticated; many have studied the *DSM-IV*.
    c. feel no guilt or remorse.
    d. have lost touch with reality.

15. Which mental disturbance is most likely to result in the afflicted person's using language in ways that do **not** follow conventional linguistic rules?
    a. schizophrenia
    b. dissociative identity disorder
    c. dissociative fugue
    d. depressive disorder

____ 16. learned helplessness

____ 17. process schizophrenia

____ 18. reactive schizophrenia

____ 19. dopamine hypothesis

____ 20. predisposition model of schizophrenia

a. Suggests that individuals may inherit tendencies that make them vulnerable to environmental stress factors.

b. Onset of symptoms is sudden and conspicuous.

c. Symptoms begin early in life and develop slowly.

d. Suggests that schizophrenia occurs when there is excess activity in certain areas of the brain.

e. A state in which people give up fighting stress, believing it to be inescapable, leading to depression.

21. Together, dissociative identity disorder, amnesia, and dissociative fugue are called

    _____.

22. Critics suggest that the _____ compartmentalizes people into inflexible all-or-nothing categories.

23. _____, which are brought about by specific objects or situations, can last from a few seconds to hours.

24. A person with _____ may actually carry several pairs of eyeglasses because vision changes with each personality.

25. One approach used to explain depression is the _____ approach, which suggests that depression is the result of feelings of loss.

26. What can research with groups of twins, some reared together and some reared apart, tell researchers about the causes of schizophrenia?

PRACTISE TEST 3: Conceptual, Applied, and Challenging Questions

1. Schizophrenia produces many dramatic and debilitating changes in a person affected with this disorder. Which alternative below is **not** one of them?
    a. delusions
    b. dissociative identity disorder
    c. decline from an earlier level of functioning
    d. withdrawal

2. Which statement below is **not** consistent with the sociocultural model of abnormality?
    a. Behaviour is shaped by our family, by society, and by the culture in which we live.

b. There is something wrong with a society that is unwilling to tolerate deviant behaviour.

c. Competing psychic forces within the troubled individual erode personal standards and values.

d. Abnormal behaviours are more prevalent among some social classes than others.

3. Mr. Dobson was having a disagreement with his boss when he suddenly became extremely anxious and felt a sense of impending, unavoidable doom. His heart beat rapidly, he was short of breath, became faint and dizzy, and felt as if he might die. Mr. Dobson was experiencing:

a. phobic disorder. c. generalized anxiety disorder.
b. panic disorder. d. obsessive-compulsive disorder.

4. "The kinds of stresses and conflicts that people experience in their daily interactions with others can promote and maintain abnormal behaviour." This statement is consistent with the _____ model of abnormality.

a. sociocultural c. humanistic
b. behavioural d. psychoanalytic

5. The psychiatrist listened patiently as his client revealed a series of episodes involving irrational fears of snakes. The psychiatrist probably labeled the client's symptoms as:

a. schizophrenic reactions. c. organic reactions.
b. phobic reactions. d. obsessive-compulsive reactions.

6. Scott is terrified to ride in an elevator in any building. He is especially bothered by the small, confined space and the fact that he is "trapped" until the elevator doors open. Usually, he avoids this unpleasantness by refusing to ride in elevators. Scott is experiencing _____ disorder.

a. phobic c. obsessive-compulsive
b. panic d. tension

7. The lawyer for a large, prosperous, law practice finds that two or three hours before an important appearance in court, he cannot talk. The firm's doctor cannot find any medical reason for the lawyer's problem. The doctor is also surprised that the lawyer seems unconcerned. If the lawyer's symptoms are the result of a psychological disorder, it would most likely be diagnosed as _____ disorder.

a. somatoform c. panic
b. conversion d. obsessive-compulsive

8. Marlane has been very tense and anxious during her professors' lectures and it is causing her to have a difficult time at college. She has been much better lately because she distracts herself by counting the number of times her professors say "the" during their lectures. Marlane's "counting" suggests she is experiencing _____ disorder.

a. panic c. obsessive-compulsive
b. phobic d. generalized anxiety

9. What is the most frequent type of mental disorder in Canada after neurotic and personality disorders?

a. bipolar disorder c. paranoid schizophrenia
b. obsessive-compulsive disorder d. alcohol and drug dependence

10. What is one difference between dissociative fugue and dissociative amnesia?

a. In fugue, memory can be restored with drugs.

b. In amnesia, the memory loss is temporary.

    c.   In fugue, past memory is eventually regained.

    d.   In amnesia, the memories are physically lost.

11.   According to your text, process schizophrenia is different from reactive schizophrenia because with reactive schizophrenia, the patient:

    a.   experiences a sudden and conspicuous onset of symptoms.

    b.   is less withdrawn.

    c.   may be dangerously aggressive and abusive to others.

    d.   is less likely to have a hereditary basis for the disorder.

12.   When minor symptoms of schizophrenia follow a severe case or episode, the disorder is called:

    a.   disorganized schizophrenia.   c.   paranoid schizophrenia.

    b.   catatonic schizophrenia.   d.   residual schizophrenia.

13.   According to the text, personality disorder is best characterized by:

    a.   firmly held beliefs with little basis in reality.

    b.   a mixture of symptoms of schizophrenia.

    c.   a set of inflexible, maladaptive traits.

    d.   an extended sense of euphoria and elation.

14.   Tanisha is uncooperative, refuses to speak to her coworkers, and frequently disrupts meetings with distracting questions and irrelevant challenges. However, she is fully capable of doing all her work assignments and maintains a reasonable family life. She will use her status as a female to threaten her superiors with "harassment" if they question what she is doing, and she will exploit anyone who is unwitting enough to be caught in one of her self-promotion schemes. Since she believes that she can do whatever she can get away with doing, which of the following categories best fits her?

    a.   sociopathic personality disorder   c.   premenstrual dysphoric disorder

    b.   self-defeating personality disorder   d.   dissociative identity disorder

_____ 15.   personality disorder   a.   Characterized by a set of inflexible, maladaptive traits that keep a person from functioning properly in society.

_____ 16.   antisocial or sociopathic personality disorder   b.   Inability to develop a secure sense of self.

_____ 17.   narcissistic personality disorder   c.   Characterized by an exaggerated sense of self and an inability to experience empathy for others.

_____ 18.   borderline personality disorder   d.   Individuals display no regard for moral and ethical rules or for the rights of others.

19.   The _____ perspective suggests that when an individual displays symptoms of abnormal behaviour, the cause will be found in a medical exam.

20.   Big Joe feels apprehensive or tense every time he has to speak publicly; he is experiencing _____.

21. People with _____ may in extreme causes be unable to leave their homes.

22. The term _____ is sometimes used to describe the last memories of dissociative amnesia.

23. The psychologist _____ has proposed that faulty cognitions underlie people's depressed feelings.

24. Describe the types of schizophrenia, their symptoms, and their causes. Compare the differing theories concerning the causes of schizophrenia.

Spotlight on Terminology and Language—
Cultural Idioms

Normal Versus Abnormal: Making the Distinction

Page 398 "Behaviour would then be evaluated in terms of **gradations**, ranging from completely normal functioning to extremely abnormal behaviour."

Gradations are a series of gradual, successive stages.
Page 398 "Contemporary approaches take a more **enlightened** view."

An **enlightened** view uses knowledge based on theoretical perspectives to understand psychological disorders.

Page 399 "Freud believed that children pass through a series of stages in which sexual and aggressive impulses take different forms and produce conflicts that require **resolution**—and that if these childhood conflicts are not dealt with successfully, they remain unresolved in the unconscious and eventually bring about abnormal behaviour during adulthood."

When a conflict requires **resolution**, a solution must be reached and the conflict must be solved. **Resolution** of the childhood conflicts identified by the psychoanalytic approach allow children to progress satisfactorily to the next psychosexual stage.

Page 400 "To understand the roots of people's disordered behaviour, the psychoanalytic perspective **scrutinizes** their early life history."

When you **scrutinize** something, you inspect and observe it carefully and critically.
Page 386 "The behavioural perspective is the most **precise** and objective approach for examining behavioural displays of particular disorders."

Precise means clearly stated and described.

Page 400 "A primary goal of treatment using the cognitive perspective is to **explicitly** teach new, more adaptive ways of thinking."

When you **explicitly** teach, you express yourself without vagueness or ambiguity. Your knowledge is shared in a clearly formulated and specific manner.

Page 400 "Suppose that whenever she takes an exam, a student forms the **erroneous** cognition 'Doing well on this exam is crucial to my entire future.'"

Erroneous is something that is mistaken. This cognitive thought is based on unrealistic thinking.

Page 400 "The humanistic perspective—growing out of the work of Rogers and Maslow—

concentrates on what is uniquely human, viewing people as basically **rational**, oriented toward a social world, and motivated to seek self-actualization."

When someone is **rational**, they have the ability to reason. **Self-actualization** is our inherent tendency to reach our true potentials.

Page 401 "Alternative explanations **abound** for the association between abnormal behaviour and social factors. For example, men may be less likely than likely than women, and poorer people might be less likely than wealthier, to seek help. **Abound** means to be plentiful in number. Many explanations can be used to suggest reasons for the association between abnormal behaviour and social dynamics.

Page 403 "Aside from these misrepresentations, everything else they did and said was their true behaviour, including the responses they gave during extensive admission interviews and answers to the **battery** of tests they were asked to complete."

A **battery** of tests is a group or series of tests especially of intelligence or personality given to a subject as an aid in psychological analysis.

Page 403 "We might assume that Rosenhan and his colleagues would be quickly discovered as the **impostors** they were, but they were not."

An **impostor** is someone who is not what they claim to be. In this study, the individuals were not ill patients, just **impostors**.

Page 403 "Even when they were discharged, most of the 'patients' left with the label schizophrenia—in **remission**, implying that the abnormal behaviour had only temporarily

subsided and could recur at any time. Most disturbing of all, none of the pseudo patients was identified by the staff of the hospitals as an impostor—although some of the real patients figured out the **ruse**."

When disease symptoms are in **remission**, they have diminished and perhaps abated. A **ruse** is an action intended to mislead or confuse.

Page 405 "Keep in mind that the chapter will present psychological disorders in a **dispassionate** and **clinical** way."

When we discuss a topic **dispassionately**, we discuss it in an objective fashion. To be **dispassionate** is to be unaffected by passion, bias, or emotion. The term **clinical** in this context suggests that the chapter will focus on the disorders in terms of how the patients or clients are actually affected after the different theories, suggestions and research on these disorders have been taken into consideration and evaluated in a scientifically detached and objective manner.

Page 405 "All of us, at one time or another, experience anxiety, a feeling of **apprehension** or tension, in reaction to stressful situations."

Apprehension is a dread of the future, an uneasy anticipation of what is coming.

Page 406 "Unlike phobias, which are brought about by specific objects or situations, panic disorders are not **triggered** by any identifiable stimulus."

A **trigger** is an event that precipitates other events.

■ CHAPTER 12: ANSWER KEY

GUIDED REVIEW

Section 1:	Section 2:	Section 3:	Section 4:
[a] medical model	[a] anxiety disorder.	[a] mood disorders	[a] psychoactive
[b] psychoanalytic	[b] Generalized anxiety	[b] Major depression	substance-use
model	disorder	[c] Mania	disorder
[c] behavioural model	[c] Panic disorder	[d] bipolar disorder	[b] sexual disorders
[d] cognitive model	[d] panic attacks	[e] learned helplessness	[c] organic mental
[e] humanistic model	[e] Phobic disorder	[f] Schizophrenia	disorders
[f] sociocultural model	[f] phobia	[g] hallucinations	
[g] *Diagnostic and*	[g] Obsessive-compulsive	[h] process schizophrenia	Evaluate
Statistical Manual of	disorder	[i] reactive schizophrenia	1. c
Mental Disorders, Fourth	[h] Obsessions	[j] Negative symptom	2. d
Edition (DSM-IV)	[i] Compulsions	[k] positive symptom	3. a
	[j] Hypochondriasis	[l] dopamine hypothesis	4. e
Evaluate	[k] somatoform disorders		5. b
1. d	[l] conversion disorder	Evaluate	
2. a	[m] Dissociative	1. d	
3. e	disorders	2. e	
4. c	[n] Dissociative identity	3. a	
5. f	disorder	4. c	
6. b	[o] Dissociative amnesia	5. b	
	[p] Dissociative fugue		
	Evaluate		
	1. c		
	2. e		
	3. b		
	4. d		
	5. a		

Selected Rethink Answers
1. Proponents of each perspective on the topic of shoplifting:
   Medical—might view shoplifting as arising from organic, physiological conditions.
   Psychoanalytic—would view shoplifting as a conflict in the unconscious and the adequacy of ego development.
   Cognitive—would focus on the irrational conscious thoughts that preceded the shoplifting.
   Humanistic—would suggest that the individual take control and responsibility for the shoplifting.
   Sociocultural—shoplifting was the result of sociocultural forces such as income or a broken home.

3. Cultural factors that contribute to the rate of anxiety disorders:
   lack of nuclear families close by, increases stress
   changing environment, fast-paced society causes stress
   in diverse cultures stress is created; members attempt to assimilate in another culture.
   Perspectives on psychological disorders best explain cultural contributions to anxiety. The behavioural perspective emphasizes environmental factors. These therapists consider anxiety a learned response to stress. The cognitive perspective focuses on peoples' maladaptive thoughts about the world.

6. People who have personality disorders have maladaptive personality traits that do not permit them to function appropriately as members of society. They have no regard for the moral and ethical rules of society or the rights of others. They are manipulative and deceptive; lack guilt or anxiety over wrong-doing; and are often impulsively distrustful and controlling; demanding, eccentric, obnoxious, or difficult.

Practise Test 1:

1.   b   obj. 5   p. 408
a.   Incorrect. This is a form of somatoform disorder.
*b.   Correct. Hypochondriacs suffer every ache as a major disease.
c.   Incorrect. This is the disorder in which psychological problems are manifest as physical systems.
d.   Incorrect. Phobic disorder is a fear of a specific event or stimulus.

2.   c   obj. 1   p. 397
a.   Incorrect. It probably was not different from how people would behave on average.
b.   Incorrect. Such behaviour is quite sane.
*c.   Correct. The ideal was for men to sacrifice themselves for their wives and children.
d.   Incorrect. Though many were probably uncomfortable after the fact, they were still alive.

3.   a   obj. 2   p. 399
*a.   Correct. The medical model views abnormal behaviour as arising from organic, physiological conditions.
b.   Incorrect. The psychoanalytic view of abnormality depends upon the extremes of conflict in the unconscious and the adequacy of ego development.
c.   Incorrect. The behavioural model of abnormality views abnormality as a result of inappropriate, learned behaviours.
d.   Incorrect. The sociocultural view of abnormality views abnormality as the result of sociocultural forces, often with the view that social systems are themselves abnormal.

4.   b   obj. 2   p. 399
a.   Incorrect. The humanistic view would understand abnormality as the self in conflict.
*b.   Correct. The medical approach seeks to understand abnormality as a result of organic, physiological causes.
c.   Incorrect. The psychoanalytic view of abnormality depends upon the extremes of conflict in the unconscious and the adequacy of ego development.
d.   Incorrect. The sociocultural view of abnormality views abnormality as the result of sociocultural forces, often with the view that social systems are themselves abnormal.

5.   b   obj. 2   p. 400
a.   Incorrect. The behavioural model utilizes a behavioural expert who can help modify behaviour.
*b.   Correct. The humanistic model views the client as the person capable of effecting a cure, the humanistic therapist is there to facilitate.
c.   Incorrect. The medical model depends upon a medical professional.

d.   Incorrect. The psychoanalytic model requires a trained psychoanalyst.

6.   a   obj. 2   p. 399
*a.   Correct. Psychodynamic views depend upon hidden or unconscious conflicts as the cause of most behaviour.
b.   Incorrect. The humanistic view would embrace the notion of "open" rather than hidden conflicts.
c.   Incorrect. The cognitive model would accept the idea of strange beliefs, but it would focus on the irrational conscious thoughts.
d.   Incorrect. The behavioural model would suggest that all the strange behaviours were learned.

7.   d   obj. 2   p. 401
a.   Incorrect. However, a behaviourist should be able to identify the system of rewards and punishments that contribute to these patterns.
b.   Incorrect. The psychoanalyst is unlikely to be concerned with the socioeconomic status in which the conditions occur.
c.   Incorrect. The humanistic model would not be interested in the socioeconomic conditions in which the abnormality occurs.
*d.   Correct. The sociocultural model emphasizes the contributions made by social and economic factors such as income and broken homes.

8.   c   obj. 3   p. 402
a.   Incorrect. Try 200.
b.   Incorrect. Try 200.
*c.   Correct. The 200 categories suggest an increasing attention to differentiating a. wide range of diseases.
d.   Incorrect. Try 200.

9.   c   obj. 4   p. 405
a.   Incorrect. A psychosomatic disorder involves a physical symptom with no apparent physical cause.
b.   Incorrect. A personality disorder involves a long-standing, habitual, and maladaptive personality pattern.
*c.   Correct. This describes an anxiety disorder.
d.   Incorrect. The term "neurotic disorder" is no longer used.

10.   d   obj. 6   p. 408
a.   Incorrect. Schizophrenia involves disordered thought, not multiple personalities.
b.   Incorrect. Not quite sure what this is, but Sybil did not have it.
c.   Incorrect. This is not an official diagnostic category.
*d.   Correct. Once called "multiple personality," this problem is increasingly common.

11.   b   obj. 4   p. 406
a.   Incorrect. In obsessive-compulsive disorder, the sufferer has uncontrollable thoughts and compulsions to act.

*b. Correct. The panic attack can be without warning and without apparent cause.
c. Incorrect. A personality disorder involves a long-standing, habitual, and maladaptive personality pattern.
d. Incorrect. A generalized anxiety disorder involves long-standing, consistent anxiety without an apparent cause or source.

12. b   obj. 6   p. 410
a. Incorrect. A dissociative identity disorder is marked by the presence of two or more personalities, not the dissociative fugue described.
*b. Correct. In dissociative fugue, the individual disappears, often just wondering off, and later reappears, often without any knowledge of why he or she left.
c. Incorrect. Someone suffering hypochondriasis has symptoms without physical illness.
d. Incorrect. Panic attack is marked by feelings of impending doom or even death paired with sudden and overwhelming bodily reactions.

13. b   obj. 7   p. 412
a. Incorrect. Or maybe, alternating fears of penguins and polar bears?
*b. Correct. The "bipolar" aspect is the swing from the high mood of mania to the depths of depression.
c. Incorrect. The "bipolar" aspect is the swing from the high mood of mania to the depths of depression, not between aspects of the personality.
d. Incorrect. The "bipolar" aspect is the swing from the high mood of mania to the depths of depression, not between panic and phobia.

14. c   obj. 8   p. 416
a. Incorrect. Paranoid schizophrenia is characterized by delusions of persecution or grandeur.
b. Incorrect. Catatonic schizophrenia is characterized by waxy flexibility and autistic withdrawal.
*c. Correct. This statement describes process schizophrenia.
d. Incorrect. Reactive schizophrenia usually has a quicker onset and has a better prognosis than the process schizophrenia described in the item.

15. c   obj. 8   p. 415
a. Incorrect. A compulsion is an idea that seems to have a life of its own—the sufferer gets up every night to hide the remote.
b. Incorrect. The hallucination is just seeing Bigfoot.
*c. Correct. Very delusional. Everyone knows Bigfoot belongs in garages.
d. Incorrect. Only if you are Bigfoot.

16. c   obj. 6   p. 410
17. e   obj. 4   p. 405
18. b   obj. 7   p. 411
19. d   obj. 7   p. 411
20. a   obj. 7   p. 412

21. Hypochondriasis   obj. 5   p. 408
22. Rosanhan obj. 3   p. 388
23. phobia   obj. 4   p. 391
24. generalized anxiety disorder   obj. 4   p. 392
25. mania   obj. 7   p. 397

26.
- The Rosenhan study suggests that mental health workers label their clients with rather unshakable labels. The labels also lead to interpretations of behaviour that continue to confirm the diagnosis (note that some stayed for many weeks even though they only complained of the symptom once on admission to the hospital).
- The issues of deception and the use of subjects who had not given their consent are major issues.
- A brief examination of the study does not explain the contexts involved: few people voluntarily walk into a mental hospital and complain of a major symptom. The sudden disappearance of the symptom could be considered abnormal as well.

Practise Test 2:
1. d   obj. 2   p. 399
a. Incorrect. Centuries ago, maybe.
b. Incorrect. Rogers never intended this to be a meaning of his concept.
c. Incorrect. The person may have bizarre behaviour as well.
*d. Correct. The notion of psychological disorders being an "illness" suggests the medical view.

2. b   obj. 4   pp. 405,406
a. Incorrect. Panic is probably the more intense.
*b. Correct. Panic involves symptoms that last for a brief period and then disappear until the next incident.
c. Incorrect. Generalized anxiety disorder is not caused by alcohol.
d. Incorrect. Panic disorder is not schizophrenic, though persons suffering from schizophrenia may experience panic.

3. a   obj. 2   p. 399
*a. Correct. If disease is organic and physiological, then abnormal behaviours are beyond the individual's control.
b. Incorrect. The sociocultural model would accept that the individual has control over his or her actions, even though those actions may be present due in part to sociocultural forces.
c. Incorrect. The behavioural model allows for the individual to take control of his or her actions through behaviour modification and self-regulation.
d. Incorrect. The humanistic model suggests that ultimately the individual must take control and responsibility for his or her actions.

4. c   obj. 2   p. 399

a. Incorrect. This explanation is more consistent with a cognitive model.
b. Incorrect. This explanation is more consistent with the medical model.
*c. Correct. Unresolved childhood conflicts would be repressed in the unconscious, and their efforts to be expressed and the costs of keeping them repressed can lead to abnormalities.
d. Incorrect. The unconscious is confused and confusing for both healthy and psychologically disturbed individuals.

5. d   obj. 2   p. 400
a. Incorrect. The medical model is currently focused on treatment through medication, and the only role the patient has is to take the drugs.
b. Incorrect. The psychoanalyst directs the patient toward an understanding of the problem.
c. Incorrect. The behavioural model depends upon the application of different reward systems to alter the problem.
*d. Correct. The humanistic model views the patient as capable of self-healing and control and responsibility over his or her own actions.

6. a   obj. 2   p. 401
*a. Correct. Some proponents of the sociocultural model claim that it is the society that is sick, not the individual.
b. Incorrect. See answer a.
c. Incorrect. See answer a.
d. Incorrect. See answer a.

7. c   obj. 3   p. 402
a. Incorrect. Treatment is not part of the manual.
b. Incorrect. The causes of abnormality are identified with specific theories, so they have not been addressed in the manual.
*c. Correct. The purpose of the manual is classification and description without implied theories.
d. Incorrect. The manual does not offer treatment.

8. c   obj. 3   p. 403
a. Incorrect. While this may be true in some cases, it is not the conclusion of the Rosenhan study.
b. Incorrect. This may be true, but it was not addressed by the Rosenhan study.
*c. Correct. Labeling carries a stigma that is difficult to erase.
d. Incorrect. The *DSM-IV* categories have little to do with stability and change.

9. b   obj. 3   p. 402
a. Incorrect. Some prefer a continuum approach and are critical of the category approach.
*b. Correct. The manual is updated with greater frequency, and the update is highly sensitive to changing views of society about mental disorders.

c. Incorrect. This is a common complaint, especially among psychologists who prefer a less medical orientation.
d. Incorrect. Often, the diagnosis is viewed as if it provided an analysis of the cause of a disorder.

10. d   obj. 6   p. 408
a. Incorrect. The anxiety that gives rise to them is environmental, but the cause of the illness remains open.
b. Incorrect. Not so.
c. Incorrect. They are equal opportunity disorders.
*d. Correct. They all have some form of escape from anxiety.

11. a   obj. 5   p. 408
*a. Correct. These include hypochondriasis and conversion disorders.
b. Incorrect. The stem describes a psychological disorder known as somatoform disorder, and not all psychological disorders have these symptoms.
c. Incorrect. A disorder related to the study of psychophysics?
d. Incorrect. No such disorder has been recognized.

12. d   obj. 6   p. 408
a. Incorrect. Depressive disorders include major and minor depression.
b. Incorrect. Schizophrenia does not share these disorders with the dissociative category.
c. Incorrect. Somatoform disorders involve a physical symptom without a physical cause, not the dissociation of part of the personality.
*d. Correct. Each of these disorders involves the separation of some part of the personality or memory.

13. c   obj. 7   p. 411
a. Incorrect. Bipolar disorders appear in men and women.
b. Incorrect. Both can have either origin.
*c. Correct. In mania, the state remains high pitched all the time.
d. Incorrect. Both are mood disorders.

14. c   obj. 9   p. 404
a. Incorrect. They feel stress and anxiety to the same extent that normal individuals experience stress and anxiety.
b. Incorrect. A rare sociopath has bothered to study the *DSM IV.*
*c. Correct. Guilt or remorse are necessary to trigger the physiological reaction that the polygraph measures.
d. Incorrect. They are quite in touch with reality, mentally at least. However, not in terms of emotions of guilt or remorse for their wrongdoings.

15. a   obj. 8   p. 415

*a. Correct. Some people with schizophrenia have their own private language.
b. Incorrect. People with dissociative identity disorder appear quite normal on the surface.
c. Incorrect. The fugue state results in wandering off, not incoherence.
d. Incorrect. Depressive individuals can become incoherent, but not because of unconventional language use.

16. e   obj. 7   p. 413
17. c   obj. 8   p. 416
18. b   obj. 8   p. 416
19. d   obj. 8   p. 416
20. a   obj. 8   p. 416
21. dissociative disorders   obj. 6   p. 408
22. *DSM-IV*   obj. 3   p. 403
23. Panic attacks   obj. 4   p. 406
24. dissociative identity disorder   obj. 6   p. 408
25. psychoanalytic   obj. 7   pp. 412-413

26. Schizophrenia has both biological and environmental origins.
  Being more common in families suggests genetic factors seem to be involved.
  Biochemical or structural abnormality (dopamine hypothesis) or exposure to a virus during pregnancy are suggested causes.
  Regression to earlier experiences and stages; lack of strong ego, id acts with no concern for reality—inability to cope
  Another theory suggests high levels of expressed emotion.
  Genetic factors may become evident in twins reared apart if genetic factors held when environments changed.
  Different family lifestyles may indicate certain factors that precipitate the condition in twins who have been identified with genetic factors that predispose them to schizophrenia.

Practise Test 3:
1. b   obj. 8   p. 4081
a. Incorrect. This is one of the major symptoms.
*b. Correct. Dissociative identity disorder, also known as multiple personality disorder, is not associated with schizophrenia.
c. Incorrect. This is a common symptom of schizophrenia.
d. Incorrect. This is a common symptom of schizophrenia.

2. c   obj. 2   p. 401
a. Incorrect. This statement is consistent with the sociocultural model.
b. Incorrect. This statement is consistent with the sociocultural model.
*c. Correct. The sociocultural model recognizes that many aspects of abnormal behaviour arise from the

conditions of society, even psychic forces within the individual would reflect conflicts in society.
d. Incorrect. This statement is consistent with the sociocultural model.

3. b   obj. 4   p. 406
a. Incorrect. A phobic disorder is an irrational fear of a specific situation or object.
*b. Correct. This describes a panic attack.
c. Incorrect. Generalized anxiety disorder is very similar to this condition, but it occurs without the rapid heartbeat, shortness of breath, and becoming faint (that is, without the panic).
d. Incorrect. Obsessive-compulsive disorder is marked by uncontrollable thoughts and compulsions to carry out ritualistic behaviours, not by panic.

4. a   obj. 2   p. 401
*a. Correct. The sociocultural model of abnormality emphasizes the interactions between people as well as the conditions of society as contributors to abnormal behaviour.
b. Incorrect. The behavioural model would attribute abnormal behaviour to faulty learning.
c. Incorrect. The humanistic model would attribute abnormal behaviour to conflicts within the self.
d. Incorrect. The psychoanalytic model would attribute abnormal behaviour to inner psychic conflicts.

5. b   obj. 4   p. 405
a. Incorrect. It is possible for someone with schizophrenia to have irrational fears of snakes, but this kind of fear is more likely a phobia.
*b. Correct. A phobia is a persistent, irrational fear of an object or situation.
c. Incorrect. While the psychiatrist is more prone to using a medical model, the term "organic reactions" is not used to describe any known ailment.
d. Incorrect. Obsessive-compulsive disorder is marked by uncontrollable thoughts and compulsions to carry out ritualistic behaviours, not by panic.

6. a   obj. 4   p. 405
*a. Correct. A phobia is a persistent, irrational fear of an object or situation.
b. Incorrect. Panic disorder involves extreme anxiety and a sense of impending, unavoidable doom accompanied by rapid heartbeat, shortness of breath, and becoming faint and dizzy.
c. Incorrect. Obsessive-compulsive disorder is marked by uncontrollable thoughts and compulsions to carry out ritualistic behaviours, not by panic.
d. Incorrect. There is no category called tension disorder.

7. b   obj. 5   p. 408
a. Incorrect. This falls in the class of somatoform disorders, but another choice offers the specific disorder.
*b. Correct. In a conversion disorder, psychological problems are converted into physical problems, often

without the sufferer showing the concern one might expect if the situation were a truly serious physical condition.

c. Incorrect. Panic disorder involves extreme anxiety and a sense of impending, unavoidable doom accompanied by rapid heartbeat, shortness of breath, and becoming faint and dizzy.

d. Incorrect. Obsessive-compulsive disorder is marked by uncontrollable thoughts and compulsions to carry out ritualistic behaviours, not by loss of voice.

8. c   obj. 4   p. 406

a. Incorrect. Panic disorder involves extreme anxiety and a sense of impending, unavoidable doom accompanied by rapid heartbeat, shortness of breath, and becoming faint and dizzy.

b. Incorrect. A phobia is a persistent, irrational fear of an object or situation.

*c. Correct. Obsessive-compulsive disorder is marked by uncontrollable thoughts and compulsions to carry out ritualistic behaviours, like counting the number of times the professor says "the" in the lecture.

d. Incorrect. Generalized anxiety is the feeling that something bad is about to happen without any direct object causing the fear or anxiety.

9. d   obj. 10   p. 421

a. Incorrect.

b. Incorrect.

c. Incorrect.

*d. Correct. Among the patients hospitalized for mental disorders each year, as many as 8 percent suffer from alcohol dependence; 10 percent suffer from neurotic and personality disorders, and 15 percent suffer from schizophrenic psychosis.

10. c   obj. 6   p. 410

a. Incorrect. Drugs are not typically used in this state, because the condition is not typically recognized until the memory is recovered.

b. Incorrect. In dissociative amnesia, the loss can be permanent.

*c. Correct. The fugue state helps the person escape an anxiety-producing situation, and sometime after the escape, memory can be recovered.

d. Incorrect. In dissociative amnesia, the memories are considered present, but psychologically blocked.

11. a   obj. 8   p. 416

*a. Correct. Reactive schizophrenia also has a better treatment outlook.

b. Incorrect. Though process schizophrenia is marked by gradual withdrawal, reactive schizophrenia can be just as withdrawn.

c. Incorrect. No type of schizophrenia is necessarily aggressive or abusive.

d. Incorrect. Neither type has been shown to be more hereditary than the other.

12. d   obj. 8   p. 415

a. Incorrect. Disorganized schizophrenia involves inappropriate laughter and giggling, silliness, incoherent speech, infantile behaviour, and strange behaviours.

b. Incorrect. Catatonic schizophrenia involves disturbances of movement, sometimes a loss of all motion, sometimes with the opposite extreme of wild, violent movement.

c. Incorrect. Paranoid schizophrenia is marked by delusions and hallucinations related to persecution or delusions of grandeur, loss of judgment, and unpredictable behaviour.

*d. Correct. Residual schizophrenia displays minor symptoms of schizophrenia after a stressful episode.

13. c   obj. 9   p. 419

a. Incorrect. This sounds like paranoia.

b. Incorrect. Personality disorder is not considered a mix of schizophrenic symptoms.

*c. Correct. Personality disorders are marked by inflexible, maladaptive personality traits, and these can take several forms.

d. Incorrect. An extended sense of euphoria and elation is found in the manic state of bipolar disorder.

14. a   obj. 9   p. 419

*a. Correct. Tanisha's apparent action without conscience and manipulation of the system are hallmarks of the antisocial or sociopathic personality disorder.

b. Incorrect. This does not describe someone who is self-defeating.

c. Incorrect. Since this is not cyclic behaviour, it could not be considered premenstrual dysphoric disorder.

d. Incorrect. While having multiple personalities is not ruled out, the condition is better described as sociopathic personality disorder.

15. a   obj. 9   p. 419
16. d   obj. 9   p. 419
17. c   obj. 9   p. 420
18. b   obj. 9   p. 404
19. medical   obj. 2   p. 399
20. anxiety   obj. 4   p. 405
21. agoraphobia   obj. 4   p. 406
22. repressed memories obj. 6   p. 408
23. Aaron Beck   obj. 7   p. 413

24.
- Describe the major symptoms of schizophrenia.
- Distinguish between process and reactive, and examine the list of types.
- Discuss the biological and psychological components.

Treatment of Psychological Disorders

13

Chapter Overview

In Chapter 13 the treatment of psychological disorders is discussed. The psychodynamic approach that seeks to resolve unconscious conflicts is presented, followed by the behavioural approaches that apply learning theory to therapy. Next, the humanistic approach focuses on issues related to the person's taking responsibility for his or her own actions regarding the meaning of life. This is followed by a presentation of the biological approaches to the treatment of psychological disorders. Drug therapy has made psychotic patients calmer, alleviated depression, and calmed anxiety. Also, the controversy surrounding electroconvulsive therapy and psychosurgery, controversial treatments of last resort, is presented. Finally, a discussion presents the issues that the community health movement now must cope with in providing care for deinstitutionalized patients. This movement has led to the development of such services as hotlines and campus crisis centres.

To further investigate the topics covered in this chapter, you can visit the related websites by visiting the following link: http://www.mcgrawhill.ca/college/feldman

Prologue: Dr. Norman Endler: Silence and Beyond
Looking Ahead

Section 1: Psychotherapy: Psychological Approaches to Treatment

Psychodynamic Approaches to Therapy
Behavioural Approaches to Therapy
Cognitive Approaches to Therapy

Applying Psychology in the 21st Century: Beating the Video Lottery Terminals (VLTs) Problem Gambling and its Treatment

Section 2: Psychotherapy: Psychological Approaches to Treatment (Continued)

Humanistic Approaches to Therapy
Group Therapy
Evaluating Psychotherapy: Does Therapy Work?

> **Pathways Through Psychology:** Janet Stoppard, Professor, Psychology Department, University of New

> **Exploring Diversity:** Clinical Practice and Training in a Multicultural Society

Section 3: Biomedical Therapy: Biological Approaches to Treatment

Drug Therapy
Electroconvulsive Therapy (ECT)
Psychosurgery
Biomedical Therapies in Perspective: Can Abnormal Behaviour be Cured?
Community Psychology: A Focus on Prevention

> **Becoming an Informed Consumer of Psychology:** Choosing the Right Therapist

Learning Objectives

These are the concepts and the learning objectives for Chapter 13. Read them carefully as part of your preliminary survey of the chapter.

Psychotherapy: Psychological Approaches to Treatment

1. Define psychotherapy and identify the main approaches/types. (p. 430)

2. Describe the psychodynamic approach to the treatment of abnormal behaviour, including the major techniques and concepts employed by psychodynamic therapists. (pp. 430–433)

3. Describe the behavioural approaches to the treatment of abnormal behaviour, including aversive conditioning, systematic desensitization, observational learning, and the use of

operant conditioning principles. (pp. 433–436)

4.   Discuss the cognitive therapy approaches of rational-emotive and cognitive therapy. (pp. 436–438)

5.   Describe the application of humanistic theory in the approaches of Rogers's client-centred therapy as well as gestalt therapy. (pp. 439–441)

6.   Describe group therapy, including family therapy. (pp. 441–442)

7.   Discuss the methods used to evaluate psychotherapy and the arguments proposed to support and dispute the effectiveness of psychotherapies, and explain the eclectic approach to psychotherapy. (pp. 442–444)

Biomedical Therapy: Biological Approaches to Treatment
8.   Name and describe drugs used in the treatment of abnormal behaviour, and discuss the problems and controversies surrounding their use. (pp. 447–450)

9.   Describe electroconvulsive therapy and psychosurgery, and discuss the effectiveness of biomedical therapies. (pp. 450–451)

10. Explain the concepts of community psychology and deinstitutionalization, and identify recommended guidelines for selecting a psychotherapist. (p. 451–452)

SECTION 1: Psychotherapy: Psychological Approaches to Treatment

Prepare

- *What are the goals of psychologically and biologically based approaches?*
- *What are the basic kinds of psychotherapies?*

Organize

- *Psychodynamic Approaches to Therapy*
- *Behavioural Approaches to Therapy*
- *Cognitive Approaches to Therapy*

Work

The common goal of therapy is to relieve psychological disorders and to enable individuals to achieve richer, more meaningful lives. Psychologically based therapy is called

[a] _____, a process in which a patient (client) and a professional work

together to deal with the patient's psychological difficulties. [b] _____
depends on drugs and other medical procedures. Many therapists today select from the large number of therapies available in order to fashion a unique approach best suited to a particular

client. This is called an [c] _____ to therapy.

[d] _____ is based on the assumption that the primary causes of abnormal behaviour are unresolved conflicts from the past and anxiety over unconscious impulses. The **[e]** _____ that individuals use to guard against anxiety do not protect the individual from these anxieties completely, and they emerge in the form of _neurotic symptoms_. Freud said that the way to deal with the unwanted desires and past conflicts was to confront them, to make them conscious. The role of the **[f]** _____ is then to explore the unconscious conflicts and help the patient understand them. Techniques such as **[g]** _____ and **[h]** _____ are used.

The principles of reinforcement are central to **[i]** _____, which suggest that both abnormal and normal behaviours are learned. To modify the abnormal behaviour, new behaviours must be learned. Behavioural psychologists are not interested in the past history of the individual, instead they focus on the current behaviour of the client.

Classical conditioning principles are applied to behaviours such as alcoholism, smoking, and drug abuse, with a technique known as aversive conditioning. In **[j]** _____, the unwanted behaviour is linked with a stimulus that produces an unpleasant response, for example, a drug that produces vomiting when mixed with alcohol. The long-term effectiveness of the approach is questionable. The most successful classical conditioning technique is called **[k]** _____, in which a person is taught to relax and is then gradually exposed to an anxiety-provoking stimulus. It has been successful with phobias, anxiety disorders, and impotence.

[l] _____ is used in therapy by **[m]** _____ appropriate behaviours. People can be taught skills and ways of handling anxiety by observing a model cope with the same situation.

Operant conditioning techniques are used in settings where rewards and punishments can be controlled. Behaviour therapy works well for phobias and compulsions; however, it is not very effective for deep depression or personality disorders. One example is that of the **[n]** _____, in which individuals are rewarded with tokens that can be exchanged for desired objects or opportunities.

Cognitive approaches to therapy attempt to change faulty cognitions held by patients about themselves and the world. The therapies are typically based on learning principles and thus are often called **[o]** _____. **[p]** _____ is one of the best examples of the cognitive approach. The therapist attempts to restructure the person's belief system into a more realistic, rational, and logical set of views.

Evaluate

_____ 1.   biomedical therapy

_____ 2.   psychodynamic therapy

_____ 3.   psychoanalysis

_____ 4.   behavioural treatment approaches

_____ 5.   cognitive approaches to therapy

a.   Basic sources of abnormal behaviour are unresolved past conflicts and anxiety.

b.   People's faulty cognitions about themselves and the world are changed to more accurate ones.

c.   Appropriate treatment consists of learning new behaviour or unlearning maladaptive behaviour.

d.   A form of psychodynamic therapy that often lasts for many years.

e.   Uses drugs and other medical procedures to improve psychological functioning.

Rethink

1.   In what ways are psychoanalysis and cognitive therapy similar, and how do they differ?

2.   How might you examine the reliability of dream interpretation?

SECTION 2:   Psychotherapy: Psychological Approaches to Treatment (Continued)

Prepare

- *What are humanistic approaches to treatment?*
- *How does group therapy differ from individual types of therapy?*
- *How effective is therapy, and which kind of therapy works best in a given situation?*

Organize

- *Humanistic Approaches to Therapy*
- *Group Therapy*
- *Evaluating Psychotherapy*

Work

  [a] _____ emphasizes the doctrine of self-responsibility as the basis for treatment. The rationale is that we control our own behaviour, make choices about how to live, and it is up to us to solve our problems. Humanistic therapists see themselves as guides or facilitators.

  [b] _____ refers to approaches that do not offer interpretations or answers to problems. First practised by Carl Rogers, [c] _____ was founded on the nondirective approach providing [d] _____. Rogers attempted to establish a warm and accepting environment in order to enable the client to make realistic and constructive choices about life.

The goal of **[e]** _____ is to help the client come to grips with freedom, to find his or her place in the world, and to develop a system of values that gives meaning to life. The therapist is more directive, and probes and challenges the client's views.

[f] _____ has the goal of integrating the client's thoughts and feelings into a whole. The approach was developed by Fritz Perls to increase perspectives on a situation. He asked the client to go back and work on unfinished business, playing the part of the angry father and taking other roles in a conflict.

[g] _____ is a form of treatment that has several unrelated people meet with a therapist at the same time. Problems, usually one held in common with all group members, are discussed with the group, while members of the group provide social support.

[h] _____ is a specialized form of group therapy that involves two or more members of a family. Therapists focus on the entire family system rather than only on the family member with the problem, and each family member is expected to contribute to the solution. Family therapists assume that family members engage in set patterns of behaviour, and the goal of therapy is to get the family to adopt more constructive behaviours.

Evaluate

_____ 1. rational-emotive therapy

_____ 2. cognitive therapy

_____ 3. client-centred therapy

_____ 4. humanistic therapy

_____ 5. existential therapy

a. Addresses the meaning of life, allowing a client to devise a system of values that gives purpose to his or her life.

b. The therapist reflects back the patient's statements in a way that helps the patient to find solutions.

c. People have control of their behaviour, can make choices about their lives, and are essentially responsible for solving their own problems.

d. Attempts to restructure one's belief into a more realistic, rational, and logical system.

e. People are taught to change illogical thoughts about themselves and the world.

Rethink

3. How can people be successfully treated in group therapy when individuals with the "same" problem are so different? What advantages might group therapy offer over individual therapy?

4. List some examples of behaviour that might be considered abnormal by members of one cultural or economic group and normal by members of a different cultural or economic group. Suppose that most therapies had been developed by psychologists from minority

culture groups and lower socioeconomic status; how might they differ from current therapies?

SECTION 3: Biomedical Therapy: Biological Approaches to Treatment

Prepare

- *How are drug, electroconvulsive, and psychosurgical techniques used today in the treatment of psychological disorders?*

Organize

- *Drug Therapy*
- *Electroconvulsive Therapy (ECT)*
- *Psychosurgery*
- *Biological Therapies in Perspective*
- *Community Psychology*

Work

Biomedical treatments that treat brain chemical imbalances and other neurological factors directly are regularly used for some problems. In **[a]** _____, drugs are given that alleviate symptoms for a number of psychological disturbances. In the mid-1950s,

[b] _____ were introduced, causing a major change in the treatment of patients in mental hospitals. These drugs alleviate symptoms related to the patient's loss of touch with reality, agitation, and overactivity.

[c] _____ are used to improve the moods of severely depressed patients. These drugs work by increasing the concentration of certain neurotransmitters.

[d] _____, a form of simple mineral salt, has been used to treat bipolar disorders. It ends manic episodes 70 percent of the time; though its success with depression is not as good.

[e] _____—Valium and Xanax—are the drugs most prescribed by physicians. These drugs reduce the anxiety level experienced by reducing excitability and increasing drowsiness.

Physicians in the 1930s found a way to induce convulsions using electric shocks. **[f]** _____ is administered by passing an electric current of 70 to 150 volts through the head of a patient. The patient is usually sedated and given muscle relaxants to prevent violent contractions. ECT is controversial because of its side effects, which include disorientation, confusion, and memory loss. But it continues to be used because it does help severely depressed patients when other treatments are ineffective.

[g] _____ is brain surgery used to alleviate psychological symptoms.

An early procedure was **[h]** _____, in which parts of the frontal lobes are removed or destroyed. The patients were then less subject to emotionality.

Evaluate

_____ 1. antipsychotic drugs

_____ 2. antidepressant drugs

_____ 3. antianxiety drugs

_____ 4. chlorpromazine

_____ 5. lithium

a. Temporarily alleviates symptoms such as agitation and overactivity.

b. Used in the treatment of schizophrenia.

c. Improves a patient's mood and feeling of well-being.

d. Used in the treatment of bipolar disorders.

e. Alleviate stress and feelings of apprehension.

Rethink

5. One of the main criticisms of biological therapies is that they treat the symptoms of mental disorder without uncovering and treating the underlying problems from which people are suffering. Do you agree with this criticism or not? Why?

6. If a dangerously violent person could be "cured" of violence through a new psychosurgical technique, would you approve the use of this technique? Suppose the person agreed to—or requested—the technique? What sort of policy would you develop for the use of psychosurgery?

Practise Questions

Test your knowledge of the chapter material by answering these questions. These questions have been placed in three Practise Tests. The first two tests are composed of questions that will test your recall of factual knowledge. The third test contains questions that are challenging and primarily test for conceptual knowledge and your ability to apply that knowledge. Check your answers and review the feedback using the Answer Key in the following pages of the *Study Guide*.

PRACTISE TEST 1:

1. Clients with psychological problems requiring some form of medical treatment are typically treated by a:
   a. psychiatric nurse.
   b. counseling psychologist.
   c. psychiatrist.
   d. clinical psychologist.

2. The category of therapy in which change is brought about through discussions and interactions between client and professional is called:
   a. eclectic therapy.
   b. semantic therapy
   c. psychotherapy.
   d. interpersonal therapy.

3. According to Freud, in order to protect our egos from the unwanted entry of unacceptable unconscious thoughts and desires, we all use:
    a. transference.
    b. aversive conditioning.
    c. systematic desensitization.
    d. defence mechanisms.

4. Which alternative below is not a term associated with psychodynamic therapy?
    a. hierarchy of fears
    b. neurotic symptoms
    c. defence mechanisms
    d. transference

5. Maura wants to reduce her anxiety and eliminate her phobia of "confined spaces". She could use a technique based on classical conditioning called:
    a. biofeedback.
    b. behaviour modification.
    c. systematic desensitization.
    d. aversive conditioning.

6. Which of the following approaches to therapy would be **least** concerned with the underlying causes of abnormal behaviour?
    a. psychoanalytic
    b. behavioural
    c. eclectic
    d. humanistic

7. In rational-emotive therapy, the goal of therapy is to restructure one's beliefs about oneself and the world into:
    a. a view that focuses on problems that arise only when events fail to turn out as expected.
    b. a realization that it is necessary for one to love and be approved by each significant person in one's life.
    c. a rational, realistic, and logical system.
    d. an understanding of the role of emotion in behaviour.

8. The approach that is the best known of the humanistic therapies and assumes at the outset that a person's troubles reflect unfulfilled potential is called:
    a. rational-emotive therapy.
    b. gestalt therapy.
    c. systematic desensitization.
    d. client-centred therapy.

9. Which therapies emphasize establishing inner rather than outer control of behaviour?
    a. psychodynamic and humanistic
    b. psychodynamic and behavioural
    c. rational-emotive and behavioural
    d. behavioural and humanistic

10. According to the text, the goal of client-centred therapy is to enable people to reach the potential for:
    a. getting in touch with reality.
    b. understanding the unconscious.
    c. taking control of their thoughts.
    d. self-actualization.

11. Spontaneous remission is:
    a. an attack, either verbal or physical, by the therapist against the client when provoked repeatedly.
    b. disappearance of psychological symptoms even without therapy.
    c. an emotional outburst by the client during the therapy session.
    d. behaviour by a family member (especially one's spouse) that worsens one's psychological symptoms.

12. Antipsychotic drugs alleviate psychotic symptoms by:
    a. increasing neurotransmitter function.

    b.   blocking the production of dopamine.

    c.   slowing down the autonomic nervous system.

    d.   sedating the patients.

13.   The most widely applied biological approach to treatment is:

    a.   psychosurgery.   c.   genetic engineering.

    b.   electroconvulsive therapy.   d.   drug therapy.

14.   Which medication would most likely be given to someone experiencing a manic episode?

    a.   lithium   c.   chlorpromazine

    b.   Valium   d.   Librium

15.   A procedure by which areas of the brain are removed or destroyed in order to control severe abnormal behaviours is called:

    a.   psychosurgery.   c.   electroconvulsive therapy.

    b.   shock therapy.   d.   personality therapy.

____ 16.   free association   a.   A patient's transfer of certain strong feelings for others to the analyst.

____ 17.   manifest content   b.   The "true" message hidden within dreams.

____ 18.   latent content   c.   The patient says everything that comes to mind, providing insights into the patient's unconscious.

____ 19.   resistance   d.   An inability or unwillingness to discuss or reveal particular memories, thoughts, or motivations.

____ 20.   transference

                                  e.   The surface description and interpretation of dreams.

21.   Freudian therapy is called _____.

22.   In treating phobias systematic desensitization uses a _____ of fears where a patient is exposed to less threatening stimuli at first.

23.   In Aaron Beck's _____ the therapist is less confrontive and more like a teacher.

24.   A technique used in psychotherapy during which the patient will say anything that comes to mind is _____.

25.   _____ requires a written agreement between the therapist and the patient that specifies goals to be reached and consequences of reaching goals.

26.   Describe the reasons why you think that psychotherapy works. Draw upon the principles of psychology that have been discussed in previous chapters, such as learning principles, theories of development, and theories of personality, to explain why you think it is effective.

PRACTISE TEST 2:

1. Biomedical therapies:
    a. are the most common therapies used by clinical psychologists.
    b. are reserved for the less severe types of behavioural disorders.
    c. presume that many disorders result from improper nutrition, food additives, or exposure to toxic environmental chemicals.
    d. use drugs, shocks, or surgery to improve the client's functions.

2. The eclectic approach to therapy:
    a. first fragments the personality and then reconstructs it.
    b. is controversial because of its connection to the paranormal world of psychic phenomena.
    c. mixes techniques of various theoretical perspectives.
    d. is based on the teachings of Horatio Eclectic, a Danish therapist who promoted meditation as a therapeutic technique.

3. The basic premise of psychodynamic therapy is the notion that abnormal behaviour is:
    a. repressing normal behaviours that need to be uncovered.
    b. the result of the ego repressing the superego.
    c. rooted in unresolved past conflicts, buried in the unconscious.
    d. the result of the ego failing to gain access to consciousness.

4. According to Freud, neurotic symptoms are caused by:
    a. defence mechanisms.   c. inappropriate choices.
    b. anxiety.   d. contingency contracting.

5. What phenomenon in psychoanalysis causes the patient remember the experiences of a past relationship?
    a. transcendence   c. translation
    b. transference   d. transrotation

6. What happens to the reaction to alcohol following aversive conditioning for alcoholism?
    a. The reaction takes on that response associated with the aversion.
    b. There is no longer a craving for the alcohol.
    c. There is a fear of the alcohol.
    d. The alcohol becomes a source of anxiety.

7. The emphasis in humanistic approaches to therapy is on:
    a. environmental control over actions.
    b. probing for unresolved hidden conflicts that arose long ago.
    c. discovering the unreasonableness of one's thoughts.
    d. personal choice and responsibility.

8. According to the text, in rational-emotive therapy, the therapist challenges the client's:
    a. defensive views of the world.   c. paranoid views of the world.
    b. self-centred views of the world.   d. irrational views of the world.

9. Which of the following approaches to treatment takes the view that it is primarily the responsibility of the client to make needed changes?
    a. behavioural therapy   c. humanistic therapy

b.   rational-emotive therapy   d.   psychoanalytic therapy

10. In humanistic therapy, unconditional positive regard is provided to the client:
   a.   as a reinforcement when goals have been met.
   b.   as part of the contingency contract.
   c.   no matter what the client says or does.
   d.   to help resolve inner conflicts.

11. According to the text, which of the following therapies is most closely associated with promoting the client's insights, the therapist's expressing acceptance and understanding regardless of the client's feelings or attitudes, and enabling people to reach their potential for self-actualization?
   a.   behavioural therapy   c.   humanistic therapy
   b.   rational-emotive therapy   d.   client-centred therapy

12. As compared with individual therapy, group therapy gives the client:
   a.   insight into his or her unconscious ideas.
   b.   automatically performed fresh new habits.
   c.   impressionistic feedback from others.
   d.   logically correct thinking, free from delusions.

13. According to the text, chlorpromazine is most commonly used in the treatment of:
   a.   mood disorders.   c.   schizophrenia.
   b.   anxiety disorders.   d.   bipolar disorder.

14. According to the text, which drug is used to help prevent future occurrences of the behavioural disorder that it is used to treat?
   a.   Valium   c.   chlorpromazine
   b.   lithium   d.   Librium

15. Antidepressant drugs improve the mood of depressed patients by:
   a.   increasing the activity of the autonomic nervous system.
   b.   suppressing the function of certain neurotransmitters.
   c.   increasing the speed of neural transmission.
   d.   increasing the concentration of certain neurotransmitters.

16. According to the text, which of the following types of treatment is rarely if ever still used?
   a.   electroconvulsive shock therapy   c.   psychotherapy
   b.   antipsychotic drugs   d.   psychosurgery

_____ 17.   aversive conditioning   a.   A person is rewarded for performing desired behaviours.

_____ 18.   systematic desensitization   b.   Breaks unwanted habits by associating the habits with very unpleasant stimuli.

_____ 19.   token system   c.   Requires a written contract between a therapist and a client that sets behavioural goals and rewards.

_____ 20.   contingency contracting   d.   A stimulus that evokes pleasant feelings is repeatedly paired with a stimulus that evokes anxiety.

21. In psychotherapy the term _____ is used when a patient has the inability to discuss or reveal particular memories or thoughts.

22. _____ is a phenomenon in which the relationship between the analyst and the patient becomes emotionally charged and the analyst takes on the role of significant others in the patient's past.

23. An acceptance by the therapist of the individual, without conditions, no matter what attitude is expressed by the client, is known as _____.

24. A method of getting clues from the unconscious used by psychoanalyists is

    _____.

25. Most therapists use a somewhat _____ to therapy, which provides a number of treatment techniques from which to select.

26. Describe the advantages and disadvantages of electroconvulsive therapy. Do you think that it should be banned from use? Explain your answer.

PRACTISE TEST 3: Conceptual, Applied, and Challenging Questions

1. Based on the descriptions in the text, if you were having trouble adjusting to the death of a friend, who would you be most likely to see?
   a. psychiatrist
   b. psychoanalyst
   c. psychiatric social worker
   d. counseling psychologist

2. Dr. Wague has clients explore their past by delving into the unconscious using dream interpretation and free association. Dr. Wague practises:
   a. existential therapy.
   b. cognitive therapy.
   c. behavioural therapy.
   d. psychodynamic therapy.

3. Ricardo is the director of guidance at a student mental-health clinic. He holds a degree appropriate to his position, so he must hold a doctorate or masters degree in:
   a. psychiatric social work.
   b. counseling psychology.
   c. clinical psychology.
   d. educational psychology.

4. Which problem below is least likely to be treated with aversive conditioning?
   a. substance (drug) abuse
   b. depression
   c. smoking
   d. alcoholism

5. _____ is the basis for behavioural approaches to therapy.
   a. Removing negative self-perception
   b. Emphasizing personal responsibilities
   c. Understanding the unconscious mind
   d. Training new habits

6. If a therapist asks you to act out some past conflict or difficulty in order to complete unfinished business, he or she most likely is using:
   a. behaviour therapy.
   b. existential therapy.
   c. rational-emotive therapy.
   d. gestalt therapy.

7. Lane, a 17-year-old client of Dr. Griswald, explains, "I was uncomfortable and didn't interview well for a job I wanted and I made a perfect fool of myself." In response, Dr. Griswald says, "Is it important for you to be perfectly competent in every area of your life?" Dr. Griswald is using:
   a. behavioural therapy.
   b. rational-emotive therapy.
   c. humanistic therapy.
   d. existential therapy.

8. Betty is in therapy with a psychotherapist to work through her feelings about her recent broken engagement. She is telling her therapist that she really didn't love her fiancé, and that she realized how different she and her fiancé are. Suddenly, her therapist says, "Betty, I heard the words that you just said, but they don't tell the same message that your facial expression and other nonverbal cues do. See if you can sense the differences." Betty's therapist is most likely:
   a. a gestalt therapist.
   b. a psychoanalytic therapist.
   c. a client-centred therapist.
   d. a behavioural therapist.

9. Generalizing from the discussion in the text, both humanistic and psychoanalytic approaches to therapy are more appropriate for clients who are:
   a. highly verbal.
   b. severely disordered.
   c. experiencing sexually related disorders.
   d. reluctant to converse with someone else.

10. Which of the following types of treatment appears actually to *cure* the disorder, so that when the treatment is discontinued the symptoms tend not to recur?
    a. antipsychotic drugs
    b. antidepressant drugs
    c. antianxiety drugs
    d. chlorpromazine

11. Melanie, after being assaulted, is nervous, overreacts to ordinary stimuli, and has trouble getting to sleep. Her psychiatrist prescribes a drug for her, which most likely is:
    a. an antianxiety drug.
    b. an antidepressant drug.
    c. an antipsychotic drug.
    d. an analgesic drug.

12. Today, electroconvulsive shock treatment (ECT) is usually reserved for severe cases of:
    a. mania.
    b. schizophrenia.
    c. depression.
    d. panic attack.

13. Electroconvulsive therapy (ECT):
    a. relieves the patient from severe depression.
    b. has been used since about 1910.
    c. is used in preference to drug therapy.
    d. can be administered by clinical psychologists.

14. Juan and his therapist spend much of their time discussing issues concerning personal responsibility, connectedness to others, and the question of finding meaning in life, and other concerns about the real meaning of human self-determination are discussed. Juan is working with:
    a. a behavioural therapist.
    b. a psychoanalyst.
    c. a humanistic therapist.
    d. a group therapist.

15. During a therapy session, Larry explores an image of his home that he had in a dream. The therapist asks him to say what the house feels, to express the unfinished business of the house. Larry's therapist is most likely:

    a. a psychoanalyst.   c. an existential therapist.

    b. a group therapist.   d. a gestalt therapist.

16. Bethany has prepared a list of experiences that run from the most frightening to the least frightening. She has prepared a _____, and her therapist is probably a _____.

    a. systematic desensitization; behavioural therapist

    b. hierarchy of fears; behavioural therapist

    c. systematic desensitization; humanistic therapist

    d. hierarchy of fears; humanistic therapist

____ 17. gestalt therapy   a. People discuss problems with others who have similar problems.

____ 18. group therapy   b. Movement aimed at preventing psychological disorders.

____ 19. family therapy   c. Attempts to integrate a client's thoughts, feelings, and behaviour into a whole.

____ 20. community psychology

                    d. Family as a unit to which each member contributes.

21. The _____ of dreams is the actual description of the dream itself.

22. In Eysenck's study on the effectiveness of psychotherapy, clients sometimes had symptoms go away without treatment, this was called _____.

23. The _____ of dreams is the message of the dream.

24. Former mental patients who return to the community in a process called _____ often do not get their needs met, and the goals of the program have not been met in most communities.

25. _____ have made it possible to end the use of brain surgery to alleviate psychological symptoms.

26. What are some of the things that the patient has to keep in mind when selecting and working with a therapist? What are the patients' responsibilities in therapy?

Spotlight on Terminology and Language—
Cultural Idioms

Page 430 "In fact, many therapists today use a variety of methods with a given person, in what is referred to as an **eclectic** approach to therapy. Assuming that psychological disorders are often the product of both psychological and biological processes, eclectic therapists will draw from several perspectives **simultaneously**, in an effort to address both the psychological and the biological aspects of a person's problems."

An **eclectic** approach is an approach to therapy in which the psychotherapist combines techniques and ideas from many different schools of thought. When something exists **simultaneously**, it occurs at the same time.

Page 431 "Patients are told to say aloud whatever

comes to mind, regardless of its apparent **irrelevance** or senselessness, and analysts attempt to recognize and label the connections between what is being said and the patient's unconscious."

When something is **irrelevant**, it doesn't seem to relate to the subject at hand.

Page 432 "**Transference** can be used by a therapist to help the patient recreate past relationships that were psychologically difficult."

In psychotherapy, **transference** is when a patient expresses strong emotions toward the therapist because the therapist substitutes for someone important in the patient's life.

Page 433 "Furthermore, patients who are less **articulate** might not do as well as those who are more verbal."

An **articulate** person is capable of speaking in clear, articulate language.

Page 433 "Psychodynamic treatment techniques have been **controversial** since Freud introduced them."

Treatment that is **controversial** is disputed, especially by the expression of opposing views.

Page 433 "One must depend on reports from the therapist or the patients themselves, reports that are obviously open to bias and **subjective** interpretation."

Subjective interpretation is produced by or results from an individual's personal state of mind. It exists only within the experiencer's mind and is incapable of external verification.

Page 434 "The basic procedure in **aversive** conditioning is relatively straightforward."

Causing avoidance of an unpleasant or punishing stimulus, as in techniques of behaviour modification, is **aversive**.

Page 434 "It is clear, though, that aversion therapy is an important procedure for eliminating **maladaptive** responses for some period of time—a **respite** that provides, even if only temporarily, the opportunity to encourage more adaptive behaviour patterns."

Maladaptive behaviour is characterized by faulty or inadequate adaptation. A **respite** is a usually short time of rest or relief.

Page 435 "**Systematic desensitization** has proved to be an effective treatment for a number of problems, including **phobias**, anxiety disorders, and even impotence and fear of sexual contact."

Systematic desensitization is a technique of behaviour therapy. Based on classical conditioning, a person is gradually and progressively exposed to anxiety evoking stimuli while practicing deep relaxation. A **phobia** is an anxiety disorder characterized by an intense and irrational fear that is out of all proportion to the danger elicited by the object or situation.

Page 435 "Behavioural approaches using **operant conditioning** techniques (which demonstrate the effects of rewards and punishments on future behaviour) are based on the notion that we should reward people for carrying out desirable behaviour and extinguish behaviour that we wish to eliminate, by either ignoring it or punishing it."

Operant conditioning is a kind of learning in which the consequences, either reward or punishment, that follow some behaviour increase or decrease the likelihood of that behaviour's occurrence in the future.

Page 436 "Behaviour therapy works particularly well for phobias and **compulsions**, for establishing control over impulses, and for learning complex social skills to replace maladaptive behaviour."

Compulsive behaviour is an irresistible impulse to act irrationally.

Page 440 "Rather, the assumption is that therapists need to communicate that they are caring, nonjudgmental, and **empathetic**—understanding of a client's emotional experience."

A person who has **empathy** can identify with and understand another person's feelings, situation, and motives.

Page 440 "The rationale for this treatment approach is the idea that people need to **integrate** their thoughts, feelings, and behaviours into a gestalt."

When you **integrate**, you organize a personality's traits and tendencies into a harmonious whole.

Page 451 "Each of the treatments that we have reviewed in this chapter has a common element: It is a 'restorative' treatment, aimed at **alleviating** psychological difficulties that already exist."

When you **alleviate**, you make an event less severe or more bearable.

Page 451 "The **influx** of former mental patients out of institutions and into the community—a process known as **deinstitutionalization**—further **spurred** the community psychology movement."

An **Influx** refers to something that is flowing into somewhere in a large quantity; for example, people, water, etc.

Deinstitutionalization means the release of mental patients from mental hospitals and their return to the community. When an activity, an animal, a person, an event, etc. is **spurred**, it is driven forward - urgently, forcefully; it is strongly encouraged.

■ CHAPTER 13: ANSWER KEY

GUIDED REVIEW

Section 1:	Evaluate	Section 2:	Section 3:
[a] psychotherapy	1. e	[a] Humanistic therapy	[a] drug therapy
[b] Biomedical therapy	2. a	[b] Nondirective counseling	[b] antipsychotic drugs
[c] eclectic approach	3. d	[c] client-centred therapy	[c] Antidepressant drugs
[d] Psychodynamic therapy	4. c	[d] unconditional positive regard	[d] Lithium
[e] defence mechanisms	5. b	[e] existential therapy	[e] Antianxiety drugs
[f] psychoanalyst		[f] Gestalt therapy	[f] Electroconvulsive therapy
[g] free association		[g] Group therapy	(ECT)
[h] dream interpretation		[h] Family therapy	[g] Psychosurgery
[i] behavioural treatment approaches			[h] prefrontal lobotomy
[j] aversive conditioning		Evaluate	
[k] systematic desensitization		1. d	Evaluate
[l] Observational learning		2. e	1. a
[m] modeling		3. b	2. c
[n] token system		4. c	3. e
[o] cognitive-behavioural approaches		5. a	4. b
[p] Rational-emotive therapy			5. d

Selected Rethink Answers

3.   Define group therapy. Because people are different and are dealing with similar issues they may be able to provide a variety of coping mechanisms to one of the group members and to develop empathy for others with similar problems.

5. Biological therapies do treat symptoms. For some illnesses the relief of the symptoms may be all that is required. Most successful therapies are a combination of the medical model with some type of therapy. When symptoms are somewhat relieved, a client may be better able to focus on the underlying problems associated with the illness.

Practise Test 1:

1. c   obj. 1   p. 431
a. Incorrect. A psychiatric nurse may provide some support in a nursing role, but the psychiatrist conducts the therapy in these cases.
b. Incorrect. A counseling psychologist is not involved in medical treatment.
*c. Correct. A psychiatrist is a medical doctor who administers medical treatment for psychological disorders.
d. Incorrect. A clinical psychologist does not administer medical treatments.

2. c   obj. 1   p. 430
a. Incorrect. Eclectic therapy may utilize approaches that do not involve discussions and interactions.
b. Incorrect. There is not a major therapy called semantic therapy.
*c. Correct. Psychotherapy specifically involves this kind of direct interaction and discussion between the client and the psychotherapist.
d. Incorrect. Also known as ITP, this approach does involve interaction, but psychotherapy is the larger category described by this item.

3. d   obj. 1   p. 430
a. Incorrect. Transference occurs in therapy, and it involves transferring emotional energy from other relationships into the therapy relationship.
b. Incorrect. Aversive conditioning utilizes behavioural techniques.
c. Incorrect. Systematic desensitization utilizes behavioural techniques.
*d. Correct. They are called defence mechanisms because they defend the ego from anxiety arising from unconscious conflicts.

4. a   obj. 2   pp. 430-433
*a. Correct. A hierarchy of fears is used in the behavioural technique known as systematic desensitization.
b. Incorrect. Neurotic symptoms, defence mechanisms, and transference are all psychodynamic concepts.
c. Incorrect. Neurotic symptoms, defence mechanisms, and transference are all psychodynamic concepts.
d. Incorrect. Neurotic symptoms, defence mechanisms, and transference are all psychodynamic concepts.

5. c   obj. 3   p. 433
a. Incorrect. Biofeedback uses signals from the body to help the person control physiological functions and achieve states of relaxation.
b. Incorrect. Behaviour modification includes classical and operant conditioning techniques to change undesirable behaviours.
*c. Correct. Systematic desensitization utilizes classical conditioning techniques by having the person imagine a hierarchy of fears and gradually become desensitized to the frightening stimuli.
d. Incorrect. Aversive conditioning uses both classical and operant principles to get the subject to avoid certain responses.

6. b   obj. 3   p. 433
a. Incorrect. The psychoanalytic approach is keyed to the problems caused by unconscious causes of abnormal behaviour.
*b. Correct. The behavioural approach is only concerned with the observable causes of behaviour, like the reinforcements or stimuli associated with learning.
c. Incorrect. An eclectic approach draws upon the most appropriate technique for the problem being treated.
d. Incorrect. The humanistic approach is concerned with how the individual views himself or herself, and this may include causes beyond the person's awareness.

7. c   obj. 4   p. 436
a. Incorrect. This may be a rational approach to problem solving, but it is not the approach of rational-emotive therapy.
b. Incorrect. Love and approval are not part of rational-emotive therapy.
*c. Correct. This is the goal of rational-emotive therapy.
d. Incorrect. This may be part of the theory behind rational-emotive therapy, but it is not the therapeutic goal.

8. d   obj. 5   p. 439
a. Incorrect. Rational-emotive therapy is a cognitive therapy, and thus it incorporates what the person thinks about themselves.
b. Incorrect. Gestalt therapy is a humanistic approach that requires the person to accept parts of himself or herself that he or she has denied or rejected.
c. Incorrect. Systematic desensitization utilizes classical conditioning techniques by having the person imagine a hierarchy of fears and gradually become desensitized to the frightening stimuli.
*d. Correct. Client-centred therapy assumes that the client has the potential to handle his or her own problems.

9. a   obj. 5   pp. 430, 435
*a. Correct. The psychodynamic approach focuses on control of unconscious impulses and the humanistic approach focuses on self-control and responsibility.
b. Incorrect. The behavioural approach is entirely focused on outer forces.
c. Incorrect. The behavioural approach is entirely focused on outer forces.

d.   Incorrect. The behavioural approach is entirely focused on outer forces.

10. d   obj. 5   p. 439
a.   Incorrect. All therapies involve, in one way or another, helping the client get in touch with reality.
b.   Incorrect. The psychoanalytic approach is focused upon understanding the unconscious.
c.   Incorrect. Cognitive therapies, like rational-emotive therapy, are focused upon the person taking control of his or her thoughts.
*d. Correct. Humanistic therapy strives to help the client achieve some form of self-actualization, or at least move toward realizing his or her potential.

11. b   obj. 7   p. 442
a.   Incorrect. This would be called unethical.
*b. Correct. Sometimes, simply allowing time to pass cures a psychological disorder.
c.   Incorrect. This may be a spontaneous emission, but not a remission.
d.   Incorrect. This is not remission.

12. b   obj. 8   p. 447
a.   Incorrect. Antipsychotic drugs block the production of dopamine.
*b. Correct. Unfortunately, this is not a cure for the problem.
c.   Incorrect. Antipsychotic drugs block the production of dopamine.
d.   Incorrect. Antipsychotic drugs block the production of dopamine; tranquilizers sedate the patient.

13. d   obj. 8   p. 447
a.   Incorrect. Psychosurgery has always been a method of last resort.
b.   Incorrect. ECT has become less common than it once was, but even in its heyday it was not the most common.
c.   Incorrect. Genetic engineering has not yet been applied to direct treatment of psychological disorders.
*d. Correct. Even general practitioners will prescribe psychoactive drug therapies.

14. a   obj. 8   p. 449
*a. Correct. How this mineral salt works remains a mystery.
b.   Incorrect. Valium is an antianxiety drug.
c.   Incorrect. Chlorpromazine is an antipsychotic drug.
d.   Incorrect. Librium is an antianxiety drug.

15. a   obj. 9   p. 450
*a. Correct. The original psychosurgery was the prefrontal lobotomy, where the frontal lobes are destroyed.
b.   Incorrect. Electroconvulsive therapy, also known as shock therapy, does not destroy any tissue.
c.   Incorrect. Electroconvulsive therapy, also known as shock therapy, does not destroy any tissue.
d.   Incorrect. There is not a group of therapies or an approach to therapy known as "personality" therapy.

16. c   obj. 2   p. 430
17. e   obj. 2   p. 431
18. b   obj. 2   p. 432
19. d   obj. 2   p. 432
20. a   obj. 2   p. 432
21. psychoanalysis obj. 2   p. 431
22. hierarchy   obj. 3   p. 434
23. cognitive therapy   obj. 4   p. 436
24. free association   obj. 2   p. 431
25. Contingency contracting obj. 3   p. 435

26.
▪   Identify the reasons you think psychotherapy works. These may include: psychotherapy offers a chance to reflect on life's problems in a safe environment, it offers a sense of control over one's problems, it provides a new way of coping with and understanding stress.
▪   Select at least two of the previously discussed concepts and describe their roles in depth.
▪   Remember, Eysenck's early study that suggested that psychotherapy was no more effective than being on a waiting list.

Practise Test 2:
1.   d   obj. 1   p. 430
a.   Incorrect. Clinical psychologists cannot prescribe drugs.
b.   Incorrect. Drug therapy is used for almost every disorder.
c.   Incorrect. This may be part of the view, but the predominant view is that the disorders are medical in nature.
*d. Correct. Biomedical therapy uses medical interventions.

2.   c   obj. 1 · p. 430
a.   Incorrect. That is not what eclectic means.
b.   Incorrect. It is not connected to the paranormal.
*c. Correct. The therapist chooses the technique best matched to the client's needs.
d.   Incorrect. It was actually his long-lost brother, Homer Simpson.

3.   c   obj. 1   p. 430
a.   Incorrect. In the psychoanalytic view, abnormal behaviours do not suppress normal behaviours.
b.   Incorrect. The ego does not repress the superego.
*c. Correct. The focus in psychodynamic therapy is on past, unresolved conflicts, often going back to childhood.
d.   Incorrect. The ego always has access to consciousness.

4.   b   obj. 2   p. 431
a.   Incorrect. Defence mechanism may play a role when they fail to protect the ego form anxiety.
*b. Correct. Anxiety is the main cause of neurotic symptoms, and the anxiety arises because of undesirable motives or repressed conflicts.
c.   Incorrect. Inappropriate choices would be the cause of symptoms as viewed by humanistic theory.

d. Incorrect. Contingency contracting might be found in behaviour therapy, but not as the cause for neurotic symptoms in Freud's view.

5. b   obj. 2   p. 418
a. Incorrect. Try transference.
*b. Correct. Transference brings the emotional energy of the past relationship into the current therapeutic relationship.
c. Incorrect. Try transference.
d. Incorrect. Try transference.

6. a   obj. 3   p. 433
*a. Correct. The response to alcohol after successful aversion therapy is to avoid alcohol because it is linked to the aversive stimulus.
b. Incorrect. The craving is probably still there.
c. Incorrect. No fear of alcohol should develop.
d. Incorrect. Properly undertaken, alcohol should not become a source of anxiety.

7. d   obj. 5   p. 439
a. Incorrect. This is the behavioural approach.
b. Incorrect. This is the psychodynamic approach.
c. Incorrect. This is the cognitive approach.
*d. Correct. Humanistic approaches focus on personal responsibility and self-healing.

8. d   obj. 4   p. 436
a. Incorrect. The views may be defensive, but those challenged are the irrational views held by the client.
b. Incorrect. The views may be self-centred, but those challenged are the irrational views held by the client.
c. Incorrect. The views may be paranoid, but those challenged are the irrational views held by the client.
*d. Correct. The therapist attempts to get the client to eliminate faulty ideas about the world and himself or herself.

9. c   obj. 5   p. 439
a. Incorrect. The therapist is primarily responsible for establishing a program of stimuli or reinforcement that will retrain the client in behavioural therapy.
b. Incorrect. The rational-emotive therapist attempts to get the client to eliminate faulty ideas about the world and himself or herself.
*c. Correct. Humanistic therapy attempts to help the client gain insight into his or her responsibility for the need to make changes.
d. Incorrect. The psychoanalytic approach seeks to understand the unconscious forces at work.

10. c   obj. 5   p. 440
a. Incorrect. Reinforcement would be used in behavioural therapy, not humanistic therapy.
b. Incorrect. A contingency contract is used in behavioural therapy, not humanistic therapy.

*c. Correct. Unconditional positive regard is the basis of any therapeutic relationship in the humanistic view.
d. Incorrect. The psychoanalytic approach is aimed more at inner conflicts.

11. d   obj. 5   p. 449
a. Incorrect. Behavioural therapy is not interested in the therapist's feelings and some unspecified actualization of the self..
b. Incorrect. Rational emotive therapy is focused upon changing the client's way of thinking about the world.
c. Incorrect. Humanistic therapy is focused upon helping the client take responsibility for his or her actions.
*d. Correct. This describes the goals of client-centred therapy, a type of humanistic therapy.

12. c   obj. 6   p. 426
a. Incorrect. Psychodynamic group therapy will focus on this aspect of the client.
b. Incorrect. This is not possible in any kind of therapy.
*c. Correct. Others in the group have had similar experiences, and the client learns that he or she is not alone.
d. Incorrect. Only in cognitive group therapy.

13. c   obj. 8   p. 441
a. Incorrect. Antidepressant drugs are used for many mood disorders.
b. Incorrect. Antianxiety drugs, like Valium and Xanax, are used for anxiety disorders.
*c. Correct. Chlorpromazine is an antipsychotic drug used to treat schizophrenia.
d. Incorrect. Lithium is used to treat the mania of bipolar disorders.

14. b   obj. 8   p. 449
a. Incorrect. Valium is an antianxiety drug without any preventive characteristics.
*b. Correct. Lithium is one of the few drugs that appears to provide a degree of cure.
c. Incorrect. Chlorpromazine does not cure schizophrenia or any of the other disorders it is used to treat.
d. Incorrect. Librium is an antianxiety drug without any preventive or curative characteristics.

15. d   obj. 8   p. 448
a. Incorrect. Antidepressants do not increase the activity of the autonomic system.
b. Incorrect. Antipsychotics decrease the production of dopamine, but antidepressants actually increase the concentrations of some neurotransmitters.
c. Incorrect. Drugs do not increase the speed of neural transmission.
*d. Correct. Antidepressants, like Prozac and tricyclic, increase the concentration of neurotransmitters.

16. d   obj. 9   p. 450

a.   Incorrect. Electroconvulsive shock therapy is commonly used today.
b.   Incorrect. Antipsychotic drugs continue to be relied upon by the medical community.
c.   Incorrect. Psychotherapy is very common.
*d. Correct. The use of psychosurgery, especially the lobotomy, is used less and less for treatment of psychological disorders.

17. b   obj. 3   p. 433
18. d   obj. 3   p. 433
19. a   obj. 3   p. 433
20. c   obj. 3   p. 435
21. resistance obj. 2   p. 432
22. Transference   obj. 2   p. 432
23. unconditional positive regard obj. 5   p. 440
24. dream interpretation obj. 2   p. 431
25. eclectic approach   obj. 7   p. 443

26.
 ▪   Describe your response to the idea of electrical shock being passed through your brain as a means of therapy. Would you want this to be done?
 ▪   What assumptions are made about the harm or benefit of using ECT? Do we assume that it must have some unseen long-term effect?

Practise Test 3:

1.   d   obj. 1   p. 431

a.   Incorrect. A psychiatrist would probably be inappropriate for this kind of short-term problem.
b.   Incorrect. A psychoanalyst would probably be inappropriate for this kind of short-term problem.
c.   Incorrect. A psychiatric social worker is trained to deal with other kinds of problems and would probably be inappropriate for this kind of short-term problem.
*d. Correct. A counseling psychologist is especially prepared for dealing with problems of adjustment such as this one.

2.   d   obj. 2   p. 430

a.   Incorrect. Some, but not all, existential therapists use psychodynamic techniques.
b.   Incorrect. Cognitive therapy would have the client explore conscious thoughts.
c.   Incorrect. Behavioural therapy would not have the client think much at all.
*d. Correct. Dream interpretation is a core technique for psychodynamic therapy.

3.   b   obj. 1   p. 431

a.   Incorrect. Someone with a degree in psychiatric social work would be more appropriately placed in a community health centre.
*b. Correct. This is the most appropriate degree for this kind of position.
c.   Incorrect. A clinical psychologist could hold this position, but a counseling degree would be more suitable.

d.   Incorrect. An educational psychologist would not be suitable for this position.

4.   b   obj. 3   p. 433

a.   Incorrect. Aversive conditioning works well with habits that are being broken, like drug habits, smoking, and alcoholism.
*b. Correct. Aversive conditioning works well with habits that are being broken, like drug habits, smoking, and alcoholism, but not with psychological problems like depression.
c.   Incorrect. Aversive conditioning works well with habits that are being broken, like drug habits, smoking, and alcoholism.
d.   Incorrect. Aversive conditioning works well with habits that are being broken, like drug habits, smoking, and alcoholism.

5.   d   obj. 3   p. 433

a.   Incorrect. Behaviourists are not that interested in self-perception.
b.   Incorrect. Humanistic approaches focus on personal responsibilities.
c.   Incorrect. Psychodynamic approaches focus on the unconscious mind.
*d. Correct. These new habits are meant to replace the old, malfunctioning ones.

6.   d   obj. 5   p. 440

a.   Incorrect. Behaviour therapy does not ask clients to act out past conflicts.
b.   Incorrect. Existential therapy is much more focused on the meaning of life than past conflicts.
c.   Incorrect. Rational-emotive therapy is focused more on the client's irrational ideas about the world.
*d. Correct. Gestalt therapy seeks to have the client integrate and "own" these conflicts to be able to resolve them for themselves.

7.   b   obj. 4   p. 436

a.   Incorrect. In behaviour therapy, other avenues would be explored, like the reinforcements that were being sought.
*b. Correct. In rational-emotive therapy, this expectation of perfection would be viewed as irrational and thus in need of being altered.
c.   Incorrect. In humanistic theory, the concern would be more about the issue of personal responsibility rather than thoughts about how others would view one.
d.   Incorrect. In existential therapy, Dr. Griswald might have asked Lane to consider what it means to be perfect in such an imperfect world.

8.   a   obj. 5   p. 440

*a. Correct. The gestalt therapist tries to integrate the nonverbal message with the verbal message and thus reduce Betty's conflict.
b.   Incorrect. A psychoanalytic therapist might be interested in the nonverbal cues as efforts of the unconscious to get a message across.

c. Incorrect. A client-centred therapist would attempt to mirror Betty's concerns back to her so she could hear what she was saying.
d. Incorrect. A behavioural therapist might suggest that there is something reinforcing about Betty's breaking the engagement that she is failing to recognize.

9. a obj. 5,7 pp. 441, 442
*a. Correct. These two approaches require much discussion and insight, so a verbal client will do well in these approaches.
b. Incorrect. Severely disordered patients should probably be treated with drugs and some psychotherapy.
c. Incorrect. People with sexual disorders would be best served if they sought a sex therapist.
d. Incorrect. People reluctant to converse with others would have difficulty talking to a psychoanalytic or humanistic therapist.

10. b obj. 8 p. 448
a. Incorrect. Antipsychotic drugs only suppress the symptoms.
*b. Correct. After taking a regimen of antidepressant drugs, depression tends not to return.
c. Incorrect. Antianxiety drugs suppress the response to anxiety, but they do not remove the cause of the anxiety.
d. Incorrect. Chlorpromazine is an antipsychotic drug and it suppresses psychotic symptoms, but they return if the drug is stopped.

11. a obj. 8 p. 449
*a. Correct. These are symptoms of anxiety.
b. Incorrect. She is not depressed.
c. Incorrect. She is not psychotic.
d. Incorrect. She does not need an aspirin.

12. c obj. 9 p. 450
a. Incorrect. ECT is used for severe depression when other treatments do not work.
b. Incorrect. ECT is used for severe depression when other treatments do not work.
*c. Correct. ECT is used for severe depression when other treatments do not work.
d. Incorrect. ECT is used for severe depression when other treatments do not work.

13. a obj. 9 p. 450
*a. Correct. It does seem to relieve depression.
b. Incorrect. It was introduced in the thirties.
c. Incorrect. Drug therapy is much preferred.
d. Incorrect. Clinical psychologists are not licensed to administer drugs or ECT.

14. c obj. 5 p. 439
a. Incorrect. These are not the concerns of a behavioural therapist.
b. Incorrect. These are not the concerns of a psychoanalyst.
*c. Correct. Humanistic psychotherapy is concerned with philosophical issues, such as finding meaning in life and self-actualization.
d. Incorrect. A group therapist would probably not bring these kinds of issues to a group.

15. d obj. 5 p. 440
a. Incorrect. A psychoanalyst would be interested in what the house symbolized for Larry, not the unfinished business it entails.
b. Incorrect. A group therapist would not likely be conducting individual dream therapy.
c. Incorrect. An existential therapist might be interested in the dream as it provides insight into the client's concerns about life and existence.
*d. Correct. The gestalt therapist attempts to get Larry to recognize and integrate the unfinished business that his dream home represents.

16. b obj. 3 p. 433
a. Incorrect. The procedure is called systematic desensitization, and the list is called a hierarchy of fears.
*b. Correct. This list is called a hierarchy of fears, and the behavioural approach is based on classical conditioning principles.
c. Incorrect. This would not be done by a humanistic therapist.
d. Incorrect. This would not be done by a humanistic therapist.

17. c obj. 5 p. 440
18. a obj. 6 p. 441
19. d obj. 6 p. 441
20. b obj. 10 p. 451
21. manifest content obj. 2 p. 431
22. spontaneous remission obj. 7 p. 442
23. latent content obj. 2 p. 432
24. deinstitutionalization obj. 10 p. 451
25. Biomedical therapies obj. 9 p. 451

26. Patients should
- make sure therapists have appropriate training, credentials, and licensing.
- feel comfortable with the therapist, not intimidated.
- feel that they are making progress with the therapy.
- be committed to making therapy work.
- do the work to resolve issues.

Social Psychology

14

Chapter Overview

This chapter discusses both attitudes and social cognitions. Attitudes are composed of affective, behavioural, and cognitive components. People show consistency between their attitudes and behaviour, and we form schemas to help us categorize people and events in the world around us. This helps us to predict the actions of others. Following this, the chapter explores the effects that social influence has on an individual. These behaviours include behaviours that result from the actions of others, as found in conformity, compliance, and obedience. The issue of prejudice is addressed as a consequence of stereotyping and both of these create challenges for people living in a diverse society. How prejudice originates and its relationship to stereotyping and discrimination are discussed. Finally, both positive and negative social behaviours are presented. These behaviours include the study of liking and loving, the influence of friendship between people and the behaviour involved in helping others.

To further investigate the topics covered in this chapter, you can visit the related websites by visiting the following link: http://www.mcgrawhill.ca/college/feldman

Prologue: And They Brought Roses
Looking Ahead

Section 1: Attitudes and Social Cognition
Persuasion: Changing Attitudes
Social Cognition: Understanding Others

Psychology at Work: Ann Altman,
Advertising Executive

Exploring Diversity: Attributions in a Cultural Context: How Fundamental Is the Fundamental Attribution Error?

Pathways Through Psychology: James Alcock, Social Psychologist, York University, Toronto, Ontario

Section 2: Social Influence

Conformity: Following What Others Do
Compliance: Submitting to Direct Social Pressure
Obedience: Obeying Direct Orders

Applying Psychology in the 21st Century:
Reading Your Mind, Reaching Your Wallet: Using Computer
Technology to Increase Compliance

Section 3: Prejudice and Discrimination

The Foundations of Prejudice
Working to End Prejudice and Discrimination

Section 4: Positive and Negative Social Behaviour

Liking and Loving: Interpersonal Attraction and the Development of Relationships
Aggression and Prosocial Behaviour: Hurting and Helping Others

Becoming an Informed Consumer of Psychology:
Dealing with Anger Effectively

Learning Objectives

These are the concepts and the learning objectives for Chapter 14. Read them carefully as
part of your preliminary survey of the chapter.

Attitudes and Social Cognition

1. Define social psychology and attitudes. (p. 458)

2. Explain how attitudes are changed through persuasion, and describe how attitudes and
behaviour influence one another. (pp. 458–460)

3. Describe the main principles of social cognition, including schemas, impression formation,
attribution, and biases. (pp. 460–465

Social Influence

4. Define social influence and conformity, and describe the factors that influence conformity.
(pp. 467–468)

5. Define compliance, and describe how the foot-in-the-door technique, the door-in-the-face technique, and other sales tactics lead to compliance. (pp. 468–469)

6. Describe Milgram's study of obedience to authority and its results. (pp. 469–471)

Prejudice and Discrimination

7. Define prejudice, and describe its relationship to stereotyping and discrimination. (pp. 472–473)

8. Explain how prejudice originates and what can be done to minimize its impact. (pp. 473–475)

Positive and Negative Social Behaviour

9. Define interpersonal attraction, and describe the factors that contribute to friendship and liking. (pp. 475–477)

10. Describe the efforts that have been made to understand love. (pp. 477–478)

11. Define aggression, and compare the instinct, frustration-aggression, and observational-learning theories of aggression. (pp. 478–481)

12. Define prosocial behaviour and altruism, and describe the factors that encourage or hinder bystanders from helping during emergencies. (pp. 481–482)

Section 1: Attitudes and Social Cognition

Prepare

- *What are attitudes, and how are they formed, maintained, and changed?*
- *How do we form impressions of what others are like and of the causes of their behaviour?*
- *What biases influence the ways in which we view others' behaviour?*

Organize

- *Persuasion*
- *Social Cognition*

Work

    [a] _____ is the study of how people's thoughts, feelings, and actions are affected by others. Attempts to persuade people to purchase specific products involves

principles derived from the study of attitudes. [b]_____ are learned predispositions to respond in a favourable or unfavourable manner to a particular person, behaviour, belief, or object.

The formation of attitudes follows classical and operant learning principles. Attitudes can be formed by association. They can also be reinforced positively or punished by the responses others may have to them, and a person may develop an attitude through **[c]** _____.
This type of learning occurs when a person learns something through observation of others. Children learn prejudices through others by hearing or seeing others express prejudicial attitudes.

Another important component consists of the characteristics of the recipient. The intelligence of the recipient influences the ability to remember and recall the message, yet intelligent people are more certain of their opinions. Highly intelligent people tend to be more difficult to persuade. A small difference in persuadability exists between men and women, with women being slightly easier to persuade. The means by which the information is processed also has influence on the persuasion. **[d]** _____ occurs when the recipient considers the arguments involved. **[e]** _____ occurs when the recipient uses information that requires less thought. Advertisers are using demographic information about people to help target their advertisements. **[f]** _____ is a technique for dividing people into lifestyle profiles that are related to purchasing patterns.

Attitudes influence behaviour, but the strength of the relationship varies. People do try to keep behaviour and attitudes consistent. Sometimes, in order to maintain the consistency, behaviour can influence attitudes. **[g]** _____ occurs when a person holds two *cognitions* (attitudes or thoughts) that are contradictory. In cases where dissonance is aroused, the prediction is that behaviour or attitudes will change in order to reduce the dissonance.

The area of social psychology called **[h]** _____ refers to the processes that underlie our understanding of the world. Individuals have highly developed schemas, or sets of cognitions, about people and experiences. **[i]** _____ are important because they organize how we recall, recognize, and categorize information about others. They also help us make predictions about others.

[j]_____ refers to the process by which an individual organizes information about another person, forming an overall impression of that person. Information given to people prior to meeting them can have dramatic effects on how the person is perceived. Research has focused on how people pay attention to unusually important traits, called

[k] _____, as they form impressions of others.

Evaluate

_____ 1.　attitudes

_____ 2.　central-route processing

_____ 3.　peripheral-route processing

    a.　Characterized by consideration of the source and related general information rather than of the message itself.

    b.　Characterized by thoughtful consideration of the issues.

    c.　Learned predispositions to respond in a favourable or unfavourable manner to a particular object.

Rethink

1.　Suppose you were assigned to develop a full advertising campaign for a product, including television, radio, and print ads. How might the theories in this chapter guide your strategy to suit the different media?

2.　Joan sees Annette, a new coworker, act in a way that seems abrupt and curt. Joan concludes that Annette is unkind and unsociable. The next day Joan sees Annette acting kindly to another worker. Is Joan likely to change her impression of Annette? Why or why not? Finally, Joan sees several friends of hers laughing and joking with Annette, treating her in a very friendly fashion. Is Joan likely to change her impression of Annette? Why or why not?

SECTION 2:　Social Influence

Prepare

- ***What are the major sources and tactics of social influence?***

Organize

- ***Conformity***
- ***Compliance***
- ***Obedience***

Work

The area called **[a]** _____ is concerned with how the actions of an individual affect the behaviour of others.

In uncertain situations, we tend to look to the behaviour of others to guide our own behaviour. **[b]** _____ is the change in behaviour or attitudes that results from a desire to follow the beliefs or standards of other people.

[c] _____ is a type of thinking in which group members share strong motivation to achieve consensus that leads them to lose the ability to critically evaluate alternatives. The group overrates its ability to solve problems and underrates contradictory information.

The behaviour that occurs in response to direct, explicit pressure to endorse a particular view or to behave in a certain way is called **[d]** _____ . Several techniques are used by salespersons to get customers to comply with purchase requests. One technique is called the **[e]** _____ technique, in which a person agrees to a small request and is then asked to comply with a bigger request. Compliance increases when the person first agrees to the smaller request. The **[f]** _____ technique is the opposite of the foot-in-the-door technique. The door-in-the-face technique follows a large request with a smaller one, making the second request appear more reasonable. The **[g]** _____ technique presents a deal at an inflated price, then a number of incentives are added. The

[h] _____ is another method that creates a psychic cost by giving "free" samples. These samples instigate a *norm of reciprocity*, leading people to buy as a matter of reciprocation.

Compliance follows a request, but obedience follows direct orders. **[i]** _____ is defined as a change in behaviour due to the commands of others. Obedience occurs in situations involving a boss, teacher, parent, or someone who has power over us.

Evaluate

_____ 1. cognitive dissonance

_____ 2. foot-in-the-door technique

_____ 3. door-in-the-face technique

_____ 4. obedience

_____ 5. compliance

a. Behaviour that occurs in response to direct social pressure.

b. Going along with an important request is more likely if it follows compliance with a smaller previous request.

c. A change in behaviour due to the commands of others.

d. A large request, refusal of which is expected, is followed by a smaller request.

e. The conflict resulting from contrasting cognitions.

Rethink

3. Given that persuasive techniques like those described in this section are so powerful, should there be laws against the use of such techniques? Should people be taught defences against such techniques? Is the use of such techniques ethically and morally defensible?

4. Why do you think the Milgram experiment is so controversial? What sorts of effects might the experiment have had on participants? Do you think the experiment would have had similar results if it had been conducted not in a laboratory setting, but among members of a social group (such as a fraternity or sorority) with strong pressures to conform?

Section 3: Prejudice and Discrimination

Prepare

- ***What are stereotypes, prejudice, and discrimination?***

Organize
- *How can we reduce prejudice and discrimination?*

- *The Foundations of Prejudice*
- *Working to End Prejudice and Discrimination*

Work

[a] _____ are the beliefs and expectations about members of groups held simply because of membership in the group. Stereotypes can lead to

[b] _____, the negative evaluation of members of a group that are based primarily on membership in the group rather than on the behaviour of a particular individual. When negative stereotypes lead to negative action against a group or members of a group, the

behaviour is called [c] _____. Stereotypes can actually cause members of stereotyped groups to behave according to the stereotype, a phenomenon known as

[d] _____. Expectations about a future event increase the likelihood that the event will occur. People are also primed to interpret behaviours according to stereotypes.

The [e] _____ say that people's feelings about various groups are shaped by the behaviour of parents, other adults, and peers and the mass media. According to

[f] _____, we use membership in groups as a source of pride and self-worth. We then inflate the positive aspects of our own group and devalue groups to which we do not belong.

Evaluate

_____ 1. self-fulfilling prophecy

_____ 2. prejudice

_____ 3. stereotype

_____ 4. social identity theory

_____ 5. discrimination

a. Negative behaviour toward members of a particular group.

b. Negative or positive judgments of members of a group that are based on membership in the group.

c. The expectation of an event or behaviour results in the event or behaviour actually occurring.

d. Beliefs and expectations about members of a group are held simply on the basis of membership in that group.

e. The view that people use group membership as a source of pride and self-worth.

Rethink

5. How are stereotypes, prejudice, and discrimination related? In a society committed to equality, which of the three should be changed first? Why?

6. Do you think women can be victims of stereotype vulnerability? In what topical areas might this occur? Can men be victims of stereotype vulnerability?

Section 4: Positive and Negative Social Behaviour

Prepare

- *Why are we attracted to certain people, and what is the progression that social relationships generally follow?*
- *What factors underlie aggression and prosocial behaviour?*

Organize

- *Liking and Loving*
- *Aggression and Prosocial Behaviour*

Work

Another area of social influence is called **[a]** _____, which encompasses the factors that lead to positive feelings about others. Research on liking has identified the following factors as important in the development of attraction between people.

[b] _____ refers to the physical nearness or geographical closeness as a factor in development of friendship. Proximity leads to liking. **[c]** _____ also leads to liking. The more often one is exposed to any stimulus, the more the stimulus is liked.

Familiarity with a stimulus can evoke positive feelings. **[d]** _____ influences attraction because we assume that people with similar backgrounds will evaluate us positively. This is called the **[e]** _____. We also assume that when we like someone, that person likes us in return. **[f]** _____ refers to attraction that is based on the needs that the partner can fulfil. We may then be attracted to the person who fulfils the greatest number of needs. It does appear that people with complimentary abilities are attracted to one another. More **[g]** _____ tends to be more popular. Physical attractiveness may be the single most important factor in college dating.

Several kinds of love have been hypothesized, one being **[h]** _____ love, which is an intense state of absorption in another person. Another is **[i]** _____ love, which is strong affection that we have for someone with whom our lives are deeply involved. Robert Sternberg has proposed that love is made of three components. The **[j]** _____ component includes feelings of closeness and connectedness; the **[k]** _____ component is made of the motivational drives related to sex, physical closeness, and romance; and the **[l]** _____ component encompasses the initial cognition that one loves someone and the long-term feelings of commitment to maintain love.

Drive-by shootings, car-jackings, and abductions give a pessimistic impression of human behaviour. The helping behaviour of many, however, counteracts the impression. Social psychology seeks to explain these extremes.

Aggression occurs at societal and individual levels, and the basic questions concern whether aggression is inevitable or whether it results from particular circumstances.

[m] _____ is defined as the intentional injury of or harm to another person.

Instinct theories explain aggression as the result of innate urges. Konrad Lorenz suggested that aggressive energy is built up through the instinct of aggression and that its release is necessary. The discharge of this energy is called **[n]** _____. Lorenz suggested that society should provide an acceptable means of achieving catharsis, like sports. There is no way to test this theory experimentally.

The frustration-aggression theory says that the frustration of a goal *always* leads to aggression. **[o]** _____ is defined as the thwarting of a goal-directed behaviour. More recently the theory has been modified to suggest that frustration creates a *readiness* to act aggressively.

The observational-learning view suggests that we learn to act aggressively by observing others. Observational-learning theory also suggests that the rewards and punishments received by a model are important in the learning of aggression. This formulation has wide support.

[p] _____ refers to helping behaviour. The prosocial behaviour studied most by psychologists is bystander intervention. When more than one person witnesses an emergency, **[q]** _____, the tendency for people to feel that responsibility is shared among those present, increases. In some cases people act altruistically. **[r]** _____ is helping behaviour that is beneficial to others but may require self-sacrifice. People high in *empathy* may be more likely to respond than others. Situational factors and mood may also affect helping behaviour. Both good and bad moods appear to increase helping behaviour.

Evaluate

_____ 1.	passionate (or romantic) love	a.	The motivational drives relating to sex, physical closeness, and romance.
_____ 2.	compassionate love	b.	Feelings of closeness and connectedness.
_____ 3.	intimacy component	c.	The initial cognition that one loves someone, and the longer-term feelings of commitment.
_____ 4.	passion component	d.	The strong affection we have for those with whom our lives are deeply involved.
_____ 5.	decision/commitment component	e.	A state of intense absorption in someone that is characterized by physiological arousal, psychological interest, and caring for another's needs.

Rethink

7. Can love be studied scientifically? Is there an elusive quality to love that makes it at least partially unknowable? How would you define "falling in love"? How would you study it?

8. How would the aggression of a Timothy McVeigh, convicted of blowing up a federal building in Oklahoma City, be interpreted by the three main approaches to the study of aggression: instinct approaches, frustration-aggression approaches, and observational-

learning approaches? Do you think any of these approaches fits the McVeigh case more closely than the others?

Practise Questions

Test your knowledge of the chapter material by answering these questions. These questions have been placed in three Practise Tests. The first two tests are composed of questions that will test your recall of factual knowledge. The third test contains questions that are challenging and primarily test for conceptual knowledge and your ability to apply that knowledge. Check your answers and review the feedback using the Answer Key in the following pages of the *Study Guide*.

PRACTISE TEST 1:

1. Advertisers often try to link a product they want consumers to buy to a:
   a. positive feeling or event.
   b. cognition.
   c. peripheral route.
   d. dissonant stimulus.

2. Schemas serve as _____ for social cognitions.
   a. organizing frameworks
   b. defences against stereotypes
   c. feeling-communicators
   d. insincerity whistle-blowers

3. According to the text, when forming an impression of another person, people rely heavily on:
   a. central tendencies.
   b. central traits.
   c. primary traits.
   d. schematic tendencies.

4. The tendency for people to attribute others' behaviour to dispositional causes and their own behaviour to situational causes is known as:
   a. ingroup versus outgroup error.
   b. fundamental attribution error
   c. dispositional attribution error.
   d. stereotypic attribution error.

5. The classic demonstration of pressure to conform comes from a series of studies carried out in the 1950s by:
   a. B. F. Skinner.
   b. Solomon Asch.
   c. Philip Zimbardo.
   d. Stanley Milgram.

6. People working on tasks and questions that are ambiguous are more susceptible to:
   a. inoculation.
   b. obedience.
   c. forewarning.
   d. social pressure.

7. The classic experiment demonstrating the power of authority to produce obedience was performed by:
   a. Albert Bandura.
   b. Solomon Asch.
   c. Stanley Milgram.
   d. B. F. Skinner.

8. The Bosnian concept of "ethnic cleansing" that results in genocide of unwanted groups reflects:
   a. reverse discrimination.
   c. prejudice and discrimination.

b.   individualism.   d.   deterrence.

9.   Beliefs and expectations about members of groups held simply on the basis of their group membership are called:
     a.   self-fulfilling prophecies.   c.   stereotypes.
     b.   culture.   d.   contingencies.

10. All of the following are strong influences on the formation of friendships **except**:
     a.   others who are like them.   c.   others whom they see frequently.
     b.   others who live nearby.   d.   others who are exceptionally attractive.

11. Which of the following elements does love have that liking does not?
     a.   proximity   c.   similarity
     b.   complementarity   d.   physical arousal

12. According to Sternberg, different types of love are made up of different quantities of:
     a.   liking, loving, and commitment.   c.   emotion, motivation, and attraction.
     b.   passion, compassion, and attraction.   d.   intimacy, passion, and commitment.

13. Maria has been trying to quit smoking since her mother was diagnosed with lung cancer. Although she knows the risks, it is very difficult when she finds herself in situations where she normally would have a cigarette. Festinger calls this:
     a.   cathartic interference.   c.   cognitive dissonance.
     b.   tension reduction.   d.   frustration aggression.

14. Prosocial is a more formal way of describing behaviour that is:
     a.   helping.   c.   innate.
     b.   cathartic.   d.   aggressive.

____ 15.   impression formation   a.   Tendency to think of people as being similar to oneself.

____ 16.   central traits   b.   Major traits considered in forming impressions of others.

____ 17.   fundamental attribution   c.   Organizing information about another individual to form
           error   an overall impression of that person.

                                      d.   A tendency to over-attribute others' behaviour to
____ 18.   halo effect   dispositional causes but to under-attribute one's own
                                           behaviour to situational causes.

____ 19.   assumed-similarity bias   e.   An initial understanding that a person has positive traits
                                           is used to infer other uniformly positive characteristics.

20. Cognitive dissonance occurs when a person holds two _____ of thoughts that are contradictory.

21. The halo effect reflects _____ theories that indicate how we think traits are inferred.

22. An experiment by _____ demonstrated the power of the judgments of others on the perceptual judgments of an individual participant.

23. When people act on negative stereotypes, this _____ can lead to exclusion from jobs, neighbourhoods, or educational opportunities.

24. Expectations that act to increase the likelihood that an event or behaviour will occur are

_____.

25. Much has been made of attitudes and behaviour and how they may or may not be consistent. Describe a situation in which your attitudes and behaviour may not have been consistent, and then compare the cognitive-dissonance explanation and the self-perception explanation of the situation.

PRACTISE TEST 2:

1. One of the basic processes that underlies the formation and development of attitudes relates to learning principles. Which of the following learning methods best explains how attitudes are acquired?
   a. peripheral-route processing
   b. classical and operant conditioning
   c. central-route processing
   d. punishment

2. The advertising industry draws upon findings from _____ regarding persuasion.
   a. experimental psychology
   b. psychometrics
   c. abnormal psychology
   d. social psychology

3. Richard is on a diet. When he sees a piece of cake, Richard wants to eat it but knows that he shouldn't. Festinger called this:
   a. cognitive dissonance.
   b. cathartic interference.
   c. tension reduction.
   d. frustration-aggression.

4. The processes that underlie our understanding of the social world are called:
   a. social cognitions.
   b. schemas.
   c. central traits.
   d. stereotypes.

5. The task of _____ is to explain how people understand the causes of behaviour.
   a. discrimination theory
   b. social cognition
   c. attribution theory
   d. directive-behaviour theory

6. Conformity is a change in behaviour or attitude brought about by:
   a. an increase of knowledge.
   b. a desire to follow the beliefs or standards of others.
   c. intense pressure to be a distinct individual.
   d. an insecure self-image.

7. According to the text, a change in behaviour that results from direct, explicit social pressure to behave in a certain way is called:
   a. conformity.
   b. congruence.
   c. commission.
   d. compliance.

8. What is the correct term for the technique in which a large request is asked, followed by expected refusal and later a smaller request?
    a. obedience
    b. social compliance
    c. door-in-the-face technique
    d. foot-in-the-door technique

9. The negative behaviour toward an individual because of his or her membership in a particular group is known as:
    a. stereotyping.
    b. discrimination.
    c. prejudice.
    d. self-fulfilling prophecy.

10. Proximity is defined as:
    a. nearness to another person.
    b. a tendency to like those who like us.
    c. a tendency of those whom we like to like us.
    d. distance from another.

11. _____ love is a state of intense absorption in someone, with bodily arousal, mental interest, and care for the other's needs.
    a. The intimacy component of
    b. The decision/commitment component of
    c. Compassionate
    d. Passionate (romantic)

12. Fear-evoking advertising messages are most effective when:
    a. they frighten people into buying the product.
    b. they reach a small and indifferent audience.
    c. viewers' cognitive defence mechanisms are activated.
    d. they include advice for steps to avoid the described danger.

13. When stereotypes are attributed to a particular group, the stereotype may induce members of that group to act in ways that confirm the stereotype. This is known as:
    a. the ingroup-outgroup bias.
    b. reverse discrimination.
    c. a self-fulfilling prophecy.
    d. the interdependent view of the self.

14. Frustration is most likely to lead to aggression:
    a. in the presence of aggressive cues.
    b. immediately after being frustrated.
    c. during late adolescence.
    d. several hours after being frustrated.

____ 15. proximity

____ 16. Mere exposure

____ 17. prosocial behaviour

____ 18. diffusion of responsibility

a. Any helping behaviour.

b. Nearness to another, one cause for liking.

c. Repeated exposure to a person often produces liking.

d. The tendency for people to feel that responsibility for helping is shared among those present.

19. Children as young as _____ years of age begin to show preferences for members of their own race.

20. When inaccurate portrayals are the primary source of information about a group, they can lead to the maintenance of unfavourable _____.

21. In an effort to maximize our own _____ we may come to think that our own group is better than others.

22. Some psychologists argue that _____ results when there is perceived competition for scarce resources.

23. One of the most important factors in establishing personal relationships is geographic closeness or _____.

24. What factors would be at work when prejudices erupt into violence against racial groups? Analyze the factors of conformity, obedience, and stereotyping, including ingroup and outgroup biases.

PRACTISE TEST 3: Conceptual, Applied, and Challenging Questions

1. A 5-year-old boy who overhears his father tell his mother that "Southerners are ignorant" may grow up to believe this opinion and adopt it as an attitude as a result of the process of:
    a. direct reinforcement.
    b. vicarious learning.
    c. cognitive dissonance.
    d. persuasive communication.

2. According to the text, if a target audience pays more attention to the celebrity doing the commercial than to the advertisement message, which processing route is being used the most by the audience?
    a. central-route processing
    b. circumference-route processing
    c. peripheral-route processing
    d. The message is not being processed.

3. Many variables influence the effectiveness of a communication to create attitude change. In which of the following situations will the impact be the greatest?
    a. The recipient appraises the message with central-route processing.
    b. The recipient of the message is male.
    c. The recipient appraises the message with peripheral-route processing.
    d. The recipient is very intelligent.

4. According to Festinger's theory of cognitive dissonance, if a smoker holds the cognitions "I smoke" and "Smoking causes cancer," he or she should be motivated to do all of the following **except**:
    a. modify one or both cognitions.
    b. enter a stop-smoking program.
    c. make the attitudes consistent.
    d. change the importance of one cognition.

5. Of the following, the best example of cognitive dissonance is:
    a. stating that women should earn less money than men for doing the same job.
    b. exaggerating the merits of a product in order to promote sales.
    c. knowing that cigarette smoking is harmful, but doing it anyway.
    d. believing that people who are disabled cannot hold good jobs and therefore not recommending them.

6. Which one of the following statements is the best example of dispositional-attribution bias?

a.   John is being good because the teacher is watching.
b.   Even though I am not feeling sociable, I will go to the party if you do.
c.   I become very anxious when criticized.
d.   Sue is staying up all night to study because she is a conscientious student.

7.   Which of the following situations best describes a situational cause for the described behaviour?
a.   Tiffany straightens the guest room, which is normally a messy sewing room, because relatives will be staying at her house for a week.
b.   Robbie helps an old lady across the street because he is always thoughtful.
c.   Donny, who is normally grumpy, frowns about an exam as he walks down the hall.
d.   Debbie is a punctual person who is on time for school every morning.

8.   What measure may be most effective for reducing the tendency of people to conform in a group situation?
a.   Make sure all members value the group highly.
b.   Include lots of members in the group.
c.   Use a show of hands when voting.
d.   Use a secret ballot when voting.

9.   Stereotypes differ from prejudices in that:
a.   stereotypes are beliefs that lead to prejudices, which are judgments.
b.   stereotypes must involve action against a group.
c.   prejudices must involve action against a group.
d.   prejudices are beliefs that lead to stereotypes, which are judgments.

10.   Of the following, which factor is the best predictor of whether two people will be initially attracted to each other?
a.   similarity   c.   proximity
b.   mere exposure   d.   complementarity

11.   According to Sternberg's theory of love, each of the following is a component of love **except**:
a.   intimacy.   c.   decision/commitment.
b.   passion.   d.   individuation/separation.

12.   Instinct theorist Konrad Lorenz would argue that opportunities to exercise and play sports ought to be given to prisoners because they:
a.   provide models of prosocial behaviour.
b.   present violent models to be seen and imitated by prisoners.
c.   enable natural aggressive energy to be released harmlessly.
d.   reduce the frustration that causes aggression.

13.   Considering the discussion of gender differences in conformity, which of these individuals would be most likely to conform?
a.   a man
b.   a women
c.   an individual who is familiar with the task at hand
d.   an individual who is unfamiliar with the task at hand?

14.   Following the Oklahoma City bombing in April 1995, thousands of unpaid volunteers assisted at the site, thereby demonstrating:

a. the fundamental attribution error.

b. diffusion of responsibility.

c. altruism.

d. the halo effect.

____ 15. rewards-costs approach

____ 16. altruism

____ 17. empathy

____ 18. schemas

____ 19. status

a. Helping behaviour that is beneficial to others while requiring sacrifice on the part of the helper.

b. Sets of cognitions about people and social experiences.

c. One person's experiencing of another's emotions, in turn increasing the likelihood of responding to the other's needs.

d. The social rank held within a group.

e. The notion that, in a situation requiring help, a bystander's perceived rewards must outweigh the costs if helping is to occur.

20. While some might argue that opposites attract, other researchers believe we tend to like people who are _____ to us.

21. People who are _____ attractive are more popular than those who are not, other factors being equal.

22. Researchers believe that liking someone is qualitatively different than _____ someone.

23. In the United States, mutual attraction and love are the most important characteristics desired in a mate by men and women; men in China rank _____ as most important.

24. _____ approaches propose that aggression is primarily the outcome of innate or inborn urges.

25. In the United States, the idea of arranged marriages often is seen with disdain. Our culture, for the most part, has always encouraged our freedom to select based on the notion of romantic love. Explain then the elements that may be present in arranged marriages that make them as successful as those partnerships we personally choose.

Spotlight on Terminology and Language—
Cultural Idioms

Page 472 "These views create **stereotypes**, generalized beliefs and expectations about groups and their members.

Stereotypes can be either negative or positive.

Page 472 "Stereotypes can lead to **prejudice**, the negative (or positive) evaluations of people based on group membership".

Prejudice is an unfair, biased or intolerant attitude toward another group of people.

Page 472 "When people act on negative stereotypes, the result is **discrimination-** , negative behaviour toward members of a particular group."
Discrimination is acting on the basis of prejudice.

Attitudes and Social Cognition

Page 458 "Such commercials are part of the **barrage** of messages we receive each day—from sources as varied as politicians, sales staff in stores, and celebrities—all meant to influence us."

They **barrage** us with a constant flood of messages.

Page 458 "Attitudes are learned predispositions to respond in a favourable or unfavourable manner to a particular person, behaviour, belief, or thing."

An **attitude** is any belief or opinion that includes a positive or negative evaluation of some object, person, or event and that predisposes us to act in a certain manner toward that object, individual, or event.

Page 459 "Instead, they are influenced by factors that are irrelevant or **extraneous** to the attitude topic or issue, such as who is providing the message or how long the arguments are."

Extraneous is something that comes from the outside, and is not vital or essential.

Page 460 "According to a major social psychologist, Leon Festinger, **cognitive dissonance** occurs when a person holds two attitudes or thoughts that contradict each other."

Cognitive dissonance is the unpleasant psychological tension that motivates us to reduce our cognitive inconsistencies by making our beliefs more consistent with one another.

Page 460 "Cases like this illustrate the power of our impressions and **attest** to the importance of determining how people develop an understanding of others."

To **attest** is to give validity to, to affirm.

Page 461 "Our schema for 'teacher,' for instance, generally consists of a number of characteristics: knowledge of the subject matter he or she is teaching, a desire to **impart** that

knowledge, and an awareness of the student's need to understand what is being said."

When you **impart** knowledge, you communicate it and make it known to others.

Page 462 "According to this work, the presence of a central trait **alters** the meaning of other traits."

To **alter** is to modify, to change.

Page 462 "However, our schemas are **susceptible** to error."

When something is **susceptible**, it can be affected by deep emotions or strong feelings.

Page 464 "In our example involving Barbara, her fellow employees attributed her behaviour to her **disposition** rather than to the situation."

A **disposition** is a habitual tendency or inclination.

Page 465 "Applied social psychology therefore extends knowledge in order '…to understand, and perhaps solve **contemporary** social proplems' ."

Contemporary here means existing or occurring at the present time.

Page 467 "**Conformity** is a change in behaviour or attitudes brought about by a desire to follow the beliefs or standards of other people."

Conformity is any behaviour you perform because of group pressure, even though that pressure might not involve direct requests. The social pressure may be subtle or indirect. What circumstances existed when you last felt the need to **conform**?

Page 468 "Conformity pressures are most pronounced in groups that are **unanimous** in their support of a position."

When something is **unanimous,** all share the same opinion or views.

Page 468 "Social psychologists call the type of conforming behaviour that occurs in response to direct social pressure **compliance.**"

Compliance is a kind of conformity in which we give in to social pressure in our public responses but do not change our personal values.

■ CHAPTER 14: ANSWER KEY

GUIDED REVIEW			
Section 1:	Section 2:	Section 3:	Section 4:
[a] Social psychology	[a] social influence	[a] Stereotypes	[a] interpersonal attraction
[b] Attitudes	[b] Conformity	[b] prejudice	[b] Proximity
[c] vicarious learning	[c] Groupthink	[c] discrimination	[c] Mere exposure
[d] Central-route processing	[d] compliance	[d] self-fulfilling prophecy	[d] Similarity
[e] Peripheral-route processing	[e] foot-in-the-door	[e] social learning approaches	[e] reciprocity-of-liking effect
[f] Psychographics	[f] door-in-the-face	[f] social identity theory	[f] Need-complimentarity hypothesis
[g] Cognitive dissonance	[g] that's-not-all		[g] physical attractiveness
[h] social cognition	[h] not-so-free sample	Evaluate	[h] passionate (or romantic)
[i] Schemas	[i] Obedience	1. c	[i] compassionate
[j] Impression formation		2. b	[j] intimacy
[k] central traits	Evaluate	3. d	[k] passion
	1. e	4. e	[l] decision/commitment
	2. b	5. a	[m] Aggression
Evaluate	3. d		[n] catharsis
1. c	4. a		[o] Frustration
2. b	5. c		[p] Prosocial behaviour
3. a			[q] diffusion of responsibility
			[r] Altruism
			Evaluate
			1. e
			2. d
			3. b
			4. a
			5. c

Selected Rethink Answers

2. Joan first experiences cognitive dissonance, her thoughts and attitudes were contradictory about Annette. Finally, with friends of Joan's treating Annette well, she was able to add positive cognitions, which enabled her to change her impression of Annette.

8. Define each approach to aggression. The observational-learning approach seems appropriate here. The social and environmental conditions are supported by McVeigh's past experiences (his military background, access to guns) One of the consequences for him was fame and notoriety, the other was that he will give up his life.

Practise Test 1:
1. a   obj. 2   p. 459
*a. Correct. Linking the product to a positive event originates with classical conditioning.
b. Incorrect. They seek to link the product to a pleasant stimuli, like a feeling or event.
c. Incorrect. The peripheral-route is one of the methods of communicating in persuasive communication.

d. Incorrect. A dissonant stimulus might be one that does not fit with the others or causes some kind of conflict.

2. a   obj. 3   p. 461
*a. Correct. A schema is an organizing framework.
b. Incorrect. Schemas actually serve as the foundation for stereotypes.
c. Incorrect. Schemas are not communicators.

d.   Incorrect. Schemers maybe, but not schemas.

3. b   obj. 3   p. 462
a.   Incorrect. Central tendencies are the measures like mean, median, and mode that are produced using statistics.
*b. Correct. Apparently we utilize major, evident traits that are central to the personality of the individual we are forming impressions about.
c.   Incorrect. The term is central traits.
d.   Incorrect. The concept "schematic tendencies" is yet to be developed.

4. b   obj. 3   p. 464
a.   Incorrect. The ingroup-outgroup bias (not error) may follow the fundamental attribution error, but its role is in determining the boundaries between groups and strengthening the sense of identity with the ingroup.
*b. Correct. The fundamental attribution error is quite common and may be understood in that we do tend to see the person's behaviour more than the environment in which it occurs, and we see our own environment and not so much our own behaviour.
c.   Incorrect. There is no dispositional attribution error.
d.   Incorrect. There is no stereotypic attribution error.

5. b   obj. 4   p. 467
a.   Incorrect. Skinner did not conduct conformity experiments.
*b. Correct. Solomon Asch performed a number of experiments throughout the 1950s on conformity.
c.   Incorrect. Zimbardo conducted experiments on compliance and obedience.
d.   Incorrect. Milgram conducted a now famous experiment on obedience.

6. d   obj. 5   p. 468
a.   Incorrect. Inoculation occurs when the person is deliberately exposed to conformity pressures in order to be better at avoiding conformity.
b.   Incorrect. Obedience requires more direct pressure.
c.   Incorrect. Forewarning is a technique for developing the ability to resist pressures to conform.
*d. Correct. In ambiguous circumstances, social pressure is more likely to have an effect on conformity.

7. c   obj. 6   p. 469
a.   Incorrect. Albert Bandura is known for his study of violence and the Bobo clown doll.
b.   Incorrect. Solomon Asch is known for his experiments on conformity.
*c. Correct. Stanley Milgram asked subjects to give an electric shock to other subjects, and he was able to get most to comply to the point of the highest shock level.
d.   Incorrect. Skinner did not perform any human conformity studies.

8. c   obj. 7   p. 472
a.   Incorrect. This discrimination is not reverse but is instead quite direct.

b.   Incorrect. Individualism is not a concept relevant to active genocide.
*c. This is a manifestation not only of extreme prejudice but also of extreme discrimination.
d.   Incorrect. Deterrence is a concept that would prevent the actions of open group by threatening retaliation.

9. c   obj. 7   p. 472
a.   Incorrect. These are stereotypes, and stereotypes can become self-fulfilling prophecies.
b.   Incorrect. Culture is the shared beliefs and practices of a group.
*c. Correct. This defines stereotypes.
d.   Incorrect. These are not called contingencies, they are called stereotypes.

10. d   obj. 9   p. 476
a.   Incorrect. See answer d.
b.   Incorrect. See answer d.
c.   Incorrect. See answer d.
*d. Correct. Living nearby, similarity, and frequent contact are the foundations of friendship, and exceptional attractiveness is not.

11. d   obj. 9   p. 477
a.   Incorrect. See answer d.
b.   Incorrect. See answer d.
c.   Incorrect. See answer d.
*d. Correct. To being nearby, sharing interests, and being similar, love adds the component of physical attraction and arousal.

12. d   obj. 10   p. 478
a.   Incorrect. See answer d.
b.   Incorrect. See answer d.
c.   Incorrect. See answer d.
*d. Correct. Sternberg's triarchic theory of love has three components—intimacy, passion, and commitment—which can be combined in different ways.

13. c   obj. 2   p. 460
a.   Incorrect. No such thing.
b.   Incorrect. If anything it would heighten tension.
*c. Correct.
d.   Incorrect. It might lead to frustration but not aggression.

14. a   obj. 12   p. 481
*a. Correct. Prosocial behaviour is altruistic, helping behaviour.
b.   Incorrect. Insofar as helping another is cathartic, this could be a good answer, but the term prosocial typically refers to helping behaviour.
c.   Incorrect. Some biosociologists argue that prosocial behaviour is innate because it promotes the survival of the species.
d.   Incorrect. Prosocial behaviour is altruistic, helping behaviour.

15. c   obj. 3   p. 461

16. b   obj. 3   p. 462
17. d   obj. 3   p. 464
18. e   obj. 3   p. 464
19. a   obj. 3   p. 464
20. cognitions obj. 2   p. 460
21. Implicit theories   obj. 3   p. 464
We all hold these personality theories reflecting our individual biases in deciding which cluster of personality traits go together in the same individual; eg, a person who is kind must also be truthful, religious, warm, etc.
22. Asch obj. 4   p. 467
23. discrimination obj. 7   p. 472
24. self-fulfilling prophecies obj. 7   p. 473

25.
- Situations that might be relevant are those in which you did something, like go on a date with someone, that you really were not that interested in doing. The mismatch between the attitude (lack of interest) and behaviour (going out), while not that great does illustrate the problem.
- Describe how you felt after the specific incident or act and whether you changed your attitudes (She/he is actually pleasant to be with). Or perhaps, you wait until after the behaviour to form your attitude (consistent with the self-perception theory).

Practise Test 2:
1. b   obj. 2   p. 458
a. Incorrect. Peripheral-route processing is not a learning principle.
*b. Correct. Both classical and operant conditioning principles are involved in the formation of attitudes.
c. Incorrect. Central-route processing is not a learning principle.
d. Incorrect. Punishment on its own cannot account for the richness and variety of our attitudes.

2. d   obj. 2   p. 458
a. Incorrect. Social psychologists, some of whom are experimental psychologists as well, have made contributions that are useful to the advertising industry.
b. Incorrect. Psychometrics is an important technique that probably was used by social psychologists as they developed key ideas that are now being used in the advertising industry.
c. Incorrect. Of all the branches of psychology, abnormal psychology has probably made the smallest contribution to the advertising industry.
*d. Correct. Social psychologists, some of whom are experimental psychologists as well, have made contributions that are useful to the advertising industry.

3. a   obj. 2   p. 460
*a. Correct. The conflict between two cognitions becomes cognitive dissonance when this conflict is accompanied by an affective state.
b. Incorrect. No such thing.
c. Incorrect. If anything, it would heighten tension.

d. Incorrect. It may lead to frustration but probably not aggression.

4. a   obj. 3   p. 461
*a. Correct. Social cognitions refer to the thoughts we have about other people and the causes of their behaviour.
b. Incorrect. Social cognitions are schemas, but schemas, the cognitive units of organization, refer to other cognitive categories as well.
c. Incorrect. Central traits are the traits we chose to make early impressions about people, and they may be included in our social cognitions.
d. Incorrect. Stereotypes are forms of social cognitions (but not all social cognitions are stereotypes).

5. c   obj. 3   p. 463
a. Incorrect. There is not "discrimination theory" that applies to this issue.
b. Incorrect. In the broadest sense this is true, but another alternative is more specific and thus a better choice.
*c. Correct. Attribution theory involves the efforts people make to understand the causes of their and others' behaviour.
d. Incorrect. There is not a "directive-behaviour" theory.

6. b   obj. 4   p. 467
a. Incorrect. More knowledge would not necessarily lead to conformity, it could just as well lead to nonconformity.
*b. Correct. Conformity is to the pressures of the group, and it is accomplished by accepting the attitudes and behaviours of the group.
c. Incorrect. The intense pressure to be an individual would be counter to the pressure to conform.
d. Incorrect. People with very secure self-images may be highly conforming individuals.

7. d   obj. 5   p. 468
a. Incorrect. Conformity results from indirect social pressure and a desire to be part of the group.
b. Incorrect. Congruence is a concept used in humanistic psychotherapy to describe different aspects of the self-concept.
c. Incorrect. A commission is an amount of money received for a specific task, like a sales commission.
*d. Correct. This is the definition of compliance.

8. c   obj. 5   p. 468
a. Incorrect. This is called the door-in-the-face technique; it is the opposite of the foot-in-the-door technique.
b. Incorrect. But it is a form of social compliance.
*c. Correct. This technique is the opposite of the foot-in-the-door technique.
d. Incorrect. It is the opposite of this, and called the door-in-the-face technique.

9. b   obj. 7   p. 472

a.   Incorrect. Stereotyping applies to attitudes, not behaviours.

*b. Correct. Discrimination is the negative action toward another person based on group membership.

c.   Incorrect. Prejudice is positive or negative attitudes toward a group or member of a group.

d.   Incorrect. A self-fulfilling prophecy is an expectation that the occurrence of an event or behaviour increases the likelihood that the event or behaviour will occur.

10. a   obj. 9   p. 476

*a. Correct. Physical proximity is nearness to another person, and it is a major factor in both friendship and love relationships.

b.   Incorrect. This defines the effect of reciprocity on us.

c.   Incorrect. This defines the effect of reciprocity on others.

d.   Incorrect. Distance is the opposite of proximity.

11. d   obj. 10   p. 477

a.   Incorrect. This is from Sternberg's theory, and is separate from passion.

b.   Incorrect. This is from Sternberg's theory, and is separate from passion.

c.   Incorrect. This type of love is seen in contrast to passionate love.

*d. Correct. Sounds like "romance."

12. d   obj. 2   p. 459

a.   Incorrect. This would be the measure of their effectiveness.

b.   Incorrect. Indifferent audiences are no more receptive to fear-based messages than any other audience.

c.   Incorrect. Defence mechanisms may make them ignore the warnings.

*d. Correct. Otherwise they are simply frightening.

13. c   obj. 7   p. 473

a.   Incorrect. In this bias, stereotypes are applied to help differentiate the two groups.

b.   Incorrect. Reverse discrimination occurs when one is making efforts to avoid the stereotype.

*c. Correct. Self-fulfilling prophecies are a danger to underprivileged groups because they sustain the circumstances.

d.   Incorrect. We are all interdependent.

14. a   obj. 11   p. 480

*a. Correct. Aggressive cues increase the likelihood of aggression (which initially creates a readiness to act).

b.   Incorrect. Aggressive cues increase the likelihood of aggression (which initially creates a readiness to act).

c.   Incorrect. Aggressive cues increase the likelihood of aggression (which initially creates a readiness to act).

d.   Incorrect. Aggressive cues increase the likelihood of aggression (which initially creates a readiness to act).

15. b   obj. 9   p. 476
16. c   obj. 9   p. 476
17. a   obj. 9   p. 481

18. d   obj. 12   p. 481
19. 3   obj. 12p. 481
20. stereotypes   obj. 7   p. 455
21. self-esteem   obj. 8   p. 456
22. prejudice obj. 7   p. 455
23. Proximity obj. 9   p. 458

24.
▪   Provide an example of recent violence against an ethnic group (or even an episode identified with a particular group).

▪   Gang violence is a clear application of the ingroup-outgroup bias. The riots in Los Angeles suggest that many have very strong stereotypes about the groups represented in the violence, including African American, Hispanic, and Asian.

▪   Describe how each of the factors, conformity, compliance, and obedience, could work toward increasing prejudice and following group behaviour.

Practise Test 3:
1.   b   obj. 8   p. 474

a.   Incorrect. Direct reinforcement would require that he express the attitude and then be reinforced for doing so.

*b. Correct. This is an example of learning through observation, or learning vicariously.

c.   Incorrect. Cognitive dissonance involves contradictory thoughts or beliefs that then cause tension (of course, the 5 year old may have a friend who is a southerner).

d.   Incorrect. Persuasive communication usually involves a more direct message.

2.   c   obj. 2   p. 459

a.   Incorrect. The approach known as peripheral-route processing is being used.

b.   Incorrect. This applies only to well-rounded messages.

*c. Correct. The peripheral route is one that avoids presenting much reasoning or detail about the product itself.

d.   Incorrect. But it is!

3.   a   obj. 2   p. 459

*a. Correct. When the recipient puts effort into cognitively analyzing the message, as required in central-route processing, the change in attitude will be the greatest for the situations given here.

b.   Incorrect. Being male does not make the message any more or less effective.

c.   Incorrect. The recipient will do little work in appraising a message that is peripheral.

d.   Incorrect. Intelligence does not affect attitude change.

4.   b   obj. 2   p. 460

a.   Incorrect. See answer b.

*b. Correct. Cognitive dissonance would lead to modifying one of the cognitions, making them consistent, or revaluing them, but it is unlikely to

make the person enter a program to stop smoking (this requires additional pressures).
c. Incorrect. See answer b.
d. Incorrect. See answer b.

5. c   obj. 2   p. 460
a. Incorrect. This is simply a sexist position.
b. Incorrect. This is simply typical of salespersons.
*c. Correct. Here, two thoughts are opposed to each other and will certainly result in tension.
d. Incorrect. This is simply being prejudicial.

6. d   obj. 3   p. 464
a. Incorrect. John's behaviour is explained according to the situation.
b. Incorrect. The decision to attend the party comes from dispositional forces.
c. Incorrect. Anxiety is explained in terms of what others do (thus situational).
*d. Correct. The disposition of conscientiousness is used to account for staying up all night.

7. a   obj. 3   p. 464
*a. Correct. Tiffany is engaging in a behaviour because of the situation, not her disposition to keep the room messy.
b. Incorrect. Thoughtfulness is 'Robbie's disposition.
c. Incorrect. Grumpiness is 'Donny's disposition.
d. Incorrect. Punctuality is 'Debbie's disposition.

8. d   obj. 4   p. 467
a. Incorrect. The more the group members value the group, the stronger will be the pressures to conform.
b. Incorrect. The larger the group, the more likely conformity becomes.
c. Incorrect. Public statements increase the pressure to conform.
*d. Correct. Secret ballots remove pressure to conform because other members will be unaware of how the individual votes are cast.

9. a   obj. 7   p. 472
*a. Correct. Stereotypes are applications of category knowledge and prejudices involve using stereotypes to make judgments about people.
b. Incorrect. Neither require action.
c. Incorrect. Neither require action.
d. Incorrect. This is reversed.

10. a   obj. 9   p. 476
*a. Correct. Similarity is the best early predictor of attraction.
b. Incorrect. Mere exposure is probably the weakest predictor of attraction.
c. Incorrect. Similarity is the strongest predictor.
d. Incorrect. Need complimentarity is an inconsistent predictor of attraction.

11. d   obj. 10   p. 478
a. Incorrect. See answer d.
b. Incorrect. See answer d.

c. Incorrect. See answer d.
*d. Correct. Sternberg's triarchic theory of love has three components—intimacy, passion, and commitment—which can be combined in different ways.

12. c   obj. 11   p. 479
a. Incorrect. Sports are not considered prosocial.
b. Incorrect. Lorenz was referring to civilized, game-oriented sports like football.
*c. Correct. Since aggression arises from an instinct in his view, it needs some form of release.
d. Incorrect. This is from a different aspect of the frustration/aggression hypothesis.

13. d   obj. 4   p. 467
a. Incorrect. Gender not relevant here.
b. Incorrect. Gender not relevant here.
c. Incorrect. An individual who is familiar with the task would be likely to defend their own views.
*d. Correct. An individual unfamiliar with the task would not risk going against the group and would choose to conform to the group opinion.

14. c   obj. 12   p. 482
a. Incorrect. Fundamental attribution error accounts for attributing the bombers' acts to their own evil nature.
b. Incorrect. Diffusion of responsibility would have left many standing by and watching.
*c. Correct. This prosocial behaviour demonstrates that more must be involved than mere rewards.
d. Incorrect. Only if they were angels.

15. e   obj. 12   p. 481
16. a   obj. 12   p. 482
17. c   obj. 12   p. 482
18. b   obj. 3   p. 461
19. d   obj. 4   p. 467
20. similar   obj. 9   p. 476
21. physically obj. 9   p. 476
22. loving   obj. 10   p. 477
23. health   obj. 10   p. 479
24. Biological obj. 11   p. 462

25. Often partners are chosen because of their proximity to each other. Selections are often made based on similarities in terms of values, attitudes, and traits. Knowing someone has evaluated us positively has a reciprocity of liking effect. Once commitments are made, intimacy and passion often follow.